T0377758

TRANSFIGURING WOMEN IN LATE TWENTIETH-CENTURY JAPAN

TRANSFIGURING WOMEN IN LATE TWENTIETH-CENTURY JAPAN

Feminists, Lesbians, and Girls' Comics Artists and Fans

James Welker

University of Hawai'i Press
Honolulu

First printed, 2024

Library of Congress Cataloging-in-Publication Data

Names: Welker, James, author.
Title: Transfiguring women in late twentieth-century Japan : feminists,
  lesbians, and girls' comics artists and fans / James Welker.
Description: Honolulu : University of Hawai'i Press, [2024] | Includes
  bibliographical references and index.
Identifiers: LCCN 2023044868 (print) | LCCN 2023044869 (ebook) | ISBN
  9780824872687 (hardback) | ISBN 9780824872694 (trade paperback) | ISBN
  9780824898243 (ebook) | ISBN 9780824898250 (kindle edition) | ISBN
  9780824898236 (pdf)
Subjects: LCSH: Feminism—Japan—History—20th century. | Sex
  role—Japan—History—20th century. | Women in popular
  culture—Japan—History—20th century. | Lesbians—Japan—History—20th
  century. | Comic book fans—Japan—History—20th century. | Queer comic
  books, strips, etc.—Japan—History—20th century.
Classification: LCC HQ1762 .W455 2024 (print) | LCC HQ1762 (ebook) | DDC
  305.42095209/04—dc23/eng/20231030
LC record available at https://lccn.loc.gov/2023044868
LC ebook record available at https://lccn.loc.gov/2023044869

Cover illustration by Shinoda Meiko.

Contents

Acknowledgments   vii

Language   xi

Chapter 1
Introduction   1

Chapter 2
Trajectories   19

Chapter 3
Terminology   53

Chapter 4
Translation   95

Chapter 5
Travel   140

Afterword   180

Notes   185

Works Cited   215

Index   241

Acknowledgments

This book has been an extremely long time in coming. I've accrued more debts along the way and owe more gratitude to more people than I can possibly enumerate here. The idea for the project that became this book came to me in the early 2000s, while I was translating a feature on the then "thirty-year history" of the *rezubian* community from the magazine *Anise*. That project was part of a distance-learning master's degree program in Advanced Japanese Studies from the School of East Asian Studies at the University of Sheffield. I am grateful for the existence of that program—which, alas, is no more—for setting me on this journey and to my advisor for that translation, Beverley Yamamoto.

Karen Kelsky's enthusiasm about my research from the instant I contacted her lured me to the PhD program in the Department of East Asian Languages and Cultures at the University of Illinois at Urbana-Champaign, and her mentorship was instrumental in my receiving generous research funding. I remain truly thankful. I am also very grateful to the other members of my dissertation committee, Martin Manalansan, Robert Tierney, and Ronald Toby, for their mentorship and ongoing support. Additional faculty members at Illinois who were especially encouraging and helpful along the way include the late Nancy Abelmann, the late David Goodman, Jeeyoung Ahn Ha, Sho Konishi, Elizabeth Oyler, Brian Ruppert, and Misumi Sadler.

Ryan Jones, Jerome Ng, Rebecca Nickerson, Yeonjoo Park, Akiko Takeyama, E. K. Tan, Chris Tan, and Myra Washington made returning to grad school when I was a decade older than many of my peers bearable, occasionally even enjoyable, and sometimes provided invaluable feedback on my work. Ryan has remained an important sounding board and friend.

In the department of Asian Studies at the University of British Columbia, where I spent two years on a post-doctoral fellowship, Sharalyn Orbaugh became an instant cheerleader for my research. She's still cheering. I am grateful to her and for the support of Stefania Burk, Shirin Eshghi Furuzawa, Christina Laffin, and Joshua Mostow, along with my then fellow postdoc Kelly Hansen and then graduate student and TA Benjamin Whaley.

At Kanagawa University, I am thankful for the encouragement of a number of colleagues, particularly Eton Churchill and Christian Ratcliff, who immediately made me feel welcome and have been consistently supportive.

The late Mark McLelland was an important mentor, collaborator, and friend since I was an MA student at Sheffield. He was the model of the kind, generous, and incisive scholar I strive to be. I am also grateful for many years of mentorship and friendship from Vera Mackie. Early encouragement from Beverley Curran helped nudge me toward doing a PhD in the first place. Louise Heal Kawai has been along for the ride from when we were on that Sheffield Japanese MA program together; she went on to become a literary translator and I, a scholar. Finally, Caroline McKenzie has been a dear friend and enthusiastic supporter of my intellectual pursuits since before I went to grad school the first time.

A number of others have been friends, collaborators, co-panelists, hosts of my lectures, and providers of advice and feedback—sometimes while chatting over a tasty craft beer—over the many years this project has been simmering. My sincere thanks to Jeffrey Angles, Tomoko Aoyama, Jan Bardsley, Thomas Baudinette, Oleg Benesch, Jaqueline Berndt, Julia Bullock, Howard Chiang, Sonja Dale, Laura Dales, the late Romit Dasgupta, Sarah Frederick, Alisa Freedman, Erica Friedman, Fujimoto Yukari, Patrick Galbraith, Barbara Hartley, Todd Henry, Andrea Horbinski, Ishida Hitoshi, Peter Jackson, Ayako Kano, Wim Lunsing, Claire Maree, Laura Miller, Kazumi Nagaike, Debra Occhi, Mark Pendleton, the late Barbara Sato, Setsu Shigematsu, Katsuhiko Suganuma, Sugiura Ikuko, Shige (CJ) Suzuki, the late Takemura Kazuko, Kathleen Uno, Uozumi Akiyo, Keith Vincent, Wachi Yasuko, Tomomi Yamaguchi, Shana Ye, Tomiko Yoda, and the others I have inexcusably failed to mention here.

This project would not exist at all had I not had the great fortune of finding dozens of women and a few men willing to allow me to interview them, provide introductions, respond to queries, or lend—sometimes even give—me rare materials. I am unable to name everyone here out of privacy concerns, but I am profoundly grateful to each individual who helped me in such ways. Those I can name include the late Akiyama Yōko, Amano Michimi, Azuma Reiko, Belne, Kittredge Cherry, Yumi Doi, Hara Minata, Ikegami Chizuko, Isoi Beau, Itō Bungaku, the late Itoh Tari, Izumo Marou, the late Kitamura Mitsuko, Audrey Lockwood, the late Sheila Michaels, Miki Sōko, Nakanishi Toyoko, Nakano Fuyumi, Nanbara Shirō, Nitō Mayumi, Linda Peterson, Sawabe Hitomi, Sawagi Takako, Lora Sharnoff, Takashima Rica, Tanaka Mitsu, the late Larry Taub, Wada Akiko, and Yonezu Tomoko. I apologize to anyone whose name I omitted for the sake of privacy but who would have liked to be included in this list. Although not everyone's story appears directly in this book, each individual who shared with me their time and their memories has helped shape it. The number of the individuals I have thanked here, directly or indirectly, who have since passed away is an acute reminder of the urgency of recording histories from personal perspectives while it is possible.

This project was funded in part by the Department of East Asian Languages and Cultures and the Center for East Asian Studies at the University of Illinois at Urbana-Champaign, which provided me multiple fellowships and grants while I was in the PhD program. My research was also supported by a Foreign Language and Area Studies Fellowship; a Fulbright-Hays Doctoral Dissertation Research Abroad Fellowship—hosted by Ochanomizu University, which graciously created a loophole to permit a male graduate student to affiliate there; the aforementioned postdoctoral fellowship in the Department of Asian Studies at the University of British Columbia; and a Japan Society for the Promotion of Science Short-Term Postdoctoral Fellowship—hosted by Josai International University.

At the University of Hawai'i Press, my editor, Stephanie Chun, has been far more patient with me than I deserve. I will be forever grateful for her seeing this book through to completion. My gratitude goes as well to my immensely sharp-eyed and helpful copy editor, Wendy Bolton. I am also thankful to the two anonymous reviewers for insightful critiques and suggestions, helping me hone and sharpen my manuscript into the book it has become. Any errors and weaknesses that remain are, naturally, my own.

I am also thankful for the support of my family, especially the unending encouragement and (excessive) praise from my mother, Marianne Welker. Mary Lou Menzie, my grandmother, was around at the beginning of this project. I wish I had managed to finish this book while she was alive to see it. She would have been so proud. I miss her boundless curiosity.

Finally, my endless gratitude goes to my husband, Jotaro Arimori, for checking my translations, for so often knowing just the right word in English, for repeatedly looking things up for me when I should have done it myself, for patiently answering my questions, sometimes the same ones again and again, and for his love and encouragement, as well as gentle nudges to get me to finish this book.

Portions of some chapters of this book have previously been published elsewhere in significantly different form. Portions of "A Brief History of *Shōnen'ai, Yaoi,* and Boys Love," in *Boys Love Manga and Beyond: History, Culture* (ed. Mark McLelland et al.; University Press of Mississippi, 2015), can be found in chapters two, three, and four. Part of chapter two also comes from "Telling Her

Story: Narrating a Japanese Lesbian Community," in *Journal of Lesbian Studies* 14, no. 4 (2010), an earlier version of which was published under the same title in *Japanstudien* 16 (2004). Finally, portions of chapter four have previously appeared in "The Revolution Cannot Be Translated: Transfiguring Discourses of Women's Liberation in 1970s–1980s Japan," in *Multiple Translation Communities in Contemporary Japan* (ed. Beverley Curran, Nana Sato-Rossberg, and Kikuko Tanabe; Routledge, 2015); "Translating Women's Liberation, Translating Women's Bodies in 1970s–1980s Japan," in *Rim: Journal of the Asia-Pacific Women's Studies Association* 13, no. 2 (2012); and "From *The Cherry Orchard* to *Sakura no sono:* Translation and the Transfiguration of Gender and Sexuality in *Shōjo* Manga," in *Girl Reading Girl in Japan* (ed. Tomoko Aoyama and Barbara Hartley; Routledge, 2010).

LANGUAGE

In this book I have opted to leave certain terms in Japanese, most notably *"ūman ribu," "rezubian," "rezubian feminisuto," "shōjo* manga," and *"shōnen'ai."* In public discourse, as well as for most of the people with whom I have spoken in regard to this project, words such as *"ribu"* and "lib" as well as *"rezubian"* and "lesbian" are treated as synonymous. I use the Japanese terms, however, in recognition that neither *"ūman ribu"* nor *"rezubian"* has the same history or valence in Japanese as their English equivalents, as I elaborate in chapter three. While this runs the risk of exoticization, it is my hope that, given their near equivalence to English words, my choice to transcribe rather than translate will be just unsettling enough to remind readers that the spheres to which I point with these terms cannot be neatly equated with counterparts elsewhere. The line between postwar feminism in Japan—of which *ribu* was the most visible manifestation in the 1970s—and radical so-called second-wave feminism springing up elsewhere from the late 1960s onward is murky, however. The same can be said about the *rezubian* community in Japan and lesbian communities abroad. Accordingly, I make use of English terms, such as "women's liberation" and "lesbian," as well as "feminist" and "lesbian feminist," when I wish to indicate feminist and lesbian spheres both outside of and in excess of these spheres in Japan. The times I have struggled to determine which term to use is indicative of the lack of clear lines between them. Similarly, as is standard in manga and anime studies, I use *"shōjo* manga" in recognition of the specificity of the Japanese art form. My reasons for distinguishing between the genre label *"shōnen'ai"* and its near translation "boys love" are made clear in chapter three. Finally, I generally strive to use terms that are chronologically apt. For example, I use the now pejorative *"homo"* about queer male culture of the 1960s to 1980s. Similarly, I use "LGBT"—rather than "LGBTQ" or another acronym—about the present to reflect the term's usage in Japan, albeit variants of LGBTQ have come into popular use in Japanese over the past decade.

I would also like to note that, with the exception of quotations, I generally refer to women and girls "in Japan" rather than "Japanese" women and girls. I do so in recognition that not all those involved in these spheres are of Japanese nationality or ethnicity, even if this was seldom recognized in the discourse I examine. In the *ribu* and *rezubian* communities in particular, the erasure of women who do not neatly fit into the category "Japanese," notably individuals of Korean descent, has been contentious at times. A woman active in *ribu* with whom I spoke at an event in 2008, for instance, was quick to point out after I identified myself as researching the movement that she felt invisible in the movement as an ethnic Korean, a feeling that lingered decades later.

Finally, as is standard in Japanese studies, when transcribing Japanese I use macrons to indicate long Japanese vowel sounds, as in the word *"shōjo,"* with exceptions made for words commonly used in English. I have tried to limit the number of Japanese terms I use, generally using English translations for names of organizations and publications with the exception of those that are particularly iconic or which are difficult to smoothly render in English. And, in keeping with norms in Japanese studies, I write Japanese personal names in their natural order of surname preceding given name except for those who have adopted the opposite order in their publications or public personae.

CHAPTER 1

Introduction

Between 1970 and 1971, on the heels of over a decade of rapid economic growth accompanied by increasing consumer comforts and spectacular citizen protests, three communities of women and adolescent girls in Japan began to take shape and to take on the entrenched norms that compelled women to be first passive girlfriends, then "good wives and wise mothers," forestalling other possibilities.[1] These three socially marginalized spheres—the women involved in the *ūman ribu* (women's liberation) movement and those who identi-fied with the *rezubian* (lesbian) community, as well as young women artists and adolescent girl readers of queer *shōjo* manga (girls' comics)—addressed gender and sexual norms in often distinct ways. What they had in common, above all, was their engagement in activities that served to undermine norma-tive understandings of the category "women." They strove for a more expan-sive understanding that would accommodate not just an increased number of public roles unbound from being a wife or mother but also—and most significantly—a greater diversity of gender and sexual expression. Critically, while they were in most cases primarily focused on the local—that is, on their own lives in Japan—many women and girls in all three communities creatively "transfigured" elements from foreign, primarily Euro-American, culture to advance their aims.

In *Transfiguring Women in Late Twentieth-Century Japan,* I examine the *ribu, rezubian,* and queer *shōjo* manga spheres in the 1970s and 1980s, when these three loosely knit, overlapping communities emerged, then variously flourished, faltered, fragmented, and took on new forms. While I focus on these three communities based on their commonalities, this is an admittedly unwieldly juxtaposition. Examining simultaneously these three spheres of con-siderably different orientations, structures, and sizes, however, allows me to shed light on their cumulative cultural and social effects, and in so doing draw attention to ways their efforts were often collective in effect though rarely in intent. My focus on queer *shōjo* manga fandom in particular foregrounds the central role of adolescent girls in engendering cultural change in Japan during this period. "Adolescents," linguist Penelope Eckert argues, "are society's transition teams, reinterpreting the world, resolving the old with the new . . . culture with culture, local with transnational."[2] In placing this sphere alongside *ribu* and *rezubian feminisuto* (lesbian feminist) activists, as well as the broader *rezubian* community, I also work to unsettle established understandings of activism in the late Shōwa era. Further, placing *ribu* alongside the *rezubian* and queer *shōjo* manga spheres pushes us to remember ways that, in spite of what can be seen from the vantage point of the present as clear hetero- and cissexist bias, the *ribu* movement too had queer aspects, not the least of which being its goal of undermining gender and sexual norms, thereby making life easier for everyone deviating therefrom.[3] The three-pronged focus of my study also highlights the significance of engagements with "Western" culture spanning a cross section of the population during a period when Japan was becoming increasingly wealthy and reclaiming its status as a global economic power.

In this book, I argue that, while they did not accomplish everything they set out to achieve, the women and girls in the *ribu, rezubian,* and queer *shōjo* manga spheres collectively had a substantial influence on Japanese culture and society as a whole. This is true in spite of these spheres being socially marginalized, even ostracized, and in spite of a majority of this population not engaging in practices typically considered to be activist. This influence stemmed, in no small part from their "transfiguration" of elements—texts, ideas, images, practices, and the like—primarily from a loosely defined "West," an idea of the West that, as Karen Kelsky points out, is often "synonymous with the international" or the "foreign."[4] Accordingly, I focus in this book on uses, effects, and experiences of transfiguration within and beyond these communities. Most crucially, I demonstrate how, through their creative transnational engagements building upon the layers of transfiguration imbricated in the construction of contemporary Japanese culture, the women and girls in these communities transformed the category "women" in Japan.

The history I map out here makes very clear, however, that the engagement of women and girls in the *ribu, rezubian,* and queer *shōjo* manga spheres with Western culture was not a matter of simply looking to the West for liberation, nor was it a matter of simple imitation of the foreign. These women and girls were on the whole, not uncritical of Western culture, even as they turned Westward in diverse ways as a part of their efforts to challenge local gender and sexual norms. Moreover, transfiguration of ostensibly foreign culture has long been part and parcel of globally engaged cultures such as modern and contemporary Japan. In other words, such engagement with the seemingly foreign was an essential part of the local Japanese culture in which these women and girls were located. The very category "women" being challenged in the *ribu, rezubian,* and queer *shōjo* manga spheres in the 1970s and 1980s was itself (re)constructed through such ongoing engagement with foreign thought and practice.

The amorphous nature of these communities makes them impossible to define precisely in terms of moment of origin or of composition, and in the case of the *ribu* movement when—or, perhaps, *whether*—it ceased to be, as I spell out below. The ways these spheres overlap complicate matters further. Regardless, each community has forged tangible impacts on the lives of individual girls and women, on their communities, and on Japanese society and culture.

The *Ūman Ribu* Movement

Initially the most culturally prominent of these three communities, the movement known as "*ūman ribu*" and simply "*ribu*"—terms I use in this volume to distinguish it from contemporaneous radical feminist movements elsewhere—first drew widespread public attention with a protest held in Tokyo's fashionable Ginza district on October 21, 1970. This was the initial salvo of the nascent moment's efforts to challenge the normative understanding of "women."

The rally was organized by one of the newly emerging groups of women advocating for "*josei kaihō*" or "*onna kaihō*," both meaning "women's liberation." The use of these terms by *ribu* activists was a rejection of a third synonym, "*fujin kaihō*," for which earlier generations of women struggled. The dated, bourgeois term "*fujin*"—meaning woman or lady, almost certainly married with children—was explicitly rejected in favor of the relatively neutral term for woman, "*josei*," or its blunter—and more assertive—counterpart, "*onna*," neither of which indicates a woman's marital status.[5] Fujieda Mioko—a generation older than most *ribu* activists—was involved in the new movement and has noted that when the *ribu* women adopted *onna* as their preferred term, it was widely considered vulgar, and some were reluctant to use it. *Ribu* activists' choice to reject *fujin* and to call themselves and each other *josei* or *onna,* she writes, was a declaration of independence from the roles of wife and mother. The use of *onna* in particular was a rejection of normative notions of femininity.[6] *Ribu* activist Yonezu Tomoko has described *onna* as having had a very base image, implying an inferior woman, with no ability, no education, and no career, in addition to being, in some male discourse, a sexual object. As Yonezu recounted to me, it was precisely because of what *onna* implied, in order "to liberate 'myself=*onna*,' to insist that 'I' am not inferior, we in the movement used not *'josei'* but the word *'onna.'*[7] When I spoke to de facto *ribu* leader Tanaka Mitsu in 2009, she corrected my use of *josei kaihō* to discuss the early *ribu* movement, insisting that to her it had always been *onna kaihō*. The former term can be found in her own handwriting in pamphlets she produced in 1970, however. *Onna* clearly reflects Tanaka's current understanding of the movement. Whether when speaking with me she had forgotten her early use of *josei* or this was a willful misremembering based on how she wants *ribu* to be represented, such discrepancies remind us that historical facts and memories do not always align. In fact, a perusal of *ribu* writing makes clear that in much *ribu* discourse in the 1970s both words were used almost but not quite interchangeably, but, in my estimation, *onna* conveyed a greater sense of power as well as pride. Note that in this book, for the sake of simplicity, I generally translate the terms *"onna," "josei,"* and *"fujin"* as "woman," indicating the original only when significant to my discussion.[8] Given that woman and its plural, women, are more open-ended than their Japanese counterparts, I believe this enriches possible interpretations of the "transfiguring women" in the title of this book.

From late 1970 at least through the middle of the decade, when the movement began to wane, many radical feminists in Japan identified themselves and their movement with the terms *"ūman ribu"* and *"ribu."* While *ribu* activists shared a number of concerns with earlier women's movements, such as motherhood and social status, what made this new movement truly radical was the centrality given to sex and sexuality in their discourse. This foregrounding of women's sex and sexuality—most forcefully evoked by the word *"onna"*—links the *ribu* movement with the *rezubian* and queer *shōjo* manga spheres.

While many of the tens if not hundreds of small *ribu* groups around the country were loosely networked and engaged in dialogues via exchange of *mini-komi* (newsletters or zines), and at various gatherings and events, there have been no definitive tallies of groups or their memberships.[9] For the purposes of this study, I associate with the *ribu* sphere women who at any point affiliated with a *ribu* group or participated in a *ribu* event or simply identified with the *ribu* movement. I situate *ribu* within feminism, broadly defined, and in this book trace certain threads from *ribu* forward into later feminist activism, in which many former *ribu* activists were involved. I resist articulating the clear distinction made by some individuals between *ribu* and other feminisms. The nature of such distinctions is largely idiosyncratic—as is evident from personal reflections by those who had engaged at some point in *ribu* activism.

The Queer *Shōjo* Manga Sphere

Just weeks after that first *ribu* demonstration in October, artist Takemiya Keiko published the short manga narrative "Snow and Stars and Angels and . . ." (*Yuki to hoshi to tenshi to . . .*) in a commercial *shōjo* manga magazine—a work that to many fans, critics, and scholars looking back from the present marks the emergence of a new genre of *shōjo* manga depicting male–male romance.[10] This genre would quickly come to be known as "*shōnen'ai*," meaning love of or by boys, which is the origin of the more recent genre labels "boys love," "BL," and "*bōizu rabu*." (I write boys love without an apostrophe to keep its meaning as open-ended as *shōnen'ai*.) Works featuring female–female intimacy and romance would emerge around the same time, often drawn by the same artists, but were generally not popular. These queer narratives were preceded by manga featuring girls dressed as boys (*dansō no shōjo*), which, in fact, date back to at least the beginning of postwar *shōjo* manga, when it was primarily drawn by men. And, while cross-dressing allowed *shōjo* characters (and readers) to evade gender norms, until relatively recently the protagonists in such narratives almost invariably ended up in female attire, paired with a male character—not a particularly queer outcome. Although I include within "queer *shōjo* manga" works depicting female–female relationships, cross-dressing, and other gender-bending that served to transgress (or at least not reinforce) social norms, my primary focus in this book is artists and fans of male–male romance manga, which for adolescent girl readers in the 1970s and 1980s was arguably the most queer and, for Japanese culture, has been the most queering.

The queer *shōjo* manga sphere is far and away the largest of the three spheres I examine in this book, and the most challenging to define. Based on mere readership of queer *shōjo* manga, a majority of adolescent and even pre-adolescent girls from the 1970s onward would fall into this camp, as well as a not insignificant number of boys and adult women and men. Rather than the casual reader, however, in this volume I delimit the queer *shōjo* manga sphere to passionate fans who sought out such manga, who bought or borrowed magazines such as *June* and *Allan* (*Aran*) catering to fans of *shōnen'ai* works, and who may have written letters to these magazines, sharing their thoughts about these texts and related topics with other readers, artists, and editors. While, for simplicity, I will primarily focus on manga, male–male romantic and erotic narratives were also created and consumed in prose form in these magazines and other media, leading by the early 1980s to periodicals dedicated to them. This fandom also extended beyond works produced locally by women, incorporating representations of male homosexuality produced by *homo* men in Japan as well as gay art, fiction, pornography, and reportage on gay cultures abroad.

This sphere was not simply one of reception and interpretation, however. The artists themselves, generally young women a few years older than their readers, were also integral. (So too, if to a lesser extent, were the male editors who oversaw the works' publication.) Born at roughly the same time as most *ribu* activists and the women who established the *rezubian* community, the professional artists who developed *shōnen'ai* and other commercial queer *shōjo* manga saw themselves as, in a sense, intervening through the genre in readers' lives, liberating *shōjo* readers from cultural restrictions that positioned females as passive players in the heteronormative romance script, as well as innocent and uninterested in sexuality. For this reason, Takemiya, for instance, later specifically identified the genre as *"feminisuto"* (feminist) in effect—although not all feminists or former *ribu* activists would agree.[11] This may also help explain why girls who would grow up to identify as *rezubian* or otherwise queer found *shōnen'ai* texts particularly influential to them during their formative years.[12]

Further blurring the line between artist and reader, the girl readers themselves were also actively producing drawings, manga, and prose narratives depicting *shōnen'ai* and other queer themes, both for sharing among friends and broader readerships. Reader submissions formed a significant part of magazines like *June,* in which readers could have their work critiqued by professionals. Moreover, the production and consumption of queer *shōjo* manga has from the beginning constituted a large part of the amateur manga scene, including at the Comic Market event, where the term *"yaoi,"* coined as a label for *dōjinshi* (fanzines), quickly came to be associated with male–male romance works. Amateur creators would sometimes go on to become professional artists, sometimes having been recruited to draw for newly created specialty magazines, several dozen of which were started beginning in the late 1980s as part of a new flourishing of media that would eventually be called *"bōizu rabu"* or "BL," namely, "boys love."

The *Rezubian* Community

Not quite a year after the magazine containing Takemiya's first *shōnen'ai* narrative hit the bookstores, a twenty-one-year-old woman used a message-exchange notebook in the back of an adult bookstore near Tokyo's Shinjuku Station to find other women who, like her, were *"rezu"* (lez). This was the first step in the creation of Wakakusa no Kai (Young Grass Club), an organization later identified as the beginning of the formation in Japan of a new community of women. A majority of these women would come to refer to themselves as "*rezubian*"—a term that I use in this book to distinguish between more global uses of "lesbian" and its local manifestation. This community might be traced further back to the limited bar scene in Tokyo dating back to the 1950s, including, by the 1960s, bars featuring "dandy beauties" (*dansō no reijin*)—women in male drag—which drew on the popular appeal of the Takarazuka Revue and similar all-female musical theater troupes.[13] Although by the late 1960s or early 1970s these bars came to be called *resubian bā* (lesbian bars), they catered to a heterosexual clientele seeking the exotic. Nevertheless, whether they identified as *dōseiaisha* (homosexual) or *josei no homo* (female homo), or, by the late 1960s, as *resubian, rezubian,* or *rezu,* or none of those, women could go there to meet other women with whom they could form romantic or sexual relationships. Evidence suggests a sense of camaraderie and connectedness among these women created a sense of community by the 1950s.[14] Regardless, the founding of Wakakusa no Kai in 1971 was a milestone: this was the first time a small group of women attempted to establish a tangible space of their own—if only at monthly gatherings—where, shielded from the outside world, they could meet others like themselves. In recognition of this, and in parallel with my situating the *ribu* and queer *shōjo* manga spheres established by and for women at the beginning of the 1970s, I follow histories produced within the *rezubian* community itself in situating Wakakusa no Kai as its symbolic starting point.[15]

A majority of those generally included in discourse within and about the *rezubian* community during the period that is the focus of this volume were unmarried, cisgender women who identified at the time as *rezubian*. Some of these individuals today have different gender and sexual identities as categories have increased. For the sake of simplicity, I use *rezubian* very broadly to point to this loosely defined community and its constituents in the 1970s and 1980s without making assumptions or assertions about the identities of specific individuals. Although this risks erasing the diversity of these women, the individuals whose experiences and discourse I directly discuss in this research claimed the label *rezubian* for themselves, including individuals who no longer identify as female. The diversity of this community is manifold. While Wakakusa no Kai was criticized by *rezubian feminisuto* for admitting married women, who were benefiting from rather than working to quash the patriarchal system, over 21 percent of respondents in a mid-1980s survey of community members conducted by *rezubian feminisuto* were either currently married or had divorced, suggesting that they were a significant presence in the community.[16] Moreover, this survey itself assumed participants to be "*rezubian*."[17]

Later surveys in community publications would not always be so identitarian, often asking rather than assuming the identities of those who counted themselves as members of the community; and respondents included those identifying themselves as bisexual or asexual, or as female-to-male or male-to-female transgender.[18] The *rezubian feminisuto* movement, which emerged in the mid-1970s out of the *ribu* movement, included women for whom being a *rezubian* was a political choice rather than rooted in an innate desire for other women—at times a major point of contention.

The *rezubian* community really came into its own in the 1990s, with new organizations, events, and spaces, sometimes created in cooperation with the *gei* (gay) community, and by the 2000s *rezubian* were included under the banner of LGBT, later LGBTQ, a loose collection of gender and sexual minorities associated in recent decades with the struggle for social and political recognition, including legal recognition of same-sex relationships. This development built on the foundations laid by *rezubian* in the 1970s and 1980s and was aided by changing economic and social conditions that made it easier to reject a heteronormative life course. It was also kicked off by a "gay boom" (*gei būmu*) in early 1990s media—a boom that developed in no small part as a result of queer *shōjo* manga fandom in the previous two decades.[19]

Chronologic Focus

The communities I examine here all emerged around 1970, and thus the year makes a fitting starting point for this study, although I do look further back, as far as the early twentieth century, to trace some of the deep and deeply transnational roots of these communities. While I at times gesture toward the present to consider the long-term impact of these communities, my primary focus runs through the late 1980s for several reasons. In addition to closing out the decade, 1989 formally marks the end of the Shōwa era, which began in 1926. More importantly, however, it represents a significant break in public memory. Along with Emperor Hirohito, the year saw the deaths of iconic singer Misora Hibari and preeminent manga artist and animator Tezuka Osamu—both emblematic of postwar Shōwa culture. Japan's so-called bubble era came to a close shortly thereafter, bringing about a prolonged economic downturn and the emergence—or, more accurately, exacerbation—of what has more recently been recognized as an economically "unequal society" (*kakusa shakai*). The subsequent Heisei era (1989–2019) also saw the worsening of Japan's demographic crisis—albeit Japan's birthrate actually dropped below the replacement level in the 1970s—and the intensification of long dire warnings about Japan's future if the trend is not reversed.[20] Consequently, the first decade of the Heisei era came to be referred to as Japan's "lost decade," a term subsequently revised by some to "lost decades," in the plural, in recognition of the economic and demographic problems that would ultimately span the entire era.[21]

More specific to the spheres that are the focus of this book, the year 1989 also saw a new "moral panic" in response to the horrific murder of four young girls by a fan of the *"rorikon"* (Lolita complex) genre, Miyazaki Tsutomu, which put a chill on the amateur artist and fan world, including at the aforementioned Comic Market fan convention, where queer *shōjo* manga thrived.[22] Conversely, the year also kicked off the early 1990s boom in commercial BL magazines, noted above, in a decade that would see the coalescence of the "BL industry." And, as also noted, the early to mid-1990s witnessed the emergence of *rezubian* and *gei* (later LGBT) film festivals, pride parades, a *rezubian* commercial magazine, and other signs of a significant shift in the nature of the *rezubian* community.[23]

Admittedly, however, I am most interested in the 1970s. Indeed, my discussion of the *ribu* movement could end in that decade would that my project were simply a chronologic history based on how that community's past is typically narrated. Carrying my discussion forward through the 1980s, however, allows me to look at some of the substantive fruits of *ribu*. Indeed, for all three spheres, stretching my primary focus through to the 1980s enables me to examine some of the most immediate results of the activities and the activism of these women and girls in the context of their development out of efforts begun in the 1970s. These range from the highly tangible—such as the publication of a book that would quickly become a *rezubian* "bible" and the establishment of women's health centers—to the amorphous—such as the emergence of a thriving amateur queer comics sphere for women and girls who were not necessarily queer themselves, and the development of new language for talking and thinking about female bodies. *Transfiguring Women in Late Twentieth-Century Japan* is, thus, not so much a history of three communities—though I do offer histories of each in chapter two—as it is an examination at different scales and from different angles of ways certain spheres of women and girls that came together in the early 1970s worked, in large and small ways, often via their transnational engagements, to redefine "women" in Japan.

Transfiguration

Each of these spheres is at once a local construct and a product of transnational flows. The now global BL media sphere—with its amateur and commercial translations and dubs of Japanese manga, anime, and other media into many Asian and European languages, as well as innumerable original works—is generally considered in the discourse of its consumers and producers to have emanated from Japan. And, indeed, *shōnen'ai* manga and its successors are indisputably a product of a confluence of events and conditions in Japan. Yet, an examination of the origins and development of queer *shōjo* manga in Japan demonstrates that it arguably would not have come to be, at least not in the form it took in the 1970s, without the immediate influence of translated literature and foreign films—to say nothing of the broader history of modern Japanese literature.

The *rezubian* community in the 1990s came to resemble lesbian communities elsewhere, with pride events (*"puraido ibento"*), film festivals, and *rezubian* spaces that might seem at first glance to have been directly imported as part of what has been called "global queering."[24] As just noted, however, these practices were established upon foundations laid by both the *rezubian* community and the queer *shōjo* manga sphere. The *rezubian* community of the 1970s and 1980s, including both the ostensibly non-political Wakakusa no Kai and the decidedly political *rezubian feminisuto,* built on the decades of transnational discursive exchange that had developed into contemporary understandings of gender and sexuality in general, as well as more specifically, what it meant to be a *rezubian*.

Finally, nowhere have there been more vehement denials of foreign influence than those coming from the *ribu* community and its feminist heirs regarding the origins of the *ribu* movement. Although few in Japan would refute that the *feminizumu* of the late 1970s and beyond was in no small part a product of translation and travel, prominent *ribu* activists such as Tanaka Mitsu and Miki Sōko have both repeatedly insisted that the *ribu* movement of the early 1970s was a *local* reaction to *local* conditions for women and denied that its emergence was inspired by the so-called second-wave feminist movement in the United States. Tanaka, Miki, and others are correct to flatly reject the idea, first circulated in the press in 1970 by way of introducing *ūman ribu* to the public, that the movement was a mere import. And yet, such an emphatic rejection forecloses an examination of *ribu* discourse as, in part, a result of engagement with feminists and feminist thought from the United States and elsewhere, thus obfuscating a key site of feminist agency in 1970s Japan. This agency is manifest not merely in women seeking information and ideas from abroad that might be of use in their own struggles. It is also evident in the way that women selected and adapted this information to suit their needs and interests, as well as the sharing by women in Japan of their own experiences and ideas with their counterparts abroad, demonstrating that, however imbalanced, this was not an import of ideas but an exchange.

To begin to unravel these multiplex webs linking girls and women as well as ideas and images across borders and across time, in this book I proffer and deploy the concept "transfiguration." At its most basic, I use transfiguration to refer to *a change in form in the process of crossing from one culture to another*. In so doing, I am drawing both on meanings of the term's constituent parts: *trans* (across) and *figure* (form), as well as the meaning of *transfiguration* itself (a change in form or appearance). The notion of transfiguration has had some rather dramatic and well-known uses. In the Bible, it is one of the miracles of Jesus, who is seen by several of his apostles to be "transfigured"—with his raiment bright white and his countenance aglow—when speaking to Moses and Elijah on a mountaintop.[25] Far more recently, in the Harry Potter series "transfiguration" refers to spells that change the shape of an object or a person into something entirely different, such as a pupil into a frog. According to fictional Hogwarts School of Witchcraft and Wizardry's professor Minerva McGonagall, "Transfiguration is some of the most complex and dangerous magic" students learn at the school.[26] Transfiguration as I use it, however, is neither miraculous nor magic, but it is at once very powerful and the effect of the workings of power, both within the cultures of origin and of reception, as well as between the two—and it at times does indeed transform objects, as well as subjects.

I borrow the kernel of my own use of transfiguration from Dilip Gaonkar and Elizabeth Povinelli, for whom transfiguration figures as part of their effort to elucidate "the circulatory matri[ces], both national and global, through which new discursive forms, practices, and artifacts carry out their routine ideological labor of constructing subjects who can be summoned in the name of a public or a people."[27] They posit that more productive than continued attention to "meaning and translation" as a means to understand the workings of transnational flows would be a focus on the circulation, transfiguration, and recognition of "cultural forms."[28] They call specifically for "form-sensitive analyses of [these] public texts, events, and practices" that highlight the conditions whereby they are transfigured to take on recognizable forms within cultures of circulation and in the process of public-making.[29] They ultimately see a focus on transfiguration as means through which to map the "generative matrices" themselves—and the workings of power within them.[30]

While Gaonkar and Povinelli never offer a precise definition of transfiguration, they use it to index *processes of change*. I would like to refine their usage of transfiguration via an expansion of sorts. First, I seek to draw attention to the subjects of transfiguration. That is, if things—images, texts, practices, and the like—are transfigured as they transit from culture to culture, there must be actors who are engaged, consciously or unconsciously, in acts of transfiguration. Like Gaonkar and Povinelli, I too am interested in the workings of power, specifically both the power that the women and adolescent girls in the *ribu, rezubian,* and queer *shōjo* manga spheres seek to confront or circumvent via transfiguration, as well as the power they exert in so doing. Accordingly, in my wish to highlight the subjecthood of these women and girls, my own use of transfiguration also calls on us to identify *acts of change* and, thus, the *actors* involved therein. Finally, transfiguration, as I use it, has no fixed direction or terminal point. A focus on transfiguration calls on us to examine the *effects of change.* As I understand it, transfiguration sets in motion "ripples of change" that do not end with the thing (re)invented via transfiguration.[31] These ripples of change can extend indefinitely in any direction, including back to the culture whence the transfigured thing originated or on to a third culture. Thus, an examination of transfiguration in the (re)production of cultural forms has no logical or fixed stopping point and has the potential to take us in surprising directions.

There are, of course, myriad other ways to describe cultural change concomitant with flows of things and of people. Yet, to me, none adequately encapsulates transfiguration as I have just outlined it. Some frequently used terms, such as "localization" and "glocalization," give the impression of a unidirectional and finite process, when, even in the face of disjunctures and imbalances, purely one-way flows are rare in any context.[32] Many of the ways processes of change in transit are framed developed out of studies of colonial and post-colonial societies. Fernando Ortiz's notion of "transculturation," for instance, describes a process whereby a people, deracinated by force or by choice, come into contact with another culture and go through a period of "deculturation," the loss of culture, and "acculturation," its acquisition. This may lead to novel cultural forms, or "neoculturation."[33] Mary Louise Pratt usefully situates transculturation within what she calls the "contact zone"—"the space of colonial encounters"—and highlights the inherent agency of colonized peoples in this process. The "subordinated or marginal groups," she writes, "select and invent from materials transmitted to them by a dominant or metropolitan culture."[34] This agentic process of selection and (re)invention has also been described as one of "hybridization," "syncretism," and "creolization" to reflect how the cultural forms and practices created by a combination or a collision of cultures are neither purely local nor left unchanged in the transit(ion) from culture to culture. Although useful in some contexts, such terms tend to be premised on a colonial or post-colonial power relationship,[35] a relationship that is not a given and certainly cannot be neatly applied to Japan. And while they have been adapted for and applied to other contexts, they still lack the structured focus and the open-endedness of transfiguration as I propose it here.

This flexibility helps transfiguration function as a heuristic device to elucidate varied facets of transnational cultural flows. Transfiguration tells us to look for changes in transit, and to pursue them beyond any initial change because the process is not finite. It does not limit the kinds of transformations it indexes to specific kinds of objects, ideas, or practices. Anything—and anyone—can change in transit from culture to culture. It makes no assumptions about relations of power, and yet careful attention to transfiguration elucidates these relations. Its use as the active verb "transfigure" reminds us that these changes are the result of acts—sometimes deliberate, sometimes not—by actors. Accordingly, it tells us to seek out these agents and to query their motivations. It is in this way that I put transfiguration to work in the pages that follow to help illuminate the development, activities, and cultural impact of the *ribu, rezubian,* and queer *shōjo* manga spheres.

Methodology

My research for this volume has entailed the examination of an archive encompassing an array of resources ranging from early twentieth-century dictionaries, sexology texts, and literature; to postwar women's and men's magazines and pornography; to translated feminist and lesbian texts; to manga and anime; to *mini-komi, dōjinshi,* and other ephemera. My work on the *ribu* community in particular has been helped immeasurably by being able to access boxes of materials from Ribu Shinjuku Center thanks to Yonezu Tomoko and the existence of several volumes of articles from newsletters and fliers lovingly compiled and reprinted by activists and published since the 1990s.[36] These volumes arguably represent an attempt to both preserve and legitimize the history of the *ribu* movement, or at least the history as imagined by their compilers and editors. More recently—too late to have been of help to me—there have been moves in both the *ribu* and *rezubian* communities to digitize materials in an effort to preserve and share them more widely. In fact, I gained access to the archive of the English-speaking lesbian community via Linda Peterson in part on the condition that I digitize it. Ongoing privacy concerns and the sense of a need to get permission from all persons concerned, however, remain an obstacle to the reproduction and sharing of these materials, even for materials many decades old—an issue I discuss in the context of the *rezubian* community in chapter two.

In addition to this unwieldly archive, between 2004 and 2009 I interviewed some seventy individuals and corresponded with many more—including several men—who directly participated in or who were otherwise linked to these communities. These individuals who generously shared with me their time, their memories, and their opinions—and, occasionally, access to rare materials—were roughly balanced among those involved in either the *ribu, rezubian,* or queer *shōjo* manga spheres. Some women, however, were connected to two of these spheres, most commonly a *rezubian* who had also been involved in *ribu* or had been an avid reader of *shōnen'ai* manga. Most were in their forties to mid-sixties at the time of the interviews, and several have since passed away.

I met these individuals through personal introductions from friends, acquaintances, and others who had themselves consented to be interviewed, all primarily based in one of the metropolitan areas surrounding Tokyo, Nagoya, Osaka, and Kyoto. My participation at the University of Illinois in a 2006 roundtable discussion on *ribu* in conjunction with a screening of the *ribu* documentary *30 Years of Sisterhood,*[37] on a tour of the United States coordinated by Tomomi Yamaguchi, gave me the opportunity to meet the aforementioned Miki Sōko, who played an important role in introducing me to key individuals in the *ribu* movement. I also contacted some individuals directly and posted self-introductions and requests for participants on several feminist and lesbian email lists as well as on the then popular social-networking website *Mixi.* Some of those whom I would have liked to interview, particularly in the *ribu* and *rezubian* spheres, declined my request, however, generally for unstated reasons. One woman who had been involved in the *ribu* movement told me she did not wish to relive her experience, suggesting that her departure from the movement was emotionally difficult, and another woman who was prominent in one of the communities explained that she was simply tired of being interviewed by researchers. Still a third woman expressed concern over how I intended to use the information, which may have been related to my request coming in the wake of a recent controversy over a book written about the *rezubian feminisuto* community or another research-related controversy earlier that decade related to a scholar working in English.

While I conducted a few interviews via email, most were one-on-one or small group conversations at cafés, restaurants, karaoke boxes, women's centers, university campuses, private homes (including twice outside Japan), as well as the lesbian space LOUD in Tokyo, and the storied women's space Freak (Furīku) in the Osaka metropolitan area. The loosely structured interviews drew upon a set of questions, which, in most cases, I had provided in advance with the request that participants give some thought to the questions before meeting me. The questions focused on participants' personal histories, including their experiences or awareness growing up or in adulthood of women's and men's differing social statuses, their involvement in or connections with any of these communities, and their current feelings about women's social status and sexuality.

My being male undoubtedly affected the content of what interview participants were willing to share, perhaps out of a concern that I would not understand their experiences. Nevertheless, my outsider status as a gay-identified white American man seems to have had an overall positive effect. My not being a Japanese man may have helped some women who expressed lingering resentment about the oppression they experienced in male-dominated Japanese society feel comfortable speaking to me. Several women in the *rezubian* community and several fans of queer *shōjo* manga directly expressed feeling comforted (*anshin*) that I am gay, something they may have gleaned from my social media or that came up naturally in conversation. One former *ribu* activist I interviewed even told me she would never have allowed a man to interview her had she not heard from the person who introduced us that I am gay, suggesting a resentment of heterosexual men specifically. Finally, based on direct and indirect comments from participants, my being a white male with blondish hair and blue eyes appears to have helped me recruit volunteers as well. Moreover, given that many of those in my target population were interested in foreign cultures, some participants may have agreed to be interviewed out of the desire to interact with a foreigner, though I do not recall more than a handful attempting to speak to me in English. Many expressed more than polite curiosity in my research, however.

Along with these interviews, Miki and I talked about *ūman ribu* and her involvement therein as she graciously guided me around a display on the *ribu* movement at Liberty Osaka Human Rights Museum and then on to Freak, where I met and spoke with Wada Akiko, the woman who established it in 1977. I have also attended and even taken part in retrospective events on the *ribu* movement in both Japan and the United States involving activists and scholars (including the one referenced above), taken part in LGBT pride parades and other events, and gone to numerous fan conventions in and outside Japan where amateur manga artists and fans shared their passion—all of which have given me additional opportunities to meet and speak with individuals linked with these communities in the 1970s and 1980s, as well as their beneficiaries. Some of these individuals make direct appearances in the following pages either under their own name, the pseudonym they used as a member of the community, or a pseudonym I assigned—the latter indicated by quotation marks at first use. What I have learned from all of these individuals, however, has enriched my understanding of both these communities and Japan before, during, and after the era upon which this book focuses.

Chapter Overview

The remainder of this book examines the *ribu, rezubian,* and queer *shōjo* manga spheres via the lens of transfiguration. To provide necessary background information for the chapters that follow, chapter two, "Trajectories," sketches historical overviews of the three communities that are the heart of this project, tracing their roots and their emergence around 1970, then following their development over the course of the next two decades and beyond. Subsequent chapters further the telling of these histories from different angles.

Chapter three, "Terminology," reaches back to the early 1900s to offer etymologies *qua* genealogies of key terms used within and beyond these spheres to name the women's and girls' communities, their activities, and the objects of their desire—primarily *ūman ribu, rezubian,* and *shōnen'ai*. *Ūman ribu* functioned simultaneously as a badge of pride and a derisive epithet. Both the *ūman ribu* movement and its adopted sobriquet have frequently been misunderstood as simple 1970s imports from the United States. This chapter illustrates that this false impression represents an insufficient grasp not just of the history of the movement but also of the sometimes complex ways "loan words" take shape and take on meaning within a language. The current pronunciation of *rezubian,* the second term, dates to roughly the same period but has a more complicated history. As this chapter demonstrates, to assume that the *rezubian* of the 1970s was simply imported into Japanese along with the (unstable) concept of what constitutes a lesbian, belies a century of evolving understandings of "homosexuality" in Japan and elsewhere, along with the continuous transnational exchange that has gone into this discourse. Finally, *shōnen'ai* is shown to be a thoroughly modern and transnational term. Much like the meaning of its ancient component parts *"shōnen"* (boy) and *"ai"* (love), it was transfigured in modern Japan as notions of boyhood and girlhood, as well as eros and affection, were reconsidered and reconfigured in no small part in response to the introduction of novel ideas from outside Japan. As this chapter details, *shōnen'ai, ūman ribu,* and *rezubian,* like other key words in motion across and within borders, "offer special insight into the remaking of worlds at different scales because they condense past motion into their material form," as anthropologist Anna Lowenhaupt Tsing observes.[38] In troubling the origins of ostensible loan words and native words alike, this chapter calls into question what it means for a word to be "Japanese." More importantly, tracing the genealogies of these words central to the *ribu, rezubian,* and queer *shōjo* manga spheres through the lens of transfiguration exposes the power struggles that have (re)shaped words, individuals, and communities.

As chapter four, "Translation," vividly illustrates, the translation and greater transfiguration of essays, empirical studies, and literature alike was a crucial tool for women and girls to unsettle gender and sexual norms in Japan. First, this chapter examines the introduction into Japan of early radical feminist writing from the United States, such as the landmark texts *Our Bodies, Ourselves* and *The Hite Report.* The former played a key role in the establishment of the women's health movement and woman-centered approaches to sexuality and reproductive health. The latter helped trigger the creation of the first commercially published book by and for self-identified *rezubian*, a touchstone for a generation of women who love women. This chapter also looks at the afterlives of translated fiction and film. Works such as German novelist Herman Hesse's *Demian* and films such as Italian director Luchino Visconti's *Death in Venice* were themselves dramatically transfigured by young women artists into *shōjo* manga narratives about love between adolescent boys. Such new narratives helped to liberate both artists and readers from the normative male–female romance pattern. Considering these various textual reworkings in terms of transfiguration, this chapter first looks at the transfiguration of texts. It then moves further by examining the impact on individuals and communities engaged in translation and transfiguration. And, finally, it considers the effects on the lives of women and girls in Japan at large. The project of elucidating the role of translation in the (re)construction of Japanese culture, notes Indra Levy, remains underdeveloped.[39] In demonstrating ways a critical focus on translation can prove invaluable for historians, literary scholars, and others, this chapter contributes to the expansion and diversification of translation studies in Japan and more broadly.[40]

Chapter five, "Travel," explores the role of real and vicarious voyages abroad in the construction of this book's three focal communities, as well as in the (re)shaping of individual members' self-understanding in the 1970s and 1980s. During this period *ribu* activists, *rezubian feminisuto,* and other women from Japan went abroad with the express goal of forming ties with women elsewhere. They often shared their experiences and what they learned with those who remained in Japan via letters and essays. Conversely, some women (and men) from the United States, Europe, and elsewhere also visited Japan and became involved in feminist and lesbian activism. Early in the 1970s, Takemiya Keiko and Hagio Moto, known for penning early queer narratives, began sharing with their young readers romanticized accounts of their own journeys to Europe, through which their fans were able to indirectly experience European cafés, overnight trains, and boy watching, as well as communication mishaps. While the motivation driving these journeys did not always overtly include the self-discovery promoted in the domestic tourism campaigns then aggressively targeting young women, travel in all these spheres was transformative. As demonstrated in this and in preceding chapters, some of this transformation was kindled by the transfiguration of the words, texts, and practices women brought back with them. And sometimes, it was individuals themselves who were transfigured through travel. As a direct result of their own personal border crossings, some women came to new understandings of themselves—as feminists, as lesbians, as women. And the ripples of change these women set in motion helped (re)shape their own communities within Japan as well as the lives of other women in and outside them.

I conclude this book with a brief afterword reflecting on ways the women and girls in the *ribu, rezubian,* and queer *shōjo* manga spheres expanded options for gender and sexual expression for women in Japan, and gesture out toward ripples extending far beyond Japan's shores.

CHAPTER 2

Trajectories

We can, we can, we can, we can stage a revolution
If women change, men will change
If women change, the world will change
If women change, the world will change

Let's, let's, let's, let's stage a revolution
You can, you can, you can
Revolutionize yourself
Revolutionize yourself

—*Dotekabo Ichiza*

Young women coming of age in Japan from the mid-1960s to the mid-1970s were the first generation to grow up under *de jure* equality with men result-ing from the 1947 Constitution. Whether considered a gift or a punishment, the postwar Constitution was effectively imposed by the United States dur-ing the Occupation (1945–1952) following World War II. Still, while the articles guaranteeing equality of the sexes in public and private life were resisted as culturally "inappropriate" by the Japanese officials negotiating the draft with representatives from the Occupation government,[1] the idea of the equal-ity of women and men can hardly be considered a sudden imposition from abroad. The possibility of suffrage for women, for instance, had been part of a broader discourse on women's rights since the Meiji era (1868–1912). To be sure, the Meiji government's shifting policies regarding women's rights involved debate over the applicability of foreign customs to Japanese society as part of Japan's broader modernization project. And the pursuit of rights and recognition by women themselves from the Meiji era through the war years was often directly linked to transnational feminist discourse on the woman question.[2] In the immediate aftermath of the Pacific War, prior to the promulgation of the new Constitution, women's rights were part of a larger human rights package proposed by the Socialist Party—itself strongly intertwined in global socialist discourse.[3] Thus, by the time the Constitution was ratified various threads positioning women's rights, including suffrage, as a question to be addressed had been thoroughly woven into public discourse in Japan.

Moreover, Beate Sirota (later Beate Sirota Gordon, 1923–2012), the Austrian-born young woman who drafted the clauses guaranteeing equality of the sexes, among other civil rights, was no mere foreigner in Japan. Indeed, the Japanese-speaking Sirota was very much at home in the country, in which she had spent most of her childhood.[4] Although it was a decision from high in the chain of command within the General Headquarters (GHQ) that led to the existence of sections addressing women's rights—a task with which Sirota had been charged on the basis of her sex—the specificity of the rights she inscribed into the articles she wrote, as well as the passion with which she fought to have all the details she drafted included in the final version, were a response to her experience of having grown up in Japan, keenly aware of the civil and social injustices meted out to girls and women through both law and custom.[5] Nevertheless, as scholar Mire Koikari points out, Sirota Gordon's later retelling of this history "repeats, quite explicitly, a gendered imperial narrative about white, emancipated women endowed with a mission to liberate oppressed and victimized women of color."[6] While Sirota and GHQ may have seen themselves as liberating women in Japan, the truth of the matter is more complicated. Although the ultimate version agreed upon by GHQ and Japanese authorities did stipulate legal equality of women and men, this new Constitution—including the provisions regarding equality of the sexes, the definition of the family, and the status of the individual—was transfigured away from the intent of its drafters, including Sirota, via translation and negotiations across "the ambiguities of cross-cultural and cross-linguistic communication" and, subsequently, via the interpretation and implementation of the Japanese-language text.[7] As a result, while women in the postwar years could now vote upon reaching the age of majority, women's life course options remained severely limited.

Moreover, like the postwar Constitution, customs, practices, and other things that were brought to Japan from overseas in the postwar years—whether as objects of curiosity, models to emulate, or something else—were only foreign and novel to a degree. They were always directly or indirectly building upon many decades of borrowing, transfiguration, and local developments emanating therefrom. This point is so obvious as to be trite and yet has often been overlooked in discussions of cultural borrowing and translation, both within the Japanese media, inclined toward hyperbolic treatment of the "foreign," and within media abroad, inclined toward an emphasis on the "exotic." The situation is not always better in academic discourse on Japan seeking "difference." A prime example of this layered nature of Japanese modernity, Japan's postwar democratic system itself "derives," as Carol Gluck reminds us, "from the past thrice over," rooted as it is in Japan's modern traditions of political party politics and social protest, bitter memories of the suppression of political debate in conjunction with the intensification of the war in the 1930s, and decades of postwar practice.[8] Thus, by the emergence of the three women's spheres I explore in this book, there was a certain cultural proximity between Japan and a loosely defined West such that, no matter how exotic or alien an "import" from the West was framed discursively, the ostensibly very foreign was also often very familiar.

This is the culture in which the majority of women who are the focus of this book grew up. The young women who in the early 1970s were involved in the early stages of the *ribu* movement and the *rezubian* community, as well as those who revolutionized the representation of gender and sexuality in *shōjo* manga were born between the mid-1940s and early 1950s. As girls, they may have witnessed—possibly on a new black-and-white television bought in time to watch the Imperial wedding a year earlier—millions protesting against the 1960 renewal of the Treaty of Mutual Cooperation and Security between the United States and Japan, commonly referred to in Japan as "Anpo." The protests were perhaps "Japan's most important postwar confrontation between democratic forces and traditional paternalism."[9] At one point, tens of thousands of protestors surrounded the Diet building, photographs and video footage of which have become iconic symbols of this era. However dramatic, the protest's failure to stop the treaty's renewal has been associated with the weakening of the Communist and Socialist parties, concomitant with the fragmentation of political opposition into narrower interest-based groups, including Japan's so-called New Left.[10]

At the end of the 1960s—near the culmination of over a decade of unprecedented economic growth and increasing prosperity made possible by a new generation of stay-at-home wives and mothers[11]—another round of protests came to a head. This time, in addition to another Anpo renewal, protesters targeted the Vietnam War and continued US military presence in Japan, which served as a staging ground for the war—another point of contention. This wave of protests is strongly associated with Zenkyōtō, the All-Campus Joint Struggle Committee (Zengaku Kyōtō Kaigi). The most tangible manifestation of the New Left, Zenkyōtō was formed in the late 1960s primarily from undergraduate and graduate students, including individuals who had participated in the earlier Anpo protests.[12] This round involved that generation of young women in their late teens and early twenties who may have watched the protests a decade earlier as girls in their living rooms.

Women's involvement in the leftist movement and these protests is generally considered to have provided a key impetus for the emergence of the *ūman ribu* movement in 1970, a movement that has been positioned as an heir to the legacy the New Left.[13] Among the women who would adopt the *ribu* moniker were a few who would, several years later, begin what they eventually called a *"rezubian feminisuto"* (lesbian feminist) movement. It was also in this context that Japan's first *rezubian* organization, Wakakusa no Kai, was formed by women based on their shared desires and experiences as women romantically and sexually interested in other women rather than an explicitly feminist or otherwise political agenda. Finally, this was the moment in which a small group of young women artists were beginning to reinvent *shōjo* manga, in part through novel experimentation with gender and sexuality that called into question the heteronormative romance script—a development particularly striking due to the young age of the graphic narratives' intended readers. In addition to this common background and the related goals of unsettling gender and sexual norms for women outlined in chapter one, the *ribu, rezubian,* and queer *shōjo* spheres had other points of overlap that I will point to as I trace their histories below.

The Liberation of Eros and the Birth of *Ūman Ribu*

When I first met prominent *ribu* activist Tanaka Mitsu (b. 1943) in September 2008 at an event celebrating the publication of a three-volume collection of reproduced fliers, pamphlets, and *mini-komi* from Ribu Shinjuku Center (Ribu Shinjuku Sentā, 1972–1977), she told me that if I wanted to understand *ribu* I should watch a video taken of a performance of *Women's Liberation: The Musical* (*Myūzukaru "onna no kaihō"*).[14] This production—created by a group calling itself Dotekabo Ichiza, with input from prominent avant-garde poet, playwright, and critic Terayama Shūji (1935–1983)—was first staged in January 1974 at Terayama's theater. It was to be performed at various other locations through 1980.[15] The video of the March 1, 1975, performance, clips from which were shown at that September event, encapsulates the social critiques waged by *ribu* as well as the spirit of the movement—in a blend of earnestness, determination, and fervor, as well as the mirth that is seldom mentioned in descriptions of the *ribu* movement. The excerpt from the rousing concluding number that forms the epigraph of this chapter articulates Dotekabo Ichiza's revolutionary intent.

The name of the group—which for that performance included Tanaka, as well as Asakawa Mari, Doi Yumi, Sawabe Hitomi, Wakabayashi Naeko, and Yonezu Tomoko, all discussed below—involves a humorous play on words that might be translated as "the good-for-nothing theater troupe." This calls to mind contemporary artist Igarashi Megumi, who goes by the name Rokudenashiko, roughly "good-for-nothing girl." In an affirmation of women's bodies reminiscent of *ribu*, Rokudenashiko drew media attention in the mid-2010s for her pussy (*manko*) art, which insists women's genitalia is not "obscene" (*waisetsu*), leading to her arrest on charges of obscenity.[16]

Staged at a time when the *ribu* movement was near its peak, *Women's Liberation: The Musical,* used humor to communicate the troupe's messages about abortion, infanticide (*kogoroshi*), Japan's economic exploitation of Asia, prostitution tours to Asian countries, and expectations about femininity.[17] In a skit about flatulence, "No Holding Farts" (*O-nara gaman hantai*), the narrator tells the audience that not only is restraining the release of gas unhealthy, it can kill: "Last year, as many as 13,787.3 women died . . . from holding their farts."[18] The use of toilet humor itself constitutes the occupation of a discursive position women were expected not to assume, making it a particularly apt tool for the critique of social expectations of femininity (*onnarashisa*). Asakawa Mari (b. 1950) found performing in these productions as well as watching them empowering because it helped her "laugh off" serious issues women were facing.[19] The audience captured in the grainy black-and-white film recording of the 1975 performance was as boisterous about and supportive of the silly fart jokes as they were the revolutionary spirit of the concluding number.

The early stages of *ribu* were not often this lighthearted, however. The innumerable personal histories that led women to the movement are filled with resentment, frustration, and anger related to contradictions that women and girls frequently confronted, and that for many came to a head in the increasingly prosperous Japan of the late 1960s. From a young age, Yonezu Tomoko (b. 1948), for instance, questioned the social norms that dictated both that women needed to marry in order to find happiness and that she herself would not "be chosen" by a man because she was partially handicapped in one leg. Her handicap placed her outside the bounds of normative femininity, which pushed her to question it. Deciding that she needed to be able to support herself in an occupation open to women, she chose to study design at Tama Art University. And, like many other young students at the time, she got swept up in the excitement of the student movement. Within the movement she was struck by the discrepancy between rhetoric calling students to arms and rhetoric positioning female students behind the barricades, doing things like making rice balls and watching male students' possessions so they could go protest. This was an experience common to many other women who would become *ribu* activists, and one that resonates as well with issues faced by women activists in the United States and France in the same period.[20] In response to this issue specifically and the more general lack of concordance between "woman" (*onna*), "student," and "designer," Yonezu and three other students at the school formed the group Thought Collective S.E.X. (Shisō Shūdan Esu Ī Ekkusu) in April 1970 to problematize being a "woman."[21]

The aforementioned Tanaka was the most high-profile figure within the *ribu* movement in the first half of the 1970s. By dint of her personality and drive, she assumed the role of "de facto leader of a movement that purported to have no leader," in the words of scholar Setsu Shigematsu.[22] Like many others, however, Tanaka came to *ribu* through questioning the meaning of "woman" in Japanese society. She got her start in activism more generally in the late 1960s via aid activities for the children of Vietnam, in part out of sympathy for their plight and in part as a catharsis for the things in her past that she felt had sullied her as a woman, including being the victim of sexual abuse as a young child and contracting a sexually transmitted infection while in her early twenties.[23] Realizing how Japan's economic growth—supported by US military demand for weapons and trucks—was being "paid for with the blood of Vietnamese children," she quickly became involved in the anti-war movement and, though she had never gone to university, found herself in the middle of the student protests.[24] Through an encounter with a newly released translation of Wilhelm Reich's *Sexual Revolution,* she came to believe that "at the core of human consciousness is sex(uality) (*sei*)."[25] This point helped her understand her tendency toward self-deprecation and that was to become the crux of her own theorizing about the marriage system, the family, and the meaning of "woman."[26]

By the middle of 1970, Tanaka was distributing fliers among demonstrators that called for women to join with her in her new struggle—for the liberation of eros. Contrary to media reports that would conflate the goals of *ribu* with sexual liberation or "free sex" (*furī sekkusu*), for Tanaka the liberation of eros entailed undoing norms that positioned women as either mothers or receptacles for men's sexual desire. Freed from such oppression, women and men would be able to engage in truly open erotic communication with each other. The group Tanaka formed would by the autumn of 1970 call themselves Group Fighting Women (Gurūpu Tatakau Onna). The early versions of the tract, titled "Eros Liberation Manifesto" (*Erosu kaihō sengen*), specifically draw on Reich in linking the Vietnam War and the Anpo struggle, as well as personal problems, to the "oppression of sex(uality)."[27] Tanaka refined her argument into an increasingly lengthy declaration that would by August become her influential "Liberation from the Toilet" (*Benjo kara kaihō*) pamphlet, which at times was printed under the Group Fighting Women name.[28] And it was under this name that they would organize a demonstration involving around fifty women in Tokyo's Ginza district on October 21, marked at the time by some activists in Japan as International Anti-War Day.[29] Through media coverage of this protest—the first public women's liberation protest in Japan—women like Yonezu learned about Tanaka's group and were able to connect with it.[30]

Akiyama Yōko (1942–2016) did not attend the first *ribu* rally in 1970 but she had already been interviewed about the nascent women's liberation movement in Japan for an article in the daily *Asahi shinbun* newspaper earlier that month, an article that would introduce the label "*ūman ribu*" and link the Japanese movement to its American counterpart.[31] A year earlier, Akiyama was a newlywed with a master's degree in Chinese literature and a new baby. Having found a part-time job she wanted to keep, teaching at a high school, she had no choice but to put her baby in an unlicensed daycare center because public facilities did not admit children that young. She had also become acquainted with Jan and Annie, a young American couple who had recently graduated from Berkeley and had come to Japan to protest the war, as well as, in the case of Jan, to evade the draft. Through English conversation classes given by the couple, she learned details about the new women's liberation movement in the United States right around the time it was first being ridiculed in the Japanese press. When the couple left to take haven in Sweden, which was providing visas to American draft evaders, they left behind several pamphlets from the US movement, including a tract by Marge Piercy critiquing sexism within the student movement in the United States.[32] Akiyama's Japanese rendering of this pamphlet was among the earliest translations of US radical second-wave feminist writing in circulation in Japan, and Akiyama would continue to play a key role in the translation of US feminist writing for the next several years.[33]

Another of the earliest *ribu* translators was Ikegami Chizuko (b. 1946).[34] A voracious reader as a child, Ikegami was in the fourth grade when a boy in her class told her that she had no need to study hard since she only needed to be able to clean and to look cute to get married—her presumed destiny and dream. As Ikegami recalls that moment, the shock she received at hearing those words was the start of her feminist career, a path that would lead to her participation in the *ribu* movement in the early 1970s. Through the media, including American television shows like *Father Knows Best,* in which women laughed boisterously and revealed how clever they were, she had gotten the impression that American women were very fortunate compared with women around her.[35] She decided to study American women's history at university, thinking there might be something useful to be learned that would help women in Japan. Upon beginning her studies at the elite and overwhelmingly male University of Tokyo in 1965, she quickly discovered, however, that women in the United States and those in Japan were confronting essentially the same issues. Nevertheless, she learned about new feminist activism in the United States, including the writing of Betty Friedan and the creation of the National Organization for Women (NOW), and she began translating short items for herself and to share with friends.[36] She was also among hundreds of women to take part in the seven-hour-long women-only debate "An Accusation of Sex Discrimination," held on November 14, 1970. This debate was transcribed and published under the same title the following year.[37] Ikegami contributed several translations to that volume and went on to publish a full-length book on American women's history, a revised version of her senior thesis, in 1972.[38]

A year earlier, Miki Sōko (b. 1943), living in the Kansai region (encompassing Osaka, Kobe, and Kyoto), one day found herself in tears on the train reading *An Accusation of Sex Discrimination*—at long last she had found other women who shared her feelings.[39] Miki had been struggling to reconcile her beliefs about equality in marriage with her own experiences, and this book touched a nerve like nothing before. Soon thereafter, Miki saw a tiny notice in the old-school feminist publication *Women's Democratic Newspaper* (*Fujin minshu shinbun,* 1946–) about the first *ribu* retreat to be held that August in Nagano and thought, "This is it!" She knew she had to go. Her first encounter with *ūman ribu* in the flesh was taking part in that gathering. At the retreat were approximately three hundred women ranging from teens to forties and a number of groups, including its organizers, Group Fighting Women and Thought Collective S.E.X. from the Tokyo area, as well as groups from more distant parts of the country, such as Ribu FUKUOKA, from southwest Japan.[40] The retreat's plans called for a discussion questioning a shopping list of issues often taken for granted: "the class struggle, sex(uality), family relationships, Marx, Freud, beauty, common sense, education, employment . . . and being a woman (*onna*)."[41] More importantly perhaps, the gathering gave women the chance to talk about their feelings and experiences—preparing food for others, abortion, discrimination, emotional wounds—offering an opportunity for the kind of consciousness raising necessary for personal liberation.[42] Miki writes that this retreat also helped establish a *"ribu* network" and led to the birth of the Osaka-based *mini-komi* titled *From Woman to Women* (*Onna kara onnatachi e,* 1972–1988)

Figure 2.1. Cover of the third issue of *From Woman to Women*
(*Onna kara onnatachi e*), published in May 1972.

(figure 2.1) and the first commercially published *ribu* magazine, *Onna erosu*
(Woman eros, 1973–1982). Miki was a founding member of both.[43]

Just over a year after the first *ribu* retreat, several *ribu* groups established
Ribu Shinjuku Center in a small Tokyo apartment. Tanaka explains that the
name of the center was chosen to emphasize that it was "just one of many
ribu groups" that happened to be located near Shinjuku rather than it being
"the" *ribu* center.[44] This intent was belied, however, by its expansive nick-
name, Ribusen—short for *ribu sentā* (lib center). And, given the centrality of
Ribu Shinjuku Center as well as the prominence of Tanaka in the movement,
the center did in fact function as a central node for *ribu* groups around Japan
for the five years of its existence. It was also often on the itinerary of foreign
feminists passing through or living in the country. It was out of Ribu Shinjuku

Center that *Ribu News: This Straight Path* (*Ribu nyūsu: Kono michi hitosuji*, 1972–1976), a key *mini-komi*, was published and distributed nationwide.[45] In addition to providing living quarters for members of Group Fighting Women and Thought Collective S.E.X.—one of a number of experiments in collective living among *ribu* groups around Japan—the center was the meeting place or founding location of over a dozen *ribu* groups working on a range of feminist issues.[46] A history of the center by women who once took part in activities at the center describes groups using the space as working on "preventing the worsening of the Eugenics Protection Law (Yūsei hogo hō), abolishing the anti-abortion law, rethinking infanticide, [fighting] the exclusion of baby strollers from public spaces and the economic invasion of Asia, protesting prostitution tours [by men], [addressing] the harmful effects of pollution and medicines, denouncing sex discrimination in the media, [attacking] violence by husbands [against their wives], [and] abolishing the death penalty."[47]

Opposition to proposed revisions of the Eugenics Protection Law would be one of the most prominent of these issues, covered in countless meetings as well as in articles in *Ribu News* and many other *mini-komi*. Building on the voices of right-wing activists who had long favored prohibition of abortion on moral grounds, some members of the Diet had begun to make moves toward drastically increasing restrictions on abortion, in part a reaction to an increasing demand for labor due to Japan's rapid economic growth.[48] *Ribu* groups began to address the problem in the latter half of 1970, among the earliest civil opposition to this move.[49] In May 1972 a bill was proposed that would remove the law's "economic reasons" clause, which effectively permits any woman to have an abortion so long as she declares her reason for having an abortion to be economic. More troubling for many was its replacement by a clause permitting selective abortion for fetuses with anomalies to allow, if not encourage, the prevention of babies with handicaps from being born. Finally, the bill included a provision that would establish a system to counsel women on the best age for marriage and childbirth, this in response to an increase in the number of women seeking careers.[50] Writing at the time in the English-language Japanese New Left journal *AMPO*, Nagano Yoshiko asserted that, "Taken as a whole . . . the reform bill is aimed at . . . controlling [women's] entire life cycle."[51] The bill failed to come to a vote in 1972 or 1973.[52] Many of those fighting the bill, including New Left groups, women's groups, labor organizations, and groups for the physically and mentally handicapped, united in March 1973 to form the Committee to Prevent the Worsening of the Eugenics Protection Law (Yūsei Hogo Hō Kaiaku Soshi Jikkō Iinkai), based at Ribu Shinjuku Center.[53] Ultimately, the bill met strong opposition from a number of fronts, including the medical establishment, and failed when it was finally voted on in May 1974.[54]

Another group focused on the abortion issue was Chūpiren, which, as reflected in its name's reference to abortion (*chūzetsu*) and the birth control pill (*piru*), vigorously protested attempts to criminalize abortion and fought equally hard for legalization of the pill, the latter of which was a cause other *ribu* groups were generally reluctant to get behind out of health and other concerns.[55] The group was established in 1972 by Enoki Misako (b. 1945), whose involvement in *ribu* activism appears to have begun in Woolf Society, co-founded by Akiyama as a translation group. While the Japanese medical establishment claimed the pill was unsafe, Enoki had obtained some, and members of Woolf Society experimented with taking them. Ultimately the group's members remained unconvinced that the pill was safe and were unwilling to advocate for it.[56] Enoki split from Woolf Society after she was criticized for using Woolf's name without the consent of her fellow members on pamphlets about the pill that she was selling at a *ribu* meeting in 1972.[57] Chūpiren's colorful public antics, such as boisterous demonstrations in pink helmets, garnered a great deal of attention from the media, which in the mid-1970s sometimes falsely conflated Enoki and her group with the entire *ribu* movement. While writing by *ribu* activists reflecting on the movement often mentions Chūpiren, the group has been positioned outside of the mainstream of the movement, likely due to a lack of strong ties between Enoki's group and core *ribu* groups, as well as the negative attention Chūpiren brought to *ribu*.[58] Enoki and the group disappeared around 1977.[59]

For *ribu* activists, as for many women around the world, the 1975 United Nations First World Conference on Women was a pivotal moment, one that would see the participation of several prominent *ribu* activists alongside Japan's official delegation. Among its impacts on women in Japan, this conference, as well as the subsequent Decade for Women (1976–1985) and related UN conventions, would drive the creation of the Equal Employment Opportunity Law (Danjo koyō kikai kintō hō) of 1985, a new law for the promotion of women's equality in the labor force in Japan. (That law would prove to be of limited effect.) For the *ribu* women, however, the 1975 meeting drew away key members and further depleted the movement's already waning energy. In the end, for many *ribu* activists the intensity of their involvement in the early 1970s was too draining, and the conference provided a smooth segue away from *ribu*. As discussed in chapter five, several prominent activists who went to Mexico City to attend the conference stayed on in North America for an extended period, either to network and to learn firsthand about feminist movements in the United States, or to simply drop out of the movement.

Those who stayed behind in Tokyo changed the organization of Ribu Shinjuku Center and stepped down their activism for various, sometimes personal reasons. After moving out of the center, Yonezu, for instance, got involved in a women-only printing collective with several other *ribu* women, including Doi Yumi (b. 1952). When tensions within that group became too much, she pulled out of feminist activities altogether until a new government move to revise the Eugenics Protection Law drew her back around 1982. Since then, Yonezu has remained heavily involved in Soshiren, a group initially focused on again preventing the worsening of the law but that has moved on to focus on broader themes.[60]

As the *ribu* movement was waning, a more intellectual form of feminism began to come to the fore, spearheaded by women of the same generation as *ribu* activists, including some *ribu* activists themselves. While these newly prominent feminists would focus on many of the same issues as *ribu* activists had been doing, the new feminists would, for the most part, not stage the same kinds of public protests or demonstrations or engage so vigorously in grassroots activism. They also embraced the words "*feminisuto*" (feminist) and "*feminizumu*" (feminism), both of which had little currency in the *ribu* movement for reasons addressed in chapter three. This new wave was represented most tangibly in books and magazines, sometimes devoted exclusively to feminist topics. One such magazine is the journal *Feminist* (*Feminisuto*, 1977–1980), founded by Atsumi Ikuko (b. 1940) and several other women, which embraced an internationalist vision of feminism. In its first year, the magazine prominently ran interviews with American feminists like Kate Millett and Erica Jong and Japan's own international feminist par excellence, Yoko Ono. Starting in 1978 it also produced several issues in English and distributed them internationally, "in the hope of bringing to readers of English accurate information about the situation of women in Asia."[61]

The subsequent issue contains a special feature on the "dawn" of "women's studies" (*joseigaku*), with articles introducing courses on women available at universities in Japan as well as women's studies courses abroad.[62] While the study of women in Japan itself was nothing new, as the editors of *Feminist* spell out in their introduction to the issue, with the advent of this new field, "women have begun to rewrite scholarship and history."[63] Like the new wave of academic feminism, those involved in establishing women's studies as a field in Japan make no qualms about pointing to learning about women's studies courses in the United States as a major impetus for moving to establish similar ones in Japan. Inoue Teruko (1942–2021) writes that she first heard about "women's studies" from journalist Matsui Yayori (1934–2002) at the *ribu* retreat in August 1971 and decided to see it for herself.[64] Nevertheless, writing about the field almost a decade later, she insisted that, "It is important to build a [field of] women's studies that is rooted in the history of women (*onna*) in Japan and not a mere import from America."[65]

When Inoue and Kaya Emiko (b. 1943), who accompanied her on a 1973 tour to several US universities with women's studies courses, later wrote about those courses, they coined the word "*joseigaku*" to name the field. Like the choice within the *ribu* movement of *josei* and *onna* over *fujin,* this naming was not without significance to Inoue. As Inoue writes in her book on the new field, she and Kaya ultimately chose a term that they felt would suggest a field in which "women (*josei*) research women (*josei*)."[66] The Women's Studies Society of Japan (Nihon Joseigaku Kenkyūkai) was founded in Kyoto in autumn 1977 and three years later published its first *Annual Report of Women's Studies* (*Joseigaku nenpō,* 1980–).[67] Though Inoue does not spell it out, the use of *josei* in the mid-1970s suggests a certain distance from the *ribu* movement, which, as discussed in chapter one, embraced the bolder *onna.*

While Inoue had high hopes for women's studies from the outset, some within the *ribu* movement, including the aforementioned Miki, saw the field, as well as the academic feminism with which it was associated, as poaching vital energy from *ribu* activism.[68] While I can neither prove nor disprove this claim, given the timing of *ribu*'s dissipation and the rise of women's studies and this new thread of feminist thought, it is not a surprising correlation to see, particularly for *ribu* activists not directly involved in the new field. Nevertheless, her choice of *josei* over *onna* notwithstanding, Inoue herself saw the field itself as "part of the *ribu* movement broadly defined."[69] Moreover, there is no definitive end point for *ribu* and no single event or new movement (or field) dealt it a fatal blow. Many of the women involved in *ribu* have continued to take part in activism, often related to women's issues sometimes explicitly framed as *feminisuto* causes. When Yonezu began again to take part in activism with the members of Soshiren, which does not define itself as a *ribu* group, she was rejoining some women she knew from her *ribu* days.[70] *Onna erosu,* the commercial magazine founded by *ribu* activists, was published until the early 1980s. The group of women in Nagoya who began publishing the *mini-komi Women's Revolt* (*Onna no hangyaku*) from May of 1971 were still producing new issues as late as 2013 roughly once a year, a reduced frequency from the *mini-komi*'s heyday. While women like Miki still proudly fly the *ribu* banner, most rarely if ever use the label anymore. Yet, even if they no longer apply the term to their current identity, some women with whom I have spoken maintain a clear attachment to "*ribu.*"

That the *ūman ribu* movement has long lived on in spirit for many former activists, however, is evident in a 2004 documentary in which *ribu* women from Tokyo, Osaka, Nagoya, and elsewhere come together to celebrate *30 Years of Sisterhood (30-nen no shisutāfuddo).*[71] The fact that a version of this video was released with English subtitles and a 2006 film tour of US universities was arranged—with Miki and Doi as well as the filmmakers participating along with local scholars, including myself—makes it clear that, while their movement is local in origin and focus, theirs is an experience that at least some former *ribu* activists and feminists from Japan continue to believe has significance beyond Japan's shores.

Weaving Together a *Rezubian* Community

Resting in the corner of an adult bookstore near the south exit of Tokyo's Shinjuku Station was a notebook in which individuals interested in *"homo, rezu,* swapping, or SM" could leave messages for like-minded others. It was December 1971 and a twenty-one-year-old office worker who would later adopt the pseudonym Suzuki Michiko (b. 1950) left a note containing the address of her new post office box, the telephone number of the boarding house where she was staying, and a message stating that she was forming a group for those who, like her, "want to live as *rezu"*—using a common Japanese abbreviation for *"rezubian"* closely associated with pornography for men. She quickly began to receive countless calls at the boarding house. Yet, to her great disappointment and frustration, the calls were all from curious men, on whom she hung up, one after another. One day, however, just as she was about to hang up yet again at the sound of a male voice, the man on the other end of the line stopped her. He was not calling for his own sexual titillation, he insisted, but rather because his wife was "like that." He asked Suzuki to meet her. Soon thereafter, Suzuki tracked down another woman who had left contact information in that notebook, and the three of them, with Suzuki as leader, became Wakakusa no Kai. The group's name, literally meaning "young grass club," references young women, who have sometimes been referred to as *"wakakusa,"* or young grass, and perhaps Louisa May Alcott's *Little Women,* which in Japanese is called *Wakakusa monogatari,* which might be translated to "tales of young women." Wakakusa no Kai is widely considered Japan's first *rezubian* organization.[72]

To reach out and provide support to as well as bring together women attracted to other women, Suzuki made a significant effort to promote the group, including outing herself publicly (albeit under her pseudonym). She was interviewed for magazines and on television, a particularly brave act for a young *rezubian* in the 1970s.[73] She also put ads in adult manga magazines, the only magazines with rates she could afford that would allow her to advertise a *rezubian* organization.[74] Many women evidently went to Wakakusa no Kai's gatherings seeking a partner rather than a community, and indeed, a defining feature of the group was the matchmaking registry maintained by Suzuki and in the personal ads in the group's publication, *Wakakusa*. Yet, according to Suzuki, a majority of women at its meetings just wanted to engage in "completely ordinary" chat in a space where it was acceptable to be a *rezubian*, a space where a woman could withdraw, however briefly, from the heterosexual world and feel at ease.[75]

By the mid-1970s, Wakakusa no Kai had over eighty members and was holding monthly social gatherings in Tokyo and bimonthly gatherings in Osaka, and it would eventually organize parties and trips.[76] A decade later, Suzuki estimated that the group had had at least five hundred members over the course of its existence.[77] In a 1983 article she penned for the venerable women's magazine *Fujin kōron* (Women's debate, 1916–), Suzuki describes the group's membership as including "single people, people living with their girlfriends, married people (those accepted by their husbands; those keeping it secret) . . . ranging in age from high school students in their teens to married women in their fifties."[78]

While the group was harshly criticized in the mid-1970s by *ribu*-oriented *rezubian* for being non-political and for perpetuation of the patriarchal paradigm through the expectation that, both in couples and within the group in general, *rezubian* take on either a female role (*onnayaku*) or male role (*otokoyaku*), under Suzuki's leadership the group advocated social change.[79] For instance, in a note opening the spring 1975 issue of the group's *mini-komi, Wakakusa,* Suzuki expresses a desire to "eliminate the deep-rooted prejudice" in Japanese society "against people attracted to the same sex," so any woman can lead a bright, carefree life with the woman she loves[80] (figure 2.2). Moreover, regardless of such critiques, the mere existence of spaces like Wakakusa no Kai, offering women a respite from social expectations, works to unravel patriarchal norms by making individuals aware of alternatives. And, clearly, Suzuki's ultimate goal was to rend a hole in the fabric of Japanese social norms.

Although this was a goal held in common with the *ribu* movement, *ribu* was not particularly welcoming for same-sex-desiring women, *rezubian*-identified or otherwise, whose experiences within the movement varied.[81] Among open *rezubian* participating in *ribu* activities were women who felt attracted to females prior to joining the *ribu* movement, sometimes from a young age.

発行所 〒144 東京都大田区蒲田郵便局 私書箱36号 若草の会

Figure 2.2. Cover of the spring 1975 issue of *Wakakusa*.

Amano Michimi (b. 1945), who got involved in the *ribu* movement and Tanaka Mitsu's Group Fighting Women around 1972, was quite open about her sexuality, although she left the group in less than a year because she and Tanaka did not get along.[82] While Amano did not feel that she was treated poorly for being a *rezubian,* other women like the aforementioned Asakawa Mari, also in Group Fighting Women, were overtly made to feel unwelcome in the organization's communal living environment. In addition, Asakawa, like a number of other activists regardless of sexual orientation, also had problems with Tanaka's leadership style.[83]

Between 1975 and 1976 four *rezubian* involved in *ribu,* including a few with ties to Wakakusa no Kai, created several surveys to find out more about the other *rezubian* they were certain were in the *ribu* movement. They circulated the surveys among *ribu* women at meetings and via *ribu* group membership lists and other channels. The first survey asked "female homosexuals" (*josei dōseiaisha*) about issues such as when they became aware of their desire for women; the other was a broader survey of women in the *ribu* movement as well as other women and men. The fifty-seven responses they received were the focus of three roundtable discussions between March and May 1976 and the subsequent creation of the first—and ultimately only—issue of the *mini-komi Wonderful Women* (*Subarashī onnatachi*), which was released that November and would sell upwards of one thousand copies.[84]

In spite of criticism and lack of support from *ribu* activists, as well as the emergence of *rezubian feminizumu* (discussed below), Wakakusa no Kai provided an important space for many women for almost a decade and a half—through around 1985—before running out of steam, as well as funds. Suzuki had taken out a large loan to privately publish "Japan's first *rezubian* magazine," *Eve & Eve* (*Ibu ando ibu*), in 1982, and in spite of poor sales possibly due to distribution problems, she quickly produced another issue. She was ultimately forced to devote her time to working in order to pay off the loan rather than running the group itself. Suzuki eventually withdrew completely, and the group dissolved.[85]

Just as the *Wonderful Women* project was underway, Wakabayashi Naeko (b. 1947) arrived back in Japan after a year spent in Mexico and the United States. Wakabayashi, who had joined Group Fighting Women after seeing an article in the *Asahi shinbun* following the first *ribu* protest on October 21, 1970, brought back with her a lesbian feminist identity, the possibility of which she had been unaware before her sojourn.[86] She contributed to *Wonderful Women* by translating into Japanese an article penned by a foreign woman living in Japan.[87] Wakabayashi has acknowledged that she is considered an "ideological lesbian" (*shisōha rezubian*), namely, someone who is a *rezubian* for "ideological" reasons. This, she knows, positions her differently from someone who grew up attracted to other women.[88]

Izumo Marou (b. 1951)—who had attended one of the *Wonderful Women* roundtables—notes that those who were *rezubian* as a "political choice" (*seijiteki sentaku*), which she links to the influence of US feminism, had not experienced the same kind of anxiety about or rejection for being *rezubian* and, consequently, were not adequately sympathetic toward the needs of those for whom being a *rezubian* was not experienced as a choice.[89] These needs included speaking and writing about negative issues in order to address the emotional wounds incurred from contravening or feeling compelled to comply with social norms. In her study of this period, Sugiura Ikuko draws a distinction between the women involved in *Wonderful Women* and those who made the political choice to be a *rezubian*.[90] Yet, in Izumo's experience, those who chose a *rezubian* identity under the influence of US lesbian feminism were not distinct from those *ribu*-oriented *rezubian* involved in the *Wonderful Women* project. Some women in this project harshly rejected ideas and experiences that contradicted the notion that lesbians are "wonderful women," and Izumo felt ridiculed and criticized for talking about her own struggles, provoking her withdrawal from the group and long-standing resentment.[91]

In 1977 Sawabe Hitomi (b. 1952) and several women who had come to *Wonderful Women* from Wakakusa no Kai formed the group Everyday Dyke (Mainichi Daiku), which produced two issues of its own *mini-komi, The Dyke* (*Za daiku*, 1978).[92] Differences of opinion led Sawabe to split off and form another group, Shining Wheel (Hikari Guruma), which produced an eponymous *mini-komi*.[93] In spite of their differences, the two groups cooperated. Everyday Dyke, for instance, promoted the premier issue of *Shining Wheel* in its own publication.[94] While both groups positioned themselves as *rezubian feminisuto,* Sugiura points out that lesbianism as an explicitly political choice was central to neither.[95]

In 1981, however, members from each group joined together to start Lesbian Feminist Center, which was guided in part by the belief that lesbianism is a rational political choice for feminists.[96] Activities organized by the groups using the center included holding consciousness-raising workshops, throwing dance parties involving fifty to sixty women, and providing support to *rezubian* from around the country who sent letters to its post office box. While the facility was repurposed into a rape crisis center in 1983,[97] several women organized Sisterhood Club (Shisutāfuddo no Kai) around that time and began producing a *mini-komi* called *Lesbian Communication* (*Rezubian tsūshin*). At a rented space near Waseda University in Tokyo, the group presented a slideshow put together by lesbians in the United States called *Women Loving Women*. Afterward, five of them, including Kagura Jamu (b. 1952), Wakabayashi, and Sawabe, the latter of whom had first learned about American lesbian feminists through participation in Ribu Shinjuku Center translation activities in the 1970s, set to work to produce a Japanese version of the slideshow.[98]

While they were unsuccessful in creating the show due to privacy concerns—a long-standing issue—these women ended up founding a new *mini-komi, Regumi Communications* (*Regumi tsūshin,* 1985–); a new group, Regumi no Gomame, later shortened to Regumi; and, in 1987, a new *rezubian* space, Regumi Studio Tokyo.[99] The group's original name, Regumi no Gomame, combines an abbreviation for "*rezubian* group"—Regumi (combining *rezubian* and *gumi,* meaning group)—with an oblique reference to the idea that working together is powerful.[100]

Inspired by a combination of American lesbian feminist writing, *The Hite Report,* attending the eighth International Lesbian Information Service Conference in Switzerland in March 1986, and the responses that came in from around the country to an article she wrote about that conference under the pseudonym Hirosawa Yumi for *Fujin kōron,* Sawabe would go on to spearhead a new pair of surveys of *rezubian* in 1986.[101] The results formed half of Sawabe's *Stories of Women Who Love Women* (*Onna o ai suru onnatachi no monogatari*), whose origin is further explored in chapter four.[102] Published in May 1987 as part of the popular Bessatsu Takarajima series, *Stories* has long, and inaccurately, been considered within the community to be the first commercially published book created by—and, more or less, for—*rezubian.*[103] This volume, available at bookstores around the country, has been described as a "bible" for a generation of *rezubian* and *baisekushuaru* (bisexual) women, for whom it was often the first positive representation of *rezubian* life they encountered.[104] Many have said that reading this book, was the first time they were aware of the extent of the *rezubian* community—and for some, its very existence.[105]

Also in the 1980s, an "English-speaking lesbian community" came together, centered around Tokyo.[106] This was initially facilitated by International Feminists of Japan (IFJ), founded in 1979 by Anne Blasing, "to provide a support network among feminists in Japan's international community and to provide a bridge between this feminist community and the many Japanese feminist organizations."[107] In 1985, a lesbian session was included in the program of an international feminist conference jointly hosted by IFJ and a Japanese feminist group. The enthusiasm at that session led those in attendance to plan an overnight gathering in November, which was the first of what would come to be called, simply, "Weekends" (Uīkuendo). Around fifty women attended the initial retreat, but for a while over a hundred women were regularly coming to the Weekends,[108] which, now under the name "Dyke Weekends," are still being held more than two decades into the twenty-first century.

Although the early workshops at the Weekends were mostly in English, the events were in principle bilingual. Nevertheless, communication across language barriers was always an issue.[109] To foster cross-cultural lesbian communication in this sphere, under the name Joni van Dyke, one woman compiled a Japanese–English "dyketionary" in the mid-1980s, which she sold at the Weekends and by mail.[110] When asked about the links between the English- and Japanese-speaking lesbian communities in general, Linda Peterson (b. 1951), an American lesbian living in Japan since 1979, recalled to me that they were bridged by binational couples in which one partner was Japanese, by enthusiastic learners of Japanese, and by Japanese women who had lived abroad at some point. She added, however, that because of differences of language and interests, "It's impossible to say that there was ever *one* community of any kind."[111] The multilingual Hara Minata (Minako; b. 1956), who had spent significant time abroad before participating in some Weekends, observed to me that the relative economic advantages of foreigners teaching English in Japan as well as their short-term outlook—a majority planned to stay in Japan only a few years at most—contributed to the gap between the English-speaking and domestic lesbian communities Hara witnessed.[112]

About the *rezubian* involved in the English-speaking community, Peterson remarked, "All the Japanese dykes who showed up were definitely political. Either lesbian political or feminist political . . . or groovy green political."[113] Hara has pointed out elsewhere that this politicization put undue pressure on some women to declare their sexuality, noting that in the beginning some women who called for information about the Weekends were asked outright, "Are you a *rezubian?*"[114] Such a direct question was doubtless unsettling for women unsure of their sexuality or uncomfortable with the word "*rezubian*" and, at times, made the label a sort of shibboleth for acceptance at the Weekends.

In addition to the Weekends, the mid-1980s also saw the emergence of bars aimed specifically at *rezubian,* and in some cases, run by them. While a limited bar scene involving women interested in other women existed as early as the 1950s, the first regular bar events aimed at *rezubian,* were likely the women-only nights on Mondays beginning in 1982 at the *gei* bar, Matsuri (Festival). Matsuri was run by Itō Bungaku (b. 1932), the (publicly heterosexual) founder and chief editor of Japan's first commercial *homo* magazine, *Barazoku* (Rose tribe; 1971–). Itō had long been supportive of *rezubian,* who, in the absence of a commercial *rezubian* publication, sometimes called him or sent letters to *Barazoku*. Against the objections of his editorial staff, who wanted to keep the focus on men, Itō occasionally included these letters and wrote about the phone calls in the magazine; he also repeatedly shared information about Wakakusa no Kai.[115] For a while in the 1970s and 1980s, Itō attempted, sometimes in cooperation with Wakakusa no Kai, to arrange marriages between *homo* (men) and *rezubian* who needed to make a show of heterosexuality to deal with familial and social pressure.[116] His publishing company, Dai Ni Shobō, was also slated to publish Wakakusa no Kai's *Eve & Eve,* but later pulled out, contributing to the financial collapse of the group, noted above.[117] Nonetheless, he promoted *Eve & Eve* in several of his columns.[118]

The women-only nights at Matsuri were run by a woman called Tomita Chinatsu. In 1985, three years after she began hosting those nights, Tomita established Ribonne (Ribonnu), Japan's first women-only bar, located adjacent to the well-known neighborhood of *gei* bars in Tokyo's Ni-chōme district. Ribonne—named after a book illustrated by male artist Kaneko Kuniyoshi, whose painting of a girl adorned the bar's sign—was established with Itō's financial backing.[119] Unlike existing bars with a significant *rezubian* clientele, drinks at Ribonne were reasonably priced and there was no service charge. Sunny (1948–2011), a *rezubian* who was running an ordinary, and thus expensive, snack bar called Sunny Ni-chōme, was a frequent customer of the newly opened Ribonne. Seeing a viable model for a bar, Sunny copied Ribonne's approach when she opened Mar's Bar in Ni-chōme's *gei* bar district later that same year. While Ribonne closed many years ago, Mar's Bar stayed open until 2016.[120] After Ribonne and Mar's Bar, similar bars began to open in Tokyo and other large cities around the country. Surveys of the community from over the past two decades suggest that bars have served an important function for many in the community, including helping them connect with women who became romantic partners.[121]

While parallels with lesbian bar culture in other countries are easy to draw, the long history of Japanese *rezubian* bars gives little indication of overt cultural borrowing in the construction of the foundation of the bar scene. Such is not the case, however, for women-only dance parties and similar events aimed primarily at *rezubian*. A Tokyo-based women-only event producer who has used monikers including Don King Chigalliano and Chiga explains that the exuberance she felt at a women-only dance party in London was the inspiration for the 1991 creation of a long-running dance party known as Gold Finger,[122] which spawned a new women-only bar under the same name in Shinjuku. Since the 1990s, women-only events have been held regularly in Tokyo, Nagoya, Kyoto, Osaka, and other major cities. A sign of changing times and attitudes, Gold Finger was harshly criticized in 2019 for sometimes not allowing trans women to enter on women-only nights—a policy it quickly rescinded and for which it has apologized.[123] Nevertheless, whether queer-only, women-only, or lesbian-only, these kinds of events challenge the heteronormative boy-meets-girl paradigm, allowing for a sense of connectedness with other lesbian-inclined women. Alongside the limited number of *rezubian* and *rezubian*-friendly bars, *rezubian* dance parties thus provide women with another space where they can feel their sexual and gender identities accepted, helping them find affirmation regardless of how they define, or refuse to define, themselves.[124]

In addition to bars and a lesbian club scene, the 1990s also saw commercial and popular successes in the *rezubian* as well as the *gei* and *rezubian* communities that owe some debt to the 1990s male-focused "gay boom" (*gei būmu*) in the popular media, which can in no small part be traced to interest in gay men on the part of fans of queer *shōjo* manga.[125] This surge in media attention in the early 1990s helped provide popular forums for *rezubian* discourse, no doubt attracting women who might otherwise have been unaware of the community. New interest sparked by the boom may have helped commercial *rezubian* publications seem viable, at least temporarily. Magazines created by and for members of the *rezubian* community but published by small commercial presses—*Phryné* (*Furīne*, 1995), *Anise* (*Anīsu*, 1996–1997, 2001–2003), and *Carmilla* (*Kāmira*, 2002–2005)—came and went and have been largely supplanted by websites. Translation of lesbian-related essays, fiction, and academic writing from abroad has continued, often published by commercial presses, but arguably more significant has been local production of an ever-increasing number of books on *rezubian* life experiences in Japan, including Kakefuda Hiroko's groundbreaking *On Being "Lesbian,"* published in 1992, and multiple others in the three decades hence.[126] Books as well as special issues of mainstream magazines on LGBT issues began to mushroom in the middle of the 2010s, nourishing a new wave of positive attention in the media that continues to the present.

Collaboration with the *gei* community in Japan has become more common since the 1990s, as with the broader community of queer people that has come together under the banner of "LGBT," truly a household word by the mid-2010s. And—while there has not infrequently been tension between *gei* and *rezubian* organizers—jointly sponsored events such as increasingly common and large-scale parades and film festivals have been held regularly in Tokyo, Osaka, Sapporo, Fukuoka, and, increasingly, smaller municipalities, with an explosion of such events since the 2010s. This is also when a growing number of politicians began voicing support for LGBT rights, including some form of official recognition of same-sex partnerships. Such partnerships have been nominally recognized by a growing number of local governments around the country starting in 2015. Similar to elsewhere, anti-discrimination laws and full same-sex marriage rights are among the most pressing political concerns of the broader community. In the early 2020s, the conservatives opposed to recognizing same-sex marriage and establishing anti-discrimination regulations have continued to prevent such measures, and some conservative politicians still make overtly homophobic comments. By contrast, recent surveys demonstrate a very high level of support for the LGBT community, particularly among the younger generations, including a sizable majority in favor of same-sex marriage.[127]

In her own history of the *rezubian* community, Sawabe describes the years from 1971 to 1980 as "the seeds," from 1981 to 1990 as "the sprouts," from 1991 to 2000 as "the flowering," and from 2001 onward as "the fruit."[128] In recent decades the *rezubian* community has come to resemble lesbian counterparts in other industrialized countries, which, as we shall see in more detail in subsequent chapters, is in part a function of transnational networking and exchange whereby seemingly imported aspects of Japanese culture continue to be transfigured to meet local needs and desires.

Queering *Shōjo* Manga

A generation of young women artists revolutionized *shōjo* manga in the 1970s, ushering in its "golden age." Early on the group came to be called the "Year 24 Group" (*nijūyo'nen-gumi*), and sometimes the "Fabulous Year 24 Group" (*hana no nijūyo'nen-gumi*), on account of most of them having been born around the year Shōwa 24, namely 1949. Hence, in English they are sometimes called the Fabulous Forty-Niners. When these women were growing up, the *shōjo* manga available to them were largely drawn by male artists, who were themselves heirs to an art form whose development by earlier generations of male artists can be traced to the introduction and influence of European and American comic arts in the Meiji and Taishō (1912–1926) eras, but that has been linked to centuries of humorous art in Japan.[129] While some manga were included in magazines aimed at *shōjo* readers in the first half of the twentieth century, *shōjo* manga's emergence as a distinct category has frequently been linked to the publication of *Princess Knight* (*Ribon no kishi,* 1953–1955), by the tremendously influential male manga artist Tezuka Osamu (1928–1989).[130] Inspired by the cross-dressing performers in the all-female Takarazuka Revue, this gender-bending narrative depicts the adventures of the cross-dressing Princess Sapphire roving around a Disney-esque European setting.[131] Prominent manga critic Yonezawa Yoshihiro, for instance, describes Tezuka's *Princess Knight* as the first *shōjo* "story manga" (*sutōrī manga*), crediting Tezuka with introducing novelistic elements into manga aimed at *shōjo* readers.[132]

Art scholar Mizuki Takahashi contends, however, that Tezuka's influence on the development of *shōjo* manga in the postwar era was "secondary" to that of the *jojō-ga* (lyrical illustration) artists of the 1920s and 1930s, including Nakahara Jun'ichi (1913–1983), who got his start in the 1930s, then revived and reinvigorated the style after the war.[133] The girls drawn in *jojō-ga* style were lithe and delicate in form, with large sparkling eyes and an "empty, wandering gaze," an appearance drawing on representations of modern girls and girlhood in the prewar *shōjo shōsetsu* (girls' fiction) that *jojō-ga* were used to illustrate, fiction that itself can itself be linked to overseas writers like Louisa May Alcott. After the war such illustrations of girls were set against flowery backgrounds, reflecting these girls "inner personality."[134] The *jojō-ga* aesthetic was integral to the *shōjo* manga of the 1970s, thanks in large part to Takahashi Macoto (b. 1934), a male artist who helped introduce elements of *jojō-ga* into the manga format in the mid-1950s.[135] Takahashi and other artists prior to the 1970s, including influential female artist Mizuno Hideko (b. 1939), built on this aesthetic sense, incorporating close-ups of characters' faces with expansive, twinkling eyes that revealed characters' "inner psychology." While the interiority of girls was of little interest to Tezuka, its presence in the genre post-Takahashi encouraged readers to identify with the characters.[136]

Regardless, Tezuka's many artistic innovations as well as his astoundingly prolific and varied manga and anime works, *shōjo* and otherwise, had a substantial impact on a majority of postwar manga artists, including Fabulous Forty-Niners such as Hagio Moto (b. 1949), Ikeda Riyoko (b. 1947), and Takemiya Keiko (b. 1950).[137] In the 1970s, these artists expanded on the visual conventions they inherited, including further experimentation with the layout and shape of panels, which were sometimes dispensed with entirely. The effect was a continued emphasis on characters' thoughts and feelings.[138] Further, this new generation introduced a greater diversity of themes as well as more complex plots and characters. They also borrowed widely from and transfigured foreign and Japanese literature, film, history, and myth. Such characteristics garnered a new appreciation from adult male and female readers and helped lead to the treatment of some *shōjo* manga works as high literature.[139] In short, it was the innovations of the Fabulous Forty-Niners that transformed the genre on a profound level, turning it into a liminal space in which readers and artists alike could experiment with gender and sexuality—if they so desired. One key innovation in this regard made by the Forty-Niners was the development of a genre of *shōjo* manga that early on came to be called *"shōnen'ai"* (boys love). The etymology of this label is traced in chapter three. These often highly literary narratives—printed in mainstream *shōjo* manga magazines in wide circulation—featured male protagonists in same-sex romantic and sometimes overtly sexual relationships. The earliest of these narratives were placed in romanticized European settings and populated with beautiful adolescent European boys.

While certainly remarkable, the *shōnen'ai* genre was not entirely groundbreaking. As with the visual style common to 1970s *shōjo* manga, the *shōnen'ai* genre built on developments in and outside *shōjo* manga, including the use of male protagonists and representations of male homosexuality in texts created by women and, sometimes, specifically for, female readers. Most notable are novelist Mori Mari's (1903–1987) early 1960s novellas portraying male homoeroticism, beginning with *A Lover's Forest* (*Kobitotachi no mori*) in 1961, and Mizuno Hideko's *shōjo* manga *Fire!* (*Faiyā!*), which featured a frequently shirtless male protagonist and depictions of sex, as well as early portrayals of racism and violence in the United States, along with references to homosexuality.[140] *Fire!* was serialized from 1969 to 1971 in *Seventeen* (*Sebuntīn*, 1968–), a magazine targeting older *shōjo* readers. Also in 1969, "Crossroads" ("*Jūjiro*"), by artist Minegishi Hiromi, crossed both racial and sexual barriers in a story culminating in the young adult white male protagonist being caught in bed with a young black man. The manga appeared in the Tezuka Osamu–produced manga magazine *Funny* (*Fanī*, 1969–1970, 1973), also targeting a more mature *shōjo* demographic.[141]

The following year saw the publication of, arguably, the first *shōnen'ai* manga. These new narratives were penned by many of the most prominent professional female artists during this period and were, visual studies scholar Ishida Minori asserts, crucial to the radical transformation of *shōjo* manga that decade.[142] While some of the same artists who penned *shōnen'ai* texts also experimented in this period with female–female romance, few of those early, generally dark narratives were popular at the time and wouldn't coalesce into a genre until at least the 1990s.[143] Critics and scholars have long argued that the *bishōnen* (beautiful boy) in *shōnen'ai* serves as a locus of identification for adolescent girl readers and that the use of male (rather than female) characters, as well as homo- (rather than hetero-) sexual relationships, placed in a foreign setting, has provided female readers the means for vicarious circumvention of gender and sexual norms.[144] While the liberatory and queer effects of the *shōnen'ai* and other gender-bending genres have, no doubt, been mitigated by the fact that the male–male couples have tended to roughly reproduce the male–female binary, the genre has nevertheless exposed a broad range of *shōjo* readers to alternative sexual and gender possibilities. For some, including individuals who would go on to take leadership roles in the *rezubian* community, this exposure would have a significant impact on their self-understanding. Lesbian activist, scholar, and queer *shōjo* manga fan Mizoguchi Akiko, to name a prominent example, has asserted that she "'became' a lesbian via reception, in [her] adolescence, of the 'beautiful boy' comics of the 1970s."[145]

The creation of the *shōnen'ai* genre is most closely associated with Hagio and Takemiya. In the December 1970 issue of *Shōjo Comic Extra* (*Bessatsu shōjo komikku*, renamed *Betsu-komi*; 1970–), Takemiya published the short narrative "Snow and Stars and Angels and . . ." (*Yuki to hoshi to tenshi to*), later reissued as "In the Sunroom" (*Sanrūmu nite*), a narrative that I consider to be the first example of the new manga genre on account of its visual style and narrative content[146] (figure 2.3). Hagio followed eleven months later in the same magazine with "November Gymnasium" (*Jūichigatsu no gimunajiumu*).[147]

サンルームにて

49

Figure 2.3. Excerpt from Takemiya Keiko's "In the Sunroom" ("Sanrūmu nite" [1970] 1976), p. 49. Reproduced courtesy of Takemiya Keiko. © KeikoTAKEMIYA

Both manga feature schoolboys in romantic relationships with other school-boys in European settings. Neither initially had intended to create narratives about homosexuality per se and both would go on to produce manga in various other genres, including science fiction, mysteries, and heterosexual romance narratives—a diversity typical of *shōjo* manga artists of their genera-tion. But those first two *shōnen'ai* narratives, as well as the pair's subsequent *shōnen'ai* works serialized in *Shōjo Comic* (*Shōjo komikku;* 1968-)—Hagio's *The Heart of Thomas* (*Tōma no shinzō*, 1974) and Takemiya's *The Song of the Wind and the Trees* (*Kaze to ki no uta,* 1976–1984)—would help drive a boom in com-mercial and amateur manga that began in the 1970s and eventually led to the thriving contemporary "boys love" (*bōizu rabu*), or "BL," scene.[148]

The fact that Takemiya and Hagio both produced narratives depicting male–male romance less than a year from each other and would go on to pen two of the most influential *shōnen'ai* works was no coincidence. The pair were roommates for several years, having moved in together right around the time Takemiya published "Snow and Stars and Angels and . . . ," when Hagio came to help Takemiya meet a deadline on another project. They lived in a small apartment "surrounded by a cabbage patch" in Ōizumi, in Tokyo's Nerima Ward. Their neighbor was Masuyama Norie (b. 1950), who was soon thereafter to become Takemiya's producer, roommate, and muse—or, in Takemiya's words, her "brain."[149] Masuyama introduced the pair to some of her favorite books and played a pivotal role in the development of *shōnen'ai*. Under the sway of Masuyama, Takemiya and Hagio's apartment became known as the "Ōizumi Salon," a space where up-and-coming *shōjo* manga artists, assistants (generally aspiring artists themselves), and others would gather to work, eat, or chat about manga, literature, films, and even *homo* magazines, at least one copy of which Masuyama brought over to share.[150] Their guests included manga artists Sasaya Nanae (b. 1950), Yamada Mineko (b. 1949), and Yamagishi Ryōko (b. 1947), the latter of whom produced sev-eral male–male romances.[151]

Many of the earliest *shōnen'ai* works were, like *The Heart of Thomas* and *The Song of the Wind and the Trees,* set in Europe. These works either took place in the past or in settings that imbued the stories with a historical feel. Some early *shōnen'ai* narratives were, however, set in Japan, albeit even then often in a romanticized past rather than the present, a past that to readers would still be exotic.[152] Such works include Aoike Yasuko's (b. 1948) *Sons of Eve* (*Ibu no musukotachi,* 1976–1979) featuring three British protagonists, Kihara Toshie's (b. 1948) *Mari and Shingo* (*Mari to Shingo,* 1977–1984), set in prewar Japan, and Yamagishi Riyoko's *Emperor of the Land of the Rising Sun* (*Hi izuru tokoro no tenshi*, 1980–1984), set in premodern Japan.[153] Some artists, including women who had apprenticed with members of the Forty-Niners, did create works set in the present day, sometimes in a not-so-idealized United States, and sometimes addressing the kinds of social issues foregrounded in the aforementioned *Fire!*. These younger artists' works frequently included one or more Japanese or half-Japanese characters, linking the narratives to their readers. Prominent among such narratives are Yoshida Akimi's (b. 1956) *Banana Fish* (1985–1994), a hard-boiled detective narrative set in New York, and Akisato Wakuni's (b. 1960) *Tomoi* (1986), which features a gay-identified protagonist whose boyfriend died of AIDS.[154] For want of labels to distinguish them, works such as these latter two have often been grouped with earlier manga.[155] They are distinct from earlier works in terms of the setting and mood, as well as the art style, however; and retrospectively, we can see they have more in common with 1990s texts that would come to be labeled BL than with 1970s *shōnen'ai*.

Concurrent and overlapping with developments in the commercial sphere, fans and amateur artists were constructing a scene of their own. In December 1975, a year after Hagio's *The Heart of Thomas* was published, the first Comic Market was held at a public hall in Tokyo's Toranomon neighborhood. In spite of what in retrospect seems like a very modest turnout that day—there were just thirty-two circles disseminating their self-produced manga- and anime-related materials and around seven hundred attendees—organizers were pleased with the event's success.[156] While not the first such event, Comic Market—referred to in Japanese as Komikku Māketto (often abbreviated to Komiketto and Komike)—has become by far the largest. It has grown exponentially into a massive multi-day event drawing well over five hundred thousand people over several days twice a year.[157] In 2019 the event suddenly swelled to over seven hundred thousand when it was extended to four days due to construction at Big Sight, the convention center at which it has been held since the 1990s.[158] The COVID-19 pandemic led to a drastic reduction in the size of the event and as of 2023, it remains uncertain whether Comic Market will reach that scale again.

The event was first organized by Yonezawa Yoshihiro and a handful of others, primarily young men, as an inexpensive means for the distribution and exchange of diverse, self-produced manga without the restrictions of existing events. It quickly became synonymous with the buying and selling of *dōjinshi* (fanzines) of wildly diverse quality and content, including original and parodic manga and prose fiction and sometimes photography, as well as criticism about manga, anime, and, eventually, video games and other electronic media. Comic Market has provided amateur and even established professional artists a "place" (*ba*) for creative expression outside the restrictions of the commercial publishing world—although the event has also been used by commercial publishers to recruit new talent and has become increasingly commercialized over the decades.[159]

Adolescent girls initially accounted for the vast majority of what the organizers call "regular participants" (*ippan sankasha*), with female participants comprising around 90 percent of those original seven hundred attendees, for example. These early attendees were predominantly middle and high school students enamored with Hagio, Takemiya, and fellow Fabulous Forty-Niner Ōshima Yumiko (b. 1947), with the former two artists outranking even Tezuka in a survey on favorite artists conducted that day.[160] Hagio's early manga works, in particular—which, as noted above, were by and large not *shōnen'ai*—had also attracted many fans among the young men involved in organizing the Comic Market.[161] One way the significance of such new developments in *shōjo* manga, including the *shōnen'ai* genre, was foregrounded was in the screening of a Dynavision animation version of Hagio's groundbreaking "November Gymnasium," produced by both male and female fans of the artist.[162]

In the first several years of the Comic Market, many *shōjo* manga-related circles participated, including those creating and selling derivative works based on manga by Takemiya and other *shōjo* manga artists, as well as the male homoerotic fiction of Mori Mari dating to the early 1960s.[163] Others displayed in their works an interest in glam and hard rock musicians associated with beauty and, in some cases, homosexuality, particularly those from the United Kingdom, such as David Bowie, T. Rex, Queen, and Led Zeppelin, echoing the objectification of male rock musicians in Mizuno's *Fire!* several years earlier. One woman who created *dōjinshi* centered around foreign hard rock musicians in the mid-1970s later recalled that, at the time, she used Western rock stars in the manga she drew because Japanese musicians were just not cool to her.[164] While early *dōjinshi*, such as by the rock-inspired Queen (*Kuīn*) by a popular circle of the same name that participated in Comic Market from the beginning, contained ample imagery of beautiful and naked males, overt homosexuality was less common at first.[165]

Before long, however, some circles did start creating *dōjinshi* with more overt homosexual themes, drawing perhaps on some combination of rumors about the lives of the rock stars, commercially published *shōnen'ai* narratives, and the homosexuality represented in *homo* magazines.[166] Over the course of the 1980s, male homoerotic narratives in *dōjinshi* would come to be labeled "*yaoi*," the coinage of which is discussed in chapter three. This self-mocking label criticizes manga bereft of plot, point, and meaning, distinguishing these works from *shōnen'ai* narratives by professional artists. *Dōjinshi* parodying or otherwise based on commercial manga and anime narratives came to predominate this scene in the 1980s. Homoerotic *dōjinshi* created by and for female readers were no exception. Although anything can be parodied, among female *dōjinshi* artists, *shōnen* manga and anime have been a major source of material for male homoerotic parodies. Pride of place goes to the magazine *Shōnen Jump* (*Shōnen janpu;* 1968–), observes manga critic and researcher Misaki Naoto. From the beginning, popular manga series in *Shōnen Jump,* many of which have been made into TV anime, have been at the heart of homoerotic *"aniparo"*—that is, *"anime parodī,"* or derivative works based on anime as well as manga. Misaki estimates *Jump* works are the source for around a third of *aniparo* in the 2000s.[167] Most prominent in histories of homoerotic *aniparo* is Takahashi Yōichi's extremely popular *shōnen* manga and anime series *Captain Tsubasa* (*Kyaputen Tsubasa*), a narrative about a soccer team first serialized in *Shōnen Jump* from 1981 to 1988.[168] While not the first target of homoerotic parody, in the mid-1980s it became the first to overwhelm the Comic Market, marking the beginning of the heyday of *aniparo* at the event.[169]

The Tsubasa genre was not the first time for *shōnen'ai* or male homoerotic narratives in *dōjinshi* to be set in Japan and feature Japanese characters, yet its incredible popularity might be seen as part of a noteworthy shift away from the dominance of foreign settings and characters in *shōjo* manga depicting male homoeroticism. Critic Nishimura Mari proposes that the original text was one that middle and high school students in Japan could easily relate to.[170] The 1980s also saw the height of Japan's economic bubble and increasing recognition that Japan was a global economic power, perhaps also helping to unsettle the high status given to the blond, blue-eyed knight on a white horse ideal in *shōjo* manga.[171] Yonezawa suggests a link between parodies of Japanese celebrities and reader-contributed content in the 1980s BL-related commercial magazines *Allan* and *Gekkō* (discussed below), which served as a site for gossip on as well as photographs and illustrations of real celebrities, very often from Japan.[172]

Before those magazines, however, came *June.* Well before the *aniparo* boom, Sagawa Toshihiko (b. 1954) was inspired by fans' enthusiasm for beautiful young men at the Comic Market and the passion among some *shōjo* readers for *shōnen'ai* manga. In 1978, Sagawa convinced San Shuppan, the publisher where he was working part time, to let him produce a "mildly pornographic magazine aimed at females."[173] At least at the time this is how he pitched the project that became *June* (1978–1979, 1981–1996), the first commercial magazine for adolescent girls and young women featuring beautiful boys and young men in romantic and sexual relationships with one another.[174] Such a magazine was not much of a stretch for San Shuppan, which published magazines with erotic themes aimed at adults, including the *homo* magazine *Sabu* (1974–2002). Reflecting on the magazine's content three decades later, Sagawa explains, somewhat more equivocally, that what the Fabulous Forty-Niners produced was not "porn" but rather something in between literature and pornography, with both being important aspects of its appeal.[175] At the time he created the magazine, Sagawa was a young man who, like many other men, was taken in by works by the Fabulous Forty-Niners, artists he hoped would contribute to this new magazine, perhaps alongside amateur artists in the *dōjinshi* scene.[176]

June, called *Comic Jun* for the first two issues, was a mix of both. Takemiya contributed immeasurably to both the content and the tone of the magazine in its early years. Another central figure in *June* was Kurimoto Kaoru/Nakajima Azusa (1953–2009), who contributed fiction as Kurimoto and essays as Nakajima. The combined presence of Kurimoto/Nakajima and Takemiya shaped the spirit of *June*, which Ishida Minori describes as a "site of collaboration" between the two women.[177] Readers, ranging primarily from adolescent girls in their late teens to young women in their early twenties, contributed a significant portion of the content in the form of letters and drawings as well as manga and short stories, the latter of which could be submitted to Takemiya or Nakajima for critique in their columns dedicated to teaching the crafts of manga artistry and fiction writing, respectively.[178] In response to the popularity of prose fiction, in 1982 *Shōsetsu June* (June fiction; 1982–2004) was created.

When disappointing sales figures forced *June* to suspend publishing in 1979, the gap was quickly filled by Nanbara Shirō, working at Minori Shobō, publisher of *Out* (*Auto*, 1977–1995), a magazine focused on anime and *aniparo*. Nanbara founded *Allan* (*Aran*, 1980–1984), which was named after handsome French actor Alain Delon, but for reasons of design, spelled on the cover in Roman letters like the middle name of American author Edgar Allan Poe and one of the beautiful boy protagonists in Hagio's *The Poe Clan* (*Pō no ichizoku*; 1972–1976, 2016–2021).[179] While initially attempting to tap into the same reader interests as *June*, *Allan* was more textual and less visually oriented than its predecessor and devoted far more page space to reader-contributed content. In 1984, Nanbara left the publisher over a difference of opinion on the direction of the magazine, which he took with him. While the new magazine, which he had rebranded *Gekkō* (Moonlight, 1984–2006), was similar in content and tone to *Allan* for the first year or so, it eventually became far more focused on dark and bizarre themes, such as suicide, espionage, and the supernatural, in keeping with Nanbara's own interests.[180] It continued to provide a space for discussion of homosexuality—that of celebrities as well as of the magazine's readers—but lost relevance for most readers coming to the magazine out of an interest in *shōnen'ai*.

Both *Allan* and *June*, which was revived in 1981, functioned as a bridge in the 1980s between commercial and non-commercial worlds of *shōnen'ai* manga, as well as between fantasy and real life. The two magazines reflected a broad range of tastes from the beautiful early teen boys in the works of Takemiya and Hagio and the innocent-looking members of the Vienna Boys Choir to the glam and heavy metal rockers mentioned above. Editorial content as well as contributions from readers also introduced and discussed foreign and domestic literature and films depicting *homo* or gay men and, especially in *Allan*, lesbians. The lives of actual gays and lesbians abroad, as well as *homo* and *rezubian* in Japan were also represented in letters and articles, albeit not necessarily realistically. The *rezubian* organization Wakakusa no Kai even placed advertisements in *Allan* and *Gekkō* to recruit new members and promote its own publications, and conversely, in 1987 *Gekkō* placed an ad in *Stories of Women Who Love Women*.[181] From its second year *Allan* ran a personal ad column, called "Lily Communications" (*Yuri tsūshin*) first "for lesbiens [sic] only," although the number of advertisers who understood themselves as "*rezubian*" is questionable.[182] In addition, artists like Kimura Ben (1947–2003), Naito Rune (1932–2007), and Hayashi Gekkō (a.k.a. Ishihara Gōjin, 1923–1998), who produced erotic illustrations for *homo* and other magazines, created illustrations of beautiful adolescent boys and young men that appeared in *June* and *Allan*, further linking *shōnen'ai* and *homo* aesthetics. Extending this aesthetic connection even more, in 1988 *June*'s publisher created *Roman June* (1988–1997), a magazine featuring content from the *homo* magazine *Sabu*. Connecting fantasy to reality, the lives of actual gays and lesbians abroad, as well as in Japan, were also referenced and sometimes discussed more extensively in letters and articles. Sociologist Ishida Hitoshi argues that, given overlapping readership and content, and cross-referencing across the various *June* magazines and *Sabu*, all four represent a "queer contact zone" between *shōjo* readers and the *homo/gei* community.[183]

The wide availability of *June* and *Allan* around the country gave countless readers not just access to homoerotic narratives by established and emerging professional manga artists, but also the opportunity to participate in the production and consumption of such narratives beyond commercial channels. That would have been otherwise impossible outside of venues like the Comic Market. Both magazines ran ads from readers seeking others to join in their manga circles and help produce *dōjinshi* as well as promotions for the *dōjinshi* themselves.[184]

These magazines, particularly *June,* along with the commercially published *dōjinshi* anthologies and—even more importantly—the phenomenal popularity and proliferation of user-created media at the Comic Market and in other forums in the 1980s helped pave the way for the commercial boom of boys love manga in the 1990s and the current prosperity of the commercial market for BL media, including manga, anime, "light novels," video games, live-action films, and other media and goods in Japan and around the world. Although BL media remains a relatively minor genre, the existence of BL media and its fans is widely known in Japan and, inclusive of *dōjinshi* and other user-created media, has had an average annual domestic market size in the 2010s ranging from 21 to 22 billion yen, then equivalent to around 195 to 200 million US dollars.[185] Thus, while remarkable in the early 1970s for running counter to gender and sexual norms, what seems most remarkable about BL media today is its economic import now that its existence within Japanese popular culture has become normalized—even as the same cannot be said for gender and sexual minorities in Japan.

As we have seen, then, the 1970s can be identified with the emergence of the literary *shōnen'ai* genre of *shōjo* manga; the 1980s with the flourishing of *aniparo* and other *yaoi dōjinshi,* as well as—straddling the amateur and commercial spheres—the magazine *June;* and the 1990s with the explosion of commercially produced and distributed BL media. The early 2000s might be tied to the rise of the *"fujoshi"*—the "rotten girl." This self-mocking moniker, which became popularized in the mid-2000s, transforms a term meaning "women and children" by replacing the *"fu"* also found in *"fujin,"* the old-fashioned term for woman (discussed above), with a homophonous character meaning "rotten." The *fujoshi* quickly became an overdetermined archetype, often caricatured in the media.[186] The term *"fujoshi,"* like the term *"yaoi,"* is deliberately self-disparaging. In addition to their focus on eroticism, *fujoshi* are "rotten," as anthropologist Patrick W. Galbraith suggests, because their fantasies—centered around BL media—entail male homoeroticism rather than the heteronormative romance that "common sense" dictates.[187]

From the rough histories sketched above, it should be clear that the primary attention of most women and girls in the *ribu, rezubian,* and queer *shōjo* manga spheres was on what was happening in their own lives in Japan, or on activities that would alter their options or distract them from the limitations they faced on account of their gender. Points of overlap between these spheres are suggested in their histories. Some of these points are obvious, such as the linking of the *ribu* and *rezubian* communities by early *rezubian feminisuto* activism, while others are more subtle, such as the varied ways men in the *homo,* later *gei,* communities were useful to women in both the *rezubian* community and the queer *shōjo* manga sphere.

Another significant point of overlap—and major impetus for their juxtaposition in this book—is how acts of transfiguration of elements appropriated from European and American cultures have shaped all three communities and helped to reshape understandings of the category "women." I expand on this in the following chapters. As I discussed in the introduction, and as the histories of these spheres show, translation as well as travel, real and vicarious, played key roles in all three of these spheres in the 1970s and 1980s. Chapters four and five will take up these threads and examine the ways both translating and traveling shaped these communities and the lives of individuals within them. Intertwined with both translation and travel are the etymologies of the predominant terms used within and about these communities, most significantly "*ūman ribu,*" "*rezubian,*" and "*shōnen'ai.*" It is to the histories of these terms that I turn next.

CHAPTER 3

Terminology

[T]he world of speech and desires has known invasions,
struggles, plundering, disguises, ploys.

—*Michel Foucault*

"What's in a name?" Names matter indeed. So too do the processes whereby
they are chosen or coined. That is certainly the case in the ways groups or
communities name themselves or are named, which is not necessarily an
either-or affair, as I will show in this chapter. As David Valentine observes, the
ways "[p]eople . . . categorize themselves and others . . . is one of the most
fundamental aspects of human language and meaningmaking."[1] In this
chapter, however, I slip beyond categorization of self and other in my examination of the etymologies, derivatives, and synonyms of the three key terms
around which certain communities of women in Japan coalesced in the 1970s
and with which they expressed identification: *"ūman ribu," "rezubian,"* and
"shōnen'ai." While the first two terms are seemingly Japanese transliterations
of "women's lib" and "lesbian," respectively, their histories show that their "borrowing" was no straightforward process. To dismiss these as mere loanwords
and, thus, imports *tout court* is to overlook their extensive local histories. The
third term, *shōnen'ai,* appears to be a calque, or loan translation, similar to
dōseiai and other early Japanese renderings of "homosexuality." Composed
of Japanese *kanji* characters, these words are generally considered to be
Japanese. My discussion of the coinage and semantic fluctuation of *shōnen'ai,*
however, works to unsettle the idea that this term is more or less Japanese
than *ribu* or *rezubian.*

Moreover, as my discussion here chronicles, with the passage of time the
meaning of ostensibly local coinages and ostensible loanwords alike can easily
become overdetermined. Rather than erase the imprint of historic usages—
whether actual or anachronistically inferred—a term's reinscription by layers
of transnational cultural flows may continue to invoke echoes of past meanings even as it transforms them. It is these layers that I set out in this chapter

to peel apart. My task, however, is not the mere unearthing of forgotten histories of words. In an oft-cited critique of the largely American lesbian and gay studies of the 1980s, Joan Scott cautions against the historical "project of making experience visible"—then typical of the field—as it "precludes critical examination of the workings of the ideological system itself"; it "exposes the existence of repressive mechanisms, but not their inner workings or logics."[2] Scott suggests:

> It ought to be possible for historians . . . to "make visible the assignment of subject-positions," not in the sense of capturing the reality of the objects seen, but of trying to understand the operations of the complex and changing discursive processes by which identities are ascribed, resisted, or embraced, and which processes themselves are unremarked and indeed achieve their effect because they are not noticed. To do this a change of object seems to be required, one that takes the emergence of concepts and identities as historical events in need of explanation.[3]

This is precisely the project of this chapter. And as I suggest below, the "emergence" of even a single term might be not so much an "event" as it is a congeries of histories, one that warrants a sort of genealogical approach.

In his essay "Nietzsche, Genealogy, History," Michel Foucault declares that genealogy "opposes itself to the search for 'origins'" and "rejects the metahistorical deployment of ideal significations and indefinite teleologies."[4] Foucault's rejection of origins—or, rather, Nietzsche's—is a rejection of the "assum[ption of] the existence of immobile forms that precede the external world of accident and succession"—a rejection, in other words, of the idea that there is some pure truth to be found behind a singular moment of conception.[5] While I concur both that the truth of a thing is not necessarily to be found in its origins and that meaning is unstable, I wager in this chapter that, on a small scale, tracing the origins and evolution of words—even when inevitably partial—can make clear some of the continuities and disjunctures that prefigure and refigure words, as well as the unstable concepts they are used to signify. In sketching out the histories of words, I work not only to elucidate how these particular words and not others came to be used within and about these three communities, but also—and more importantly—to offer a richer understanding, at various moments, of the individuals and communities who used these words, as well as about and by whom these words were used.

Part and parcel of this project is an examination of the workings of power that have shaped these histories. The dominant role of men in shaping discourse and the words with which it is constructed means that men occupy a relatively large proportion of the histories told in this chapter. Indeed, one of the more fascinating, if unsurprising, points that the etymologies of the three focal terms of this chapter cast in particular relief is the extreme extent to which discourse is presumed to be a male domain and, more strikingly, the almost ingenious way some men have managed to reframe even words whose meaning seems predicated on the centrality of women so that men themselves remain central—as subject or objectifier. The primacy of the male in erotic discourse is evident, for example, in two terms borrowed from Chinese and in common use in the Edo era (1603–1868): "*nanshoku*" (male eros), which names the broad tradition and practice of male same-sex erotic relations, and "*nyoshoku*" (female eros), which names not erotic interaction between two females but between a male and a female. Although this pair evidently assumed a male subject position ab initio, some examples I share below demonstrate male semantic reinscription. Yet, the terminological histories below also illustrate that men's roles in the (re)shaping of these key terms were sometimes positive for women in intent if not as frequently in effect. More importantly for the broader project of this book, they show that women have—to borrow a term from feminist translation practice—"hijacked" words and even whole fields of discourse for their own purposes.[6] Women have reclaimed and redefined words, and, in the case of "*shōnen'ai*," recast females in the subject position of an ostensibly all-male sphere.

As I will illustrate below, it is productive to consider the coinage and adoption as well as denotative and connotative redefinition of these words in the *ūman ribu, rezubian,* and queer *shōjo* manga spheres in terms of the concept of transfiguration, introduced in chapter one. To examine key words with an eye toward ways they have been transfigured invites us to look not just for a single moment of coinage, import, or redefinition, or for the person(s) responsible, but for the multiplex processes over time factoring into what and how words come to mean in inherently, indelibly transnational contexts. It also draws our attention to the words' reverberations in the lives of individuals and in communities and the culture at large.

Framed thusly, it should be evident that the life of a word is often far more complex than may initially be evident. Not only do individuals create and recreate words, but each person has their own idiolectic sense of a word, which can be particularly and profoundly meaningful in the case of words naming identities. Moreover, shifts in the meaning and usage of a word in one sociocultural sphere do not necessarily have a significant or immediate effect on others. To address the depth and breadth of this complexity, in this chapter

I draw upon an archive chronologically and materially more far-ranging than subsequent chapters on translation and travel. I also draw from interviews with individuals in these spheres to clarify empirical details as well as to incorporate reflections on the personal significance of *ūman ribu, rezubian,* and *shōnen'ai,* as well as other terms.

The "Arrival" of "*Ūman Ribu*"

The moniker "*ūman ribu*" is a Japanese transliteration of the "not quite"[7] English phrase "woman lib" and was coined not by women in the movement but by a male journalist writing for a mainstream broadsheet. "Not exactly [a] loanword . . ." the term is, in fact, "*wasei Eigo*"—that is, "English made in Japan." Linguistic anthropologist Laura Miller describes *wasei Eigo* as English "re-fashioned to such an extent that" such words "are linguistically marked as genuine Japanese offspring."[8] Ninagawa used his neologism to indicate the women's liberation movement, upon what he understood as its "arrival" in Japan from the United States in 1970. The term's creation and quick dissemination, including its adoption by nascent groups of women formed to advance women's social and sexual freedom in Japan, appears relatively straightforward. Unraveling why and how this particular expression came to be used as a term of derision within the popular press and in public discourse, as well as, conversely, a badge of pride within the movement itself, however, begins to reveal some of the complexity of the processes and effects of cultural borrowing in the Japanese context—even for something as simple as an ostensible loanword. Moreover, the evolution and use of the term "*ūman ribu,*" like "*rezubian*" and "*shōnen'ai,*" exemplify the profoundly transnational nature of what it means to be a woman in Japan.

By all accounts, the first instance of "*ūman ribu*" in print was its use in the headline of an October 4, 1970, article in the Tokyo edition of the major national newspaper, the *Asahi shinbun,* written by male journalist Ninagawa Masao (b. 1938)[9] (figure 3.1). This was the initial article in a series introducing the movement which, Ninagawa tells readers in the headline, had "at last arrived" in the "male paradise" that was Japan and was already spreading around the country. Akiyama Yōko, who was herself interviewed for that article, concurs that Ninagawa most likely coined the term, and, regardless, the article and those that followed were pivotal in its popularization—a function, no doubt, of their prominent appearance in the Tokyo daily.[10]

Figure 3.1. *"Ūman ribu"* juxtaposed with "Women's Liberation" adorning "Ūman ribu, 'dansei tengoku' ni jōriku" (October 4, 1970, morning ed., p. 24).

The word *"ūman"* itself has long been a part of modern Japanese vernacular. For instance, Kadokawa Shoten's *Dictionary of Loanwords* cites the use of *ūman* as early as 1885, by prominent male writer, translator, and public intellectual, Tsubouchi Shōyō.[11] Its currency a quarter of a century thereafter is evidenced, for example, in the title of *Ūman karento* (Women's trends), a magazine founded in 1923. This usage of *ūman* is echoed five decades later in the term *ūman ribu*. Both terms might be considered *wasei Eigo,* which does not always adhere to English grammar rules, including, in this case, an inflection to indicate the term is plural. In the postwar decades leading up to 1970, *ūman* appeared with some frequency in the media as a stand-alone word and in *wasei Eigo* phrases. Moreover, of course, in 1970 a majority of the population, having received at least some English-language instruction, would likely have been familiar with such a basic word.[12]

The term *"ribu,"* however, indeed seems to have "arrived" in 1970, initially appearing in print around six months prior to *ūman ribu.* Its first use in the *Asahi shinbun,* for example, may have been in a March 28 article, not two months after the phrase "women's lib" was first seen in the pages of the *New York Times.*[13] The *Asahi* article explains that *"ribu"*—which it first writes as "LIB," in capital Roman letters—is short for "LIBERATION" and has been making daily appearances in the mass media in the United States. The American liberation movement, it tells readers, splintered off from the student civil rights group Students for a Democratic Society (SDS) and, based in part on an anti-capitalist philosophy, the "braless" "Redstockings" in the US "lib movement" intend to "crush 'male society.'"[14] A month later, under the heading "Lib, not love!" in its "New Words '70" column, the daily *Yomiuri shinbun* regales readers with details about the US women's liberation movement, recounting how "braless" lib activists have been protesting at beauty pageants and the offices of *Playboy* and *Ladies' Home Journal*.[15] While only the former article attempts to explain the rationale behind "lib" philosophy, each draws attention both to the choice by women's liberation activists to go braless, thus marking them as crude or hysterical, and to the apparent threat these women represent to men. Noting that lib is spreading in Europe, the author of the latter article wonders when a spark from the lib flame will reach Japan's shores.

In the pages of the July issue of the women's magazine *Fujin kōron,* a venue more sympathetic toward the idea of raising women's social status, yet another male writer, Suzuki Tadashi, uses *ribu,* this time in an article in which he describes the US women's liberation movement as potentially edifying for the leftist student activist organization Zenkyōtō.[16] This article also links the initial use of the word "lib" to SDS, with which Suzuki, a student at the prestigious Kyoto University involved in the Japanese student movement, had established direct ties.[17] Suzuki reports that SDS members in San Francisco bombarded him with questions about what he called in his article *"Nihon no ribu"* (Japanese lib). While Suzuki was unable to adequately answer the questions posed to him by SDS members, he was himself interested in increasing the number of women in the Japanese student movement. This curiosity about the "secret" of women's liberation—and perhaps a lack of awareness that many women were leaving SDS because of sexism—moved him to ask a lib activist about it. She explained that the movement was not just about the liberation of middle-class women through free sex and reproductive planning, perhaps all Suzuki learned from this encounter.[18] Regardless of what Suzuki was able to share with readers in Japan, it was already too late. By the time the article hit the newsstands, women were beginning to break away from the Zenkyōtō-led student movement, which was itself beginning to collapse.

Outside the commercial press, *ribu* was also in use at least by mid-1970 within the movement that would by year's end be widely referred to by that term. Its early use, however, seems to derive from male-authored Japanese media accounts, such as those noted above, rather than direct contact.[19] In May of 1970, a handful of women in Fukuoka formed a group they called "Ribu FUKUOKA," writing *ribu* in the phonetic *katakana* script and their location in all capital Roman letters on the masthead of their *mini-komi*. This may be the first group to use *"ribu"* in its name.[20] One group member later wrote that they chose the name *ribu* based on the fragmented and sensational bits of information they got from the media about the American women's liberation movement. While the use of *ribu* in their name "gave the impression that we were directly influenced by [that] lib movement, we hardly knew anything about the actual lib movement. It was just that, now, this new women's movement was springing up globally and we drew strength from a sense of connection to it."[21]

By August, prominent activist Tanaka Mitsu was using *"ribu undō"* (lib movement) in early versions of her influential "Liberation from the Toilet" pamphlet to refer specifically to the American movement—about which, she too makes clear, she has learned what little she knows from the Japanese press.[22] In the distinction she deliberately draws in these early writings between the Japanese terms *"onna kaihō undō"* and *"josei kaihō undō"* (both meaning women's liberation movement), and the American *"ribu undō,"* we can see a point that she and other prominent *ribu* leaders were quite vocal about: in spite of the media's insinuation or insistence to the contrary, the Japanese women's liberation movement that emerged in 1970 was local women's organic response to conditions for women in Japan.[23] It was decidedly not an import.

So now we have established the presence of both *"ūman"* and *"ribu"* and the emergence of a new movement of women activists. The question remaining is how these came together.

Since, as is clear in his initial article on October 4, Ninagawa saw Japan's new women's movement as emanating from the United States, his use of *ribu* a logical extension of the new word, which was then tied strongly to the American movement. Given how unusual it was to use English in headlines, his or his editors' decision to conspicuously write out "women's liberation" in grammatically correct English as a caption—or decorative heading—for no fewer than five of the dozen or so articles that appeared in the *Asahi* between October 4 and November 4 reinforced the casting of this movement in a foreign light. Ninagawa's own understanding of the connection was likely cemented for him by the fact that he interviewed not Tanaka, whose knowledge of the US women's liberation movement was very limited, but Akiyama, who was interested in the US movement and who, with a small group of others, had already produced and distributed, *Women's Liberation Movement Materials 1: American Edition* (*Josei kaihō undō shiryō 1: Amerika hen*), a pamphlet on the US women's liberation movement to provide accurate information about the American movement and counter the ridicule it was receiving in the Japanese media.[24]

The fifty-page handwritten, mimeographed pamphlet contains two articles translated from English and an interview with American activist Charlotte Bunch (b. 1944).[25] Ninagawa, in fact, mentions in the first article that this pamphlet served as a reference for him.[26] In both translated articles in the pamphlet, the original English "women's liberation"—rather than "women's lib"—is rendered *"josei kaihō"* (women's liberation). However, Kurita Reiko uses *"ribu"* throughout her translated interview with Bunch, conducted during a visit by Bunch to Japan. While we can speculate that Ninagawa likely read at least one of the few earlier articles in the popular press in which *ribu* is used, it seems quite plausible that the word's use in this pamphlet, as well as, possibly, by Akiyama when he spoke with her, played a role in his use of the term in reference to this new Japanese movement.

Curiously, though, at the opening of the Bunch interview, Kurita introduces readers to the new term and its connection to the women's movement by first writing out *"uimenzu ribu,"* a Japanese phonetic rendering not of "woman lib" but rather of the actual English term "women's lib," as a superscript on *"josei kaihō"* to assign the transliterated term the Japanese term's meaning. Thereafter she simply wrote *"ribu."*[27] Whether Ninagawa did not notice this fully transliterated English term or did not find it striking enough for his purposes, the fact is that before he coined *"ūman ribu"* Ninagawa had access to a transliteration of "women's lib" that was in circulation within the nascent *ribu* community. And, thus, it was a *new* term coined by a male journalist rather than an existing transliteration penned by a *ribu* activist-cum-translator that became the name of the new movement. Nevertheless, both Ninagawa's *"ūman ribu"* and the activists' *"uimenzu ribu"* link the Japanese movement to radical American feminism.

Regardless of why Ninagawa opted to use *ūman* over *uimenzu* to introduce this new movement, it is clear that he needed a term that would sound novel to the reading public or at least distinguish these activists in Japan from their foresisters. Drawing from an interview she conducted with Ninagawa, sociolinguist Saitō Masami suggests that it would have been difficult for Ninagawa to run articles about the movement under the banner of *josei kaihō* or its near synonym, *onna kaihō,* the most widely used terms in early *ribu* writings, or *fujin kaihō,* the most common older term, as none of these would convey a sense of something new or newsworthy.[28] Moreover, certainly the use of *"ūman ribu"* in headlines in bold *katakana* script—which, like italics in English, can indicate foreign words as well as emphasis—was bound to attract more attention.

There were several existing transliterated loanword alternatives Ninagawa might have chosen to reflect his understanding of the movement as having come from abroad, words that were also used within and about the new American women's movement: *"feminizumu"* (feminism) and *"feminisuto"* (feminist). Both had been introduced into Japanese by at least the Taishō era. While *feminizumu* seems to have indicated advocation of women's rights from the early twentieth century, *feminisuto* came primarily to indicate advocating praise of women, a meaning that would persist through at least the 1970s. A perusal of dozens of dictionaries of new words and jargon from the 1920s and 1930s, finds some ten volumes with an entry for *feminizumu,* all defining the term as advocation of women's rights. *Feminisuto,* on the other hand, only appears in two of those volumes, in both cases with the primary definition being a man who praises women or treats them well. The advocation of women's rights appears as a secondary definition.[29] Although I was able to find some instances in the popular press of *feminisuto* used to indicate a person or people who believe in feminism/*feminizumu,* these cases were either translations from another language or referring to feminists outside Japan, and sometimes glossed to explain the intended meaning. One 1977 article even spells out that the understanding of a feminist as an adherent of the principle of "ladies first" is a Japanese invention.[30] As *feminizumu* may thus have been somewhat familiar to educated readers, it lacked the novelty of Ninagawa's new term. Moreover, if *feminisuto* would have given most readers entirely the wrong impression, the similarity of *feminizumu* and *feminisuto* might also have been cause for confusion. Akiyama, for instance, notes that the lack of currency of *feminizumu* and the lack of correspondence between *feminisuto* and feminist made translating these terms a challenge when translating *Notes from the Second Year,* a project discussed in the next chapter.[31]

   There was one other ostensible loanword new to Japanese that Ninagawa might have considered, one that might have influenced his coinage of *ūman ribu,* namely, the *wasei Eigo* term *"ūman pawā"*—a transliteration of "woman power." This term was introduced to readers of the *Asahi* in October 1968 in an article on women in the workforce by female social critic Kageyama Yūko (1932–2005), garnering additional attention in both the *Asahi* and the *Yomiuri* surrounding the "National Meeting on the Development and Utilization of Woman Power" held in Tokyo in June 1969, for which Kageyama was acting as a spokesperson and, again, which focused on women's labor issues.[32] A 1969 article in the *Yomiuri* makes a link between *ūman pawā* and both Black power (*buraku pawā*) and student power (*suchūdento pawā*) yet defines the term as "women's labor power" (*fujin rōdōryoku*) rather than something related to activists' calls for broad civil and social rights.[33] The meaning of *ūman pawā* would very quickly blur in newspaper articles with *ūman ribu,* however, and examples can also be found of its use in reference to the US women's liberation movement even before Ninagawa coined *ūman ribu,* including by Tanaka Mitsu.[34] Perhaps the expression's association in the *Asahi* specifically with women in the work force—an association which is decidedly more old-school liberal feminist than the issues of immediate concern to this new movement—rendered *ūman pawā* inappropriate for his introduction of this new wave of women's activism. Given Ninagawa's evident interest in and awareness of women's issues, however, it is easy to see how, whether consciously or not, he might have been mimicking the grammar of this expression when he coined *ūman ribu.*

Like the emergence of the movement itself, the adoption of the terms *"ūman ribu"* and *"ribu"* by the women in the movement seems organic rather than planned, and occurred in the face of various factors that might have forestalled it. The simplest of these factors to explain is the question of why the labels were adopted in spite of their negative association in popular discourse. In popular and academic writing on the treatment of the *ribu* movement in the media, as well as the recollection of several dozen women in and outside the movement with whom I have spoken, the standard narrative is that the male-run mass media establishment ridiculed *ūman ribu,* accusing its adherents of being any combination of hysterical women engaged in irrational antics, unattractive women unable to get men, and women obsessed with sex. The image of the *ribu* activists as objects of—and, to some outside the movement, worthy of—widespread mocking and scorn lingers to this day. Yet, as Saitō reminds us, some of the initial treatment of the *ribu* movement, particularly Ninagawa's series in the *Asahi,* was largely positive and sympathetic in its attempt to give *ribu* activists a voice in the media.[35] While not exactly denying this point, in a 2009 interview with me Tanaka disagreed. She explained that regardless of Ninagawa's sympathy, the way the women were portrayed even in those early articles left them open to ridicule in popular discourse.[36] Yet, even if we allow that the word was first used ambivalently at best, circulation of the term *"ūman ribu"* within the establishment could at the very least be seen to symbolize public recognition of these activists.

The mistaken association with the US movement is the other major factor that might have forestalled the adoption of *ribu* and *ūman ribu* in the community. Although, as we have seen, the origin of these terms points to early ties—however tenuous—between activists in Japan and the United States, to adopt these labels supported the misconception that the Japanese movement was indeed imported. As noted above, the members of Ribu FUKUOKA appropriated the word *"ribu"* out of a feeling of connection with their American counterparts but with little knowledge of what was actually going on in the United States. The members of Radical Ribu Group (Radikaru Ribu Gurūpu)— which formed in November 1970, a month or so after the word *"ūman ribu"* appeared in print—espoused the new term as it symbolized something completely different from the old-fashioned image of the *fujin undō,* noting that *ribu* was "born in America and . . . is spreading globally." They argue, however, that the idea promulgated in the mass media that Japan's *ribu undō* was simply imported from the United States—and, by implication, out of place in Japan—is "meaningless criticism." This criticism, they suggest, likely stems from the fact that the same issues raised by the American liberation activists resonate in Japan. And, they speculate, perhaps the men who criticize them are afraid of the fact that the grudges women bear in Japan are even stronger than those among women in the United States.[37] Also by November, *ūman ribu* was appearing in materials put out by Tanaka's Group Fighting Women, and, in spite of her misgivings both about its use in the media and the sense of importedness it carried, she herself ultimately adopted it to name her own theory of women's liberation, articulated in her influential book, *To Women with Spirit: A Disorderly Theory of Ūman Ribu.*[38]

However local a coinage, the fact that component parts of the term *"ūman ribu"* did not originate in Japan had another benefit. For Miki Sōko, the term did not have the baggage of existing Japanese terms and was thus appealing to activists such as herself in the new movement.[39] The fact is, however, that *ūman ribu* functioned merely as the most attention-grabbing name—and, for some, derisive epithet—for a movement of loosely knit groups around the country that continued to describe themselves as working toward *onna kaihō* or *josei kaihō.* Miki, wont to claim *ribu* as specifically and uniquely Japanese, forgets or overlooks the fact that from the term's coinage it was sometimes used as a universal label for contemporary activist feminism both within and outside of Japan and in some cases was applied to earlier generations of women's rights activists.[40] In other words, *ūman ribu* was weighed down with baggage from the moment it appeared in print. And yet Miki and many of her sisters chose to claim the term as their own anyway, similar to *rezubian* reclaiming the label used in androcentric discourse to name them, as discussed below.

Miki's suggestion that the term was relatively neutral when introduced to Japanese helps to emphasize a critical point I have repeatedly touched upon, however. When *ribu* and *ūman ribu* were adopted, most activists knew very little about "women's lib" in the United States. As discussed in chapter four, Akiyama and the others engaged in translating early radical feminist writing from the United States began to do so precisely because there was virtually no information about the American liberation movement available in Japanese. To be sure, to Ninagawa and much of the mass media establishment, his *ūman ribu* pointed specifically to a foreign women's movement and its imported Japanese manifestation. Yet, to a majority of women engaged in this new activist movement in Japan, it represented, at most, a sense of solidarity with an American or global women's liberation movement. To these activist women, then, the term was able to function as a not quite empty signifier, open to reinscription with their own meanings, and ultimately infused with the energy and passion of these women activists in Japan. Thus, while bearing denotative and connotative similarities to women's lib, *ūman ribu* was clearly not the same thing, particularly to members of the *ribu* community. I would also argue that the meanings of women's liberation and of women were themselves transfigured in Japan both through placing them under the banner of *ūman ribu* as well as *onna kaihō* and *josei kaihō,* and, more significantly, through the discourse in which the term *"ūman ribu"* was coined, narrowly adopted, and widely disparaged. It is to this latter phenomenon we now turn.

In the sphere of public discourse, the *ribu* women were unable to control the meaning or image of *ūman ribu*. Among the public at large, almost as soon as it appeared in the media, *ribu* was more closely associated with the flamboyant protests ridiculed on the evening news and talk shows and in the press, such as the antics of the pink-helmeted pro–birth control pill, pro–abortion rights group Chūpiren led by Enoki Misako, than the radical philosophy behind Tanaka's activism.[41] Nakanishi Toyoko, founder of the influential women's bookstore Shōkadō in Kyoto, recalls that the negative valence and images associated with the term made it impossible even at the beginning of the 1990s to find an existing commercial publisher to put out a compendium of *ribu mini-komi,* pamphlets, and other ephemera from the movement, leading her to publish it herself via her bookstore.[42] This negative impression of the term and the movement has continued to linger, as evidenced by the reaction of many people with whom I have discussed the subject, including many of my interviewees who were not themselves involved in feminist activism in the 1970s.

The fossilization of the term's meaning can be attributed not just to negative media coverage but also to the weakening of the *ribu* movement itself and the emergence of new visible manifestations of feminist activism and scholarship. Writer, performer, and former politician Nakayama Chinatsu (b. 1948), who was involved in *ribu* in the 1970s, wrote in the late 1980s that, while the word had "died" around 1975, she "was still calling [herself] *ribu* in her heart."[43] The year 1975 was when, as discussed in chapter two, the *ribu* movement began to rapidly lose steam. It was also around this time that some *rezubian*-identified women began to identify as *rezubian feminisuto*.[44] Soon thereafter, the field of *joseigaku,* or women's studies, began to take form at Japanese universities and a new more intellectual and—from the perspective of *ribu*—less activist Japanese feminism began to develop, reviving the word *feminizumu* and reclaiming the word *feminisuto*.[45]

The editors of the new journal *Feminist*—so titled as part of an effort to redefine and, thus, reclaim the term—saw *"feminizumu"* as more cultural than *"uimenzu ribarēshon"* (women's liberation), probably pointing here to the movement in the United States as well as in Japan.[46] Based on the contents and tone of the magazine, it seems clear that "cultural" implied a certain cosmopolitanism these women saw neither in the US women's liberation movement nor in *ribu*.[47] Intriguingly, when *Feminist* was first published, the association with the then primary meaning of a *"feminisuto"*—that is, a man who sweet-talks women—remained strong enough that apparently at some bookstores the magazine was at first mistakenly shelved with the men's magazines.[48] Evidence of feminists' ultimate success in redefining the term can be found with younger people in and outside this volume's focal communities with whom I have spoken, who are, for the most part, unaware of the earlier meaning of the word. This does not, however, mean that women whose ideas and activism resonate with a broadly defined notion of feminism consider themselves to be *feminisuto,* however. As Laura Dales shows, in early twenty-first century Japan, some such women feel that "a feminist is one who is aware of inequality or of the difficulty of being a woman, and this awareness has grown from a tangible, personal experience of hardship." Thus, the term could not possibly apply, for instance, to housewives.[49] In a 2009 conversation over dinner with four women in their forties to sixties who were regularly meeting to discuss English-language texts (often on feminist themes), my own querying as to whether these women identify as "feminists" led to an unresolved definitional discussion in which one of the four rejected the label even as she espoused views that clearly fell under the definition she herself agreed to, namely being an advocate of equality of social opportunity for women and men.

While a few women continue to publicly identify themselves as *ribu* rather than *feminisuto,* such as Miki, who only applies the label "feminist" to herself when speaking in English, by and large the term only serves to name a specific sphere of 1970s feminist activism in Japan (and abroad) that the general public believes to have faded away long ago. This is likely a consequence of a handful of factors, not the least of these being the media's use of the term as a mark of derision. The shift in the locus of the discourse on women's social status from activists engaged on the ground, to scholars and others more heavily invested in intellectual dialogue—not infrequently dialogue with American and other foreign feminists—certainly contributed. If "women's lib" had remained a popular term in the United States, transnationally engaged feminists in Japan may well have worked to hold on to rather than replace the term. Their success at redefining *feminisuto* suggests this may have been possible. Nevertheless, even if the increasing predominance of the term "feminism" over "women's lib" in the American public was the final nail in the coffin for *"ūman ribu,"* the roots of the term's demise lay in shifts in local discourse and practice.

On the Possibility of a *"Rezubian"* Continuum

A decade into the so-called second wave of the American women's liberation movement, lesbian feminist Adrienne Rich provocatively declared the presence of a "lesbian continuum," by which she meant "a range—through each woman's life and throughout history—of woman-identified experience," somewhere along which any woman might be located regardless of whether she consciously desires a sexual relationship with another woman.[50] Her bold claim is but one example of the many self-identified lesbian feminists around the world who have attempted to reclaim and redefine "lesbian." Observing the very personal process of identification with the term, lesbian feminist writer Nicole Brossard has declared that, "A lesbian who does not reinvent the word is a lesbian in the process of disappearing."[51] For their part, *rezubian feminisuto* in Japan have themselves repeatedly responded to their own perceived need to cast *rezubian* in and on their own terms.[52]

One possible way to approach the history of female same-sex eroticism and romance in postwar Japan would be the delineation of a different kind of "lesbian continuum" from that of Rich, one that seeks not to redefine the word itself but, instead, to offer a basic genealogy in order, in Foucault's terms, "to identify the accidents, the minute deviations—or conversely, the complete reversals—the errors, the false appraisals, and the faulty calculations"[53] whereby the word has come to take its current form and meaning, and whereby some women have come to claim it as their own. Even a brief history of the term *"rezubian"* makes clear that there is, in fact, no straightforward continuum, no figurative baton toss stretching from the introduction of variant formulations of the word "lesbian." Hereafter in this section I maintain "scare quotes" around this and select other English terms when using them in the broadest sense to emphasize both their fluidity and the multiple calques and transliterations used to represent them—from Latin, German, English, and French, and, more than half a century later, extending to the popularization of the word *"rezubian"* from the 1970s onward as a locus of identification and a badge of pride in and celebration of women's love and sexual desire for other women.

"Homosexuality" is a modern concept, one whose introduction in Japan as early as an 1894 translation of sexologist Richard von Krafft-Ebing's *Psychopathia Sexualis* (1886) led, in fits and starts, to a dramatic reconceptualization of same-sex sexual behavior and what are now understood as non-normative gender practices.[54] Strikingly, this novel approach to same-sex eroticism drew new attention to same-sex affection and sexual activities between females, who were for the first time placed conceptually on a par with those among males, even if widely considered qualitatively distinct.[55] It took several decades for *dōseiai* (literally, "same-sex love") to become established as the translation of "homosexuality" among the half dozen or so calques in circulation.[56]

It took still longer for the current Japanese form of the term "lesbian" to be settled on in the mid-1970s. Its ultimate form and meaning reflect the efforts of some women to take control of the discourse on female same-sex desire as well as men's continued dominance of that discourse in mainstream culture. As I will show, the presence of the word *"rezubian"* in contemporary Japanese in its multiple permutations and meanings is not the result of a simple one-time import, but rather dozens of transnational exchanges, as well as domestic discussion and debate over much of the twentieth century—a stretch of time when the meaning of "lesbian" remained similarly unstable in English and other languages.[57] In Japan, it should be noted, until as late as the 1960s, this discourse rarely included the women whose romantic and sexual practices the word now purports to name.[58]

In her groundbreaking work on same-sex love and suicide among women in modern Japan, anthropologist Jennifer Robertson describes "lesbian (*rezubian*)" as already a "household word" in early 1900s Japan.[59] The truth of the matter, however, depends on what is implied by both "household word" and "lesbian (*rezubian*)."[60] To be sure, in the early 1910s the "female homosexual" was "discovered and quickly problematized" in the media.[61] Press accounts of double suicides of schoolgirls, actresses, and female factory workers repeatedly drew the public's attention and caused anxiety about "homosexuality" among girls and women. Yet, prior to the war, transliterations of the word "lesbian" from any language were rare in popular magazines and newspapers—and virtually nonexistent in reference to women in Japan, to whom variant calques of "homosexual" were applied. Transliterated forms of "lesbian" as well as the related terms "Lesbos," "Sappho," and "tribade" were in use but largely limited to sexology and translated literature—often in the context of offering a global, primarily Western, history of female "homosexuality" in general, or Sappho and the isle of Lesbos specifically.[62] They can also be found in contemporary dictionaries of new words referencing usages from both genres of writing. These were specialized discourse spheres dominated by men. The extent, then, to which the public at large was familiar with and used any of these terms is questionable.

As in European languages, while these terms would continue to have limited currency for much of the twentieth century, "lesbian" would ultimately prevail in Japan, likely a result of the cross-citational nature of pre- and postwar discourse on female "homosexuality" in Japan as well as, crucially, ongoing transnational exchange. Indeed, from its introduction into Japanese, "lesbian" has always been a thoroughly transnational term. One of the earliest transliterations of "lesbian" upon the initial boom in discourse on female "homosexuality" beginning around 1911,[63] can be found in the 1913 translation of a recent edition of Krafft-Ebing's *Psychopathia Sexualis,* in which the term *"amōru resubikusu"*—a transliteration of the Latin *amor lesbicus*—appears a handful of times, glossed the first time as *fujo kan no ren'ai* (love between women), along with the Germanic *resubisshu* (*lesbisch*).[64] In this early text *amōru resubikusu* is used not as a universal term for female "homosexuality" but rather refers to non-congenital "homosexuality" among adult females. The specificity of this usage, however, like its Latin name, would ultimately not endure.[65] While the Latin-derived *amōru resubikusu* lacked staying power—with rare exception[66]—variations on the phrase "lesbian love" would remain the primary form of "lesbian" in Japanese through the 1960s.[67] A particularly noteworthy exception can be found in a translation of Havelock Ellis's writing on female "homosexuality" from his *Studies in the Psychology of Sex* (1897–1928) published in the feminist journal *Seitō* in 1914 with an introduction by outspoken feminist Hiratsuka Raichō (1886–1971). The translator chose to avoid creating either a transliteration or calque, leaving the word "Lesbianism" in English.[68]

Of the several dozen dictionaries of new words and slang published between the 1910s and 1930s I examined, almost a third contain references to female "homosexuality" (*dōseiai*) and/or schoolgirl romance.[69] Eight of these dictionaries include the words *"resubiyan ravu," "resubian ravu," "amōru resubikusu,"* and/or, from German, *"resubisshu rībe"* (lesbische Liebe).[70] Earlier dictionaries tend toward transliterations from German and later ones from English, indicating a gradual shift in the locus of sexological discourse. The heavily German-inflected dictionaries of Satō Kōka (a.k.a., Tamio Satow; 1891–?)—a collaborator of Slavonian-Austrian folklorist Friedrich S. Krauss—were first serialized in the journal *Hentai shiryō* (Perverse materials, 1926–1928) and then in his *Global Sexuality Dictionary,* adorned on the cover with the German title *Universell Sexual Lexikon.*[71] These texts contain entries for both the German and Latin terms, along with *saffisumusu* (*Sapphismus*) and *toribāde* (*Tribade*), with a comment under *resubisshu rībe* in both dictionaries that female "homosexuality" (*josei dōseiai*) is also colloquially called "*Resubosu no ai*" (Lesbos love), a seemingly novel term combining "Lesbos" and "*ai*" (love) according to the "lesbian love" pattern, which would have much currency in the "perverse press" in the 1950s and 1960s.[72]

While none of these dictionaries explain these transliterated terms as unrelated to women in Japan, neither do they support drawing such a connection. The illustration of two young women gazing into each other's eyes that accompanies the definition of the calque "*dōseiai*" in a 1931 *Illustrated Dictionary of Modern Words* is ambiguous but may represent Japanese schoolgirls in sailor suits, the modern schoolgirl uniform, still in use today.[73] "*Resubian ravu*," on the other hand, is represented by two women wearing evening gowns and running off together with hands interlocked. Their hair is completely un-inked, possibly blonde, but more tellingly they have large breasts and large, round derrières—a body type evoking images of European and American women. Juxtaposed as they are with the kimono-clad, black-haired women illustrating unrelated words on the opposite page, they appear particularly Western—or at least very Westernized[74] (figure 3.2).

Most commonly included in these dictionaries, however, are modern native terms to describe passionate friendships between schoolgirls, such as *ome(-san)*, *(o-)netsu,* and *S* or *esu*—with the former two composed of Japanese roots and the latter a modern Japanese transfiguration of the notion of a "sister."[75] Historian Gregory Pflugfelder notes that different modern terms appeared to have emerged or at least become popular in different schools by the close of the Meiji era. While only *esu* draws directly on a "foreign" word, it must be remembered that the modern girlhood that rendered possible such passionate schoolgirl friendships, however they were labeled, was itself a product of Japan's transfigured modernity. By contrast, *to ichi ha ichi* (tribadism), another native term included in some of these dictionaries, dates at least back to the Edo era.[76]

A male-dominated literary discourse on "lesbians" ran alongside more scientific writing on female "homosexuality," albeit scientific discourse too

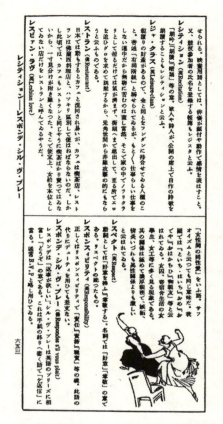

Figure 3.2. The women in the illustration for *"resubian ravu"* (bottom left) in contrast with the women in the illustrations for unrelated words on the opposite page (top and bottom right) in the *Illustrated Dictionary of Modern Words* (1931), pp. 652–653.

drew from literary texts, including mythic accounts of the life of Sappho, as noted above. Unsurprisingly, Sappho and the isle of Lesbos were at the center of "lesbian" literary representation in Japan for most of the first half of the twentieth century, often but not always via translations of texts by European writers such as Franz Grillparzer, Charles Baudelaire, Alphonse Daudet, and Pierre Louÿs, as well as poems by or reputed to be by Sappho herself and those of or about other women of Lesbos.[77] The European writings were translated and retranslated—in some cases, such as Daudet's *Sapho* (1884), dozens of times—and regularly serialized in magazines and published as stand-alone volumes from the early twentieth century onward, with some repeatedly retranslated and republished decades into in the postwar era.[78]

It must be noted, however, that "lesbianism" in much of nineteenth-century European writing "served to represent heightened sensuality in woman" in general and was—as in what we know of the actual life of Sappho and the fictional lives represented in Louÿs's *Les chansons de Bilitis* (*The Songs of Bilitis*) (1894)—neither considered to be engaged in to the exclusion of relationships with men, nor was it pathologized in those texts in the way emblematic of late nineteenth- and early twentieth-century scientific understandings of "inversion."[79] David Halperin observes that as late as the 1920s "a cultivated social observer," such as Aldous Huxley, "could portray a party at which the term 'Lesbian' gets thrown about in civilized banter and applied" as a geographic reference "not only to heterosexual"—rather than homosexual—"love affairs but to the male participant in them without causing the slightest puzzlement or consternation."[80] Similarly, perhaps, in the late 1920s, the two female and two male members of the Japanese singing group the Resubian Bōkaru Fōa (Lesbian vocal four) may have been unaware of any "homosexual" implication of "lesbian," which they might have used in their name merely to reference Sappho's lyrical nature.[81] Moreover, whatever their implications, these early translated and transfigured "lesbian texts," focused as they were on European or Greek *qua* "Oriental" women, were a world apart from the domestic discourse on "homosexuality" among Japanese women.

This is not to discount the possible influence of these texts on Japanese writers, such as cosmopolitan novelist Tanizaki Jun'ichirō (1886–1965), who depicts in a Japanese setting a love triangle involving two women and one man that ended in suicide in his novel *Manji* (1959), first serialized 1928–1930.[82] Such a relationship might suggest at least a tangential link between European literary "lesbians" and Japanese women. Tanizaki would certainly have been familiar with a least some of the literary depictions of female–female erotic relationships noted above and aware of the existence of Sappho and current variants on the word "lesbian" from reading of literature and, likely, from sexology texts as well. Yet, while he does use "*dōseiai*" (homosexuality) in the novel, when he makes direct reference to female–female relationships, the author primarily describes the relationship between the two women merely as being between persons of the "same sex" (*dōsei*) as opposed to between members of the "opposite sex" (*isei*).[83] In contrast both with postwar discussions of the text, including those in which he was involved, and with the 1990s English translation, in the original text Tanizaki did not use the word "lesbian."[84] Indeed, in my surveys of prewar writing, I have not encountered in any context, presented as fact or fiction, direct connections being made between real women in Japan and literary representations of "lesbians."

In the immediate postwar era, in addition to the ongoing literary depiction of "lesbians," sexological texts continued to be produced locally as well as translated into Japanese. In the earliest works that discussed "homosexuality" among females, references to Sappho and Lesbos were frequent as were references to "lesbian love," yet their use was by no means universal, nor was their form consistent. Among the first of the new translations was of Morris Ernst and David Loth's *American Sexual Behavior and the Kinsey Report* published in English in 1948 and in Japanese translation in 1949, demonstrating the rise in global prominence of American sexology as well as, perhaps, a prurient interest in Japan's occupiers.[85] Suggesting that the prewar form "lesbian love" lingered in Japanese sexological discourse, however, where Ernst and Loth make a passing reference to the historical association of the Greek isle of Lesbos with "female homosexuality," their translator notes parenthetically that Lesbos is in the Aegean Sea and the birthplace of Sappho, so "Lesbos love means female homosexuality."[86] However, with the exception of introducing this alternative way to indicate *josei no dōseiai* (female homosexuality), the term is not used in this volume.

Interest in the work of groundbreaking American sexologist Alfred Kinsey was strong enough that his influential studies on the sexual behavior of men and of women were published in Japanese translation within a year or two of their publication in English.[87] For Kinsey, who saw "homosexual" as a description of behavior rather than as a name for a kind of person,[88] it is unsurprising that again, Sappho-related terms for homosexuality are mentioned only in passing as terms Kinsey recommends avoiding in scientific discourse. In the translation of this fleeting reference, however, rather than render "lesbian" into the existing Japanese *resubian ravu,* as had the translator of the Ernst and Loth volume, the translator of *Sexual Behavior in the Human Female* simply renders it *resubian,* providing an early postwar example of a stand-alone use of the term, a usage that may have made its way into the "perverse press" (discussed below).[89] It is also worth noting that the translation of Kinsey's discussion of his discomfort with the term "homosexual" itself is the only time that the word is transliterated (*"homosekushuaru"*) rather than translated (*"dōseiai"*).[90] This suggests that at the time *dōseiai* sounded more scientific or legitimate—or perhaps more neutral—to the translator than transliterations of "homosexuality," a sense reflected in popular press accounts of "homosexuality," which favored *dōseiai* throughout most of the twentieth century.

Outside the scientific and literary discussion and representation of female "homosexuality," an increasingly graphic discourse on female–female sexual practices within Japan's semi-underground postwar "perverse press" ran alongside similar discussion of male–male sexual practices and any number of sexual behaviors between opposite-sex partners. While clearly designed to titillate an ostensibly male readership and largely written by men, as Mark McLelland shows, there were also voices that might be considered to come from same-sex-desiring females.[91] In 1954, the year the Japanese translation of Kinsey's *Sexual Behavior in the Human Female* appeared in print, an article titled "Chitchat on lesbianism" appeared in *Fūzoku kagaku* (Sexual customs science, 1953–1955), one of the earliest of the postwar perverse magazines.[92] Penned by an individual using the female name Miyagawa Yoshiko, this article links Japanese female homoerotic experiences to the terms *"resubianizumu," "resubian rabu," "safizumu"* (Sapphism), and *"toraibādo"* (tribade), terms she explains via a lengthy discussion of Sappho and Lesbos, as well as, in the case of tribadism, the aforementioned Japanese synonym *"to ichi ha ichi."* Two photos illustrating the article show Japanese women in *yukata* (robes) who appear to be intimately connected—one woman brushing the other's hair in the first picture, and both lying down and gazing into one another's eyes in the second. Miyagawa also makes extensive reference to Krafft-Ebing, the most likely source of the introduction of "lesbian" into Japanese decades earlier. This usage of *resubianizumu* apparently did not immediately catch on even within that magazine, however.

Occasionally, such as in a 1955 roundtable discussion including both Japanese women and male "experts" in *Fūzoku kagaku,* for instance, women-loving women were referred to and referred to themselves as *"josei no homo"* (female homos), positioning them as the female counterpart to the (male) *homo* discussed in this sphere with greater frequency during this period and who were and continue to be the primary referent of *homo.*[93] With the exception of *dōseiai,* the most frequently used term during this same period seems to have been *"Resubosu no ai"* (Lesbos love) or simply *"Resubosu"* (here, lesbian[ism]). The former of these echoes the *amōru resubikusu* pattern dating back to translations of Krafft-Ebing. While noted in dictionaries, such as that by Satō Kōka, several decades prior, these terms had not taken root in the discourse until this point.[94]

A significant number of writers in the 1950s perverse press might better be described as scholars of literature than of science, yet, as McLelland observes, they derived a certain scientific authority from "extensive reading about Japanese and foreign . . . 'sexual customs'" including "psychoanalytic and sexological works such as [by] Kinsey . . . as well as anthropological, historical and literary treatises,"[95] and their writing echoes the blurring between scientific and literary discourse in the prewar era. Whether or not the use of

Resubosu no ai in this sphere originated with these more literary-minded con-tributors to the magazines, in retaining the name of Sappho's mythic Aegean home, *Resubosu no ai* points toward the literary roots of the term and of that particular strand of interest in female "homosexuality."

Regardless, by the late 1950s, *resubian* began occasionally to stand on its own in the perverse press, used both as an adjective and as a noun, indicating a woman whose primary affectional and sexual desire was directed at other women. Perhaps this change reflects the influence of postwar sexological texts, which, as noted above, had already begun to shift toward this "English" form. One early article to use this form discusses *"resubian kurabu"* (lesbian clubs) that existed in the late nineteenth century in the "lesbian paradise" (*Resubosu no tengoku*) of France. And yet, while the article positions the exis-tence of these clubs as a product of a specific time and place akin to the *"gei bōi"* (gay boy) culture that emerged in the context of postwar Japan, it makes no reference to "lesbian" culture in Japan.[96]

The earliest instance in this sphere I have encountered in which *resubian* is used specifically in reference to same-sex-attracted women in Japan was a feature in the August 1960 issue of *Fūzoku kitan* (Strange talk about customs, 1960–1974) on *resubian no seitai*, which might be translated as "the life (or ecol-ogy) of lesbians." This was introduced on the cover with the more provoca-tive headline, "Techniques of Lesbian Love" (*"Resubian no ai no gihō"*). While *resubian* is prominently used in the title, the term by no means supplants alter-native words in the remainder of the feature—nor would it for several years in the discourse at large. In fact, only two of the four articles contained therein frame their discussion as being about *resubian*.

The most substantial of these is an article on "love techniques of *resubian* east and west" by Kabiya Kazuhiko, a prolific writer on "homosexuality" and frequent contributor to perverse magazines beginning in the 1950s. In this piece, Kabiya discusses relationships between women in Japan and elsewhere primarily relying on *dōseiai* and the transliteration *"resubian,"* while also ref-erencing local coinages noted above including *S* (*esu*), *o-netsu*, *ome-san*, and *to ichi ha ichi*.[97] Reflecting the novelty of *resubian*, Kabiya introduces the term and its meaning by using it as a superscript over *josei dōseiaisha* (female homosexual).[98] At one point, by way of an explanation of why *josei no dōseiai* (female homosexuality) is referred to as *resubian rabu* (lesbian love) or *Resubosu* (Lesbos), he offers the familiar story of Sappho.[99] Both of the articles in the same issue of *Fūzoku kitan* that did not use *resubian* go further into that same mythic history. One offers an "invitation to *Resubosu*" via French litera-ture.[100] The other, entitled simply *"Resubiennu"*—a transliteration of the French "*lesbienne*"—is ostensibly a Japanese translation from French of a dialogue between two women. This text was purportedly translated into French from ancient Greek by "Pieru Robizu" (Pierre ?Lovise)—a mistranscribed attempt to credit Pierre Louÿs.[101] The article itself is actually plagiarized from a magazine dating to Japan's interwar "erotic grotesque nonsense" boom.[102] Even decades later *Resubosu* had not completely disappeared: as late as the mid-1990s there was a "magazine/book" (*mūku*) under the name *Resubosu kurabu* (Lesbos club). While the 1997 issue I examined—lent to me by a *rezubian*-identified woman I interviewed—had articles that appeared to be about actual *rezubian*-identified women, the overall salacious tone of the editorial content makes the text appear to be aimed primarily at male readers, making it clear that the androcentricity of *Resubosu* has lingered as well.[103]

Discussion of "homosexuality"—among women or men—during this period and through much of the 1960s was far less complicated in the mainstream press, which in general continued to refer to it simply as *dōseiai*.[104] Exceptions included weeklies catering primarily to male readers—such as *Heibon panchi* (Ordinary punch, 1964–1988), *Shūkan taishū* (Popular weekly, 1958–), and *Weekly Playboy* (*Weekly pureibōi*, 1966–)—as well as in a few magazines aimed at women such as *Josei jishin* (Women's self, 1958–). In these magazines, interest in *resubian* was primarily prurient, echoing interest expressed in this sphere in gender ambiguous *gei bōi* and, perhaps, evidencing the influence of the "perverse press," which appears to be a source of information for those charged with writing articles on the topic.[105] In newspapers and more conservative magazines in general, however, the term "*dōseiai*" maintained its dominance throughout the 1970s and 1980s.

The final transition in the term, that from "*resubian*" to "*rezubian*," the current form, is marked by several clear and significant signposts and, in part, evidences women's efforts to take control of the discourse at a moment when more women were claiming the right to their own sexuality—at the same time that it indexes several new points of transnational exchange. In January 1967, Narabayashi Yasushi (1919–2002), a man trained in obstetrics and gynecology who later became a marriage counselor and author of sex manuals, published a book called *Rezubian rabu* (Lesbian love).[106] This title echoes the prewar expressions "*resubiyan ravu*" and "*resubian ravu*"—carried on into the postwar era, as noted above, in sexological writing and the perverse press—as well as the postwar "*Resubosu no ai*," yet differs in his deliberate switch from "*su*" to "*zu*." While *resubian* is the generally used pronunciation, Narabayashi explains on the opening page of his book, the pronunciation *rezubian* is the "correct" (*tadashii*) one.[107] (Ironically, even in insisting that his readers switch to this English-based—and thus, to Narabayashi, correct—pronunciation of "lesbian," he can be accused of "incorrectly" transcribing "love" not as *"ravu"* but as *"rabu."* Like *"resubian," "rabu"* was the established Japanese pronunciation for a word whose English "original" could, if a speaker desired, be more closely approximated in Japanese.) Narabayashi had previously spent a year (1964–1965) in New York City, working as a marriage counselor and while there became acquainted with a "collective" of male and female homosexuals, the latter of whom provided the material for part of the book. Although he does not state this explicitly, he presumably adopted the English pronunciation of "lesbian" while in the United States.

One month after the publication of this volume, an interview with Narabayashi introducing his new book and his research appeared in the men's magazine *Heibon panchi,* and an editorial comment in the opening paragraphs also informs readers that *"rezubian"* is the "correct" pronunciation.[108] This is to become the pronunciation used in all subsequent articles on "lesbians" in the magazine. Shortly thereafter articles began appearing in other popular magazines that draw on Narabayashi's book, sometimes referencing it directly, including the women's magazine *Josei jishin.*[109] From that point forward, some such magazines switched completely to the newer pronunciation. In other magazines, however, *resubian* would persist through at least the end of the decade and in some cases far into the 1970s—with some magazines switching back and forth between pronunciations from issue to issue.[110]

Around the same time as Narabayashi's introduction of the evidently novel pronunciation, the abbreviations *"rezu"* and, to a lesser extent, *"resu"* began to gain currency in the press. The former of these remains in use to the present primarily as a slur or a sexually objectifying term outside the "lesbian" community and as an identity marker within it, while the latter fell into disuse. Given the tendency in Japanese to abbreviate words, these shortened forms may, but do not necessarily, reflect a separate introduction of the English form "lez," sometimes spelled "les," which in American English existed alongside other diminutives including "lezzie" and "lesbo." As for Narabayashi, whatever his motivations, in addition to furthering interest in "lesbians" in the popular press, his book, perhaps drawing on his authority as a doctor, was a major impetus behind this seemingly insignificant yet revealing change in how "lesbians" are referred to and how they refer to themselves.

When "lesbians" were discussed at all within the *ribu* community, as in popular discourse at large, the spelling was inconsistent through the first half of the 1970s. The newer pronunciation was common in translated works and writing about the United States but not universal.¹¹¹ As with Narabayashi, rather than the use of one pronunciation (*resubian*) to index women in Japan and the other (*rezubian*) to index women in the United States and elsewhere, the choice to use one or the other seems to stem from individual translators' and writers' personal connections to native speakers of English. Akiyama Yōko, discussed above, who participated in the translation of both *Our Bodies Ourselves* and *Notes from the Second Year* (discussed in chapter four) herself had a handful of American friends who both introduced American lib materials to her and assisted her and her fellow translators in their translation, and when speaking to me in 2009 did not recall when she picked up the newer pronunciation.¹¹² By contrast, the rare references to "lesbians" in books focused on women in Japan and by women with few direct international connections are more likely to use the old pronunciation, such as in Tanaka Mitsu's aforementioned *ribu* treatise *To Women with Spirit*.¹¹³

In the first several years after its founding in 1973, the commercial *ribu* magazine *Onna erosu* generally used the older pronunciation in reference to Japan and the new one in reference to the United States.¹¹⁴ A note at the end of an article in the first issue on the American lib movement explains that the newer pronunciation is English and the older French.¹¹⁵ Amano Michimi— who had lived in the United States and Europe before translating the chapter "In Amerika They Call Us Dykes" from *Our Bodies Ourselves* for the journal— recounts that she vacillated over how to translate "lesbian" and "dyke."¹¹⁶ Amano's understanding of the latter term as a pejorative in the United States accorded with the existing nuance of "*rezu*," which she used in the title of the article. For the translation of "lesbian," she rejected "(*onna no*) *dōseiaisha*" ([woman] homosexual) as too serious or stiff (*katai*), reflecting its use, noted above, in the press and other formal contexts. While she associated *resubian* with French culture when she first heard it, the word was too strongly linked in her mind with the gloomy image of *resubian bā* (lesbian bars) and with sex in general for it to be appropriate in an affirmative article on "lesbian" life in the United States. The word "*rezubian*," which she does not recall as being in wide use at the time, seemed in her mind to indicate women who "try to live lives in which they take their homosexuality earnestly," hence her choice to use the term.¹¹⁷ It bears noting that, while the switch from "*su*" to "*zu*" indexes a new awareness of the English pronunciation, contrary to the aforementioned note in *Onna erosu*, as we have seen, the original "*su*" of lesbian can be traced back not to French influence, as Amano and others with whom I have spoken believe, but the term's transliteration from Latin in the early twentieth century.

Within the *rezubian* community—I use *rezubian* here for the sake of simplicity—the older pronunciation seems to have lingered longer, perhaps because of fewer direct ties to women overseas. Photographer and writer Kiyooka Sumiko (1921–1991), perhaps the first self-identified "lesbian" in Japan to produce books about "lesbian" experience, acknowledges the new pronunciation but favors *resubian* in the over half a dozen books she published starting in 1968 as the term "comes from [the name of] the isle of Lesbos (Resubosu), where the ancient Greek poet Sappho was born."[118] A 1975 issue of *Wakakusa* (Young grass), the *mini-komi* produced by Wakakusa no Kai (introduced in chapter two), also favors the earlier pronunciation, even using the outdated *resubian rabu* in reference to the narrative of a recent novel—Kiyooka's *Nichiren Actress* (*Nichiren joyū*)—as well as, in a retelling of the myth of Sappho.[119] By contrast, in the sole issue of the first overtly *rezubian feminisuto* publication in Japan, *Wonderful Women* (*Subarashī onnatachi*, 1976)—produced, as noted in chapter two, by a collaboration of women from the *ribu* sphere and those involved in Wakakusa no Kai—*resubian* is used on the cover and in the table of contents while *rezubian* is used in most of the articles, albeit inconsistently even within individual pieces.

On the one hand, as the ease with which the producers of *Wonderful Women* seem to have switched between pronunciations demonstrates, such a minor change as this was, to many, insignificant. Indeed, most of the dozens of women and men in and outside the *rezubian* community I have spoken with about this over the past several years did not even recall until reminded that there had been another pronunciation. A few of these women who identify as *rezubian* now, including some who were attracted to other women in the late 1960s and early 1970s, do recall the two pronunciations, but most do not recall it as being significant enough that each was a distinct term. "Fujisaki Rie," however, remembers that when she was struggling with understanding her own attraction to women at the end of the 1960s, she wondered which word—that is, which of the two pronunciations—applied to her experience.[120]

As late as the 1990s, the older pronunciation lingered in community discourse. Vocabulary lists in the first commercial *rezubian* magazine *Phryné*, for example, offer *resubian* as an alternative pronunciation.[121] Further, echoing Kiyooka's choice in the late 1960s, Hara Minata chose *resubian* over *rezubian* in translations of works by activist Pat Califia and, with fellow translator Tomioka Akemi (b. 1951), by scholar Lillian Faderman to honor the term's Sapphic roots—even though both books were written by Americans about women in the United States.[122] In daily life, however, Hara uses *rezubian*. Reflecting on the distinction in 2009, Hara explained that—like the schoolgirl term "*S*"/"*esu*," which resonates with the *"su"* of the older pronunciation—*"resubian"* seems too strongly associated with "two *women* together" (*onna dōshi*). It thus does not contain the overt sexuality or gender difference between partners crucial to Hara's own *rezubian* experience.[123]

While in the intervening years since the 1990s, for Hara, and since the 1970s, for Amano, there is of course a chance that the passage of time may have distorted each of these individuals' recollections of their motivations to choose *rezubian* over *resubian* and vice versa. Two points stand out, however. One is that the association with the then currently favored pronunciation in (male-dominated) public discourse—*resubian* for Amano, *rezubian* for Hara— foregrounded the sexual aspect of "lesbian" experience. The other point is that for both women the choice to use one or the other in reference to their own lives as well as the lives of other women in Japan and abroad was and is clearly related to the politics of being a "lesbian"—something scholar and activist Horie Yuri shows has continuing relevance two decades into the twenty-first century.[124]

This emphasis on sex over all other aspects of "lesbian" experience is arguably a function of men's desire to objectify women's sexuality and the androcentricity of public discourse in Japan. That is, discourse assumes the centrality of men to the extent that, as noted above, even *feminisuto* was quickly transfigured in Japanese into a referent for a man who was kind to women in order that he might more easily entreat them to meet his wishes. With this in mind, it might be somewhat less surprising that even "lesbian" was used in some spheres to reference male subjects. Arguably, the subject of the term "lesbian" in much of twentieth-century Japan was not women but the men who were gazing upon these real and fictive women, whether in scientific, literary, or pornographic contexts. But men were not simply voyeuristic subjects of "lesbian."

For instance, in the 1960s, in a column in *Fūzoku kitan* dedicated to male-to-female cross-dressers *"Resubosu no purei"* (Lesbos play) was used to suggest relations between two cross-dressers, for example.[125] Two decades later, *"rezu purei"* (lez play) and variant terms (e.g., *"rezubian no purei"* and *"rezubian gokko"*) were similarly used in personal ads beginning with the very first issue of *Queen* (*Kuīn*, 1980–2003), a glossy bimonthly commercial magazine for cross-dressing men.[126] Given the sexual implications of "lesbian" in Japanese discourse, it can be safely assumed that this "play" was itself at least in part erotic. Related uses can be found in more recent lowbrow magazines as well as pornography aimed at men.[127] While, to be sure, we might understand the earliest users of *"Resubosu no purei"* and *"rezu purei"* as marginalized individuals, who might today identify as trans women, using language to reflect their own desires and identities. But we must also be careful not to conflate cross-dressing with transgender identity, a distinction less clear in the period I am discussing. Nevertheless, and however marginalized these individuals were, they had access in the 1960s to a regular column in *Fūzoku kitan* and in the 1980s to a commercial magazine for cross-dressing men, neither of which was readily available to *rezubian* at the time, however they identified.

Kakefuda Hiroko, a *rezubian* activist prominent in the early to mid-1990s and best known for writing what is often called the first *rezubian* "coming out" book in Japanese, *On Being "Lesbian,"* has expressed ambivalent, sometimes conflicting, opinions about the use of Western concepts and terms such as "lesbian."[128] In her book she describes her unease before eventually embracing the term.[129] Part of this discomfort stemmed from the long association between *rezubian* and *rezu* and pornography aimed at men. While not denying the *rezubian* identities of herself or other women in Japan, two years after her book was published, she comes to question the applicability of imported concepts such as "lesbian" and "heterosexual," given that they come from the West, which, she argues, is "completely different" from Japan.[130]

Taking a different tack, other women had by the early 1990s reclaimed *rezubian* for themselves in a fun way: changing its abbreviation from *rezu* to *bian*. The latter is homophonous with the Japanese transliteration of the French *bien* (good), allowing these women to affirmatively "put the *bian* back into lezu [*sic*]!"[131]

Today *"rezubian"* is the primary term used in the public sphere, including the mass media, to refer to female "homosexuals," as well as in the *rezubian* community—though *"bian"* still has some currency in the latter. The sense of connection felt by women in Japan with women abroad from the earliest days of the *ribu* movement has meant that, while the history of "lesbian" in English in other languages and *rezubian* are not the same, the general sense in the community today is that, even if there are cultural differences, *"rezubian"* and "lesbian"—as well as "Lesben," "lesbienne," and other linguistic variants— are effectively the same word. That said, while "lesbian" in the United States, for instance, has its own complex history in which men have often been the subjects—not infrequently of a pornographic gaze—it is not the same history. Thus, the discomfort that some women in Japan have continued to feel with *rezubian,* as well as the sense of solidarity and pride stemming from participation in the *rezubian* community, come from women's relationships with Japanese cultural representations of female desire and with other women in

Japan, as well as women's own (in)ability to, as Brossard remarks, "reinvent the word" in their own context.[132]

"*Shōnen'ai*": Love of Boys from Pederasty to Pedophilia and Beyond

One difficulty of writing about *shōjo* manga is how to map the diverse range of narratives created by and for women and adolescent girls depicting male–male romance and sex. That such narratives and themes are not actually limited to manga but also exist in prose fiction, animation, video games, and audio and live-action dramas, as well as toys and other goods, complicates matters further. Specific narratives are sometimes produced in multiple media, and some fans create derivative works based on narratives or characters they feel passionate about. As we shall see, the publishing industry has played a significant role in the naming and classification of these narratives. In their own creation, consumption, and discussion of these works, however, artists and fans have the ultimate say in a sphere of textual and image consumption that has for decades straddled commercial and non-commercial domains.

Among the earliest labels for these narratives that caught on was *shōnen'ai*, a then decades-old term combining "boy" and "love." As I will show, women and girls' use of this term is both a claim to discursive and erotic subjecthood and a dramatic transfiguration of the very idea of a (homo)eroticized youth, theretofore almost exclusively the purview of adult male subjects. These works have had a number of other labels. This media came to be referred to in some spheres as *yaoi* followed by *bōizu rabu,* a transliteration of the English words "boys love." The former term emerged in the amateur manga sphere, while the latter, often abbreviated "BL" (pronounced *bī eru*), was first used by a commercial publisher.

Although there is a clear link between the terms "*shōnen'ai*" and "*bōizu rabu,*" it is one that might seem counterintuitive for a number of reasons. First, "*bōizu rabu*" may have been transliterated from English words, but it, in fact, existed within Japanese before it was borrowed into English by foreign fans, and in that sense may, like *ūman ribu,* be considered *wasei Eigo,* or English made-in-Japan. Indeed, its first appearance in print was in English text rather than in *katakana* transliteration. Further, while discourse flows on sex and sexuality between Japan and certain Western countries have resulted in multiple calques and transliterated terms in Japanese stemming from European languages, such as "*dōseiai*" and "*rezubian,*" discussed above, "*bōizu rabu*" is a Japanese-English rendering of the ostensibly Japanese "*shōnen'ai,*" an inversion of this pattern. So too, then, is "boys love" in English and other languages.

Outside of Japan, however, *"shōnen'ai," "yaoi,"* and "boys love" are used by many fans to make distinctions based on the level of sexual explicitness in a work, adding novel layers of meaning. Clearly then, it is not only technology and popular culture flowing out of Japan but novel ways of envisioning and naming eros, ways that continue to be transformed in transit from culture to culture.

The practice of adult males erotically objectifying and having sexual relations with male youths in pre- and early modern Japan is arguably comparable to the ancient Greek tradition of pederasty—a point often indicated via juxtaposition in modern historiographical and sexological writing in Japan on Edo-era sexual customs.[133] In discourse on male homoerotic practices in Japan prior to the modern era, the term *"wakashudō"* (way of the youth), particularly abbreviated to *"shudō,"* has carried on into the contemporary era as the most common referent, after *"nanshoku,"* widely pronounced *"danshoku"* in contemporary Japanese. In the title of his 1988 *A History of* Shōnen'ai Renga *and* Haikai (*Shōnen'ai no renga haikai shi*), however, Kita Tadashi describes ninth- to seventeenth-century verse written by adult men about beautiful *shōnen* (youths) or *chigo* (young male temple acolytes) as *shōnen'ai*—an ascription that employs a modern understanding of the term.[134] To be sure, as explained in the comprehensive dictionary *Nihon kokugo dai jiten,* during the Edo era (and likely before this) *"shōnen"* sometimes indicated the younger, passive partner in male–male erotic relations.[135] Prefixed with the character *"bi,"* for beautiful, the form *"bishōnen"* (beautiful youth), also dating at least back to the Edo era, renders all the more salient the youth's positioning as the potential object of aesthetic admiration or erotic desire.[136] Given that well into the modern era public discourse on the erotic has been an almost exclusively male domain, until even recent decades this desire for beautiful boys has presumed an adult male subject.

   A notable example of how the polyvalence of *shōnen* has carried on into the modern era can be found in *Vita Sexualis* (*Wita sekushuarisu*), a 1909 novel about a youth's sexual awakening—or, more accurately, relative lack thereof—by prominent writer, translator, and physician Mori Ōgai.[137] Ōgai uses *shōnen* dozens of times and occasionally *bishōnen,* sometimes but not always referring to or implying male homoeroticism with these terms. While, from his introduction to the concept of male homoeroticism at age eleven, the narrator makes occasional reference to male–male sexual relations among *kōha* (roughnecks), and their attempts to seduce, if not rape, *bishōnen,* he describes these practices as *"nanshoku"* or "Urning" (in German, untranscribed into Japanese), not "*shōnen'ai,*" a term that does not yet seem to be in use at the opening of the twentieth century.[138]

While the "*shōnen'ai*" is absent from key studies of *nanshoku,* I cannot prove that the phrase was never used before the modern era.[139] Nevertheless, the "*ai*" (love) part of the equation has shifted enough in meaning during Japan's early and rapid modernization in the Meiji era that—even as "*shōnen'ai*" draws on this Edo history for some of its historico-erotic cachet—such a term would not have had the same valence to Ōgai and his readers as it might have had even a half century prior. As Takayuki Yokota-Murakami observes, the contemporary meaning of "*ai*" came to approximate the English word "love" in Meiji Japan through a problem of translation: namely, the lack in Japanese of a term for a relationship of friendship and mutual respect between opposite-sex partners found in the Western literatures with which Japanese intellectuals were coming into contact and attempting to render in Japanese. The transfiguration of "love" into the rapidly transforming Japanese language eventually gave rise to a reconceptualized understanding of "*ai,*" through which "a friend and a (heterosexual) lover came to stand in a paradigmatic relationship with each other in the Japanese language system for the first time in history."[140] "Dismantling . . . contempt for women," Saeki Junko remarks, "was a primary goal of those who propounded *ai*" to name this new sense of "love."[141] The result is a modern understanding of *ai* premised in principle on an affective equality of the sexes. Beginning in the late nineteenth century, the lack of a corresponding term led some translators and writers to use transliterations of the English word. Yet—echoing *ribu* activist Miki Sōko's aforementioned explanation of the appeal of "*ūman ribu*" over existing native terms—the meaning, like the spelling, of this new signifier was unclear and unstable, if not empty, "denot[ing] hardly anything, having, instead, a good deal of connotations."[142]

This leaves us with the question of the extent to which it is this modern "*ai*" that finds its way into the term "*shōnen'ai*" as used in the twentieth century. When paired with "*shōnen,*" "*ai*" remains tinged with the asymmetrical Edo eroticism that Meiji intellectuals sought to attenuate. Yet, at least to the extent that—in contrast with *koi,* its approximate synonym—*ai* is not inherently carnal, *shōnen'ai* simultaneously seems to connote a certain avuncular affection and a sense of responsibility on the part of the man for the youth. And while composed of Sinitic characters, *shōnen'ai*—the various modern understandings of which date back to the early decades of the twentieth century—is from the beginning a transnational term.

Unlike "lesbian," which first entered Japanese at a specific moment in time, most likely as a transliterated term within a translated text, and unlike *ūman ribu,* whose coinage can with some certainty be linked to a specific journalist and a specific newspaper article, the first use of *shōnen'ai* is challenging to pinpoint definitively. Its initial modern use may date to as late as the 1920s. During this period multiple combinations of *shōnen* and *ai* were used to name adult male desire and affection for adolescent males—perhaps patterned after the still somewhat novel *"dōseiai"*—but there is no evidence suggesting that during the prewar and wartime eras *"shōnen'ai"* was ever the primary label for this desire. In 1923, Sawada Junjirō offers a book-length explication of *Mysterious Homosexuality (Shinpi naru dōseiai)*, one that draws heavily on European sexology and history and includes a number of foreign words written out in Roman letters.[143] In one section he sets out to define a number of terms, which he writes in *katakana,* parenthetically including the original term in Roman letters at first mention. Among these terms are *"sodomī* (Sodomy),"* which he identifies as religious in origin, and *"pederasuchī* (Pederasty),"* which he identifies as literary. Sawada explains that *"pederasuchī"* comes from the Greek and means *"shōnen no ai"* (love of/by youths), using the genitive particle *"no"* to link "boy" and "love." The result is a phrase that could mean love *for* a boy or love *by* a boy,[144] though in this context it is clear that the boy is the object of an older male's desire. In a chapter on the meaning of "homosexuality" *(dōseiai)* in a 1931 book on the topic, Morita Yūshū combines *shōnen* and *ai* with the object marker *o* and the auxiliary verb *suru* (do): *"shōnen o ai suru,"* that is, "love a boy."[145]

Somewhere in between these two couplings of *shōnen* and *ai,* the word *"shōnen'ai"* seems to have first appeared in its modern form and meaning. In a heavily German-inflected article in the journal *Hentai shinri* (Perverse psychology, 1917–1926) in 1925, Tanaka Kōgai (a.k.a. Tanaka Yūkichi) pairs German terms (spelled out in Roman letters) with Japanese equivalents. For the German *"Knabenliebe"* (boy love) it gives *"nandōai"* (lit., male child love); and for *"Funglingsliebe [sic],"* a misspelling of *Jünglingsliebe* (adolescent love), it offers *"shōnen'ai."*[146] *"Nandōai"*—which combines a classical term for young boy *("onowarawa")* with *"ai"*—does not appear in other prewar (or postwar) texts that I have consulted and may have been coined by Tanaka.[147] *"Shōnen'ai,"* which may also have been coined by Tanaka, is a reasonable combination of existing combinations of *"shōnen"* and *"ai,"* such as those named above, into a term.

For the remainder of the 1920s *shōnen'ai* would compete in dictionaries and glossaries as the Japanese meaning of "pederasty" with other terms—including *"keikan"* (anal intercourse), *"nanshoku* (Urning)," *"sodomī* (Sodomie)," and *"shikijōsei shōni shikō"* (erotic taste for small children).[148] In 1932, however, *shōnen'ai* is used in a book offering *A History of Human Sex Lives* in a section of the chapter on "homosexuality" (*dōseiai*) discussing same-sex relations between teacher and pupil in ancient Greece and Iberia.[149] This time the word stands alone. It is not glossed with or used as a gloss for any loanword, with its meaning either assumed by the author to be known by readers or easy enough to surmise from the characters and the context.

More significantly, prominent writer Inagaki Taruho (1900–1977) employed the term as early as 1930, in an essay originally published in *Grotesque* (*Gurotesuku*, 1928–1930), the namesake journal of the aforementioned interwar erotic grotesque nonsense boom.[150] In this article, as in many of his later musings that sought to develop a modern homoerotic aesthetics of beautiful boys, Taruho draws extensively on Japanese and European history and literature as well as philosophical and sexological texts, including the writing of Krafft-Ebing and early "homosexual" rights advocate Edward Carpenter, with the result being a hybrid aesthetics of boy loving that is heavily intertextual, transhistorical, and transnational, like the *shōnen'ai* manga created by female artists forty years later.[151] Though Taruho's attempt to develop a modern aesthetics of the adolescent male was impressively erudite, the intertextual nature of his approach was not significantly different from contemporary sexological writing on "homosexuality." And while he can be credited neither with coining the term "*shōnen'ai*" nor its association with the tradition of *nanshoku*, it is Taruho's writing, more than anything else, that imbued its eroticized object with the characteristics of, at once, a prewar European schoolboy in uniform and of a beautiful Edo-era *wakashu* (youth) with unshaven forelocks—that is with the folding of German *Knabenliebe* and Japanese *shudō* concepts into one another. The apex of this imagery is inscribed in his *Aesthetics of Boy Loving* (*Shōnen'ai no bigaku*, 1968), which includes the 1930 article that first used the term (figure 3.3). Evidencing the lack of taboo regarding adult male erotic adoration of youths, the volume was awarded the prestigious Grand Prize for Japanese Literature (Nihon Bungaku Taishō).[152] That the title on the slipcase, dust jacket, and cover of the original work was written in German "*Ästhetik der Knabenlibe [sic]*" rather than Japanese—which was used on the *obi* (the promotional sash) and interior title page—only reinforces the transnational nature of Taruho's *shōnen'ai* aesthetic and the implied semantic equivalence between *shōnen'ai* and *Knabenliebe*. Carrying on into the postwar era, Taruho's *shōnen'ai* was occasionally used in the perverse press of the 1950s and 1960s, including by the aforementioned Kabiya Kazuhiko.[153] Yet, "*shōnen'ai*" had not been established as the standard term to name either pederasty or pedophilia prior to the 1970s.

Figure 3.3. Slipcase and original *obi* on Inagaki Taruho's *Aesthetics of Boy Loving* (*Shōnen'ai no bigaku*, 1968).

Over the course of that decade, however, *shōnen'ai* would gain currency as a label for adult male desire for adolescents in this rapidly expanding commercial *homo* publication sphere, which in 1971 saw its first commercial magazine *Barazoku* (Rose tribe), put out by Dai Ni Shobō, the publisher of books such as sex and popular culture writer Akiyama Masami's *Homo Technique* and activist Minami Teishirō's *An Introduction to Homology*.[154] *Barazoku* made no effort in its early years to restrict expression of *shōnen'ai* desire for even prepubescent boys. Perhaps this was a function of the lingering memory of the *nanshoku* tradition modernized in the writing of Taruho among others—who were discussed on occasion in both reader-contributed and editorial content[155]—as well as the lack of a clear legal prohibition at the time. Nevertheless, the magazine would not facilitate correspondence between those over and under eighteen years of age through the magazine's personal ad section or the *"Shōnen no heya"* (Boys' room) column established for adolescent readers. In the personal ads in *Bara-zoku* as well as *Sabu* (1974–2002), while *shōnen'ai* was used by adult males to indicate their desire for adolescents, this was alternated with other terms in popular use, such as *"yangu"* (young) and *"hai tīn"* (high teen), as well as the vaguer terms *"onī-san"* and *"aniki"* (both, older brother) and *"otōto"* (younger brother).[156]

Men, however, were not the only ones homoerotically objectifying *bishōnen* (beautiful boys) in the 1970s. As outlined in chapter two, new female artists who were taking over the production of *shōjo* manga began to incorporate homoerotic romances between beautiful boys into their works beginning in late 1970. The new genre, for which Takemiya Keiko's *In the Sunroom* represented the initial salvo, would quickly come to be called *"shōnen'ai* manga."[157] Though predominant this term competed in the 1970s and 1980s with other labels including *"bishōnen* manga," *"June-mono"* and *"June,"* as well as *"tanbi."*

While as a genre label, the first of these terms, *"bishōnen* manga," indexes a work's beautiful young male protagonists, and works thus described do not necessarily entail male–male romance, the term *"bishōnen"* is closely linked in this context to *shōnen'ai* manga imagery and draws on the same history of the homoerotic objectification of male youths.

Sometime after its founding in 1978, the groundbreaking magazine *June* would see its title come to be used as another label for these narratives, which quickly came to be described as *"June"* or *"June-mono,"* that is, *"June* things"—often with the magazine title spelled out in capital Roman letters: "JUNE." Some, including *shōjo* manga critic Fujimoto Yukari, treat *June* as a subgenre of homoerotic manga works by and for women based on stylistic or narrative differences between works appearing in *June* and existing *shōnen'ai* manga.[158] *"Sōsaku* JUNE" (original *June*) has also served as a broad genre code to categorize original, rather than derivative, *dōjinshi* (fanzines) at the massive and influential Comic Market event since 1987; it would take another twenty-five years for that category to become *"Sōsaku* (JUNE/BL),"[159] a belated acknowledgment that BL had become the primary generic label used among fans, and a usage that has survived into the 2020s, long after the original magazine ceased to exist.

"Tanbi," meaning aesthete or aestheticism, is a fourth term that began to be used in this sphere relatively early. (Intriguingly, while the term continues to have limited currency in Japanese in this sphere, particularly in reference to prose fiction, it endures most conspicuously in its Chinese pronunciation,

danmei, which is used by Chinese-speaking fans as a general label for BL and by other fans as a label for Chinese BL.) The use in Japanese of *"tanbi"*—which conveys a mix of beauty, romance, eroticism, and decadence—to describe BL media plays on the term's broader application as a label for works of highbrow literature that are aesthetically appealing and often subtly erotic, and sometimes as a description of the lives of the authors. These include works by—and the lives of—Japanese writers such as the aforementioned Tanizaki Jun'ichirō, along with Kawabata Yasunari (1899–1972) and Mishima Yukio (1925–1970), as well as Europeans such as Oscar Wilde (1854–1900) and Jean Genet (1910–1986).[160] Within the pages of *June,* the term *"tanbi"* was applied both to this genre and to literature by Mishima, Genet, and Wilde, and others known both for their own "homosexuality" and for their writing that depicted it, including Taruho. While such writers are associated in this sphere with *tanbi,* Taruho is most closely associated with *shōnen'ai,* or, rather, the term's hijacking in the 1970s by young women artists for use as a label for the genre of male homoerotic manga narratives.

Inspired by the relationships among schoolboys depicted in some of Herman Hesse's novels and the writing of Taruho, Masuyama Norie took upon herself the role of muse and encouraged Takemiya and Hagio Moto to give life to her ideas. Takemiya recalls having just read Taruho's *Aesthetics of Boy Loving* when she conceived the idea for *The Song of the Wind and the Trees,*[161] meaning its use of *shōnen'ai* is almost certainly the origin of the label of this new genre. Moreover, Masuyama recalls that initially they also described the narratives as depicting *kunābenrībe,* which may have come from its use as a synonym for *shōnen'ai* in Taruho's book.[162] The German term might have been particularly appealing as a label for works set in Europe, as were the earliest *shōnen'ai* narratives. Regardless, the ambiguity of the term *"shōnen'ai"* served the genre well since, as previously noted, it can simultaneously indicate the boys as the subject or object of affection.[163] It is also important not to overlook here that, while the primary romantic relationships in the seminal *shōnen'ai* works by Takemiya, Hagio, and other artists are between adolescent boys, from the beginning some sexual and romantic relationships in works labeled *"shōnen'ai"* in fact involved an adult male and an adolescent or younger boy, rendering the theme closer to the original pederastic meaning of the term. Other works called *shōnen'ai* involved relationships between handsome young men (*biseinen*), however, rendering the *shōnen* in the genre name a misnomer.

Masuyama and *shōnen'ai* artists claim to have understood *shōnen'ai* in *shōjo* manga as well as Taruho's writing as quite distinct from the "homosexuality" depicted in the works of writers such as Mishima and Shibusawa

Tatsuhiko (1928–1987).[164] This did not forestall interest among some *shōnen'ai* manga readers in the *homo* sphere, nor the conflation of the fictive *shōnen'ai* of *shōjo* manga and of Taruho both with the "real" male–male sexuality and with *shōnen'ai qua* pederasty/pedophilia as depicted in magazines like *Barazoku*. Letters from adolescent female readers printed in the pages of *Barazoku* and other *homo* magazines in the 1970s and 1980s make that quite clear.[165] Some female readers of *Barazoku* indicated in their letters to the magazine that they started reading it after first becoming fans of *shōnen'ai* manga. Such readers occasionally explained that they learned about *"homo"* from manga, often noting directly or by implication that reading these works gave them a spe-cial sympathy for and/or interest in *homo* men. "Sylvie," for instance, who inci-dentally "want[ed] to marry a *homo*," wrote manga and "homosexual fiction" about boys that she hoped to publish in *Barazoku*.[166] She also recommended to male readers a handful of *shōnen'ai* manga titles, including Takemiya's *The Song of the Wind and the Trees* and Hagio Moto's *The Heart of Thomas,* as well as films such as *Death in Venice* (1971).[167] In addressing the magazine's readers with *"shōnen'ai no mina-san"* (roughly, dear boy lovers) but clearly indicating *homo* men, Sylvie conflates the *homo* of *Barazoku* and the beautiful boys of *shōnen'ai* manga, as well as pedophiles, for whom the term *shōnen'ai* had (and continues to have) a different meaning.[168]

While some of these letter writers suggest they were devoted readers of the magazine, I have encountered only one woman who described herself as a regular reader of *Barazoku*—a then university student–aged *rezubian* who bought the magazine frequently in the mid-1980s for its personal ads from other *rezubian* rather than for its depiction of male homosexuality.[169] Many of the twenty or so women I interviewed who were avid readers of *shōnen'ai* manga during this period, however, did tell me that they had perused a copy or two, sometimes as it was passed around at middle or high school.

However limited in number, these female readers of *homo* magazines declared their interest in *homo* men via letters printed not only in the pages of *Barazoku* and other *homo* magazines but also in *June* and two additional magazines connected with *shōnen'ai* manga and female erotic consump-tion of beautiful boys in the 1980s, *Allan* and *Gekkō*. Editorial content in these three magazines also sometimes explicitly made such linkages and drew read-ers' attention to "gay" cultures in Japan and abroad.[170] Moreover, as noted in chapter two, some male artists drew illustrations of beautiful youths for both magazines aimed at a *homo* readership and those targeting *shōnen'ai* fans; and *June* itself was published by San Shuppan, the same publisher that produced the *homo* magazine *Sabu*. Importantly, both this kind of editorial content and reader submissions helped spread the vocabulary and symbolism as well as cultural information from the *homo* sphere among the broader *shōnen'ai* manga fandom, perhaps helping them decode or re-encode the symbolism found in *shōnen'ai* manga texts.[171]

The *"shōnen'ai"* label as used in the *shōjo* manga sphere found its way into the popular press, both in the pages of magazines partially or entirely devoted to the representation of *shōnen'ai* for female consumption, such as those noted above, and in occasional articles about the genre in high- and lowbrow periodicals, sometimes compiled into books.[172] Based on my perusal of hundreds of issues of various magazines from the 1950s to the 1990s aimed at a wide variety of readerships on women's issues and on "homosexuality" as well as database searches of major newspapers, however, I do not believe the term *"shōnen'ai"* was in wide use in print as a label either for gender-bending manga or for male–male pederastic or pedophiliac desire outside these discourse spheres.[173] When used in the context of a discussion of either these *shōjo* manga or adult male erotic appreciation of beautiful youths, however, I would suggest that even for those unfamiliar with the genre or Taruho's writing, the term's meaning would be easy to infer in context.

While some fans of the *shōnen'ai* genre in the 1970s and 1980s with whom I have spoken used the term in our discussions, either of their own volition or at my prompting, it is the pederastic/pedophilic meaning that has lingered into the present day. This is evident, for instance, in its use to name the subject of a book on contemporary pederasty and pedophilia, *Boy Lovers: Searching for Their Reality, Concealed by Myth and Taboo,* and, more prominently, the fact that the Japanese *Wikipedia* entry on *"shōnen'ai"* focuses on pederasty and pedophilia. While the entry contained a section on the *shōjo* manga genre as late as 2015, this was displaced into a separate entry, while the German, English, and Greek terms *"Knabenliebe,"* "pederasty," and *"paiderastíā,"* respectively, remain as synonyms.[174]

While, similar to *"ūman ribu,"* it is thus clear that the term's primary users were unable to control the meaning of the specific word in popular discourse, the women and girls in this sphere did not lose control of the broader discourse. As explained in chapter two, while the depiction in manga of male homoeroticism by and for a female audience first emerged in the commercial publishing sphere, by the latter half of the 1970s, female fans-cum-artists were creating their own narratives in either manga or short story form, compiling these narratives into *dōjinshi,* and selling them at the Comic Market and other events and through magazines like *Allan.* Many of these narratives parody *shōnen* manga (boys' comics) by homoeroticizing the male–male relationships therein, and others entail male celebrities, while some are "original." It is in this sphere that *"yaoi,"* one of the terms used to label this broad generic sphere, emerged.

"Yaoi" is an acronym for *"yama nashi, ochi nashi, imi nashi,"* or, roughly, "no climax, no point, no meaning," an apt description of the relatively plotless original narratives and parodies replete with implied or roughly depicted male-on-male sex. Its coinage and initial use had little specifically to do with the genre, however. As recalled by Hatsu Akiko (b. 1959), once a frequent guest at Takemiya and Hagio's Ōizumi Salon, the term emerged organically at the end of the 1970s among the members of the popular Ravuri (Lovely) manga circle as a general, self-deprecating assessment of all types of *dōjinshi*.[175] Playing on the new term, Ravuri member Maru Mikiko created a male homoerotic manga that she titled *"Yaoi,"* writing the term in *kanji* characters meaning "chasing the night." At the time Hatsu felt that, "It's true that this manga has no climax, no point, and no meaning. But there's something—what's going on between these guys?" So, in December 1979, she, Maru, and a small group of others collectively compiled a *dōjinshi* full of male homoerotic narratives based on the concept that, "Even if there's no climax, no point, and no meaning, there's eros." This *dōjinshi*, titled *RAPPORI: Special Yaoi Issue* (*RAPPORI: Yaoi tokushū gō*), in effect narrowed the definition of the term.[176] By the early 1980s, the term *"yaoi"* was beginning to be used in the amateur comics sphere to name these amateur homoerotic parodies.[177] It has subsequently been given alternative readings within the community to highlight the sometimes—but by no means universal—pornographic content of these *dōjinshi*, including *"yamete, oshiri ga itai,"* that is, "stop, my butt hurts," and *"yaru, okasu, ikaseru,"* or "do (him), rape (him), make (him) cum."[178] Although it is still common in fan discourse in other languages, *"yaoi"* has largely fallen into disuse in Japanese.

The term *"shōnen'ai"* as a genre label is used even less frequently in Japanese than *"yaoi,"* yet it has a perhaps surprising afterlife stemming from the publishing world and the vagaries of Japanese and global fandoms. Starting at the end of the 1980s, a number of new commercial magazines were established to take advantage of the ever-increasing desire to consume male homoerotic manga evidenced at the Comic Market and beyond. Such magazines often printed a catchphrase on the cover, generally in Japanese. In the 1970s, *June*'s was "now, opening our eyes to dangerous love," while by the 1990s, this was altered to "now, transcending dangerous love." Embracing the word *"tanbi,"* *Allan* labeled itself "an aesthete magazine for girls." Among the slogans appearing on magazines first published at the opening of the 1990s were "YAOI♥COMIC" (in capital Roman letters) and "a comic for bad girls." And on the cover of the

1991 debut of *Image* (*Imāju*, 1991–?1995) was "BOY'S LOVE♥COMIC," a title that renders *"shōnen'ai* manga" into would-be English.[179] The following year, the sister publication *Shōsetsu Image* came out similarly adorned with "BOY'S LOVE NOVELS" on its own cover.

While "English" is often used for little more than ornamentation on the covers of magazines, in advertising, and on consumer goods, this particular decorative turn of phrase seems to have caught on: Soon after *Image's* debut, *Manga jōhōshi pafu* (Manga information magazine puff, 1979–2011) used "BOY'S LOVE" as the title of a special feature on these works and artists, and the term gained currency as a generic marker, often abbreviated as BL or spelled out phonetically as *"bōizu rabu."*[180] The "English" form of the term caught on and is used globally alongside *yaoi* and local transliterations and translations to name male homoerotic manga, anime, and novels, as well as related video games. Although the presence of an English translation of *"shōnen'ai"* does not itself seem remarkable, the fact that "boys love"— also written "boys' love" and "boy's love"—was first coined in Japan as an "English" translation renders the already unclear current of cultural and linguistic flows still murkier.

Through the first decade or so of the 2000s, many fans in Japan used *yaoi* and boys love/BL as relatively interchangeable, but for some *yaoi* marked amateur and BL commercial works based on their points of origin.[181] The fact that amateur works are often more sexual and less plot driven than commercially published texts has meant that some in this sphere classified works in roughly the same way but based on content rather than form. By the 2010s, *"yaoi,"* like *"shōnen'ai"* and other terms, had largely fallen out of favor. Today, all such works are generally called BL or boys love. One major exception are works by and for gay men, often labeled variations on "gay comics" (*gei komikkusu*), though the line between BL and gay comics is somewhat nebulous. While, gay comics notwithstanding, some scholars and fans continue to treat *"shōnen'ai,"* *"yaoi,"* *"June,"* and "boys love" as distinct genres,[182] I would argue that this runs the risk of erasing the extensive overlap among and between the terms, the media, and their histories.

In other languages too, *yaoi* and *shōnen'ai* linger on. Among English-speaking fans, for instance, while boys love and BL have garnered increasing currency, *"yaoi"* continues to be used as a catchall term or to specify works that have explicit sexual content. This is in contrast with *"shōnen'ai"* (often spelled *"shonen-ai"* or *"shounen-ai"*), which has been widely used to specify works that focus on romance with little to no sex.[183] These transfigurations into English and other languages draw on misunderstandings of the terms' use in Japanese.

Whether the usage of such terms by fans speaking Japanese, English, or other languages will converge remains to be seen.

"Words," writes anthropologist Anna Lowenhaupt Tsing, "offer special insight into the remaking of worlds at different scales because they condense past motion in their material form."[184] We have seen in this chapter how words in their travels across time and space have had a sometimes profound impact on individuals and communities, and, ultimately, on the culture at large. To be sure, my histories of *"ūman ribu," "rezubian,"* and *"shōnen'ai"* have not been comprehensive, nor in the case of the latter two terms have they been precise as to their origins. While I may have been able to pinpoint the originary moment of *"ūman ribu,"* as I hope my discussions of *"rezubian"* and *"shōnen'ai"* have demonstrated, this is less important than the (inevitably partial) elaboration, in Foucault's terms, "of the myriad events through which—thanks to which, against which—they were formed,"[185] and have come to make and to remake meaning. My aim in this chapter has not been to offer misleadingly teleological histories of *"ūman ribu," "rezubian,"* and *"shōnen'ai,"* but to begin to unravel and complicate—rather than merely uncover—the individual and collective struggles over meaning that these histories reveal. For women and girls in the *ribu, rezubian,* and queer *shōjo* manga spheres, this grappling is—in no small part—with the meaning of their desires and the terms that name them. And, as Kath Weston reminds us, "no one has a greater stake in the outcome of conflicts over terminology than the people who constitute themselves through and counter to available cultural categories."[186]

In recent years, there has been substantial debate in queer activist communities in Asia over the applicability of "imported" terms such as "lesbian," "gay," and "queer."[187] Some of the debate centers on whether these terms and the meanings that they carry are being imposed from the outside and thus fail to reflect local understandings of gender and sexuality. As I have shown, in the case of Japan, the history of the terms *"ūman ribu"* and *"rezubian"* demonstrates that they were neither imported at a single specific moment nor, more importantly, were they imposed from the outside. If, as Lydia Liu argues, through translation terms and their meanings "are not so much 'transformed' when concepts pass from the guest language to the host language as invented within the local environment of the latter,"[188] then these terms have been invented and, indeed, reinvented in Japanese multiple times. Even the seemingly native term *"shōnen'ai"* has been inflected by decades of transnational cultural and intellectual flows. And the meanings in Japanese of all three terms have been shaped and reshaped by local discourse on women's rights and gender and sexual expression, a discourse repeatedly incorporating transnational exchange of ideas, and, increasingly, the voices of women and girls.

If the *ūman ribu* movement has been misunderstood as a simple import from the United States, this is as much a function of insufficient attention to the sometimes complex ways "loanwords" come to be and to mean within a language as it is to the history of the movement itself. And while *rezubian* has, roughly, come to converge in meaning and in pronunciation with the English "lesbian," to assume that *rezubian* was simply imported into Japanese along with the (unstable) concept of what constitutes a lesbian, belies nearly a century of evolving understandings of "homosexuality" (in both Japan and elsewhere) along with the transnational exchange that has gone into it. The history of *shōnen'ai* goes back centuries further, and yet, much like the meanings of its components *shōnen* and *ai*, it was transfigured in modern Japan as notions of boyhood, girlhood, eros, and affection were reconsidered and reconfigured in no small part in response to the introduction of novel ideas from beyond the confines of Japan. And like *"rezubian,"* while residue from past meanings continues to adhere to it, the term's meaning has remained unfixed. Its afterlife in the contemporary term "boys love" demonstrates both linguistic creativity and the nativeness of ostensibly foreign terms within Japanese.

CHAPTER 4

Translation

Modern Japan is a culture of translation.... The idea seems
so self-evident as to require no further comment, and yet we
have only begun to unravel its manifold implications.

—*Indra Levy*

According to literary scholar Mizuta Noriko, the translator is "a transmitter, a transvestite, a trans/gender/lator who blurs the boundaries between self and other and transgresses into different cultures and across gender distinctions."[1] For more than a century translation has been central to individual and collective efforts by women in Japan to explain and, to varying degrees, to liberate female gender and sexuality from restrictive norms. While the work of some of the earliest women translators, such as Wakamatsu Shizuko (1864–1896), Koganei Kimiko (1870–1956), and Senuma Kayō (1875–1915), may not be regarded as overtly feminist, their introduction of foreign literature in the late nineteenth and early twentieth centuries certainly contributed to the discourse on what it means to be a woman in Japan.[2] In that same period other women more actively and overtly deployed translation and translated texts to question, resist, or subvert attempts to control female sexual and gender expression. Prominent among feminist translation activities in the 1910s were members of Seitōsha (the Bluestocking Society) and their journal, *Seitō* (Bluestocking, 1911–1916), founded by iconic feminist Hiratsuka Raichō. As evidenced in the pages of *Seitō,* these Japanese bluestockings looked toward the writings of figures such as Swedish feminist Ellen Key and British sexologist Havelock Ellis to help elucidate certain desires for social and sexual autonomy—and, at times, for each other. They also turned a critical eye to many of the same literary works that drew the attention of the (male) Japanese literati of the time, such as works by Anton Chekhov, Henrik Ibsen, and Edgar Allan Poe—authors who have continued to resonate with women and girl readers and writers many decades later.[3] While the specific texts have varied, this combination of translated literature, social criticism, and empirical studies would long remain of great import to women seeking to rethink the category "women."

In her introduction to the volume *Translation in Modern Japan,* Indra Levy writes that a focus on translation in the Japanese context "mobilizes a set of heuristic tools that take us far beyond the often vague and slippery trope of 'influence.'"[4] Levy observes, moreover, that within Japanese studies, translators as well as their audiences are finally being seen as agents of translation, through which they contribute to the reshaping of the culture at large[5]—a point long taken for granted in the field of translation studies. It should come as no surprise that, from the time they began to coalesce, women in the *ribu* movement and the *rezubian* community, as well as artists and readers of queer *shōjo* manga deployed both translation and translated writing to engender cultural change via their creative use of ideas and imagery as well as practices from abroad. This chapter specifically takes up the use of translation in the 1970s and 1980s within and around the *ūman ribu, rezubian,* and queer *shōjo* manga spheres.

Unsurprisingly, given their dominance in publishing as well as academia and other areas of the public sphere, men have also been the translators of feminist and other texts of great influence in these communities. Even key feminist texts of the 1970s were translated by men, as had been Simone de Beauvoir's *The Second Sex* (1949) two decades prior.[6] These male translators' lack of expertise or interests related to the topics of these works has sometimes resulted in misunderstandings and omissions, occasionally sparking criticism and motivating new translations.[7] As a man who is, in a broad sense, also acting in this book as a translator of women's words and experiences, I would be putting myself and my project here on shaky ground to claim that a male translator would be unable to successfully convey the nuances, valences, and affects expressed in feminist texts in another language. Yet, we cannot deny that, regardless of an individual translator's skills, their knowledge and lived experience function as resources the translator draws upon in the course of translation. At the very least, translating feminist texts into Japanese in the 1970s and 1980s would have demanded a far greater degree of awareness of women's experiences and openness to women's concerns than could have been expected of most male translators at the time.

Even a poor translation may be better than none at all, however. Indeed, whatever its shortcomings, the 1953 translation of Beauvoir's work became a feminist touchstone for many women in Japan in the latter half of the twentieth century[8]—even motivating at least one woman to travel to France, as discussed in chapter five. And, similar to the coinage of the terms examined in the previous chapter, we must recognize that men at times played a signifi-cant role in the translation of feminist ideas into Japanese, as some examples below demonstrate. That their role has been almost completely unacknowl-edged speaks at least as much to the fact that these men were, by and large, not otherwise participating in the movement or in the field of women's studies that was to emerge in the late 1970s as it does to the general condition of what Lawrence Venuti describes as the "translator's invisibility."[9] We should also rec-ognize that, even if this role was not wholly positive—resulting in, for instance, infelicitous mistranslations—the aggregate effect of their work was certainly not negative for women. However inspired by or indifferent to feminist ideas they may have been, male translators did help convey them into Japanese. And, conversely, female translators of feminist writing did not necessarily have feminist aims, as I also address below.

In the case of the literature read and transfigured by artists and readers of queer *shōjo* manga, the sex of the translator generally appears not to have been relevant, particularly since the texts themselves were often initially penned by male authors and depict male experience anyway. I show below, however, that the sex—and sexuality—of the translator of a text can add meaning to the text's transfiguration into *shōjo* manga.

I revisit here the notion of transfiguration to help make sense of the various roles of translators, acts of translation, and uses of translated texts within and surrounding the three communities I take up in this volume. As I note in chapter one, Dilip Gaonkar and Elizabeth Povinelli propose that focusing on "circulation and transfiguration, rather than meaning and translation," might be a more productive way to think about the transformational nature of bor-der crossing.[10] They specifically suggest that the focus on meaning—and its transformation, often via translation—has run its course. While, as they point out, there are already "countless socially informed studies of the conditions of possibility for various forms of translation and countless studies of the pro-foundly political nature of translation,"[11] I see translation as a key mode of transfiguration, and, consequently, an important focus through which to elu-cidate transfiguration within the *ūman ribu, rezubian,* and queer *shōjo* manga spheres. An eye toward translation *as* transfiguration insists that we look at not just the *agents* (translators and publishers) and *processes* (acts of translation themselves) but also the *effects* of these processes—be these effects new texts or, indeed, new subjectivities. This offers us a better sense of translation as a practice that transfigures not only ideas and texts but also communities and cultures and even the people who inhabit them.

Although translation theorists such as Maria Tymoczko make a compelling case for an expansive notion of translation that encompasses diverse processes and products across cultures and time,[12] I find it productive here to delimit "translation" to its more common definition of conveying in one language, however successfully, specific words from another. While all translation is creative—André Lefevere, for instance, describes translation as "rewriting"[13]— it is important to distinguish attempts to directly transmit textual meaning and affect from attempts to transform it. This distinction speaks to both agency and intention, and can have profound implications on the resultant texts, as well as the effects of those texts. By positioning a narrowly defined "translation" as a mode of transfiguration, we can expand our purview to include acts and products related to translation without losing this specificity.

I turn now to the translation and more radical transfiguration of texts within the *ribu, rezubian,* and queer *shōjo* manga communities. I used the previous chapter's focus on the etymology of *"ūman ribu," "rezubian,"* and *"shōnen'ai"* to begin to get at how these three pivotal terms, among others, were shaped by manifold acts and fortuities at the junctures and disjunctures of global and local discourse. To incorporate the long histories undergirding these terms—histories that include many layers of translation—the focus of that chapter stretches back more than a century. In this chapter, I narrow my chronological purview and simultaneously widen my focus beyond individual words. I turn specifically to the roles that both acts of translation and translated texts themselves played in shaping the *ribu, rezubian,* and queer *shōjo* manga spheres as well as the individuals who inhabited them. Translation in these spheres has been largely overlooked, which I believe is in part because of resistance in the case of the *ribu* and *rezubian* spheres to the suggestion of import or copy, and in part because, while the key texts I examine in this chapter arguably had a significant impact on these spheres, as I have already noted, the focus of most of these women was local.[14] In the queer *shōjo* manga sphere, on the other hand, it was not direct translation but rather the further transfiguration of already translated texts that makes translation most significant. The production and reverberations of the numerous and varied translations and more radical transfigurations in these spheres exemplify the web of connections and coincidences that not infrequently accompany translation, as well as the sometimes random, spontaneous, and amorphous nature of these three spheres themselves.

To cover this vast and uneven terrain, I have selected diverse translated critical, empirical, and literary texts that allow me to outline the role of translation and translated texts in shaping these communities and the individuals within them. The texts I have chosen also at times call particular attention to the intertwined nature of the *ribu* and *rezubian* spheres—despite the degree to which *rezubian* women felt ignored within or ostracized from the *ribu* community.[15] I first scrutinize direct translations within the *ribu* and *rezubian* spheres, with an emphasis on how choices made by these translators shaped these texts and their relevance to women in Japan. I then take up the translations and the multiple transfigurations of *Our Bodies, Ourselves,* a germinal book on women's health intended from its conception to have a global impact, and *The Hite Report,* a pioneering study designed to reveal the many realities of women's sexuality in the United States. Both texts inspired local transfigurations sometimes so dramatically different from the originals as to be unrecognizable as such. Finally, I look at ways literature in translation has been transfigured in the realm of queer *shōjo* manga. While the role of translations of fiction and poetry by women writers in shaping *shōjo* literature in the early twentieth century has been given significant attention,[16] this chapter looks at the afterlives of texts by male authors including Herman Hesse, Anton Chekhov, and Thomas Mann, which, through their transfiguration into *shōjo* manga, helped facilitate an awareness in readers of other gender and sexual possibilities.

Re-Presenting Radical Feminist Writing from the United States

Each in its own way, the key terms discussed in the previous chapter—*"ūman ribu,"* *"rezubian,"* and *"shōnen'ai"*—are products of translation. In the case of *"ūman ribu,"* Ninagawa Masao, the male journalist who coined the term, came across translations of American so-called second-wave feminist writing while conducting research for the first of his series of newspaper articles that introduced the *ribu* movement to the Tokyo reading public. These translations and Ninagawa's interview with Akiyama Yōko, a translator of some of that writing, may have reinforced or given rise to Ninagawa's false impression that the Japanese movement itself was—like the translated articles—imported from the United States. While *ribu* was clearly not an import, an examination of translation within *ribu* and the ripples it set in motion demonstrates, however, that, in Akiyama's words, "we cannot ignore the influence of the American women's liberation movement" on the nascent Japanese movement.[17] As Akiyama observes in relation to the translation of materials from the US movement, information and ideas from the United States helped to inform, even ignite "the smoldering resentment among Japanese women and to put that resentment into words."[18]

The influence of American radical feminism was, of course, nowhere stronger than among translators, whose work entailed a relatively high level of interest in and intimacy with their American counterparts, who were, consequently, less "foreign" to the translators. The earliest of the *ribu* translators were not, however, typical of *ribu* activists in the early 1970s. Most *ribu* activists were of university age, if not university students, and many of the first activists had participated in the student and anti-war movements of the late 1960s before joining *ribu*. Most of the first translators, by contrast, were in their late twenties or early thirties and already occupied with employment or families. They were also less likely to have been involved in the most recent wave of social protests, which had flared up after they had graduated from university. And the translators were, of course, more likely to be both relatively proficient in written, if not spoken, English and in contact with foreigners liable to pass on new feminist writing. Consequently, as noted in previous chapters, while the earliest translation of radical feminist materials from English was coincident with the organizing that is widely seen as the beginning of the movement, the scant information that most of the first *ribu* activists in Japan initially had about their counterparts abroad came from the limited and distorted images available in the mass media, rather than direct contact with activists from overseas or their writing.

It was, indeed, this combination of slant and silence in the mass media that Akiyama's first feminist co-translation project aimed to correct. This is directly spelled out in the project's afterword: "Not a word is written [in male-produced media accounts] about why these American women—who appeared more liberated than us—have risen up."[19] In response to this situation, in mid-1970, shortly after the founding of small student feminist groups like Thought Collective S.E.X. and around the same time activist Tanaka Mitsu was drafting her influential "Liberation from the Toilet" manifesto, Akiyama and a handful of others were assembling in a fifty-page, handwritten and mimeographed pamphlet what were likely the first translations into Japanese of so-called second-wave feminist writing. The pamphlet, *Women's Liberation Movement Materials 1: American Edition* contained two translated articles from members of the US liberation movement and an interview with an American activist.[20] This pamphlet represents the *ribu* movement's earliest "engaged translation," a term Tymoczko uses to describe translations intended to "rouse, inspire, witness, mobilize, and incite to rebellion" and which are created by "engaged translators," who themselves "have political agendas and use translation as one means to achieve those agendas."[21] And yet, the pamphlet was created by a group that came together by happenstance, did not set out to be or identify as "translators," and was not even entirely comprised of feminist women.

Akiyama recalls that the group, which named itself Women's Liberation Movement Preparation Group (Josei Kaihō Undō Junbi Kai)—hereafter
Women's Preparation Group—was "very ordinary," just one among "numerous gatherings of [female] co-workers, fellow students, and friends who came
together to study women's issues and history" at that time. "Ordinary" though
they may have seemed, such groups helped plant the seeds that grew into the
ribu movement. Women's Preparation Group was itself formed from members
of two different reading groups in the Tokyo area. One was a group of professional women working at Nippon Television (NTV) who, groping for a way to
understand their own experiences, were reading classics of women's history.[22]
Akiyama was invited to take part in the group's discussions through a friend
working at the station. The other group was comprised of women who were
former members of the Haiyūza Theatre Company (Gekidan Haiyūza), editors,
teachers, students, and so forth. Several members of the latter group were also
working part time at the TV station, which is how members of the two groups
became acquainted with each other.[23]

The two translated articles in *Women's Liberation Movement Materials*,
Marge Piercy's "The Grand Coolie Dam" and Kathy McAfee and Myrna Wood's
"Bread and Roses," were originally published in 1969 in the American New
Left magazine *Leviathan* and were quickly circulated as pamphlets, which is
the form in which they fortuitously reached their Japanese translators.[24] Both
articles discuss institutionalized sexism and the exploitation of women within
the American anti-establishment New Left movement, an issue that resonated
with the experiences of women in Japan involved in leftist groups. Akiyama
was motivated by her own interest in the topic to translate Piercy's article. For
Akiyama, in its narration of the resentment that in the United States drove the
women to break from the New Left and begin the women's movement, it really
spoke to how the personal is political.[25] This lends a certain irony to the fact
that "Bread and Roses," accompanied in the pamphlet by James Oppenheim's
1911 poem of the same name, was actually translated by a Japanese man who
had come into contact with the leftist movement while living in Berkeley in the
late 1960s. The uncredited translation was the work of the then up-and-coming
actor Nakamura Atsuo (b. 1940). Though not a member of Women's Preparation Group or the two reading groups, Nakamura had become acquainted
with several members of the latter reading group who had been fellow members of the Haiyūza Theatre Company. He was asked to translate McAfee and
Wood's article for these women at around the same time that Akiyama was
working on Piercy's.[26] The draft translations were circulated among both reading groups, and some members of both groups ended up cooperating to put

these translations together and more widely distribute them, forming Women's Preparation Group for that purpose.[27]

The remaining third of the pamphlet consists of a translated interview with American feminist activist Charlotte Bunch conducted by Kurita Reiko, a woman unaffiliated with Women's Preparation Group but who was very familiar with the United States and felt a strong sense of connection to the women's liberation movement.[28] One of a number of American activists who were either transiting through or sojourning in Japan during this period, Bunch was interviewed while en route back to the United States from Hanoi.[29] In her conversation with Kurita, Bunch describes issues similar to those covered in the two translated articles. While the interview is largely composed of Bunch sharing information about the movement and the current situation for women in the United States, it ends with a discussion of the merits and safety of the birth control pill, then unavailable in Japan, and abortion, then largely unavailable in much of the United States.[30] This brief exchange—surely among the first between this new wave of radical feminists in Japan and the United States to be recorded—shows that even at the early stages of the movement in Japan, the *ribu* women were both learning from and actively engaging with their American counterparts.

Chance helped Women's Preparation Group's translations play a role in the introduction of the *ribu* movement to the nation in late 1970 and the coinage of the term "*ūman ribu*." And, while such informally circulated translations would continue to be important within the movement, from that point forward commercial translations were to have the most far-reaching impact on women (and men) within and beyond the *ribu* sphere. The small collection of texts that are apparently the first translations of radical feminist writing from the United States to be commercially published in Japan comprised the last third of a book that, though focused on the interests of Japanese women, somewhat blurred the *ribu* movement with contemporary American feminist activism. Released in March 1971 by the left-leaning publisher Aki Shobō, this volume, *An Accusation of Sex Discrimination: The Demands of Women's Lib* (*Sei sabetsu e no kokuhatsu: Ūman ribu wa shuchō suru*), was also the first commercially published book focused on *ribu* and the first to use "*ūman ribu*" in the title.[31] While foregrounding Japanese women and the Japanese movement, a keen interest in and a sense of connection to women's activism abroad is also evidenced by the fact that nearly a third of this volume is devoted to the American movement. Even the two-thirds focused on Japan directly and indirectly points to the US movement or often uses generic language universalizing women's oppression.

The volume is divided into three sections, the first of which, "A Debate for Liberation," is a transcript of a groundbreaking "teach-in" (*tīchi in*) involving hundreds of women, which was held in a large public facility in Tokyo's Sendagaya neighborhood on November 14, 1970.[32] Perhaps half of the participants were in their early twenties, but many were in their thirties or older, with some women in their sixties.[33] Some were then or had previously been involved in the current or older waves of pre- and postwar women's activism. Their ranks included members of Women's Preparation Group as well as Tanaka's Group Fighting Women. The participants were of diverse backgrounds in terms of career and life course. Most are identified not by name but simply as "activist" (with or without mention of a specific *ribu* group affiliation), "consumer activist," "researcher," "participant," "high school student," "university instructor," "student," "housewife," "worker," "older housewife," or "instructor"; at least one of the participants was a non-Japanese-speaking American activist.[34] These women's discussion includes differences between the new and previous movements; sex discrimination at the workplace, home, school, and within social movements; and the historical origins of and what to do about this discrimination.[35]

After proclaiming her excitement about being "able to take part in this profoundly moving meeting,"[36] an American participant introduced as Diana Connolly shares information about the movement in the United States. Like Bunch in her interview with Kurita, Connolly mentions, among other things, the importance of the abortion issue in that country.[37] She also describes the movement's troubled relationship with the mass media, which she felt was using the movement and providing distorted coverage thereof.[38] The resonance with *ribu* criticism of the Japanese media's treatment of the *ribu* movement highlights the relevance of the American experience to women in Japan. While Connolly contributes little more than words of support and information already in circulation, her participation in the discussion and its reproduction in the first commercial "*ūman ribu*" publication, like the interview with Bunch, also draws our attention to early personal ties between the *ribu* movement and foreign activists.

The rendering of Connolly's words into Japanese also illustrates the potential of translation to (mis)shape the message it attempts to convey—in sometimes subtle ways. While I have no original against which to compare the Japanese version, translation's effect on the nuance of Connolly's words is most evident in her (translator's) reference to the new US women's liberation movement as the American "*fujin kaihō undō*" (women's liberation movement). As noted in chapter one, this was seen within the *ribu* movement as a dated term generally used to refer to earlier generations of women's activism in Japan and abroad.[39] The labeling of this new wave of radical feminism with the more formal *"fujin"* rather than *"josei"* or *"onna"*—the then preferred terms among *ribu* women—casts the US movement as more old school than revolutionary. Connolly's words were likely interpreted by an older woman more accustomed to the old-fashioned and more deferential term and not consciously distinguishing between *fujin* on the one hand, and *josei* and *onna* on the other. Regardless of the appropriateness of the interpreter's choice of words, the ultimate impact was probably minimal in this particular case—the context and content make it clear that Connolly is speaking of a radical new movement—but it reminds us that we need to pay attention not only to what is being translated but also to how and by whom, and that even female translators were (and are) not always attuned to linguistic nuances of feminist import.

The second section of this book, "Materials, Japanese Edition"—echoing Women's Preparation Group's aforementioned "American Edition" pamphlet—attempts to offer a representative sample of the text from fliers and short pamphlets produced by various *ribu* groups.[40] The first, in fact, is a Women's Preparation Group flier that introduces their pamphlet of translations. The flier also notes Women's Preparation Group's own plan—never realized—to release a Japanese edition of its pamphlet. This suggests that the title of this section of the book is not a coincidence, but rather a choice that cannot be separated from the information flowing in from the United States.[41] A number of fliers released by "Women's Liberation Network (Preparation Group)" (Josei Kaihō Renraku Kai [Junbi Kai], an organization distinct from the original Women's Preparation Group), Group Fighting Women, and other groups and individuals are also reproduced here. While some refer to the specifics of the situation of women in Japan, including announcements for upcoming meetings and events, much of the content of these pamphlets speaks in very general terms about women's oppression and about the complex relationship between women, imperialism, and capitalism (sometimes overtly linked to Marxist philosophy)—with little direct reference to women in Japan. The discourse on imperialism and capitalism is, of course, strongly connected to Japan's student and anti-war movements, which, in turn, are part of a more global discourse with deep roots in Japan.[42] This reinforces the point that, however grounded in local experience, the discourse on women's liberation in Japan was also from the very beginning impossible to pull apart from global discourses on many topics in addition to women, discourses long circulating in Japan.

The final section of the book directly attempts to offer a more global perspective on women and includes some of the earliest commercially published translations of writing from this new wave of US feminism. This section, "The History and Current State of the American Women's Liberation Movement: Materials, American Edition," contains a lengthy introduction to the US movement as well as two articles on the movement from the US left-wing literary and political magazine *Ramparts* and the mainstream magazine *Time*.[43] It also has a three-page appendix with brief lists of local and national women's liberation groups in the United States and Canada, and American feminist periodicals. This section was written and, in the case of the articles on the United States, translated by Ikegami Chizuko. Ikegami explained to me that she translated those articles, as well as researched and wrote about American feminism, because she wanted to share information that would help stimulate women in Japan.[44] This contrasts somewhat with the goal, discussed above, of simply providing information and correcting mass media accounts, stated by Akiyama and Women's Preparation Group as the purpose of their translation project and introduction of American feminist ideas to women in Japan.

The year 1971 also saw Japan's first commercially published translations of collections of US radical feminist writing. Just three months after *An Accusation of Sex Discrimination* was released, partial translations of two pioneering collections of American feminist writing, *Women's Liberation: Blueprint for the Future* and *Notes from the Second Year,* were published by commercial presses.[45] Both collections were published in Japanese quite soon after their publication in the United States, indexing strong interest in and awareness of the American movement in Japan, and belief on the part of publishers that such materials would sell.[46] While, like *Women's Liberation Movement Materials,* these collections were each translated by groups of women who were somewhat older than typical *ribu* activists, the choices made in these two translation projects, including the framing of the finished products and the degree to which they were transfigured by their translators (and, possibly, editors), represent two very different approaches to translation and two very different ideas about the potential value of information from the US movement. These differences appear to stem at least in part from the translators' degree of connectedness to feminism in Japan and in the United States.

    The Japanese version of *Women's Liberation,* the first collection of this new wave of American feminist writing to be translated into Japanese, was not an engaged translation. The decidedly non-activist academic women who translated the volume into Japanese make no effort to indicate the major changes they made to the framing, structure, and content of the original text and, in drawing no concrete connections between the volume and the lives of women in Japan, fail to offer the sort of "blueprint for the future" that the writers of the original volume proffered. To be sure, the relevance of the book to women in Japan is spelled out in the copy on the outer *obi* (sash) and the dust jacket, as well as the commentary in the back of the book—part of what Keith Harvey calls the "bindings," which contextualize, contribute to, and construct the discourse.[47] Covering the bottom quarter of the dust jacket, the *obi* describes the book as a "groundbreaking anthology" responding to the current "darkness" (for women) and as a successor to *The Second Sex* and Betty Friedan's *The Feminine Mystique*. The copy inside the dust jacket describes the contents of the book as part of the discourse of "the storm of women's lib, which is now blowing in America, Japan, and other countries."[48] However, the original subtitle, which presents the text to readers as a plan—or "blueprint"—for action, becomes a pair of tepid questions: "What are women thinking? What are they seeking?" The other noteworthy change to the book's bindings was the replacement of the name of Sookie Stambler, the compiler of the original volume, with "Kate Millett et al." as authors. In fact, Millett was just one of several dozen contributors, albeit of the longest chapter, excerpted from her magnum opus, *Sexual Politics*.[49] Millett had already been the subject of attention in the mainstream Japanese press for the text, referred to as "Mao's little red book" and the "bible of women's liberation," translated excerpts from which had appeared by that same November in *Fujin kōron*.[50] It is unclear whether such changes were an intervention by the book's editor or its translators.

The six women who translated *Women's Liberation* were established academics in their late thirties to mid-fifties, four of whom were then assistant or full professors at the prestigious and conservative women's school, Tsuda College, while the remaining two were assistant professors elsewhere.[51] All did research on English-language literature, English-speaking countries, or the English language itself, and most had already undertaken or would later undertake translation projects related to their research, not uncommon in Japanese academia. All but one had previously or were to publish research on either women's literature or women's labor issues in Britain or the United States. While none were at the time working in the yet-to-be-established field of women's studies (*joseigaku*), this research demonstrates an ongoing interest in issues related to women, though not necessarily to feminism. A case in point, in 1976, one translator who was a scholar of American literature, Itabashi Yoshie (b. 1931) would later translate Marabel Morgan's *The Total Woman,* a conservative best seller advocating women's subservience to their husbands for the sake of strong marriages.[52] That in the afterword to this translation Itabashi describes Morgan's method to attain marital bliss as "extremely effective in Japan as well" demonstrates either a lack of commitment to the sexual and social autonomy of women advocated by contemporary American radical feminists or a dramatic change of heart in the intervening five years.[53]

The primary translator of *Women's Liberation,* Takano Fumi (1914–2013), was a former Fulbright scholar with an MA from Radcliffe College and by the time of the translation a full professor at Tsuda. Takano wrote the "commentary" (*kaisetsu*) that appeared in the book after the translation, contextualizing the work with a historical overview of the struggle for women's rights in the United States.[54] While Takano makes no attempt to relate the content of the book to Japan, toward the beginning of her commentary, she does offer a parenthetic aside implying that "those who insist that Japan's movement is independent, is not an imitation of America's [movement], and has no connection to it" are mistaken.[55] Regardless of the degree of accuracy of her assessment, this comment makes clear that she is not in accord with *ribu* leaders, who routinely made (and make) the claims she refutes.

Commentaries, commonly included in translated fiction and nonfiction texts, are sometimes brief introductory or explanatory remarks, while other times they are quite long and offer a very detailed explication of or response to a text. In translated works, the translators sometimes include a "translator's afterword" (*yakusha atogaki*) or, less frequently, a "translator's preface" (*yakusha maegaki*) that variously offers background information, interpretation, or an explanation of at least some of the choices made in translation. This may be provided in addition to a commentary by a critic or scholar. That Takano's comments are included *qua* commentary, rather than as a translator's note, positions her not as a translator but as a scholar-cum-critic. Moreover, in her comments, she does not discuss the process of translation or note that the translated version includes a number of significant changes made by Takano and her fellow translators, allowing for the false impression that the translated text is unaltered from the original.

The most substantial of translators' changes were to the text itself rather than to its framing, however. Most noticeably, the translators excised approximately a quarter of the book, including seven articles of various lengths, a one-act play, a short story, and two poems. As four of the six translators were literary scholars, it is ironic that these latter works—the only literary pieces in the original—were removed. This removal also runs counter to the idea of women's creative writing as a vital part of articulating, performing, and circulating feminist ideas—an idea evidenced by *Women's Liberation: The Musical,* discussed in chapter two. A second irony is the translators' choice to reorder the first and second sections in the original volume such that "Women on Men" precedes

"Women on Women," reversing the order of the original and—in contrast with the Japanese stereotype about gender norms in the United States—putting men rather than "ladies first." Moreover, while there is no obvious direct translation for "on" in these section titles, the Japanese they chose—"*Dansei tai josei*" (men *tai* women) and "*Josei tai josei*" (women *tai* women), respectively—replaces "on" with the oppositional word "*tai,*" meaning against, versus, or to. They could have chosen a more neutral alternative such as "*josei ga kataru dansei*" (women speaking [about] men). Their choice of *tai,* by contrast, allows for a reading of conflict that is not present in the original titles and (re)sets the tone for the translated articles. In addition, section four, "Women on Sex and Sex Roles," was completely omitted, eliminating three chapters, one of which was the single chapter on lesbians.[56] Finally, in the section "Women on Liberation," a chapter on Black women's liberation was kept, while a chapter on consciousness-raising groups was eliminated.[57] In spite of the latter's exclusion here, however, the collective discussion practice was soon to be adopted by some women within the Japanese movement in order for women to "develop [a] . . . clear self-identity [and] to lay bare their own 'inner feminine-consciousness.'"[58] Similar to Takano's offhand comment about the influence of the US liberation movement, the translators' choice to omit this chapter further demonstrates that they were not in touch with issues that women in the *ribu* movement found most pressing.

In striking contrast, the Japanese version of *Notes from the Second Year* is a product of engaged translators, and, almost certainly in consequence, this work reverberated in and outside the *ribu* community. These translators called themselves Woolf Society (Urufu no Kai), a name intended to evoke writer Virginia Woolf and the wild and powerful image of a wolf—and later treated as the pronunciation of the acronym for Women's Liberation Front.[59] These women were both directly involved in the *ribu* movement and very overt about the interventions they made in their translation to create a text of immediate relevance to women in Japan, and, ultimately, to help bring about social change. Their purposefully conspicuous presence evokes Barbara Godard's declaration that "the feminist translator immodestly flaunts her signature in italics, in footnotes—even in a preface."[60] Such supplementation via prefaces and footnotes (or parenthetically, as in examples given in the next section), along with "hijacking"—namely, making a text the translator's "own to reflect her political intentions"—are, as Luise von Flotow observes, hallmarks of "feminist translation."[61]

Though they credit Shulamith Firestone and Anne Koedt as the editors of the volume and themselves as merely the translators, Woolf Society openly made substantial changes to the text, translating, in full or in part, only sixteen of the original thirty-four chapters that felt most meaningful, reorganizing them, and then framing them with their own words. Woolf Society members gave the collection an entirely new title, *From Woman to Women: A Report from the American Women's Liberation Movement* (*Onna kara onnatachi e: Amerika josei kaihō undō repōto*), positioning the text as a message from American women's liberation activists to women in Japan as well as suggesting the collective nature of women's activism.[62] And rather than burying their thoughts about the text in an afterword, the translators included both a translators' foreword in the front of the book and in the back an extended roundtable in which the text and the movement are discussed by the translators, who relate this to their own experiences in Japan.[63]

Akiyama, formerly involved in Women's Preparation Group, which dissolved around the end of 1970, played a key role in the translation activities of Woolf Society, a group of nine women who came together as a reading group under circumstances and with a composition similar to that of Women's Preparation Group.[64] As before, it was Akiyama who got her hands on a copy of the just-published *Notes from the Second Year,* which she shared with the reading group. As Akiyama later recalled, these "brave, bold" self-proclaimed radical feminists writing about sex, housework, and self-awareness had "put words to [feelings] that had been smoldering in our hearts, that now finally made sense," and the group set about to translate it, as they explained in their foreword, "because we wanted as many women as possible to read it."[65] Similarly, journalist Matsui Yayori, one of Woolf Society's founders, later wrote that the group gathered materials about the US movement to get an unmediated look at those women's struggles, and then translated them to share what they learned with other women in Japan.[66]

The chapters they chose to translate include Jo Freeman's "Bitch Manifesto," Koedt's "Myth of the Vaginal Orgasm" (first published in *Fujin kōron*), Ti-Grace Atkinson's "Institution of Sexual Intercourse," and the "Redstockings Manifesto," along with writing by Firestone and Millett.[67] Topics covered include abortion, consciousness raising, capitalism and the oppression of women, and feminism and social revolution.[68] They arranged the essays into three sections, "Women's Experience," "Love and Sex," and "Women's Struggles," each of which they prefaced with a brief commentary on the essays contained therein and information about the authors. They opted not to translate chapters overlapping significantly with the ones that were selected, and chapters on specific organizations, as well as chapters on drug addiction, classism within the women's movement, and feminist theater. In their foreword, the translators indicate that they cut around one-third of the total text, and concentrated on translating the longer, richer essays.[69] While the foreword gives no further indication of why they chose the articles they did, in the roundtable in the back, the translators discuss their reaction to various essays, making it clear that they translated those that most strongly resonated with them and helped them reevaluate their own experiences pertaining to themes commonly discussed in feminist writing, including marriage, housework, sex, childbirth and child-rearing, and work and discrimination.

Reflecting on the roundtable, Akiyama later recalled that, "We felt that by talking about how we all came to this book, we could play a role in connecting the American writers and Japanese readers."[70] In the foreword, however, Woolf Society members express ambivalence about the project as a whole. While they strongly wished for other women to read this text, they wondered whether it would be better to spend their time writing something themselves or engaging in more direct activism. But they wanted it translated and knew they could not leave the job to a professional male translator: even though he would be able do the job much more quickly, they did not believe a man—not torn as they were between work and home—would be able to translate it accurately.[71] (They imply by omission that finding a professional female translator to do the work was not an option.) The translators felt further encouraged to do it themselves by Koedt's positive reply to their request for permission to translate the text, including her declaration that the text was written by women and should be translated by women.[72]

The responses the translators received from the translation's readers were also overwhelmingly positive and encouraging, reassuring the translators that their decision to undertake the project was a good one. The transfigured text was clearly as inspirational to the readers of the upwards of five thousand copies published as the original had been to its translators.[73] While the book received nearly no publicity, readers around the country found copies of the book, and sent Woolf Society dozens of passionate letters, desperately seeking information about the *ribu* movement and solidarity with other women.[74] A third of these they compiled in a booklet, *Letters to From Woman to Women*, to send around to those who had written to them and to connect women around the country with each other.[75]

Woolf Society's translation spoke to readers in various ways. One female student from Tokyo wrote, "I just finished reading 'The Bitch Manifesto' and I'm so excited my hands are still trembling. I feel like saying 'The Bitch Manifesto' is truly 'My Human Manifesto.' . . . [It] made some things very clear for me. . . . 'Activism' like in 'The Bitch Manifesto' isn't possible for me right now, but I hope to carry on with an awareness of what's inside me."[76] A woman from Kyoto wrote that the volume helped her think deeply about the meaning of "woman" (*onna*), as well as the status of minorities in Japan, while another woman from Tokyo read the roundtable at the back and realized that the "woman problem" is not just an "intellectual woman problem."[77] And a thirty-two-year-old housewife from Nagoya was overjoyed to learn that what she had always believed about sex was true.[78] Women critical of the volume also wrote to the group, including one who was "completely disappointed" that the members of the roundtable "just expressed admiration for and agreement with American lib activists' opinions, and not a word of criticism or opposition."[79] They also received multiple letters similar to one from a university student living near Tokyo, who had assembled a small group whose members had begun to "raise their [as yet] naïve voices." She wrote that, more than anything, what they need is information, and she asked Woolf Society to contact her if the group puts out their own publication.[80]

This the group very quickly decided to do, and in the spring of 1972, they produced the first of what would become three issues of *From Woman to Women* published over the following two years. This new *mini-komi* covered some of the same issues as *Notes from the Second Year* but was written from the perspective of women in Japan and concentrated on their concerns. Included as a supplement to the first issue was the aforementioned booklet of letters, furthering the dialogue between readers and translators, as well as readers and other readers over the meaning of the text.[81] The ripples from the translated text extended further still, inspiring, for instance, the creation of a long-running *ribu mini-komi* out of Osaka also titled *From Woman to Women* (1972–1988). While among the earliest, this particular translation was not, however, unique in furthering dialogue on issues such as women's bodies, sexuality, and reproductive health in the early 1970s, as we shall see.

From Translation to Transfiguration and Back:
Our Bodies, Ourselves

Our Bodies, Ourselves was made to be translated. When the small group of women in Boston who put together the open-ended "course" that became *Our Bodies, Ourselves* were negotiating with the publishing giant Simon and Schuster to produce the first commercial edition of the book, they fought for and won a contract clause calling for it to be released simultaneously in Spanish for distribution in the United States.[82] While the Spanish version was ultimately delayed several years, through a combination of coincidence and fortuitous personal ties, three women in Japan came to produce one of the very first translations of this landmark in the transnational movement for women's health.[83] *Our Bodies, Ourselves* resonated as well with major concerns of *ribu* activists on account of its emphasis on female sexuality and reproduction, including chapters on sexual anatomy, sexuality, rape, venereal disease, birth control, abortion, and childbirth. And the conditions that prompted its compilation by the Boston Women's Health Book Collective were also true for women in Japan: women's frustration incited by their need to entrust medical issues—particularly those surrounding sexual and reproductive health—to predominantly male, "paternal, judgmental and non-informative doctors" because of a lack of knowledge about their own bodies.[84] In fact, at the suggestion of a couple of Americans then in Japan to protest the Vietnam War, Woolf Society had already published in fall 1972 an issue of *From Woman to Women* focused on women and sex(uality) (*sei*), divided into sections on abortion and birth control, pregnancy, and infertility, as well as sex(uality) and the female body[85]—many of the issues addressed in more depth by the women in Boston. That these issues were of interest to a broad spectrum of women in Japan is evidenced by the fact that, in addition to circulating through informal *ribu* networks, part of this issue was reprinted in *Fujin kōron* in spring 1973.[86]

This translation came about because Yamada Mitsuko (b. 1945), who was to become one of the three translators of the volume into Japanese, received a copy of an early version of *Our Bodies, Ourselves* from an American friend around 1972 and found it "just wonderful." It was around that time that she also got a copy of the "sex(uality) for women" issue of *From Woman to Women*, which is how she learned about Woolf Society and decided to post a letter to them, enclosing with it *Our Bodies, Ourselves*. Yamada explained that she had been asked to translate the book by an American woman living on the rural island of Shikoku and had been looking for co-translators for a while. When Akiyama received the letter and the book, which did a much more thorough job addressing women's sexual and reproductive health than Woolf Society had thus far managed to do, she knew she wanted to help introduce this book to women in Japan. At the time, Yamada had just moved to the Shikoku city of Matsuyama, which is where, by chance, she met Kuwahara Kazuyo (b. 1942), an English teacher previously unconnected to *ribu,* who became the third translator.[87]

The first Simon and Schuster version, published in 1973, reached the three women as they were planning the translation. The greatly expanded volume included new chapters on nutrition, exercise, lesbians, aging, and medicine and society. Although Akiyama, Kuwahara, and Yamada wanted to translate the whole volume, they realized they needed to abridge it for it to be cheap enough for ordinary women to afford. So, working off the structure of the older version, they chose to concentrate on the "topics of greatest urgency" to women in Japan: the female body, birth control, pregnancy, and childbirth. They were also committed to supplementing their translation with information specific to Japan.[88] In 1974, ten months after an excerpt on the birth control pill was published in *Fujin kōron,* the Japanese translation of *Our Bodies, Ourselves* made its way to bookstores.[89] A "best seller" among *ribu* books, it sold well enough that it was reprinted several times.[90] Theirs was also one of the first two foreign-language editions to be published, with an Italian rendition published that same year. In the decade that followed the publication of the initial Simon and Schuster edition, twelve country-specific authorized and unauthorized versions were released in various languages—including Japanese, just two of these were produced in Asia.[91] With Japan among the very first, clearly *ribu* activists were very much a part of the transnational feminist loop.

The Japanese version names both the Boston Women's Health Book Collective and the three Japanese translators on the cover of the book, which was retitled *Women's Bodies: The Truth about Sex(uality) and Love* (*Onna no karada: Sei to ai no shinjitsu*). The translators chose this title to more clearly convey the contents of the book than would a direct translation of the original English title.[92] *Women's Bodies* opens with a letter from members of the Boston group expressing great pleasure that the book is being published in Japanese and the hope that it will be useful. They also emphasize that the book, which they say could only have come to fruition as a collective project, is just a "beginning" step toward the improvement of women's understanding of their own bodies and lives.[93] The very engaged translators make their presence visible throughout the remainder of the volume, from the "Foreword to the Japanese Edition," which follows the collective's letter, to the brief annotations and supplementary information inserted throughout in dark brackets, to the two distinct afterwords they include at the back.[94] Sandwiched between the new content produced by the Japanese translators, the translated content includes the original preface, titled "Our Changing Selves," and nine core chapters: "Anatomy and Physiology," "On Sexuality," "Birth Control," "Abortion," "Pregnancy," "Childbirth," "Postpartum," "Venereal Disease," and "Illness and Sanitation." This breakdown, the editors explain, uses the skeleton of the older version and the meat of the new.[95]

In their foreword, the translators explain the background of and impetus for the original version. And, echoing the letter from the Boston women's group that opens the book, the translators situate *Women's Bodies* as a collective project.⁹⁶ While they are clearly trying to help individual women across Japan, their emphasis on the collective nature of the book's production resonates with the spirit of *ribu;* and, to the translators, *Women's Bodies* "symbolizes" what the women involved on both sides of the Pacific hope is "a new expansion and intensification of the movement."⁹⁷ In the remainder of the foreword, the translators turn to Japan, where circumstances are "completely the same" as those that had driven women in the United States to develop the book: in Japan, as in the United States, the medical system has deprived women of both their feelings about and accurate information on their own bodies. Yet, as the Boston group says, "knowledge is power," and through this project the translators hope to empower women in Japan. Finally, they give a nuts-and-bolts explanation of how, among other things, they indicate their own additions of Japan-specific information in the volume.⁹⁸ Following up on this—and contradicting their statement that the United States and Japan are the same—the first afterword explains that, while there are many points in common between the medical systems in Japan and the United States, there are also many differences. It urges women to take steps, such as paying attention to their own bodies and asking questions of doctors, to avail themselves of the best medical treatment they can.⁹⁹

In their "Translators' Afterword," Akiyama, Kuwahara, and Yamada describe their own encounter with this book as taking place "in the middle of the expansive flows of the women's liberation movement which links the United States and Japan." This is exemplified by their description of the translation's history, including the circumstances whereby Yamada came to be asked to translate the earlier version and found the other two translators, as well as the international group of women and men who helped with the project.¹⁰⁰ The translators then declare the book to be a "Japanese language version" (*Nihongo ban*) rather than a "translation" (*hon'yaku ban*).¹⁰¹ This is on account of the restructuring of the book they carried out—in consultation with their editor, the American authors, and others—in order, as noted above, to make it available to as many women as possible by keeping the cost down. This, they believe, is in accord with the intention of the original authors.¹⁰²

Although the translators retain from the Simon and Schuster version a few pages in the sexuality chapter on homosexuality (*dōseiai*), they omitted the groundbreaking chapter, "In Amerika They Call Us Dykes."¹⁰³ "Far and away the most controversial chapter," Kathy Davis writes, the lesbian chapter "became a landmark publication on sexuality and relationships between women, providing encouragement to countless women to 'come out' as women loving women."¹⁰⁴ By way of a justification for its "unfortunate" omission, the translators explain that this chapter was written by a lesbian group not otherwise connected to the Boston Women's Health Collective. They direct readers "who are interested" to the translation of that chapter already published in the commercial *ribu* magazine *Onna erosu*.[105] Although she had no connection to any lesbian groups in Japan at the time, Akiyama recalled to me feeling concerned about cutting the chapter but satisfied that it was introduced to a lesbian group to translate.[106]

The "lesbian group" was, in fact, the singular Amano Michimi. Amano had become involved in Tanaka Mitsu's Group Fighting Women and the activities of Ribu Shinjuku Center while acting as a go-between for several individuals wanting to translate Tanaka's influential *For Women with Spirit* into English.[107] Though Tanaka unceremoniously booted her out six months later, Amano had maintained ties with other *ribu* activists. Amano joined the team producing *Onna erosu* at the invitation of Funamoto Emi, one of the founding editors. Funamoto also specifically requested that Amano translate the lesbian chapter, which Funamoto thought would be a shame not to make available in Japanese. Amano agreed, she told me, because she thought doing it would be a good chance to work on her English and might lead to something else.[108] Amano's translation, published in two parts, in the April and September 1974 issues, was most likely the first commercially published translation by a self-identified *rezubian* of lesbian-authored writing into Japanese. Kagura Jamu, who was strongly attracted to women but had no one with whom she could discuss it, recalled years later what a shock it was to read that article in a copy of the journal at her neighbor's: "One look at the word 'lesbian' gave me a start, and I slammed the magazine shut." Kagura would later become a founding member of the *rezubian* group Regumi no Gomame.[109]

While issues of specific concern to women romantically and sexually attracted to other women were, in the end, largely absent from *Women's Bodies,* the core of *Our Bodies, Ourselves* resonated with many issues of great concern to women in the *ribu* movement, as noted above. Building on this immediate relevance, within the *ribu* movement the transfigured text became a springboard for further discussions about women "stealing back their bodies" from gynecologists and obstetricians.[110] In a roundtable discussion printed in *Onna erosu* in March 1975, co-translator Yamada and three others talk about the lessons the book has for women in Japan. One of the three, *Onna erosu* editor Saeki Yōko (b. 1940), opens the roundtable by commenting that, while such a book "will be written by women's hands for women in Japan as well," for now, using *Women's Bodies* as a stepping-off point, she would like to talk about the topic of "me and woman's bodies."[111] The discussions took off from there, in the form of study groups and teach-ins at, for instance, Ribu Shinjuku Center and the women's space Hōkiboshi (Comet). At Ribu Shinjuku Center, the first of a series of "women's bodies" teach-ins was held in the fall of 1976; these would continue at other locations from 1977 through 1982. Using a slide show produced by one of the Feminist Women's Health Centers in the United States and methods used there to better acquaint women with their own bodies, participants were encouraged to talk and learn about their own bodies, sexuality, and reproductive health. For instance, women at the teach-ins were invited to use speculums to view their cervixes and taught how to do breast self-examinations.[112]

In 1977, Wakabayashi Naeko, who had worked at the Feminist Women's Health Center in Oakland, California, during a year spent in North America, published an article on the teach-ins in *Onna erosu*. The subtitle, "Toward the Establishment of a Clinic for Women," clearly indicates the direction toward which at least some of the women involved in the teach-ins were aiming.[113] When, almost a decade later, the Woman's Health Center (Ūmanzu Herusu Sentā) opened in Osaka, one of its founders described the need for women to learn more about their own bodies and, thereby, take control of their own reproductive health[114]—the same language used in *Women's Bodies*. While it would be overly simplistic to situate such clinics in a direct line of descent from *Our Bodies, Ourselves* or as a mere imitation of the women's health centers in the United States with which women in Japan such as Wakabayashi had connections, we cannot deny that these ties, as well as these translations and other transfigurations are a significant part of the context in which they emerged.

Beyond the *ribu* movement, *Women's Bodies* soon reached more readers in its transfiguration into two volumes of the popular Bessatsu Takarajima series (1976–), *Women's Dictionary* (*Onna no jiten*) and *Women's Bodies* (*Onna no karada*) in 1977 and 1978, respectively. These two books sold well enough to remain in print for at least another decade.[115] On the cover of both is the subtitle, written in English, "The New Women's Survival Guide Book." The cover of the former is illustrated with a color drawing of a woman's breasts. The latter features a color drawing of three women wearing only panties; all three, whose nationality is unclear, have rather large thighs and the one facing forward has large breasts (figure 4.1). The image, which resembles art circulating in the United States liberation movement, evokes a feminist retreat, perhaps one of the retreats associated with *ribu* or with a radical feminist group in the US or elsewhere. The volumes serve as broader, more locally focused lifestyle guides than Woolf Society's translation, but openly draw on *Our Bodies, Ourselves/Women's Bodies*. The opening section

Figure 4.1. Cover of Bessatsu Takarajima, no. 9, *Women's Bodies* (*Onna no karada*, 1978).

of *Women's Dictionary* specifically concentrates on women's bodies and is given a title that is a literal translation of "our bodies, ourselves" (*watashi-tachi no karada, watashitachi jishin*), words also included in English on the cover, the table of contents, and the first page of the section. That section also contains illustrations by Nina Reimer found in both the original *Our Bodies, Ourselves* and its Japanese translation, as well as a brief section on "homosexuality"—this time penned, rather than translated, by Amano.[116]

While Amano writes somewhat equivocally about this volume in *Onna erosu,* these new transfigurations as well as the 1974 version served as references for and are recommended in a handwritten, mimeographed guide to birth control methods first produced in 1983 by Students to Prevent the Worsening of the Eugenics Protection Law (Yūsei Hogo Hō Kaiaku o Soshi Suru Gakusei no Kai), newly established as part of a larger response to new proposed revisions to the law.[117] The pamphlet, which immediately sold out of its initial print run of two hundred, was given a title that can be read as *Women's Bodies* or *My Body.*[118] The group writes the pronunciation of the word "I" (*watashi*) in superscript over the character for "woman"/"women" (*onna*) to link the reader herself to women's bodies, thereby echoing the titles of both the translated and English versions.

A year later the Boston Women's Health Collective released *The New Our Bodies, Ourselves,* the first major revision of the book in a decade.[119] The project to translate this version into Japanese began with a suggestion by prominent feminist scholar Ueno Chizuko (b. 1948) in 1986, which along with the timing, positions it as a post-*ribu* feminist project.[120] And yet, the project involved women who had been active in the *ribu* movement and was supervised by activist, translator, and women's and gender studies scholar Fujieda Mioko (1930–2011), who had assisted with the 1974 translation of *Our Bodies, Ourselves* during the same period she was translating Millett's *Sexual Politics.*[121] This clearly positions the new translation in the same complex trajectory as earlier *ribu* discourse on women's health in which the first translation played such a vital role.

While the translators of the 1974 version made significant abridgements of the American text to keep the cost affordable, the Boston Women's Health Book Collective encouraged the translators of *The New Our Bodies, Ourselves* to translate the whole volume, and, preferably, to publish it at the hands of women.[122] A decade earlier, finding a woman-run publisher would have been a tall order—even the Boston Women's Health Book Collective has published subsequent editions of *Our Bodies, Ourselves* through an imprint of Simon and Schuster—but for the new Japanese translation this call was answered by Nakanishi Toyoko (b. 1933). In 1982, Nakanishi founded the Kyoto-based Shōkadō, Japan's first women's bookstore, which became the publisher of the new translation. And, unlike the first translation, which was presented as the work of three women with the assistance of others, some fifty women are credited as translators or editors of the new volume, making it more overtly the kind of collective project these women were trying to render into Japanese. Like the book upon which it was based, the translation included a page full of photos of these women, personalizing the translators and editors in the same way as the original had done for its contributors.[123]

This time, they followed the wishes of the Boston collective and attempted to faithfully translate nearly the entire volume.[124] One unfortunate result of this was the price tag of 5,000 yen (then around US$38), which made the oversized 600-page book less affordable than the earlier edition had been. While the translators aimed for a more literal translation of this book, to which they assigned the more literally translated title *Bodies, Ourselves* (*Karada, watashitachi jishin*), it was nonetheless a very engaged and feminist translation. Like its predecessor over a decade earlier, the translators and editors assert their presence throughout, beginning with a three-part foreword penned by the three women in charge of translation and editing.[125] While they continued to use anatomical illustrations from the original book, according to the editors most photographs were replaced with photos taken in Japan, to make it easier for readers to relate— although this might have been a positive spin on an editorial problem.[126] Like the 1974 translation, the translators and editors inserted up-to-date local information in dark brackets throughout. They also added longer sidebars with local information and, in several cases, lengthier sections, including a two-page section on lesbians in Japan added to the lesbian chapter.[127] Finally, at the end they added thirty pages on obtaining gynecologic and obstetric care around the country, including details on fees, available services, and the kinds of information that can be provided to whom at various clinics.[128] Such a list both provides readers with invaluable information and spells out what is important when making choices about reproductive and sexual health care.

When the Japanese translation of *The New Our Bodies, Ourselves* was published in 1988, as significant an undertaking as it was, the awkwardly oversized volume probably did not have the impact the translation from fourteen years prior had had on elevating awareness on women's health issues. First, the earlier translation played a key role in the formative years of the women's health movement in Japan, while by 1988, even if many doctors remained largely unwilling to cede control of women's bodies and health to women themselves, information was by far more readily available in numerous other books, at women's centers, and through various women's organizations around the country. Moreover, the new translation was priced out of range of women with a limited budget.

One very significant intervention this new translation made was on the Japanese language itself. The Sino-Japanese terms long used to refer to most sexual organs contain the character *in*, meaning private or shadow, or *chi*, the character for shame—thus associating the parts of women's bodies linked to sex and reproduction with darkness and shamefulness. The translators replaced these characters with the more neutral *sei*, meaning sex or sexuality, introducing new words to talk about parts of the body such as the vulva, the labia, and pubic hair. They also replaced "*seiri*," the then standard word to describe menstruation, the primary meaning of which is physiology, with "*gekkei*," a new term meaning "monthly occurrence." In so doing, the translators hoped to displace the shame and euphemism that might make it difficult for women to speak openly about their bodies. Finally, the translators replaced "*kangofu*," the then standard term for nurse, a term meaning "a woman who takes care of," with "*kangoshi*," a somewhat more unisex term for "a person who takes care of."[129] While the older terms do remain in use today, many of the terms the translators introduced in this translation have become standard, and thus the translation has helped shape the language used to think and speak about women's bodies decades after they penned their translation.

Giving Voice to *Rezubian,* Transfiguring *The Hite Report*

Three years after *Our Bodies, Ourselves* was first published commercially in the United States, extending the women's health movement to the mainstream, Shere Hite's trailblazing *The Hite Report* (1976) revealed the results of a survey of over three thousand women across the United States on their sexual feelings, experiences, and opinions on topics including masturbation, intercourse, clitoral stimulation, lesbianism, women's subservient role in (heterosexual) sex, the "sexual revolution," older women's sexuality, and the changing nature of sex itself.[130] What made this book meaningful to women in the United States was arguably not the statistics Hite tabulated but respondents' often very intimate, sometimes quite moving responses to Hite's questions, responses that proved women could indeed talk about their sexual desires and experiences without shame. Ranging from brief comments to lengthy paragraphs and collectively occupying the bulk of the book, these real and diverse women's voices demonstrated to the women reading the book both that they were not alone in their experiences and that there were other sexual possibilities open to them.

An ostensibly complete Japanese translation was published the following year by Ishikawa Hiroyoshi (1933–2009), a male sociologist who had already published and translated prolifically on diverse topics that included sexuality but nothing specifically focused on women and nothing written from a feminist perspective.[131] While analyzing Ishikawa's ability to translate intimate details of women's sexual lives is beyond the scope of my discussion here, I only encountered one article in Japan critiquing having a man translate the text, this in an article in *rezubian feminisuto* group Shining Wheel's *mini-komi* discussing the issue of translations by men in the other ten countries that had, to date, seen translations of the book. The article makes no comments on Ishikawa's translation itself.[132] Perhaps this general lack of attention to Ishikawa's role as a translator simply reflects the acceptance by women readers—or by that particular critic—of the ubiquity of male translators in Japan. As we saw above, however, such acceptance of male translators by feminists was by no means universal. And it merits noting that at the end of his translator's preface in the first volume, Ishikawa thanks three women and one man whose assistance he solicited "because women's sexual behavior and sexual sensations (*sei kankaku*) are the main theme" of the book, implying not so subtly that, as a man, he needed women's input.[133] In the commentary at the end of the second volume, however, he asserts his scholarly expertise.[134] Ishikawa furthers his positioning himself as an expert by introducing *The Hite Report* to readers of the trendy new women's magazine *Croissant* (*Kurowassan*, 1977–), in the first of a series of articles he wrote on female sexuality, timed to appear the same month as the first volume of his translation came out.[135]

This translation gave rise to significant public interest and similar local projects. For instance, *The Hite Report* was the direct inspiration for *More* magazine (*Moa*, 1977–) to run a survey of its readers on "women's lives and sex" in 1980.[136] Their responses were released as the *More Report* in a thick hardcover volume in 1983—adorned with "The MORE Report on Female Sexuality" in English on the cover—and then an abridged paperback two years later.[137] Linking this volume directly to Hite, in the preface to the initial release, the editors note that, while there are reports by Kinsey and Masters and Johnson, as well as, more recently, Hite's reports on female and male sexuality in the United States, there is nothing like this about women in contemporary Japan.[138]

Also in 1983, Linda Wolfe's *Cosmo Report,* itself following in the footsteps of Hite's work, was translated into Japanese. This volume was, like Hite's work, translated by a man.[139] Following Hite's 1981 report on male sexuality—translated into Japanese, ironically perhaps, by a woman in 1982—*More* released its own report on male sexuality in 1984.[140] And thus, through a new series of translations and transfigurations of *The Hite Report* beginning in the late 1970s—alongside multiple translations and transfigurations of *Our Bodies, Ourselves*—Japan saw an increase in frank public discussion of female sexuality, wherein women were able to share anxieties as well as desires and to find a measure of affirmation and comfort. This was very much in tune with what had been taking place within and advocated by the *ribu* community since the beginning of the 1970s.

Unsurprisingly then, *The Hite Report* in translation was also well received in the *ribu* community itself. The spring 1978 issue of the Osaka-based *mini-komi From Woman to Women,* for example, devoted over three full pages to responses from activists. The first of these begins, "This is an excellent book. In the six months since I first started living with my new lover, I've been worried and confused about sex, but I feel like at last [through this book] I've encountered opinions that give me strength."[141] Later in her response the activist notes that reading this book was the first time for her to encounter the voices of lesbians in any detail. Miki Sōko observes that the androcentric equation of sex with (hetero)sexual intercourse for the sake of reproduction and giving men pleasure is called into question by Hite's chapter-length attention to both masturbation and lesbianism.[142]

I believe it is this prominent attention to the voices and experiences of lesbians that gave this book special meaning to some women in the *rezubian* community and, ultimately, led to its transfiguration into the project that would become *Stories of Women Who Love Women*[143] (figure 4.2). Widely considered the first commercial publication produced by and for members of the *rezubian* community, *Stories* is an example of a transfiguration that seems quite distant in time and form and yet still bears obvious traces of its roots. Published in 1987 as part of the Bessatsu Takarajima series, the project that became *Stories* began as a pair of surveys conducted in late 1986 that drew on the Japanese translation of *The Hite Report* and other of its transfigurations.[144] The *More Report* surveys also contained questions about homosexuality among women in Japan specifically, which suggests it might have served as a local model for the *Stories* surveys.[145] However, the length and organization of the *More Report* makes it very difficult to find references to homosexual experience and identity. *The Hite Report,* by contrast, has a chapter focused on "Lesbianism," rendered "*Rezubian*" in Japanese. This chapter ends, moreover, with a section under a heading that declares "Lesbianism can have political significance," a sentiment that resonated with the ideology of *rezubian feminisuto,* some of whom were to create *Stories.* Consequently, the translation elaborating on American women's lives seems to have been more meaningful than the locally produced

Figure 4.2. Cover of Bessatsu Takarajima, no. 64, *Stories of Women Who Love Women* (*Onna o ai suru onnatachi no monogatari*, 1987).

text for women in Japan wishing to read about other women's experiences to make sense of their own same-sex desire. And thus, while the *More Report* may have played a larger role in women's discourse on their own sexuality in Japan, *The Hite Report* was a more immediate model for the surveys compiled into a section of *Stories* called "*Rezubian* Report."

Sawabe Hitomi, the architect of and driving force behind *Stories*, situates its genesis at the nexus of events in her own life, including reading lesbian feminist Marilyn Frye's *The Politics of Reality* with a small group of women considering translating it into Japanese, attending the eighth International Lesbian Information Service Conference in Geneva in March 1986, and receiving around a hundred letters in response to an article about the conference she published under a pseudonym in *Fujin kōron*.[146] Reflecting back two decades later, Sawabe explains that her desire to become a reportage writer combined with the letters in particular—overwhelmingly earnest in their various expression of loneliness and regret, as well as encouragement and excitement—motivated her to produce a book.[147] Thus, while thinking and talking about American lesbian feminist theory with other Japanese *rezubian feminisuto* and her attendance at the Geneva lesbian conference, including interacting with other Asian lesbians, formed a significant part of the context, the most powerful impetus seems to have been Sawabe's visceral reaction to the personal accounts of the experiences of women in Japan.

In a 2009 oral history, Sawabe makes no mention of *The Hite Report* when she narrates the history of *Stories*.[148] There are, however, several reasons I position it in a fuzzy line of descent from Hite's initial study and its earlier transfigurations. The most initially salient of these is in its naming. The title of the section of the book containing the survey responses, "*Rezubian* Report: A First for Japan! The Testimony of 234 *Rezubian*" (*Rezubian ripōto: Nihon de hajimete! 234 nin no rezubian ni yoru shōgen*), almost certainly draws directly from the titles and subtitles of both the Hite and *More* volumes. In Japanese, *The Hite Report* is assigned the subtitle "Testimony of new women on love and sex(uality)" (*Atarashī josei no ai to sei no shōgen*), while the first *More Report* is given the lengthier "For the first time, Japanese women talked about sex(uality) in their own words" (*Nihon no joseitachi ga, hajimete jibuntachi no kotoba de sei o katatta*). To be sure, this titling—paraphrased slightly and placed in eye-catching type on the cover of *Stories* for promotional purposes—could be an editorial intervention from the publisher to tap ongoing public interest in such surveys.

Yet, it is clear that Sawabe had *The Hite Report* in mind when working on the survey. To begin, *Shining Wheel,* which, as noted above, discussed the translation in its pages, was produced by a *rezubian feminisuto* group Sawabe herself founded, so it is obvious that Hite's text had her attention soon after its publication in Japan. More tellingly, when she sent out the questionnaires for the "*Rezubian* Report," Sawabe enclosed copies from the translated *The Hite Report* for use as a reference, illustrating the kind of responses she had in mind.[149] Finally, while each of the three "reports" frames the responses differently via categorization into chapters, they all rely on the same kinds of testimony about personal experiences and feelings. The testimony in "*Rezubian* Report" of a twenty-five-year-old office worker specifically links the *Hite Report* and *Stories*:

> [W]hen I first read *The Hite Report* I was moved in a way I couldn't put into words. . . . If this kind of book were published in Japan, it would be

a big step for Japan's *rezubian*. Until now, the only way to get at the heart of "lesbianism," politically, culturally, socially, has been through information from abroad. . . . Hearing about [lesbians] abroad was very moving, but to hear directly from Japan's countless *rezubian,* for all women who are in that situation, in the shadows, it would provide them support.[150]

Although looking back more than twenty years later, Sawabe did not indicate *The Hite Report* was part of the inspiration for *Stories,* I would argue that the circumstances surrounding its production—and its reception—position *Stories* as a greatly transfigured version of *The Hite Report.*

Hite conducted the nationwide survey that became *The Hite Report* to find out how "[American] *women* themselves . . . feel, what they like, and what they think of sex," so that—through this sharing—women would be able to "see our personal lives more clearly, thus redefining our sexuality and strengthening our identities as women." A secondary goal was "to stimulate a public discussion and reevaluation of sexuality."[151] As we have just seen, Hite's study provided inspiration and context, along with a productive model for Sawabe and the women who worked with her, yet they transfigured her approach—reshaping her model to make it meaningful to the lives of *rezubian* in Japan.

In her preface to the results of the *rezubian* survey, Sawabe explains that she created the survey to, first, "convey, as it is, the existence of *rezubian* living in Japan . . . [because] we ourselves need to know the truth . . . about our current situation. It's true that in America and in the countries of Europe, the lesbian feminism born out of the feminist movement has developed a great deal of power. We have a lot to learn to learn from those lesbians, but I would like to begin with an understanding of our own current situation."[152] Sawabe's second goal was to represent *rezubian* in all their diversity, which bears out in the great variety of individual and collective experiences represented in the book, both in the *rezubian* report itself and in the remainder of the volume. Sawabe carefully explains the procedures by which the surveys were distributed and tallied, lending an air of scientific validity to the project akin to Hite's. Yet, in the preface to the report Sawabe rejects the idea that this was a formal *rezubian* study, "academic research," or any other sort of "objective 'research' [or] 'survey.' " It was far more personal. This survey was created, "to shed light on our real selves, and to reconsider and come to a new understanding of the lives of [those of us who] have continued to love women in the midst of the extreme pressure of [this] heterosexual society, which only permits love between men and women."[153]

Another goal that seems to underlie the project—which later surveys and personal narratives would show was realized—was to create a book that affirms the presence of a community of *"rezubian"* in Japan, a community with a real history and a bright (*akarui*) future.[154] While *mini-komi* and other community-produced materials arguably had already been serving the same function since the mid-1970s, they reached an extremely limited number of women. The fact that *Stories* was a widely available commercial publication rendered it a public declaration of its creators' and the community's existence, well before the use of the term "pride" (*puraido*) in Japanese queer contexts— a declaration capable of reaching out to women with same-sex desire who may or may not identify as *rezubian* and who might otherwise be unaware of the *rezubian* community.

The results contained in this section come from two surveys distributed to individuals recruited via *rezubian* bars and groups, as well as the reader correspondence columns in magazines and word of mouth in October and December 1986. The former elicited 202 responses and the latter 122, of whom 90 had responded to the first survey.[155] Thus the responses represent the experiences of 234 individuals. The survey asked women about their realization they were attracted to women and how they first met other *rezubian,* their marital history, their work and educational history, their love and sexual experiences, and their experiences within "heterosexual society" including their own families and friends.[156] The second survey was much shorter and designed to be more "fun," with questions on, for example, the sex appeal of the respondents' favorite singers or actresses, their opinion about butch (*tachi, bucchi*)/femme (*neko, femu*) roles, and whether—since it is said that *rezubian* are less likely than *gei* (gays) to cheat on their partners—if they themselves have ever cheated.[157] Similar to the Hite and *More* reports, most of the respondents' statements are given out of context, protecting respondents' privacy but making it impossible get a clear picture of individuals. The complete responses to five individuals who consented to be profiled are in the final section of the report, under the English heading "A Lesbian Was Here."[158]

While the surveys that became the *"Rezubian* Report" marked the beginning of the *Stories* project, they comprise only the second half of the book. The first half contains over a dozen articles about what the editors have described as "living as lesbians," divided into five sections on women in Japan—"lesbian lives," "lesbian experiences," "lesbian beliefs," "lesbian sex," and "lesbian groups and spaces"—followed by one on women overseas, "lesbians abroad." And thus, in spite of its roots in a survey on the sexuality of women in the United States, *Stories* positions the lives of local lesbians as foremost in importance.

This is of particular significance given the fact that in the 1980s most commercially available publications depicting lesbian lives in anything other than a salacious or scandalous manner were translations or gave little attention to women in Japan[159]—as well as the fact that, as will be detailed in chapter five, many of the most prominent lesbian activists of the 1970s and 1980s had formative experiences abroad.

While I have described *Stories of Women Who Love Women* as a radically "transfigured" version of *The Hite Report,* I do not mean to imply that it is an imitation of the original. Indeed, it is quite a different kind of book produced for very different reasons. Rather, as we have seen in this section, I use the idea of "transfiguration" to draw attention here to the how, the why, and the who when "things"—ideas, signs, and texts—change as they cross cultural borders. Acts of transfiguration can have real-world effects, effects that are experienced on personal and collective levels. This and the preceding section have focused on translations and other transfigurations of activist writing, writing that overtly aims to change hearts, minds, and societies. In the following section I turn to literature, which can also have personal and cultural effects, but rather than focus on translation from a foreign language, such as English or German or Russian, I start with texts that are already translated, and follow the ripples from there.

Literary Transfiguration as a Liberatory Strategy: The Creation of *Shōnen'ai*

As I noted at the outset of this chapter, translated literature has long been a touchstone for women rethinking what it means to be a woman in Japan. This was true to varying degrees among women in the *ribu, rezubian,* and queer *shōjo* manga communities of the 1970s and 1980s. In the remainder of this chapter, however, I will specifically focus on the consumption and transfiguration of translated literature and foreign films within the queer *shōjo* manga sphere. The role played in the creation of queer *shōjo* manga was building upon many decades and many layers of such influence. Translated literature has been transporting *shōjo* readers to foreign lands since the end of the nineteenth century.[160] And, indeed, not long thereafter it played a key role in the creation of *shōjo* fiction (*shōsetsu*), which in turn, was a critical part of the background of the *shōjo* manga of the 1970s, as explained in chapter two. Moreover, in 1970s *shōjo* manga works in general, the foreign, including foreign settings and characters, frequently provided "a means to embody the dreams and *akogare* (longing) of the *shōjo.*"[161] It is easy, therefore, to see its use in *shōjo* manga as foreshadowing if not helping to shape the "narratives of internation-alism" that led to a boom in overseas travel and study of foreign languages among young women in the 1980s and 1990s, lifestyle narratives that Karen Kelsky argues were themselves founded on *akogare,* which she aptly describes as a "long[ing] for something unattainable."[162] Actual foreign countries and cultures held out the potential for escape, even if this escape usually proved to be merely vicarious, particularly for adolescent girls—a topic explored in chapter five.

To be sure, translated texts—and in some cases narratives surrounding the lives of their authors—offered narrative options for all readers in Japan. Trans-lation scholar Keith Harvey, whose own "incipient and fragile identity position as a gay man" was bolstered as a teenager in 1970s Britain through reading translated texts by André Gide, Jean Genet, and Marcel Proust, recalls that rather than being put off by the foreignness of their works, the "distance was actually . . . the space in which I was able to work out the message I wanted to hear and could get nowhere else."[163] Similarly, for many *shōjo* manga readers and writers the space of the foreign in textual form was at once the object of an insatiable longing and a means of sending and receiving messages about sexual and gender alternatives unavailable elsewhere, most notably via the creation of and fandom surrounding the genre of *shōnen'ai.*

Shōnen'ai, the genre at the heart of the queer *shōjo* manga sphere in the 1970s, itself, first emerged as a genre through direct and indirect repurposing of elements from translated literary works. As noted in chapter two, the first commercially published *shōnen'ai* manga narrative was Takemiya Keiko's "Snow and Stars and Angels and . . ." (1974), later republished as "In the Sunroom."[164] Like most early *shōnen'ai* manga, the work's protagonists were beautiful boys (*bishōnen*) in love with each other and the story was set in Europe. As noted in the same chapter, Masuyama Norie played a key role in the genesis of this genre, including this first work. Although not a visual artist herself, Masuyama was an avid consumer from childhood of highbrow literature, classical music, and film. While she was a fan of manga as well, her disappointment with *shōjo* manga instilled in her a desire to elevate *shōjo* manga from its lowly position as a frivolous distraction for girls into a more serious, literary art form. Drawn to the talents of Takemiya and Hagio Moto, Masuyama recommended to the pair various works of music, cinema, and literature in hopes of inspiring them to incorporate elements of these works into their own art.[165]

Among the novels Masuyama recommended were Herman Hesse's *Beneath the Wheel* (1906), *Demian* (1919), and *Narcissus and Goldmund* (1930), each of which having attracted sufficient interest to have been translated into Japanese multiple times and republished repeatedly from the late 1930s onward. All three novels feature adolescent male protagonists in school environments in Germany. While none depict overt homoeroticism—in fact romantic or erotic relationships with female characters help drive their plots—their narratives all revolve around strong bonds between the protagonist and another youth or, in the case of *Narcissus and Goldmund,* a young teacher. Masuyama did not directly encourage Hagio and Takemiya to make manga versions of these novels; yet, as Ishida Minori carefully maps out, the texts played a pivotal role in the development of *shōnen'ai.*[166]

Drawing on her own interviews with Masuyama and Takemiya, as well as existing essays and commentary by Takemiya and Hagio, Ishida makes a compelling case that these novels were crucial source material for pivotal early *shōnen'ai* works, including Takemiya's "In the Sunroom" (1970) and *The Song of the Wind and the Trees* (1976–1984), and Hagio's "November Gymnasium" (1971) and *The Heart of Thomas* (1974).[167] In addition to the European boys' boarding school setting, which serves as a key site for seminal *shōnen'ai* narratives, and the use of male protagonists in and of itself, Ishida argues that Takemiya and Hagio "drew great inspiration" from the rich and deft depictions of the psyches of the youths in Hesse's works.[168] Attention to characters' internal worlds is emblematic of classic *shōnen'ai* manga—beginning with the internal monologue that opens "In the Sunroom"—and, Ishida suggests, it is one of the ways *shōnen'ai* manga helped to foster literary qualities in *shōjo* manga in general.[169] Ishida proposes, moreover, that the typical gender balance between pairs of male protagonists in *shōnen'ai* manga, whereby one is positioned as relatively masculine and the other relatively feminine, can be traced back to Hesse as well.[170] Finally, Ishida argues, Takemiya in particular draws on a latent romanticism and eroticism between some male characters in Hesse's writing, "emphasiz[ing] a tendency in Hesse's works."[171] Takemiya has written specifically of *Beneath the Wheel* that she finds something vaguely erotic—a sort of "chaste eroticism"—in the youths depicted by Hesse.[172]

From the opening scene of two adolescent boys having sex, the overt eroticism of *The Song of the Wind and the Trees,* far exceeds anything possibly read into Hesse's novels, however. This can be linked to the eroticized beautiful boys celebrated in the writing of Inagaki Taruho, whose *Aesthetics of Boy Loving* inspired the name of the new genre, as noted in chapter three.[173] As I discuss in that chapter, Taruho's work draws on both European and Japanese traditions and customs surrounding the adoration of beautiful youths as depicted in literature and historical scholarship; and, like his own use of the term *"shōnen'ai,"* Taruho's writing cannot easily be classified as simply

"Japanese." While Takemiya did not begin to serialize *The Song of the Wind and the Trees* until 1976, she had first conceived of the narrative and began to pen drawings seven years earlier, even before "In the Sunroom" was published.[174] As Takemiya recalls, by the time she finished reading Taruho's book, around 1969, she had developed a clear idea of what she wanted to depict in the work that would become *The Song of the Wind and the Trees*. Early to mid–twentieth-century British public schools are frequently referenced in *Aesthetics of Boy Loving*, "so the first thing I decided was to make a public school-like place the setting for *The Song of the Wind and the Trees*."[175] Yet, the manga's setting is not a British public school, nor an early twentieth-century German one as depicted in Hesse's novels, but a boarding school in nineteenth-century France.

Hagio, however, set her two early *shōnen'ai* narratives in German boarding schools. Yet Hagio claims the 1964 French film *Les amitiés particulières* (These Special Friendships)—first shown in Japan in 1970 under the title *Kanashimi no tenshi* (Angels of sorrow) (figure 4.3)—to be her inspiration for *The Heart of Thomas*, which she had begun working on before *November Gymnasium*, though it was published several years later.[176] Based on a semi-autobiographical novel by Roger Peyrefitte, the film depicts two adolescent boys in a Catholic boarding school who fall in love and ends with the suicide of the younger one, whose love for the older boy made their separation unbearable.[177] This suicide would be mirrored by the titular character in *The Heart of Thomas*. In Japanese, Thomas's name, it should be noted, is pronounced "Tōma," which aligns with the French rather than German version of "Thomas." Scenes from the film as well as stills printed on the Japanese ticket stub and in the twenty-two-page pamphlet bear an uncanny visual resemblance to the overall mood of both of Hagio's texts.[178] Takemiya, on the other hand, says she was initially most influenced by the romanticism in the films of Italian director Luchino Visconti, including his well-known 1971 film based on German novelist Thomas Mann's 1912 novella *Death in Venice* (*Der Tod in Venedig*).[179] Indeed, with his flowing blond hair and clothes that resemble a sailor uniform, the seductive Polish youth Tadzio in the film—played by the stunningly beautiful Swedish teenage actor Björn Andresen (b. 1955)—evokes the *bishōnen* (beautiful boy) characters in *Kaze to ki no uta* and other of Takemiya's manga from the 1970s.

In this Occidentalist mélange of all things European, Hagio and Takemiya, and other artists, drew freely from settings, characters, and plot elements, transfiguring into *shōnen'ai* manga the often nostalgic depictions of intimate friendships as well as romantic and erotic relations between beautiful European boys in translated literature and film, as well as in Taruho's writing. In literary studies, this borrowing might be considered a sort of intertextuality, a practice long

Figure 4.3. Cover of the pamphlet for the Japanese screening of *Les amitiés particulieres* (1964), released in Japan in 1970 under the title *Kanashimi no tenshi* (Angels of sorrow).

central to *shōjo* culture, broadly defined.[180] The concept of intertextuality is often used to index the presence in one text of overt references to other texts, what Norman Fairclough calls "manifest intertextuality." Fairclough distinguishes this intertextuality from what he calls "constitutive intertextuality," or "interdiscursivity," namely "the heterogeneous constitution of texts out of elements (types of convention) of orders of discourse" rather than of specific texts.[181] I would argue that depictions of Western adolescent boys tinged with nostalgia and eroticism, such as via the pen of Hesse and the lens of Jean Delannoy, can be seen to very loosely constitute an order—or a field—of discourse from the perspective of Take-miya, Hagio, Masuyama, and Taruho, as well as from their readers. It is from this field that these artists and others drew, both obviously and obliquely, and it is this field—rather than any specific work or collection of works—that Takemiya and Hagio transfigured into a new genre of *shōjo* manga.

As Fairclough points out, "intertextuality points to the productivity of texts, to how texts can transform prior texts and restructure existing conventions (genres, discourses) to generate new ones." And yet, he notes, this productivity is constrained by the conditions of power operating in society.[182] As has been discussed in numerous analyses of *shōnen'ai* manga, however, it is precisely gendered relations of power constraining women's gender and sexual expression in Japan that Takemiya, Hagio, and other *shōnen'ai* artists worked to undermine through their transfiguration of this world for *shōjo* manga readers.[183] As Takemiya herself has stated, *shōnen'ai* narratives serve "to mentally liberate girls from the sexual restrictions imposed on us" as women.[184]

This does not mean the artists themselves have ultimate control of the parameters of the discursive field of *shōnen'ai* they created. As mentioned in chapter three, Masuyama sees the metaphysical sphere of *shōnen'ai* within *shōjo* manga, as well as in Taruho's writing, as quite distinct from "the world of homosexuals" such as depicted by Mishima Yukio and Shibusawa Tatsuhiko, for instance. That world, she believes, requires the presence of physical male bodies.[185] Yet, many readers of *shōnen'ai* manga in the 1970s and 1980s had their own ideas, reading Mishima as well as Jean Genet and Jean Cocteau along with watching Visconti, and discussing them in the same breath as Hagio and Takemiya. This crossover interest is most salient in letters from adolescent girls and young women published both in magazines for *shōnen'ai* fans and in magazines for *homo* men. It can also be seen in the vocabulary flowing between the two ostensibly separate spheres. For many readers at this time a clear line could not be drawn between *homo* and *shōnen'ai*, nor between *homo* men in Japan and gay men elsewhere.[186] Support for drawing such links can also be found in *shōnen'ai* texts themselves. To offer an obvious example, the protagonist of Takemiya's *The Song of the Wind and the Trees*, Gilbert, is given the surname Cocteau, an overt reference to the French writer and his works.

Sometimes the intertextual references to specific translated works were more blatant. And, while significantly less common than *shōnen'ai*, some *shōjo* manga of the 1970s and 1980s represented female–female romance and sexuality and non-normative gender identity.[187] One example comes from the mid-1980s, Yoshida Akimi's *Sakura no sono* (The cherry orchard), initially serialized in the *shōjo* manga magazine *LaLa* (1976–) from 1985.[188] Through casting her characters in Chekhov's *The Cherry Orchard* (1904), Yoshida temporarily transports them into the liminal, liberatory space of the foreign. It is the encounter of the characters—students entering their last year at a girls' high school—with this translated play that helps to bring gender and sexual alternatives to the fore.

Yoshida's *Sakura,* then, is not a direct translation of Chekhov's foreign text into *shōjo* manga but rather a reuse of some of the elements of the translated work in a way that makes them meaningful to the lives of both Yoshida's characters and her readers. Like the less obvious constitutive intertextuality of early *shōnen'ai* manga, such obvious redeployment of a specific text is one way translated literature has been subsequently transfigured in *shōjo* manga. It is in no small part through this process of transfiguration of foreign texts and foreign spaces within *shōjo* manga—by writers and readers (and no clear line can be drawn between the two)—that readers can begin to find both a sense of affirmation and, in *shōjo* manga scholar Fujimoto Yukari's insightful terms, "a place where they belong."[189]

While most of Yoshida's manga, such as *Banana Fish* (1987–1994), focus on male homosocial environments, sometimes in the United States, *Sakura no sono* is a narrative about a female homosocial sphere, a Japanese girls' high school.[190] Through their performance of Chekhov's *The Cherry Orchard,* the high school girl characters are transported to another space and time and, in the process, come to a deeper understanding of themselves. *Sakura*'s affirmative depiction of alternative gender possibilities and same-sex affection, along with its critique of the heteropatriarchal limits imposed on women, mark it as a "lesbian" text and help liberate it from prior *shōjo* manga narratives in which "lesbian panic" forecloses the possibility of female–female desire.[191] Moreover, in contrast with its *shōnen'ai* predecessors, *Sakura* portrays the trials and tribulations of "very ordinary high school girls" in Japan, thereby prompting its readers to empathize, if not identify, with the characters.[192] On a television program focused on this manga, one reader explained that *Sakura* "reveals the me that I want to hide, [that] I don't want to know." This reader faulted *Sakura* for being too realistic, making her re-live the self-contempt she felt in high school.[193] Another reader, however, recounted being reassured to learn from *Sakura* that there were others who felt unable to accept being female.[194]

While Yoshida has not been directly linked to the lesbian community, in her own transfiguration of Chekhov's play, she produces a narrative that is in many ways emblematic of the role of translation in constructions of "lesbian" in modern Japan.[195] Further, her use of Chekhov ties *Sakura* to Japanese translation and theatrical tradition as well as, perhaps inadvertently, to Japanese lesbian history. Chekhov's plays have long been popular and frequently translated in Japan.[196] In fact, *The Cherry Orchard* was "the first major postwar production of the modern theater," staged just four months after the end of the war[197]—reflecting the work's position within the Japanese modernity to which the theater troupes were striving to return.

While a partial translation of the play appeared in the magazine *Shin shichō* (New thought) around 1910, the first complete translation of the play—reputedly the first from the original Russian—was penned by Seitōsha member Senuma Kayō and serialized between March and May of 1913 in the pages of *Seitō*.[198] Although *The Cherry Orchard* has since been retranslated from Russian more than a dozen times, the characters in Yoshida's *Sakura no sono*, by coincidence or design, read from Yuasa Yoshiko's mid-century translation.[199] Yuasa was a renowned translator and scholar of Russian literature with personal ties to some of the feminists of Seitōsha and is claimed in the pages of *Stories of Women Who Love Women* as a Japanese lesbian foresister.[200] While I am not certain Yoshida made a conscious choice to use a translation by a woman—the majority of *The Cherry Orchard* translations have been by men—she may have done so. And she may have been aware that Yuasa's romantic and sexual partners were exclusively women. In fact, late in life, in an interview published in *Stories*, Yuasa expressly applied the word *"rezubian"* to herself.[201] Even if a mere fortuity, this choice reinforces a lesbian reading of *Sakura* while allowing Yuasa to vicariously participate in the production of this liberatory text nearly four decades after she penned her translation.

Echoing *The Cherry Orchard*, the fleeting nature of time and the inability to return to the innocence of one's childhood are among the themes in Yoshida's *Sakura*. Nostalgia is, in fact, doubly inscribed in the very title of her work. *Sakura* (cherry) blossoms are themselves traditionally associated with the passage of time, and, while the school's name, Ōka Gakuen (literally "cherry blossom academy") and the lines spoken from the script are written in contemporary *kanji* characters, in both the title of the manga and each reference to Chekhov's play Yoshida writes *"sakura"* with the old-fashioned character, suggesting a bygone era. Svetlana Evdokimova points out that *The Cherry Orchard*'s central figure, Madame Ranevskaya, is the embodiment of the contrast between "the bliss of childhood . . . [and] the heavy burden of . . . post-puerile adult life," a burden that also looms for the students in Yoshida's narrative.[202] Ranevskaya's resistance to the passage of time and her concomitant adult responsibilities leads to the downfall of her estate and the felling of the orchard. In contrast with the destruction of Ranevskaya's orchard, each graduating class at Ōka Gakuen High School traditionally leaves a new cherry tree behind; however, the protagonists, who are in their final year of school, will not be there to see the trees when they bloom again. These adolescent girls face the imminence of their own adulthood with a great deal of ambivalence. Similar to Ranevskaya, they are to varying degrees excited about adulthood, including the possibility of romantic and sexual relationships. However, their maturing bodies, including menstruation, are also a source of anxiety and at times embarrassment, even humiliation.[203]

Sakura is divided into four acts, like Chekhov's play, each of which is centered around a different girl taking part in the school's annual production of *The Cherry Orchard*. While the narrative is set in the present, the adult future of the four girls and their classmates is represented in the first "act" by Nakano's sister, ten years her senior. The sister's appearance with her fiancé toward the end of the last "act" disrupts the lesbian script, reminding readers of the heteronormative life course society holds in store.

Yoshida uses the play to force her characters to reflect on their own gender and sexual identities through engaging in cross-dressing. Such performance recalls the all-female Takarazuka Revue, established in 1913—by chance, the year Senuma's translation of *The Cherry Orchard* was published—and long linked to female–female desire.[204] The association between the students' performance and Takarazuka cross-dressing is obvious to the girls of Ōka Gakuen, some of whom still swoon over Kurata Chiyoko's past performances as an "*otokoyaku*"—a label for a woman playing a "trouser role." Given *Sakura*'s striving for realism, this transgender performance exposes, in the words of renée c. hoogland, "the fundamental contradictions marking female sexuality from its earliest stages."[205]

Moreover, the peek behind the scenes that Yoshida provides illustrates how gender is not natural but "performative," as Judith Butler has famously elaborated. The struggle of several characters with their gender(ed) performances renders gender "thoroughly and radically *incredible*."[206] Although last year she performed as an *otokoyaku*—a role better suited to her height and masculine traits—Kurata Chiyoko is cast this year as the heroine, Madame Ranevskaya, a part she is obviously uncomfortable performing. In a twist on the trouser role, in costume Kurata looks like a boy in drag, mocking, in Butler's words, "both the expressive model of gender and the notion of a true gender identity."[207] Kurata's clear discomfort with and desire to reject this female "role" illustrates "the duress under which gender performance always and variously occurs."[208] "Of all the classifications concerning human beings," children's literature scholar Honda Masuko remarks, "nothing is more desperate than the distinction between 'man' and 'woman.' . . . For a girl to affirm her sex is to recognize that the world is a cold Other."[209] While openly wishing she were more feminine, Kurata bemoans her most visible sign of being a woman, her large breasts, which her ill-fitting costume makes all the more prominent. Sympathetic to Kurata's situation, Shimizu Yūko—whose past unpleasant experiences have led her to reject men and who is drawn to Kurata throughout the narrative—constructs a frilly ribbon to attach to the bosom of the dress to cover and draw attention away from Kurata's breasts. Honda observes that "fluttering" (hirahira) frills and ribbons function to conceal the body and yet "inevitably draw . . . the attention of others,"[210] allowing for the simultaneous emphasis of femininity and denial of womanhood. As Yoshida illustrates, the figure of the girl, thus, embodies the tension between being feminine and being a woman. Further, the intimacy between Kurata and Shimizu shows readers that girls can affirm each other as well as their sometimes powerful affection for one another.

Trapped in an internal conflict over her femininity and her willingness to adapt to heteropatriarchal norms, Sugiyama Noriko is the other cross-dresser in Yoshida's narrative. Sugiyama is made to perform an *otokoyaku*, Yasha, in this year's production of *The Cherry Orchard*. While she takes on the role reluctantly, expressing jealousy toward others who are given women's roles, in her own life she vociferously rejects sexual double standards, dresses somewhat androgynously, and—though she is widely suspected of being sexually experienced—is reluctant to date and kiss boys. (When she finally does, however, she is quite happy about it.) Through performing this male role, she realizes that the other side of the gender fence is no more comfortable for her. It is Yoshida's critique of the patriarchal social structure via Sugiyama, more than any other character, that marks *Sakura* as a feminist text.

Stepping back, through her fictive narration of Adrienne Rich's "lesbian continuum," Yoshida inverts and, thus, subverts the expected high school romance narrative—moving across the four "acts" from one girl's first sexual experience with a boy, to another girl's first kiss with a boy, to a third girl's declaration of affection to a receptive fourth girl.[211] While boy–girl relationships are important in the first "act" of the manga, they gradually lose prominence while female relationships deepen. As a result, by the end of the manga, rather than a typical narrative in which the lesbian characters are erased, it is the boys who are blotted out of the story through both dialogue and visual imagery. In the latter two "acts," the few male characters are either literally cut out of the narrative frame, obscured by dialogue bubbles, or turned away from the viewer/reader. Thus the narrative gradually moves toward the state of "lesbian utopia" that Patricia Smith observes is common in "homosocial school fictions" in British literature,[212] resonating as well with the *shōnen'ai* narratives discussed above.[213] Ultimately, even in the face of the heteronormative world looming outside the school grounds and at the end of the school year, protected by the "cherry orchard" enveloping their school lives, the girls are at liberty to explore a range of women-identified experiences.

Rather than directly engaging in acts of literary translation, then, Yoshida and the other manga artists discussed above deploy imagery and plot elements from translated texts. The transfiguration of translated literature functioned as a means to circumvent the restrictions inherent in their own identities as Japanese women. Through the transfigurations of a foreign space, a well-known name, or other aspect of a field of discourse into something to which shōjo readers could relate, these artists worked to liberate their readers. The manga of Takemiya, Hagio, and Yoshida examined above demonstrate how translation and the transfiguration of texts can create spaces for new narratives, both fictional and real. Such linguistic, cultural, and generic transformations inherent in their production of the manga narratives discussed in this chapter enable the construction, de-construction, and re-construction of multiple sexual and gender options. While readers may also enjoy the liberatory aspects of a Western liminal space as they read more directly translated texts, these manga and their reception illustrate that shōjo readers remain aware on some level of how even fictional foreign spaces may be transfigured into something meaningful to them and through which they can construct new meanings—and even new worlds.

Indra Levy suggests in this chapter's opening epigraph that, in spite of translation's centrality to modern Japan, the project of elucidating its role in the (re) construction of Japanese culture remains to be fully developed.[214] Yet there is a growing and diverse body of scholarship on translation in Japan, even if translation studies has not been fully recognized as a discipline within Japan.[215] Thus far, the bulk of the scholarship on translation in Japan has, like the section above, focused on literary translation, or, rather, the rippling effects of translated literature. As the other portions of this chapter demonstrate, however, the translation of essays and empirical studies also served as critical tools for those seeking to challenge gender and sexual norms in the twentieth century. Both through direct translation and more extensive transfiguration of many kinds of foreign texts, the women and adolescent girls in the ribu, rezubian, and queer shōjo manga spheres worked to expand the possibilities for the category "women" in Japan.

And translation goes both ways. A small group of women at Ribu Shinjuku Center—including, from March 1974, Sawabe Hitomi—gathered to read and sometimes translate materials and letters sent to the center from abroad.[216]

Realizing they could also introduce the current situation of women in Japan to women elsewhere, they created English-language materials, which center members took with them in June 1975 to attend the First United Nations World Conference on Women, in Mexico City. Founded in the mid-1970s by Takagi Sawako (b. 1947), who had been abroad and found herself unable to adequately explain the Japanese *ribu* movement, Femintern Press also released a series of pamphlets on the Japanese movement as well as other feminist issues encompassing Asia more broadly.[217] Notably, Akiyama Yōko's pamphlet introducing Ding Ling and her translation from the Chinese of Ding's "Thoughts on the Eighth of March" helped introduce Ding to feminists outside of Asia.[218] And within the English-speaking lesbian community in Japan, Joni van Dyke, for instance, created a bilingual "Dyketionary" to "help bridge the communication gap" between Japanese and foreign lesbians "to fight the patriarchal strategies for blocking DYKE ENERGY!"[219]

And as boys love (BL) manga, anime, and other works have gained a global following over the past several decades, earlier *shōnen'ai* texts have sometimes been translated as well, this time by fans abroad, who often share their unauthorized translations online. English-language "scanlations" (page scans in which the original text has been replaced by translations) of both *The Heart of Thomas* and *The Song of the Wind and the Trees* have been put online by fans on a popular manga scanlation site, for instance, the appeal of which may have helped lead to the publication of an authorized translation of *The Heart of Thomas* in 2012.[220] The anime version of *The Song of the Wind and the Trees* (1987), recently released commercially in Italian and Spanish translation, has been posted with subtitles in English, Italian, and other languages on YouTube, and clips from it as well as panels from the manga have been remixed by fans into dozens of anime music videos (AMVs) to accompany pop songs in English, German, and other languages,[221] a tiny hint of the scope and scale of the global BL fandom that has developed in recent decades—to which I return in the afterword.

Sandra Bermann urges that we seek both evidence and the effects of globalization "in the interstices, the nodes, those endless, precarious junctures where translation between cultures and languages takes place.... Here conflicting histories make their claims, with their stories of passions felt and decisions taken.... In these junctures lie unheard, muted voices of past and present."[222] This chapter has shown that to even begin such a complicated and important task requires attention to multiple fields of discourse and multiple approaches. Situating translation as a mode of transfiguration encourages us to pay attention to the important distinction between attempts at direct translation and attempts to more greatly transform a text, without losing sight of the way both are often contained in everyday speech within a very loose notion of translation. Yet even loosely defined, confining ourselves to pure translation would miss the way translated texts can, in turn, be transfigured into texts like *Stories of Women Who Love Women* and *The Heart of Thomas*. Transfiguration also steers us to look for effects beyond translated texts themselves, beyond their translators, and beyond even dramatically transfigured texts such as these to the communities and the lives of individuals who have been transformed. It is here, in the sometimes subtle ripples and reverberations, we can see how much translation really matters.

CHAPTER 5

Travel

Certainly, travel is more than the seeing of sights; it is a change that goes on, deep and permanent, in the ideas of living . . . an evolution.

—*Miriam Beard*

In October 1970, the same month as the first *ūman ribu* demonstration in Tokyo and in the immediate wake of Osaka's massive Expo '70 world's fair, Japanese National Railways (JNR) began an advertising campaign encouraging young women to hit the rails and "Discover Japan." This was a time in which expectations lingered that, until married, a young woman would sleep in the family home under parental supervision and would certainly not spend the night unsupervised in a strange place—a fact that added, in the advertising campaign designer's own calculations, a certain erotic liberation to the journeys he was promoting.[1] During this period, domestic and, notably, foreign travel was also increasingly a part of the broader interwoven public discourses on consumption and status, with overseas holidays serving as a key symbol of financial success in the 1970s.[2] And, while fixed exchange rates unfavorable to the yen along with currency export restrictions and other obstacles hampered travel abroad through the early part of that decade, over the course of the 1970s foreign journeys gradually became conceivable for an increasing number of people in Japan, including women.

This period also saw a new wave of magazines targeting young women consumers, beginning with *An An* (1970–) and *Non-no* (1971–) at the opening of the 1970s, followed later that decade by *Croissant* (*Kurowassan,* 1977–) and *More* (*Moa,* 1977–)—the latter of which released transfigured versions of *The Hite Report,* discussed in the previous chapter. These magazines simultaneously inspired and reflected among their readers an interest in travel and eroticism alongside other kinds of consumption. Fujioka Takao, the mastermind of "Discover Japan," described the readership of *An An* and *Non-no* as "perfectly" aligning with the campaign's target audience.[3] Those two magazines in particular have indeed been associated with an increase among young women in both domestic and overseas travel, linked with the magazines' promotion of Japanese tourist attractions as well as—particularly from the mid-1970s onward—foreign destinations including Paris, London, and New York.[4]

The JNR campaign was built around the Japanese idea of *tabi,* a term hearkening back to Japan's past and originally implying a journey, most often on foot, with a clear purpose—such as a religious pilgrimage or a trip taken as part of one's occupation.[5] From ancient travel literature to the present, *tabi* have also been tinged with the stuff of dreams.[6] JNR has not been alone in capitalizing on—and stretching the meaning of—this traditional idea of a sometimes fantastic, often nostalgic journey with a purpose. As Sylvia Guichard-Anguis points out, in contemporary Japan people continue to make *tabi*—whether by train, plane, or the internet—journeys that are quite often to destinations beyond Japan's borders.[7]

Government tourism white papers from the 1970s indicate that, as overseas tourism grew, women and adolescent girls occupied a rapidly increasing proportion of the Japanese nationals traveling abroad, reaching a quarter of the total by the middle of the decade, a decade that saw an increasing number of individuals going abroad for tourism and increasingly choosing the United States or Western Europe over closer Asian destinations. The number of women and girls traveling abroad had reached almost 631,000 in 1975, nearly double the 339,000 who traveled abroad just two years earlier.[8] By 1980 the nearly 1,150,000 journeys abroad by Japanese women and girls constituted almost 30 percent of the total number of overseas voyages, a figure that rose decade upon decade to near parity with men toward the end of the last century as the total number of Japanese traveling abroad each year skyrocketed.[9] Around 40 percent of the women journeying abroad in 1980 were in their twenties, a figure that the 1981 tourism white paper attributes to a high number of women wishing to travel overseas prior to marriage or for their honeymoons.[10] In this speculation, the white paper authors associate overseas travel with the fulfillment of young women's fantasies, fantasies to be rendered unobtainable by marriage and children.

While JNR's motivation was to shore up demand for domestic travel by rail, a key part of the initial inspiration for the "Discover Japan" campaign came from overseas. Specifically, the promotion's creators transfigured a 1967 "Discover America" campaign aimed at keeping American travel money within the borders of the United States into a series of advertisements encouraging young Japanese women to fill JNR's coffers by traveling around Japan by train.[11] Moreover, the "Discover Japan" campaign was sold to these women as a journey to discover oneself—a journey that required leaving home to discover a self whose origins lie imbricated in a nostalgic notion of Japan, a Japan that was also home.[12] Historian Marilyn Ivy remarks that the "Discover Japan" campaign positioned young women simultaneously as the subjects of these journeys and as objects. They were subjects who must leave a home that is "essentially lacking: lacking both in the satisfaction necessary to keep women at home . . . and in the resources necessary to actualize 'woman' as the desirable object of the male gaze."[13] In short, through journeying in Japan, the targets of this campaign were expected to come to understand themselves as subjects in possession of a self that is authentically Japanese as well as female—and thus the object of Japanese male desire.[14]

Like translation, in the 1970s and 1980s travel played a key role in shaping the *ūman ribu, rezubian,* and queer *shōjo* manga spheres, as well as in reshaping the self-understandings of many individuals linked to these communities. The travel among these spheres that is the focus of this chapter dates to the same period as the JNR campaign and is also intimately linked with self-discovery and transformation through venturing away from one's childhood home—and, sometimes, home country. These women's and girls' journeys, however, often served to challenge, rather than bolster, the gender and sexual norms that would position them as sexual objects. In some cases, their journeys also unsettled, rather than reinforced, these travelers' sense of being Japanese. Moreover, in contrast with the predominantly rural destinations emphasized in the "Discover Japan" campaign, the domestic journeys for the women in these spheres generally entailed travel to, not from, urban centers. Arguably the cultural capital of each of these three communities, Tokyo, in particular, had a centripetal pull that drew in many of the women whose lives I discuss in this book—though, to be sure, the Kansai region, encompassing Osaka and Kyoto, comes in a close second, especially within the *ribu* movement. In this chapter, however, my primary focus is on real and vicarious voyages across, rather than within, national and cultural borders.

Regardless of the purpose of the foreign journeys by the women and girls in these three communities taken in the 1970s and 1980s and, on occasion, even earlier, their destination was most often located in the West. Some of the interest within these communities in entering Western cultural milieux seems to prefigure the *akogare* (longing) for an ultimately unobtainable "West" that Karen Kelsky analyzes in her study of internationally minded women in the late 1980s and the 1990s. Those women rejected Japan for what they often later discovered to their disappointment had been an overly idealized understanding of Western culture and, frequently, Western men. While the sense of *akogare* experienced by the women in Kelsky's study was imbued with and perpetuated an "attitude of Japanese inferiority,"[15] such an attitude—while also present to a degree within these three communities—does not appear to have been a driving force among the women and adolescent girls in the *ribu, rezubian,* and queer *shōjo* manga spheres, who generally did not express the same rejection of Japan as had the women who were the focus of Kelsky's study.

Aside from the United Nations First World Conference on Women in Mexico City, discussed below, travel to countries outside the West received relatively limited attention within these spheres in most of the 1970s and 1980s. And there were few women from countries outside the Euro-American sphere whose voices were prominent in the discourse of these three communities. As discussed in previous chapters, queer *shōjo* manga narratives were often set in the West—particularly so in the 1970s—with most of the remainder set in Japan. Within the *rezubian* community, it would take until the mid-1980s for organizations to begin significant networking with other lesbian groups in Asia, and even the most meaningful of those connections were initially forged at a lesbian event in Europe, discussed below. Some feminist groups in Japan did attempt to directly reach out to and network with other Asian women from the very beginning of the 1970s, but the most notable such efforts were made by a group not identified with the *ribu* movement.[16] Among activist women's groups and within *ribu,* the most prominent discussion of Korea and elsewhere in Asia in the 1970s was a campaign to end prostitution tours by men.[17]

As I have shown in the preceding chapters, elements from the West—primarily the United States and Western Europe—were transfigured in these communities by women and girls (as well as men) in Japan in the process of redefining the category "women." Many of these elements were introduced via transnational travel—that is, flows of people across national borders. For instance, the American radical feminist writing that was among the first to be translated into Japanese, discussed in chapter four, was brought to Japan by a pair of Americans who had traveled to the country to both protest US military aggression in Southeast Asia and to evade the draft. And the shift in pronunciation from "*resubian*" to "*rezubian*" discussed in chapter three began with direct contact between American lesbians and a Japanese man who had journeyed to New York. That shift also involved other transnational voyages and face-to-face contact between women from Japan and people from the United States, through which women from Japan directly heard how the word was pronounced in English—the foreign language to which most women in Japan have long felt closest.

Like the transfigured words, texts, images, and practices discussed in previous chapters, the intents and effects of travel abroad within these spheres were often the result of coincidence rather than design. These trips often had multiple goals and served multiple functions, and at times had unforeseen consequences. Escape was one such goal. This escape might have been from the parental home, from aspects of the self, from Japanese patriarchal norms broadly defined, or from a combination thereof. Among the women with whom I have spoken, as well as in the discourse of these three communities, however, these journeys abroad were framed as *journeys to* more often than as *journeys from*. This distinction is significant. For those in the *ribu* and *rezubian* spheres in particular, rather than frame travel abroad as an attempt to escape oppressive gender and sexual norms, women undertook many journeys for the purpose of networking with and learning from women in other cultures—or at least described their trips thusly. They aimed both to bring back knowledge that might strengthen women's activism within Japan and to share information about Japanese activism with their sisters abroad. Further, for some women these journeys—including both short- and long-term sojourns abroad—were for work, either for an individual's own job, her partner's, or a parent's. Finally, as travel abroad became more affordable, particularly since the 1980s, the primary purpose of an increasing number of these journeys was pleasure.

In the sections below, I consider real and vicarious travel experiences in the *ribu, rezubian,* and queer *shōjo* manga spheres. In contrast with the previous chapter, in which I used a relatively narrow definition of "translation" to highlight the intentions of those involved in transfiguring texts, for my purposes in this chapter I employ an expansive definition of "travel," one that often exceeds the notion of *tabi*. I place on the continuum of travel long-term, even permanent, dwelling abroad when the choice to move away from—and in some cases to—Japan can be linked to experiences in these communities. I do so to recognize women from Japan who have become long-term residents of other countries as well as women who are long-term foreign residents of Japan who have contributed in meaningful ways to the discourse in these spheres on being a woman in Japan. For instance, articles and correspondence from women on journeys or residing abroad often provided information about foreign cultures, including details about topics such as the status of women, the normative family structure, the state of feminist activism, the shape of queer communities, and—in the case of discourse within the queer *shōjo* manga sphere—the attractiveness of adolescent boys and young men overseas. Narrated firsthand by women who had grown up in Japan, such information allowed readers in Japan to vicariously share in the experiences of someone perhaps very much like themselves.

Liberating Journeys in the Late 1960s and Early 1970s

Amano Michimi traveled to Europe by herself in 1968—an exceptionally early time for a young Japanese woman to travel solo, particularly abroad.[18] Her motivation was a combination of a yearning for Europe, a dream to become a writer, and a hope to escape her current life in Japan. Her actual travel experience and its aftereffects were rather different from her expectations, however.

Born right at the end of the war, Amano had had an unusual upbringing.[19] Her father, born in the Meiji era, held very traditional ideas about the position of women in the family and in society; her mother, on the other hand, had abandoned the family when Amano was four. She subsequently received little in the way of discipline from either her grandmother, who raised her and her two brothers for the next six years, or her stepmother, who joined the family when Amano was around ten years old. Further, as she recalls, no one made much effort to inculcate in her normative feminine behavior—the imposition of which was a common complaint in the discourse in the *ribu, rezubian,* and queer *shōjo* manga spheres, and among the many women with whom I have spoken in conjunction with the research for this book.

Nevertheless, Amano developed a rebellious streak and longed to escape her family and Kyoto, the conservative city of her birth. When she finished high school, her father allowed her to go to a four-year university—somewhat unusual for young women at the time—but not to a school in Tokyo, where she desperately wanted to live. As a university student in the early 1960s, Amano tried to "act like an intellectual" and read what people around her were reading—such as works by Marx and Engels as well as Japanese writers like Yoshimoto Takaaki and Ōe Kenzaburō—but found this writing too opaque. Upon the recommendation of a friend, she read Simone de Beauvoir's *Second Sex* and was instantly in thrall. Amano subsequently read everything else by Beauvoir that had been translated into Japanese and, in the process, her intellectual infatuation with the philosopher developed into a strong desire to become a writer and, concomitantly, an irrepressible yearning to experience firsthand the France in which Beauvoir wrote.

Certain that her father and stepmother would try to prevent her from undertaking such a journey, she planned her voyage to Europe in secret and sprang it on them the day before she left. The route she took—a ferry from

Yokohama to Russia, and from there the Siberian Express to Europe—was common among intrepid young male Japanese travelers at the time, who, lacking sufficient funds to live once they arrived, frequently found jobs to cover their livelihood and pay for further travel.[20] This experience was exemplified by the 1967 novelized account of a journey to Europe, *A Young Man Seeks the Wilds* (*Seinen wa kōya o mezasu*), by popular writer Itsuki Hiroyuki (b. 1932). Itsuki's book was a source of inspiration, even a de facto guidebook, for young travelers with the will and the means.[21] Amano was among them.[22]

Amano's actual experience of life in France was far from the rose-colored image she had held of the country before she arrived, however. She worked as an au pair for a series of families over the course of about ten months, and often felt lonely and miserable. She had a great deal of difficulty communicating with people around her, who often mistook her for a Vietnamese refugee. She was poorly paid but when she had enough money, she spent time with a Japanese friend at a café in Paris that Beauvoir was said to frequent, eventually managing to see the object of her passion in person twice. In less than a year, her worried parents offered to pay for a flight back to Japan. Amano declined because she did not want to appear that she needed their help. To cover the cost of her return journey, she moved to Copenhagen, where she cleaned rooms at a Scandinavian Airlines–owned hotel for a year, long enough to entitle her to a free flight back to Japan. Before she left, she also scraped together enough money to make a circuit around Europe and hit spots then popular with the bohemian set she was trying to emulate. While this journey was on the whole not as rewarding as Amano had hoped, and she does not speak of it as a transformative experience, she did come back with a limited ability to speak French and, more importantly, greater self-confidence.

Although Amano's trip appears to have been little more than an unusual adventure for a young Japanese woman in the late 1960s, it set in motion a chain of events that got her involved in *ribu* and engaged in further transnational networking. After returning to Japan, Amano was invited by someone she had met in Europe to a party for British writer Angela Carter (1940–1992), who had moved to Japan in 1969. Among the last people remaining at the party that evening were Amano and Larry Taub (1936–2018), an American in Tokyo in part to protest the Vietnam War. Later Taub asked for her assistance in getting permission from Tanaka Mitsu to translate Tanaka's highly influential *ribu* treatise *To Women with Spirit*.[23] While that translation project did not pan out, Amano found herself pulled into the *ribu* movement, first as a member of Tanaka's Group Fighting Women, discussed in previous chapters. Amano believes that Tanaka invited her to join because she was so self-assured and subsequently kicked her out of the group within about six months because, at almost the same age as Tanaka and with a university degree and significant experience living abroad—neither of which Tanaka possessed—Amano's presence threatened Tanaka's superiority and authority.

Amano stayed involved in the *ribu* movement itself, however, taking part in the four-woman collective, Red June (Akai Rokugatsu), a group with which she would soon become dissatisfied. Before long, Amano had saved enough money to travel again, and this time chose to go to New York. She initially told those around her she was going to learn about the women's liberation movement in the United States, but, as she later wrote, she merely wanted to extract herself from the movement, which had proved overwhelming.[24] Through Taub, Amano got introductions to New York–based radical feminists, most of whom, she says, identified as lesbian. She supported herself and earned money for the return trip by working under the table at a Japanese restaurant, and then at a hostess bar catering to Japanese businessmen. In spite of being impressed by how openly women expressed lesbian desire in the radical feminist community she had connected with, and in spite of being given small-scale celebrity status by constantly being introduced by one woman as "the only lesbian in the Japanese lib [movement]," she was disappointed with her experience in the United States and stayed only five months.[25] While in New York, she was interviewed for the American feminist magazine *The Second Wave*, with which she shared her understanding of the status of women and of lesbians in Japan, and of the Japanese *ribu* movement, as well as her impression of feminism in the United States.[26] Back in Japan, Amano wrote up her experience in New York and her opinions about women's status and feminism in the United States. While Amano told me in 2009 that she had found New York and the United States in general boring, in *Onna erosu* she described New York as "dangerous . . . dirty . . . [and] traumatic"—shocking beyond compare—nothing like France, Denmark, or the other countries she had visited in Europe.[27]

Although, as noted in chapter four, Amano may deserve recognition as the first open *rezubian* to translate lesbian writing into Japanese, she did not become involved in the *rezubian-feminisuto* activism that would begin to come together soon after her return from New York. At the time, Amano felt oppressed in Japanese society primarily because she was a woman, not because she was a *rezubian* and, thus, she was not particularly interested in *rezubian* activism.[28] She did, however, remain involved with *ribu* activists, including translating "In Amerika They Call Us Dykes" for *Onna erosu* in 1974, discussed in chapter four. She would also become a member of the magazine's editorial team, a position she held through the late 1970s. While she would go on to pursue other interests, among them acupuncture and abstract art, Amano continued to contribute to *ribu* and other feminist publications such as the Osaka-based *From Woman to Women* well into the 1980s.

While both of Amano's sojourns in the West can be linked to her rebellion against normative restrictions on women in Japan, and while she used her experience in *ribu* to reflect on her journeys, Amano seems to have taken away little personally except increased self-confidence, improved language skills, and, she wrote in *Onna erosu,* the knowledge that Japanese men abroad were as dependent on women as they are in Japan.[29] In recent years, Amano has not reflected back on those journeys as shaping her identity as either a feminist or as a lesbian, though, as we have seen, it did lead to her involvement in the *ribu* movement.

Takagi Sawako was another early overseas traveler whose prominent role in the production of *ribu* publications was a result of chance encounters. And, like Amano, travel abroad and her interest in foreign cultures played a somewhat unpredictable role in her life. Takagi had attended a high school unusual in that it offered courses in French and German in addition to English.[30] Studying French for two years along with seeing a risqué film by Jean-Luc Godard piqued her interested in France. After finishing high school, Takagi continued to work on her French for another two years while preparing to pass the entrance exam that would gain her admission to the prestigious Waseda University, which had a professor of French with whom she wanted to study. Although she was in university during the peak of the student movement and then the rise of *ūman ribu,* she was so busy with work and study that she was unaware of the new women's movement that was beginning to take shape. After graduation she found a publicity position with the Japan Family Planning Association (JFPA; Nihon Kazoku Keikaku Kyōkai). Rather than representing a personal interest in reproductive health, such a job was merely one of the few besides teacher, doctor, and nurse open to women with a four-year degree at the time. In 1971, on assignment at a gathering celebrating a milestone anniversary for *Fujin minshu shinbun* (Women's democratic newspaper, 1946–), Takagi learned about the existence of *ribu* from fliers being distributed. She did not immediately get involved, but through her work she would continue to have occasion to interact with both old-school feminists and new-school *ribu* activists, including Amano, who was to eventually become her roommate.

In 1973, through her involvement with the French-speaking community in Tokyo, Takagi met a French woman who had followed her journalist boyfriend to Japan on assignment. This woman, who had been involved in the feminist movement in France, told her about the upcoming International Feminist

Planning Conference, co-sponsored by the National Organization for Women, to be held in Cambridge, Massachusetts, at the beginning of June. This time Takagi was sufficiently curious to make up her mind to attend the event on her own rather than as part of her job. In fact, she decided to quit her position at JFPA and combine the conference with a three-month sojourn in the United States. Unable to speak English sufficiently enough to get much out of the event, Takagi had requested an interpreter, but the person provided by the organizers, a Japanese woman residing in the United States, disappeared after the first day. However, prolific feminist writer Higuchi Keiko (b. 1932) hired an interpreter who Higuchi, Takagi, and Yoshihiro Kiyoko (b. 1940), the only three participants coming from Japan, were able to make use of for the remainder of the conference.

While mere curiosity had gotten Takagi to the conference, it was clearly inspirational to her, and she threw herself into the *ribu* movement upon her return to Japan, speaking to the women at Ribu Shinjuku Center about her experience, as well as laying the groundwork for further transnational exchange.[31] Fellow conference attendee Yoshihiro also shared with readers of *Onna erosu* details about her experience at the conference and subsequent participation in women's liberation activities in New York. The most striking point about the US movement for Yoshihiro—one that occupies most of her article in the journal—seems to have been the prominence of lesbians among American radical feminists, something that stood in sharp contrast with the *ribu* movement.[32]

During Takagi's time in the United States, including at the conference, she found herself repeatedly asked about feminism and women in Japan but felt unable to respond adequately. This was the inspiration for Femintern Press (Femintān Puresu), which she founded to publish English-language materials about feminism in Japan and elsewhere in Asia, "not only to satisfy the curiosity and chance questions that interested American, Canadian, European, and other feminists may have, but also from the conviction that feminists in these countries have an *obligation* to become informed about and support the actions of women in Asia, and particularly in undeveloped countries."[33] The name of Takagi's new press, which echoes Comintern, was suggested by Taub, whom Takagi had met through Amano, and who would go on to assist with translating and proofreading the press's publications.

From 1974 to around 1977, Femintern produced at least seven English-language pamphlets written primarily by individuals variously linked to the *ribu* movement, which the press promoted in English-language women's periodicals and newsletters.[34] (Coincidentally, it was also around 1974 that the

Figure 5.1. Cover of *A Short History of the Women's Movement in Japan*, by Kazuko Tanaka (Tokyo: Femintern Press, [1975] 1977).

translation group at Ribu Shinjuku Center began producing their own materials in English in response to requests for information from abroad, as noted in chapter four.) One of the earliest Femintern Press pamphlets was Kazuko Tanaka's *A Short History of the Women's Movement in Modern Japan,* first published in 1975, which sold sufficiently well that it was in its third edition two years later[35] (figure 5.1). The press also released in pamphlet form *The Hidden Sun: A Brief History of Japanese Women* by Akiyama Yōko, first published as an article in *International Socialist Review*. It had also been presented at the 1973 Cambridge conference by Takagi, in Akiyama's stead.[36] In keeping with Takagi's belief that feminists in more developed countries need to be aware of issues confronting women in developing countries in Asia, one of the pamphlets focused on Chinese feminist Ding Ling, by Akiyama, and another on prostitution tours to Korea, by well-traveled journalist Matsui Yayoi.[37] In sum, Takagi sold enough of the pamphlets that she was able to turn a small profit.

In 2009, over thirty years after the press ceased publication, Takagi asked me to assist her in donating her personal collection of Femintern pamphlets to an archive in the United States, demonstrating her ongoing interest in the dissemination—and preservation—of information related to the *ribu* movement. They ended up at the Schlesinger Library, which houses materials related to women's history within Harvard's Radcliffe Institute—formerly Radcliffe College, a historic women's college. Takagi chose this location based on her recollection of visiting the college on her first visit to the United States in 1973—on the trip that spurred her establishment of the press.

By the time of Takagi's first trip to the United States, women who were already committed feminists were also journeying abroad, sometimes with the goal of networking with other feminists and learning about feminist activism in other countries. For instance, Inoue Teruko also traveled to the United States in 1973. Inoue ostensibly went there to take part in the Ninth International Congress of Anthropological and Ethnological Sciences in Chicago, which she attended with around forty individuals from Japan, including politician and social critic Tanaka Sumiko (1909–1995).[38] Her real motivation for visiting the United States—her first journey abroad—was to learn about the women's movement there and the emerging field of women's studies, the latter of which she had learned about from Matsui.[39] This visit, as noted in chapter two, would help lay the foundations for establishing the field of women's studies (*joseigaku*) in Japan later in the decade. But before that, in 1974, Inoue and several other scholars, including Japanese women who had spent time studying and conducting research in the United States, founded the Women's Sociology Study Group (Josei Shakaigaku Kenkyūkai) to promote the study of women within sociology. American scholars Kathleen Uno and Gail Nomura were members while studying in Japan in the mid-1970s.[40]

Inoue had initially become interested in women's issues in the 1960s and at the University of Tokyo belonged to a research circle examining women's issues from a Marxist position, reading works by Marx and Engels, as well as Inoue Kiyoshi's influential *History of Japanese Women* (*Nihon joseishi*, 1948).[41] While in the United States, Inoue met with activists, such as Marxist feminist activist Evelyn Reed, who had visited Japan the year before, and women's studies scholars, including Joan Roberts, and learned about what opportunities for women's studies were available at Wisconsin, Chicago, and Berkley. At the conference itself Inoue was to present a paper titled, "Women's Movement and Women's Status in Modern Japan," again evidencing a desire to share information about what women activists were doing in Japan rather than to merely learn from or mimic their counterparts in the West.[42]

Still other women went abroad for reasons completely unrelated to the *ribu* movement. Akiyama, who contributed two publications to Takagi's press, was herself well-traveled by the mid-1970s, though the traveling she had done was not in conjunction with *ribu* activism. Akiyama's first voyage overseas was a brief trip to Cuba in 1969, on which she found herself invited by chance while she was a graduate student.[43] Several years later she accompanied her husband, a translator, to Moscow for his work, where they, along with their two children, lived from 1974 to 1981.[44] While activism did not motivate these trips, Akiyama sent "letters from the Soviet Union" to publications like *Ribu News* and *Onna erosu* in which she discussed women, family structure, and society in Russia, illustrating how she used her involvement in *ribu* to reflect on Russian culture, itself just one of the ways she helped to link women across linguistic and cultural borders.[45]

Larry Taub, who, as noted above, gave the name to Takagi's small press, was one of a number of foreigners who found their way to Japan and interacted with the *ribu* movement in the first half of the 1970s, including individuals introduced in previous chapters, who attended and contributed their voices and experiences at early *ribu* meetings and retreats. Many of these individuals first came to Japan in conjunction with the anti-war movement, beginning in the 1960s. And even those foreigners who came to Japan for other reasons entirely sometimes found themselves involved in this sphere. For instance, Angela Carter, also mentioned above, came to Japan not as part of the anti-war movement but to "estrange" herself from her present life and continue to develop as a writer through a process of self-discovery.[46] She later claimed that through her experience in Japan—which she initially funded with the prize money from her 1968 Somerset Maugham Award—she "learnt what it is to be a woman and became radicalised."[47] American scholars whose work focuses on women in Japan, including Susan Pharr and the aforementioned Kathleen Uno, also made connections with activists at Ribu Shinjuku Center.[48] In addition to researchers, foreign feminist activists, including lesbian feminists, regularly visited Ribu Shinjuku Center, as did foreign residents of Japan.[49] Pharr was one of a handful of foreigners, mostly Western visitors or residents of Japan, who directly contributed writing to *ribu* and *rezubian* publications, thus participating in local discourse on the meaning of "women" from the perspective of someone who was not from Japan.[50] While foreign visitors to the center were seldom mentioned in the interviews I conducted and rarely come up in the written materials about the center, when I asked individuals involved in center activities, such as Yonezu Tomoko and Akiyama, I was told that there were often foreign women at the center. That such individuals are seldom mentioned in discourse on *ribu* and *rezubian* history speaks to the fact that most played only temporary and marginal roles. Nevertheless, foreigners visiting and residing in Japan did add to the discourse and occasionally set in motion ripples of change of which they themselves may never have been aware—including some of the translations discussed in the previous chapter.

1975, Mexico City, and New Beginnings

The year 1975, United Nations International Women's Year, was pivotal for women around the world. Whatever the critiques of the United Nations–sponsored First World Conference on Women in Mexico City—and there were many[51]—the gathering provided opportunities for one-on-one interactions among women across economic and cultural differences, both at the official meetings and at counterdemonstrations. Collectively, this helped set the stage for a more global movement for women's human rights. For the *ribu* movement, however, the Mexico City conference has been widely seen to mark either the movement's demise, or at least a major turning point leading toward its decline.[52]

Women from Japan attended the Mexico City conference, held from June 19 to July 2, with both official and nongovernmental delegations. Old-school feminists, including several members of parliament, spearheaded the organization of women from all walks of life into the grassroots Group of Women Taking Action for International Women's Year (Kokusai Fujinnen o Kikkake Toshite Kōdō o Okosu Onnatachi no Kai). The group, which sent a delegation to the conference, set its mission as promoting women's full participation in society and more equitable cooperation between women and men, goals that were decidedly part of a liberal feminist philosophy.[53] This loosely knit organization was able to use the conference and associated International Women's Year and subsequent Decade for Women (1976–1985), as well as the Convention on the Elimination of All Forms of Discrimination Against Women (CEDAW)—which Japan signed in 1980 and ratified in 1985—to put international pressure on the Japanese government.[54] The convention, and subsequent international conferences on women's rights, prompted legislative changes that would at least nominally improve women's legal status, including the passage in 1985 of the Equal Employment Opportunity Law.[55]

Some *ribu* activists went to Mexico City in conjunction with the conference as well, but the consequences for certain of these individuals and the *ribu* movement itself appear to have been largely unforeseen. Those attending from Ribu Shinjuku Center were Tanaka Mitsu, Wakabayashi Naeko, and Takeda Miyuki (b. 1948).[56] Takeda was a core member of Tokyo Komuunu, a communal living and child-rearing group linked to the center whose name combines *"ko umi"* (giving birth to a child) with *"komyūn"* (commune). Her departure for Mexico led to the dissolution of that group, one of a number of significant changes set in motion in this period.[57]

For Tanaka, leaving for Mexico marked her exit from *ribu* activism. Exhausted from all the energy she had put into the movement, Tanaka needed to pull herself away but felt unable to do so if she remained in Japan, so she settled down in Mexico City, where she would live for the next four years.[58] Thus, in contrast with many other women discussed in this chapter, rather than an object of any sort of yearning or a place where she hoped to network with and learn from local women, Mexico was for Tanaka a convenient place that was "not Japan" that could serve as a backdrop for her recuperation. Tanaka did not, however, cut off ties completely with individuals from the *ribu* movement, several of whom visited her in Mexico. When Tanaka finally returned to Japan, she studied acupuncture and, in 1982, opened her own clinic.[59]

Tanaka's long-term departure from Japan in connection with the UN conference is sometimes linked to the end of the most visible phase of the *ribu* movement. Indeed, her absence had a huge impact on Ribu Shinjuku Center. Asakawa Mari believes that Tanaka's absence made it possible, or at least easier, to organize what were called "wonderful women" surveys, introduced in chapter two, to find out about *rezubian* within the *ribu* movement and to produce a *mini-komi* of the same name in 1976.[60] As for others heavily involved in the center's activities, exhausted themselves, they ended their collective living arrangement and began taking turns managing the center, before permanently shuttering it in May 1977.[61]

Some of these women started up new feminist projects. Yonezu Tomoko, Doi Yumi, and Mori Setsuko (b. 1948), the latter of whom had been in Thought Collective S.E.X. with Yonezu, formed the core of a women's printing collective called Aida Kōbō. By the end of the decade, however, relations within the group had grown poor, as had Yonezu's health. Yonezu withdrew from the collective, and in 1981 Doi headed to the United States to "take a year off" and cool her head. Enjoying her new life, Doi decided to stay long term and was able to parlay her experience in the collective into a job at a printing company and eventually a green card.[62] Though she had not planned to live abroad permanently, and while she has maintained ties with some former *ribu* activists, decades later Doi is still living in the United States.[63]

Wakabayashi Naeko was another Ribu Shinjuku Center member who combined the Mexico City conference with an extended sojourn in North America. Unlike Tanaka, however, Wakabayashi used her time abroad to network with and learn from foreign feminists, came back recharged and ready to engage again in local activism.[64] Wakabayashi went to Mexico via Los Angeles, where she spent a brief time at the Feminist Women's Health Center. After Mexico, she went back up to Los Angeles and then on to San Francisco and Berkeley, the latter of which she loved for its hippie atmosphere, so she decided to stay a while. In the house where she chose to rent a room, it turned out that two of the women were lesbians. Through the people she had met at the health center down in Los Angeles, she found herself employed at the Feminist Women's Health Center in neighboring Oakland. Two things stood out at the health center. One was its promotion, in conjunction with the Los Angeles center, of the use of speculums to help better acquaint women with their own bodies as part of the broader women's health movement, which can be traced in part to the Boston Women's Health Book Collective's *Our Bodies, Ourselves*. This experience motivated Wakabayashi to introduce speculums to women back in Japan and to work toward the establishment of women's health centers in the country.

The other thing Wakabayashi found remarkable was that her coworkers were lesbians. Wakabayashi had held a negative impression of lesbians prior to getting involved in the *ribu* movement based on images circulating in public discourse, including pornography. Through translating materials for *Ribu News* that had come from lesbian-feminists abroad, as well as through interaction with *rezubian* friends within the movement, however, this prejudice "quickly disappeared."[65] Nevertheless, prior to living in the United States she did not think women loving women had anything to do with her. But at the clinic, for the first time in her life, she became romantically attracted to a woman, specifically an African American woman who was the partner of a Filipina woman who regularly visited the clinic. While that crush led nowhere with that woman, it did lead her to the realization that liking women was the same as liking men had been for her in the past. Having experienced racism herself for the first time while in the United States, Wakabayashi had become increasingly aware of race and identity, and she does not believe her liking a woman who was African American was insignificant in this regard.[66] As a result of these experiences, while she had arrived in the United States identifying as a heterosexual woman in the *ribu* movement, Wakabayashi returned to Japan identifying as an "Asian lesbian feminist."[67]

Journeys Abroad and the Expansion of *Rezubian/* Lesbian Activism

Beginning around 1974, Sawabe Hitomi took part in the translation of lesbian-feminist materials at Ribu Shinjuku Center with Wakabayashi and others.[68] Sawabe was specifically in charge of perusing the American feminist newsletter *off our backs* (1970–2008), from which Sawabe learned about lesbian feminists in the United States and was instilled with the desire to visit the country. At the time, no one she knew in the center was openly *rezubian*. An American woman named Kim, who was studying at Waseda University, provided Sawabe details about American lesbian life, reinforcing her yearning to see it herself. After she made up her mind to go, she began to study both English and the martial arts Shorinji kempo and karate—the former to be able to communicate and the latter to be able to defend herself in a place she thought would be frightening. And to combine earning money with an education on *rezubian* culture, she got a job at one of Tokyo's "*rezu* bars" with cross-dressing women on the staff, though she was extremely uncomfortable with the atmosphere and quit within a couple of months.

A few months before Tanaka, Wakabayashi, and other *ribu* and feminist activists headed to Mexico City, Sawabe found her way to the United States.[69] In her diary, she wrote that her motivation for the trip was to "discover some kind of legitimacy to being homosexual."[70] Over three months, she had visited places as far-ranging as Berkeley, Seattle, New York, and Minnesota, and found many lesbian feminists with whom she could identify, women whose expression of gender seemed very liberated—neither particularly feminine nor masculine. This was a far cry from the women at the bar where she had briefly worked, which expected women to be clearly one or the other. And thus, the US lesbian feminists provided a model of lesbian identity she felt would work for her. Reflecting back more than thirty years later, she said that meeting those women "was like a baptism" into a new world for her.[71] She took this richer understanding of what it might mean to be a lesbian back with her to Japan, laying a new foundation for her activism.[72]

Both Sawabe and Wakabayashi got involved in *rezubian-feminisuto* activism immediately after returning from the United States, with both involved in the "wonderful women" project, mentioned above.[73] Wakabayashi devoted much of her energy over the next few years to women's health issues, playing an important role in the women's health movement in Japan, while Sawabe focused on *rezubian-feminisuto* writing and activism, including *rezubian-feminisuto* groups discussed in chapter two, and, later, more broadly defined feminist work. Both, however, were involved in the creation in 1985 of the *rezubian-feminisuto* group Regumi no Gomame, which would become Regumi Studio. And both went to Switzerland to attend the eighth International Lesbian Information Service Conference in Geneva in March 1986, a conference whose roots stretch back to lesbian organizing at the 1975 UN conference in Mexico City.[74] The connections they made there with the handful of other Asian lesbians led to the creation of the Asian Lesbian Network (ALN), which held its first international meeting in Bangkok in 1990, followed by meetings in Tokyo, Taiwan, and the Philippines through the end of the 1990s.[75] As discussed in chapter four, responses to the article Sawabe wrote about her experience in Geneva, published in *Fujin kōron,* helped motivate the production of the highly influential *Stories of Women Who Love Women,* just after the establishment of Regumi Studio Tokyo in 1987.[76]

For Sawabe and Wakabayashi, then, spending time among lesbian feminists in the United States was transformative. It ultimately changed their understanding of themselves and their options for living true to their same-sex attraction and desire. In other words, how they made sense of their experiences abroad transfigured for them the meaning of "*rezubian*" and, in the process, their own identities. And, like other kinds of transfiguration, the ripples from their own experiences set in motion affected many other women.

The survey results in *Stories of Women Who Love Women* demonstrate, however, that Sawabe and Wakabayashi's own transnational understanding of what it might mean to be a *rezubian* was not unique. While there was nothing about the survey questions that directed respondents to talk about life in other countries, such references do come up. A number of responses name foreign films and fiction as helping respondents rethink their own same-sex desire, and some make comparisons between the respondents' experiences and lesbian life abroad. Other respondents incorporate foreign travel or living abroad into their understanding of what might be a good life as a lesbian. One woman explains that she and her girlfriend were considering having a child, and that her girlfriend wants to raise it in the United States, perhaps given the lack of models of lesbian mothers in Japan.[77] And another woman mentioned having gone to Europe the year before and being shocked by the "culture of lesbianism" at women's collectives, bookstores, and cafés she visited, an experience that—even though she "had already started living with a man"—helped her reinterpret feelings she had previously felt for women as romantic love.[78]

Hara (Minako) Minata was among the individuals contributing their experiences to *Stories of Women Who Love Women,* when they identified as a lesbian.[79] Hara would go on to become a prominent member of the *rezubian* community and to translate several important lesbian texts into Japanese.[80] From the age of eight to the time the volume was published, when they were around thirty, Hara had spent more time living abroad than in Japan, an experience indelibly shaping who they were as an individual, including their understanding of possibilities for expression of gender and of same-sex desire. Around 1963, when Hara was an elementary school student, they lived with their mother in East Lansing, Michigan, while she worked on a PhD. Hara, raised female but uncomfortable with female gender norms, found themself more comfortable at school there than they had been in Japan because there was little expectation expressed by those around them to dress and act femininely. Uncomfortable back in Japan both because of more rigid gender norms and because they felt ostracized on account of speaking English, they later followed their mother to the Philippines, where they finished high school. In Japan they often tried to hide their English ability, whereas in the Philippines most people around them spoke multiple languages so they felt normal being able to speak Japanese and English, as well as Spanish, which they began studying there.

Back in Japan around 1973, they heard about the *ribu* movement and went to a *ribu* space, but they did not get involved because they were disappointed with the absence of open discussion about homosexuality—Hara had only been attracted to women from a young age—and the lack of men, which made the space too feminine to feel comfortable. While Hara wanted to go to a university in Mexico for the country's similarities to the Philippines and to master a language their parents did not speak, this did not work out, so they chose to study in Spain. During the last week of their first year, they told a close friend at their dorm that they liked women, and the friend told the teachers and the dorm head, who temporarily removed Hara from the dorm, a crisis that solidified Hara's identity as a lesbian. Hara overcame this crisis, and, after receiving a degree, moved to London for a year, before returning in 1982 to Japan, where they have lived ever since.

Hara told me that the prejudice they experienced that cemented their sense of being a lesbian just happened to have occurred abroad. Yet, it is also true that experiences abroad, particularly at a young age, helped Hara see the extent to which it was possible to circumvent or simply ignore oppressive gender norms—and to experiment in both directions. In their early twenties when Hara was living in London, to connect with the feminine part of themself, they decided to have a child but not to get married, something they accomplished with a male friend/boyfriend. While some *ribu* activists had shown in the early 1970s this was possible in Japan, more flexible ideas about parenthood, womanhood, romantic relationships, and sexuality made this much easier in London.

In recent years, Hara has identified as X-gender (*ekkusu jendā*)—a relatively new local gender category that represents a rejection of identification as either male or female—and uses the masculine name Minata rather than Minako, the name they grew up with. Hara has continued to be passionately and intensely engaged in activism related to sexual and gender minorities in Japan, including playing a key role in the group Kyōsei Net, a national organization of sexual minorities, allies, and experts founded in 2008 with the goal of rooting out discrimination against members of sexual minorities and having a positive impact on local and national policies.[81]

As Hara's experience shows, even if differences do not always work out in an individual's favor, merely being away from the country and culture of one's birth—being an outsider for whom local norms do not exert as much pull—can be liberating. Even Japan, which Wakabayashi and Sawabe, as well as Tanaka, Takagi, and others have found oppressive for women in general and for *rezubian* in particular, has served as a liberating space for foreign women coming from relatively privileged backgrounds. Many foreign lesbians in the English-speaking lesbian community in the 1980s found freedom from blatant homophobia, sometimes coming from their own families, combined with the solidarity facilitated in expatriate communities and the special treatment often afforded Westerners, particularly white people from wealthy countries. For many Western lesbians, Japan was a relatively safe, clean place to live where they could earn a significantly greater amount of money than they could in their home countries.[82] While Western women were subject to some of the same sexism and ideas about female sexuality that oppressed (and oppresses) *rezubian,* the majority, those whose position involved teaching English at a university, language school, or a primary or secondary school in or near an urban area, were also somewhat protected from the worst of this by virtue of their ability to pull back into what is sometimes called an expatriate bubble. This bubble was itself certainly not free of sexism and homophobia, however. Unsurprisingly, then, in the 1980s most of the writing on oppression of lesbians in the English-language newsletter circulating in this community, nicknamed *The DD* (1986–1996) (figure 5.2), was focused on oppression within Western, primarily anglophone, culture, rather than the Japanese culture toward which most members of the English-speaking community had positioned themselves (and had been positioned) as outsiders.

Participation in the English-speaking lesbian community also offered the possibility of a temporary escape for lesbians from Japan with strong

Figure 5.2. Cover of *The DD*, no. 8 (December 1987).

transnational ties, particularly at the "Weekends," the lesbian retreats first held in 1985 as a joint venture of the Japanese- and English-speaking communities. While the Weekends provided a transnational space for women from Japan, from English-speaking countries, and elsewhere, language and cultural differences created a division between the Japanese- and English-speaking communities, something noted in the discourse of both communities.[83] The problem was not simply differences of language, communication style, and worldview. While most English-speaking lesbians would leave the retreats and return to the expatriate bubble in which some were able to identify themselves at least to a limited extent as lesbians while working at relatively well-paying jobs, most lesbians from Japan returned to lives in which that was not possible. Foreign women who chose to avoid or were unable to be as shielded by the expatriate bubble, however, might find themselves in a similar situation.[84]

And not all *rezubian*-identified women found life in the West liberating either. For instance, "Sano Rie," who was born in the mid-1960s and grew up in the center of the country along the Sea of Japan, had been interested in foreign countries from a young age.[85] While many of her friends in middle school had their eyes on Europe, she became interested in the United States, ironically perhaps, through karate. In the late 1970s, Sano was in her middle school's karate club, when an American karate team visited Japan. She befriended a team member and began to correspond with that person, who was from a state in the American South. Although she had not directly connected with the *rezubian* community yet, while still in school she had realized that she was attracted primarily to other women and from around 1980 she began reading the magazine *Allan,* neither for the beautiful boys nor for the representations of Western culture but for the correspondence from adolescent girls and young women who were romantically interested in other women.

After she finished high school, Sano's parents tried to convince her to go to a junior college and would not support her desire to go to a four-year university, so she chose to go study the travel industry at a technical college, hoping a career as a travel agent would take her far away from home, possibly abroad. After completing the program at the technical college, she found work at a travel agency, but the job was extremely taxing, and she quit within two years. Her next job was as a secretary for a large firm, and by chance she was offered the opportunity to work in their division in a major southern city in the United States, which she immediately accepted. While Sano was excited to be able to live in the state her American friend was from, her actual experience was miserable. People around her frequently made very homophobic comments, and she felt the need to remain silent and to pretend to be heterosexual. Since she expected the position to be temporary, she did not try to find a girlfriend or otherwise connect with the lesbian community in the region. Later, she was actually given the opportunity to make the position permanent and to apply for a green card, but she turned it down thinking that if she remained in the United States she would need to get married for the sake of her relations with her American coworkers. Thus, for Sano, life in the United States was actually more restrictive than life had been and would again be in Japan. And, indeed, when she returned to Japan a year and a half later, she came back with the audacity to say "no" to her parents and was able to resist their pressure to participate in matchmaking meetings with potential husbands, a pressure still commonplace in the 1980s.

Traveling from the Realm of Fantasy to the Real in *Shōjo* Manga Magazines

As in the *ribu* and *rezubian* communities, travel played a significant role in the queer *shōjo* manga sphere from the outset, yet similarly few individuals in this sphere were able to venture abroad themselves in the early years. Overseas travel and the lure of an exotic(ized) West had long been a presence in *shōjo* culture in general, not just through translated literature but also via transfigured elements of largely Western culture that have been woven into the fabric of *shōjo* dreams— and into the media through which they were expressed and exchanged.[86] In the 1970s, the pages of *shōjo* magazines—including *shōjo* manga magazines—were no exception. These publications frequently took readers on overseas journeys via text and image, much like the contemporary magazines aimed at young women discussed in the introduction to this chapter. This formed the immediate context of early *shōnen'ai* and other queer *shōjo* manga works.

Shōjo Comic—the magazine that initially serialized two landmark *shōnen'ai* works, Hagio Moto's *Heart of Thomas* and Takemiya Keiko's *The Song of the Wind and the Trees* beginning in the mid-1970s—was one of a handful of major magazines at the heart of *shōjo* manga culture in the 1970s.[87] Even if the bulk of its content was focused on Japan, scattered throughout its pages were also depictions of foreign travel—including living abroad as a Japanese girl—not just within manga narratives but also in features, in printed correspondence from readers and authors, and as the top prize in contests for readers at the beginning of the decade.

Although everyday life in Japan was a common theme of manga works, works set abroad, including those by Hagio and Takemiya, were also popular. Making it easier for readers to mentally transport themselves outside Japan, perhaps, some narratives featured contemporary adolescent Japanese girl protagonists. For instance, in Matsui Yumiko's "The Passionate Couple," appearing in April 1970, clever sixteen-year-old Chiaki wins a quiz contest and is awarded a trip to America.[88] She hopes to use the freedom she expects to experience there to find herself a boyfriend. While she and Larry, the handsome boy she meets there, part ways when the time comes for her to return to Japan, the closing lines of the narrative tempt readers to go on their own "grand adventure" abroad.[89] The following month, in Tani Yukiko's "My Lover Is Made in Japan," twin brothers, the evocatively named Alain and Delon, fight over the affections of Akiko, a diplomat's daughter of perhaps eighteen or twenty years of age who has come to stay at their family's home in Bern, Switzerland.[90] Running counter to the *akogare* for the West that is so common in this sphere, however, at the end of the story Akiko declares that, while she has enjoyed her experience abroad and the attention she has received from the two handsome young men, she ultimately prefers things that have been "made in Japan"—including potential romantic partners. Upon her farewell, her father gives her would-be suitors tickets to the ongoing Expo '70 in Osaka by way of expressing his gratitude for looking after her in his absence. Akiko then flies off into the sunset—with the suggestion lingering that they might soon meet her at the fair.[91] Regardless of where the protagonists choose to live in the end, such use of travel in these early 1970s works not only suggests and reinforces *akogare* toward Europe but also continues to evoke a certain glamour that cultural studies scholar Masafumi Monden associates with overseas travel in *shōjo* manga in the 1950s and 1960s.[92]

The reference to Expo '70 in "My Lover Is Made in Japan" may have been planted at the request of the magazine's editors. Held in Osaka, Expo '70 was a major touchstone of the postwar era and the first such event in Asia— much like the Tokyo Olympics six years prior. Expo '70 served, in the words of sociologist Yoshimi Shunya, as a "grand monument" confirming the successful "results of Japan's postwar economic recovery and high growth."[93] As a celebration of foreign cultures, Expo '70 was consonant with the general *akogare* for the West ubiquitous in this and other *shōjo* magazines at the time.[94] So too was the message to the Japanese population promulgated in the mainstream media that everyone should go to gaze upon the various pavilions and—in an often objectifying manner—upon foreign pavilion staff and visitors. It is unsurprising that the media boom surrounding Expo '70 reached the pages of magazines targeting *shōjo* readers. In addition to the reference in "My Lover Is Made in Japan," over the spring and summer of 1970, *Shōjo Comic* offered Expo-related raffle prizes to readers who returned survey cards and ran a number of Expo-related pictorials, gag manga, and other features, including a pictorial in which gender-bending celebrity Peter and five handsome young male singers, Tomita George and the group the Four Leaves, strike poses around the fairgrounds.[95] For many of *Shōjo Comic*'s target readers this opportunity to encounter foreign cultures and foreigners within the confines of Japan brought the foreign within reach. Osaka-raised writer Shimamura Mari (1956–2008), for instance, was positively obsessed with Expo '70 as a second-year middle school student and went around a dozen times with her friends over the six months of the fair.[96] Together they wandered around collecting autographs from "*gaijin*" (foreigners), asking foreign pavilion staff and tourists alike to "*sain purīzu*" (sign please), while musing about taking round-the-world excursions.[97]

Several times during this period, *shōjo* manga magazines made the dream of traveling abroad a reality for a select few readers. In a very early instance, the issue of *Shōjo Comic* containing the pictorial with Peter at Expo '70 also ran a two-page spread announcing a contest in which three lucky girls could win a Hawaiian holiday for designing the best mini-logo for the magazine.[98] Promotions for the contest would run the rest of the month, tempting readers with the chance to fly on a Japan Airlines jumbo jet and spend five days in exotic Hawai'i, or at least win a small travel bag emblazoned with the logo of Pan Am, Qantas, Scandinavian, or another airline with global allure. Photos of the three winners enjoying their Hawaiian *"vacance"* (*bakansu*)—a Japanese-French term conveying a romantic, relaxing time far away from home—appeared in the October issue.[99] Hawaiian vacations would be the top prize for two more years. Each time it was subsequently promoted with photographs of the three lucky *Shōjo Comic* readers swimming in the ocean, participating in luaus, and meeting local students. More so than characters in manga, such depictions of real girls going on real trips abroad, no doubt helped to gradually nudge the idea of an overseas holiday toward the realm of the possible for the magazine's readers.

Shōjo Comic was but one of dozens of magazines aimed at *shōjo* readers in the 1970s, a magazine, which, like many other *shōjo* manga magazines, sometimes published queer *shōjo* manga such as the aforementioned works by Hagio and Takemiya. As discussed in chapter two, it was not until the late 1970s, however, that *shōjo* magazines targeting specifically focused on queer *shōjo* manga or containing significant queer content appeared. The most significant of these in the 1970s and 1980s was, without a doubt, *June,* followed by *Allan* and, to a lesser extent, *Gekkō.* The lure of Western culture, particularly Western Europe and the United States, was a significant presence in these magazines from the start—although the line between fantasy and the real was seldom clear. In magazines like *June, Allan,* and *Gekkō,* as well as *dōjinshi* (fanzines), queer *shōjo* manga blurs with representations of and discourse about musicians, actors, and other flesh-and-blood Western and Japanese male celebrities. As noted in chapter two, in editorial and reader-submitted content in these magazines, particularly *Allan* and *Gekkō,* as well as in *dōjinshi,* foreign musicians and actors such as David Bowie, Queen, and the Vienna Boys Choir, as well as Rupert Everett and River Phoenix, are profiled and gossiped about alongside photos and drawings of beautiful boys and young men, most of whom are White. Some of these foreign performers—rock stars, boys' choirs, and actors alike—boarded planes themselves, planes that brought them in front of some of their fans in Japan. This made them all the more real for those young women who could afford and get (or get around needing) permission to attend their concerts or to show up to greet them and send them off at the airport—and, especially, for the young women who were able to follow them backstage or to their hotel rooms.

Further, letters and other contributions from readers published in *Allan, Gekkō,* and *June* sometimes reference the foreign in more concrete terms, even as travel abroad for most readers was as yet unrealistic. Editorial content as well occasionally offers descriptions of foreign countries and cultures in realistic terms, sometimes framed as travelogues. Most content offering glimpses of foreign life was focused on the United States and Europe and appears to have been intended as more titillating than informative.[100] The second issue of *Allan,* for instance, contains an article by a Japanese woman describing aspects of gay culture she witnessed walking around New York City—including gay publications for sale, gay bars, and gay couples, as well as male prostitutes walking around in the vicinity of Christopher Street.[101] A subsequent issue contains an interview with "K," who lived in Florida for a year and talks about differences in morals between the United States and Japan.[102] Reflecting an increasing visibility of readers interested in female–female romance in the magazine, a handful of articles on foreign culture focused on lesbians, including one with a cursory description of the contents of magazines about lesbians and gays that "you can get your hands on at train station kiosks" in Italy, and another offering a "London Lesbien [*sic*] Report" with information about Gay Pride Week and details about the contents of lesbian and feminist magazines, including a summary of and the author's own response to an article on lesbians in Japan.[103]

June, which devoted most of its space to manga and fiction, ran fewer such articles. One from the late 1980s, however, summarized the content of foreign gay magazines by way of a description of gay culture abroad.[104] Another offered a personal account of following the band the Communards around the U.K., attending a gay film festival, and experiencing other aspects of the gay scene in London.[105] Similar articles would appear in the magazine with somewhat greater frequency in the 1990s, when the magazine's tone began to change, perhaps in reaction to the decade's "gay boom," which entailed an increase in popular media depictions of realistic images of (predominantly male) homosexual culture, both foreign and domestic.

Artists Drawing Fans into Overseas Journeys

Even at the start of the 1970s, the lucky *Shōjo Comic* contest winners described above were not the only individuals in this sphere traveling overseas. Artists also began making trips abroad, voyages to Europe and elsewhere that would shape the works of some of the most popular *shōjo* manga artists in this period.[106] As for queer *shōjo* manga specifically, the artists' earliest foreign voyages postdate the initial use of Europe as a setting in influential *shōnen'ai* works and, thus, cannot be claimed as part of the genre's impetus, but these journeys contributed to the accuracy and amount of detail in the artists' renderings of cityscapes, buildings, and rooms, as well as the characters themselves. A few of these same artists would also share with their fans often romantic accounts of their trips via various media, allowing their readers to vicariously accompany them on their journeys.

The first overseas trip by prominent members of the new generation of *shōjo* manga artists, the Fabulous Forty-Niners, began on September 12, 1972, when Hagio and Takemiya set off for Europe with Takemiya's muse and Ōizumi Salon regular, Masuyama Norie, and popular *shōjo* manga artist and occasional Ōizumi guest Yamagishi Ryōko. The four roughly followed the path beaten in the 1960s by so many intrepid young adults before them, including the aforementioned Amano Michimi. They journeyed first by ship from Yokohama to Russia, then rode an overnight train to Vladivostok. From there, they abandoned the rails and continued by plane to Moscow and, after three days of sightseeing, flew on to Stockholm. Over the course of forty days, the four young women traveled from Russia to Stockholm and then on to Brussels, Paris, Versailles, Strasburg, Heidelberg, Lausanne, Rome, Venice, and Vienna, before returning to Japan by plane.[107]

Their journey might be described as a research trip and, thus, a *tabi* in the sense outlined at the top of this chapter. Hagio and Takemiya believed that, to "give life" to their own stories, they needed their drawings to convey a certain realism.[108] Such a professed desire for authenticity is, of course, more than a little ironic given the Occidentalist blurring of cultures that went into their creation of the *shōnen'ai* genre and specific works, discussed in the previous chapter. Nevertheless, they believed such firsthand research to be necessary. According to Masuyama, the artists had already visited all the bookstores in Tokyo that stocked foreign books and bought and read over what few they could find on the history of European clothing, accessories, wallpaper, furniture, and so forth. And they watched a lot of films. What they talked about after watching a film, in Masuyama's retelling, was not the plot so much as things like the way the cobblestones looked and the shape of the windows and the doorknobs. Realizing the limited resources available to them in Japan were insufficient, they decided to visit Europe and see things for themselves.[109] On this first trip, Takemiya explains, rather than simply taking in the beauty of famous sites, they spent their time examining things like how thick the walls were and how the doors opened, an interest reflected in the photos they took, and later in detail they incorporated into their manga.[110] Masuyama similarly recalls that they took photos not of landmarks but of "benches, boys, and windows," collectively forming a catalogue of objects for later reference.[111] While this research may have been the ostensible impetus for the trip, the voyage was also certainly motivated by the yearning that the artists themselves felt for the continent—a yearning instilled or reinforced by the same literature and films they transfigured into their early *shōnen'ai* works.

As noted above and as Ishida Minori points out in her discussion of this voyage, for young women to travel independently and with their own money to Europe so early in the postwar era was exceedingly unusual.[112] Thinking back about the trip and how young the four were—all around twenty-one years old—Masuyama herself seems impressed, if not a little boastful: "At a time when the dollar was at 360 yen, a trip to Europe that wasn't part of a tour— well, it was pretty reckless."[113] This trip by these particular women to Europe was all the more extraordinary because they went for professional reasons rather than sightseeing.[114]

Their absence did not go unremarked in the pages of *Shōjo Comic*. An editorial comment on the margin of the final installment in the second round of Takemiya's popular *bishōnen* (beautiful boy) manga *I Like the Sky!* (*Sora ga suki!;* 1971–1972)—about swindling scamp and Montmartre denizen Tag Parisien— refers to their departure and excitement about what kind of presents they will bring back.[115] On the last page of the story, Takemiya thanks readers for their support for the manga and bids them "*adiyū*" (adieu).[116]

Upon their return, rather than simply use what they observed as a resource for their manga, however, Takemiya and Hagio shared their travel experiences with *Shōjo Comic* readers via illustrated reminiscences about their experiences. That December, Takemiya published a one-page manga about the journey, which was followed by a five-part manga travelogue, drawn by turns and published in *Shōjo Comic* at the beginning of 1973[117] (figure 5.3). The artists drew themselves and their traveling companions in a gag manga style, and Europeans as well as the scenery in a more beautiful—if exaggerated—*shōjo* manga style.[118] The use of the gag style for artists to represent themselves is a common way for them to insert editorial comments, simultaneously placing themselves within the narrative and yet at a remove from the action. It also arguably helps bring the artists closer to fans since the style functions as sort of an aside to readers in a tone that shows the artists do not take themselves too seriously. Through this graphic travelogue, their fans were able to experience both fantastic and mundane aspects of the artists' journey vicariously, from savoring the

Figure 5.3. "Keiko-tan's European Travel Journal" (Kēko-tan no yōroppa ryokōki), *Shōjo komikku*, December 24, 1972, p. 206. Reproduced courtesy of Takemiya Keiko. © KeikoTAKEMIYA

tranquility of Vienna, to posing for photographs with beautiful boys dressed in traditional clothing, to calculating expenses in various currencies.

While a trip abroad, particularly to somewhere as far afield as Europe, might have seemed a once-in-a-lifetime experience for most people in Japan in the 1970s, that forty-day journey was just the beginning of Hagio and Takemiya's travels that decade. And they—and others in the same milieu—would continue to take their fans along for the ride, sharing with young readers travel tips as well as cultural information and observations, both mundane and serious.

The narratives they would go on to share of their journeys appeared in various media and took many forms, vacillating between the depiction of a fanciful Europe that their fans might only dream of visiting and of a tangible Europe that might soon be within their fans' reach.

In late 1973, Hagio went to Brighton, England, for around four months to study English. During her absence, long letters and brief notes from her to readers frequently appeared in *Shōjo Comic* between November of that year and the following February. In a full-page letter on November 18, Hagio tells readers about the language school where she was attending classes and the various nationalities of the students there. She mentions, for instance, being repeatedly scolded by her blue-eyed, chestnut-haired teacher for being unable to distinguish between *l* and *r* sounds (a common issue for first-language speakers of Japanese), as well as for her American-influenced pronunciation (due to American English being taught in Japanese schools). Hagio also praises England for the way individuals with a disability seem to feel able to participate freely in society, in contrast with Japan.[119] In subsequent correspondence, she talks about seeing the Vienna Boys Choir when the choir visited Brighton.[120] In addition, Hagio published a three-part manga diary, "Hello! England," in sister publication *Shōjo Comic Extra* between December and February, sharing with readers varied aspects of her time there.[121] In these manga, she provides cultural information about England, explaining, for instance, Guy Fawkes Day and the one-hour time change in spring and autumn, not done in Japan.[122] She also narrates an incident in which a young blond-haired man, perhaps trying to pick her up, tries out Japanese phrases on her: "*Konnichiwa!* . . . You're cute! . . . I'm hungry. Feed me."[123] And in the final installment, she recounts discussing with her landlady the topic of religion, which she links in her own mind with the Vienna Boys Choir.[124] She also reports attending a concert featuring British pop singer Cliff Richard, whom she characterizes—and draws—as moving flamboyantly on stage "like an insect or like a *danshokuka*."[125] Her description of Richard using "*danshokuka*," an old-fashioned word for male homosexual, is an early overt reference in this sphere to adult male homosexuality.

While Hagio was abroad, letters from readers asking for updates appeared in the magazine, and occasional editorial comments in the margins alerted readers about her status, most notably when she would be back to produce new manga for her fans. During Hagio's first time studying in England, a letter in *Shōjo Comic Extra* beseeches the magazine for information about her: "Why did Hagio-*sensei* go to England? Why? Why, oh why? Please tell me. Or I'll go mad with worry."[126] While the reader does not reveal her cause for concern, it may have stemmed from a desire to show what a passionate fan she was—or she may have simply been impatient for the next installment of *The Poe Clan*, Hagio's *bishōnen* manga hit in *Shōjo Comic Extra* about vampires.[127] An editorial comment in 1976 entitled "Viva! European Journey" appearing in the same magazine tells readers about a lengthy sojourn undertaken by Hagio and three other women, entailing a month wandering around Paris, followed by more time in Germany and the United Kingdom, during which time Hagio will be mulling over both her next work as well as the latest episode of *The Poe Clan*.[128]

In January of 1979, Takemiya published the book *Vienna Fantasy* (*Uīn gensō*), focused on a city she had by then visited at least three times.[129] *Vienna Fantasy* is largely a collection of Takemiya's manga and writing published in *shōjo* manga magazines over the previous three years, with a particular emphasis on the Vienna Boys Choir, to which Takemiya expressed a strong attraction. The bulk of the book is given to three manga works initially published in the *Shōjo Comic Extra*, *Ribon Deluxe* (*Ribon derakkusu*, 1975–1978), and *LaLa* between 1976 and 1978;[130] two of these narratives take place within the choir itself, while the third is focused on a young male Japanese piano prodigy studying piano at a prestigious music academy in Vienna. The remainder includes a full-color pictorial including photos of Takemiya in Vienna and the choir on a visit to Japan, and essays by Takemiya on her impressions of Vienna, a visit to the choir's home at the Palais Augarten, including an interview with Walter Tautschnig, the group's then director, portions of which were also published in *LaLa* in 1978. While the book vacillates between fantastic and touristic representations of Vienna and its boys' choir, it is far more of an homage to Vienna than a how-to guide to the city. And yet, even "Auf Wiedersehen," Takemiya's three-part manga fantasy about the handsome choirboys serialized in *LaLa* between June and August of 1978 and reprinted in the book, might have infected readers with the travel bug. Masuyama, for instance, speculates in a publication of Takemiya's fan club (discussed below) that reading "Auf Wiedersehen" led to an increase in the number of Takemiya's fans who "definitely want to go Vienna."[131]

Hagio and Takemiya would share their love of travel outside the pages of manga magazines as well. *Paper Moon* (*Pēpā mūn*, 1976–1983), a sophisticated text-heavy culture magazine aimed at older *shōjo* readers, and its manga-heavy counterpart *Grapefruit* (*Gurēpufurutsu*, 1981–1988), form one such site. Takemiya effusively recounts various travel experiences in Europe in a series of articles framed as "first-hand account[s] of Western Europe for *shōjo*" from 1978 to 1984, starting in the pages of *Paper Moon* and continuing on into *Grapefruit*.[132] The latter magazine also contained occasional travel narratives by other manga artists who drew queer *shōjo* manga, such as Aoike Yasuko.[133] Lending realism to Takeymiya's descriptions are her personal snapshots of scenery, people, and, quite often, Takemiya posing for the camera, whether in front of landmarks, enjoying a meal with Japanese traveling companions, or spending time with locals.

In the first of these, a four-page article with a dozen or so photographs, published in September 1978, Takemiya writes about spending time in a snowy Germany.[134] She opens with a dialogue between herself and an unnamed interlocutor that paints her as very much the cosmopolitan world traveler, one who is particularly bold and spontaneous in the context of the 1970s:

Interlocutor to Takemiya:	[You're going to] Europe again? Where to this time?
Takemiya to interlocutor:	Well . . . I never decide where I'm going.
Takemiya to readers:	It's true. I don't make "plans" on my journeys (*tabi*). If the plane arrives in Paris, first I find a cheap hotel, take a shower, flop down on the bed, and then think. So, what should I do? Head north or head south? Maybe I'll cut across Switzerland to Vienna. Maybe I'll go to Germany and eat sausages.[135]

In the body of the article Takemiya regales readers with descriptions of European train stations, restaurants, cafés, hotels, and *bishōnen*. She has come to Regensburg to see the local boys' choir, she tells readers. Given the popularity of European boys' choirs in Japan, particularly among *shōjo,* it is no surprise that, as Takemiya shares, from around ten years prior the choir had been receiving many letters from Japanese *shōjo* wishing to begin corresponding, and "many members of the choir have an interest in Japan."[136] Even if individual readers have not themselves corresponded with the choir, they are brought closer to those handsome choirboys by a reminder of the possibility thereof. Appended to the bottom of the article is a list of "boys [she] like[s]," including the boys' choirs of Regensburg, Göttingen, and Vienna, and twenty-something Dutch singer Heintje, whose "bright, hearty singing voice and [whose] smile, reminiscent of [her popular *bishōnen* character] Tag Parisien, [Takemiya] is unable to forget."[137] And thus in the space of four pages, a web of interconnections is spun between Takemiya, Europe, *bishōnen,* manga, travel, and *shōjo* readers.

In another photo-filled article published in April 1979, just three months after *Vienna Fantasy,* Takemiya recounts being in Vienna at Christmastime, which had been a long-standing dream of hers.[138] However out of reach such a trip might actually be for her readers, the article's title beckons them: "Won't You Come Spend Christmas in Vienna?" In a third article in the series the following year, Takemiya shares yet another effusive account of visiting her beloved

Vienna.[139] Her description in this piece of the relative deliciousness of the breakfast served on Scandinavian Airlines compared to Austrian Airlines, the simplicity of immigration procedures into Austria, and the welcome prepared for tourists at Vienna's airport, as well as descriptions of everyday experiences shopping and dining made such a trip seem almost mundane, at least for Takemiya.[140] As the series moved from *Paper Moon* into *Grapefruit,* Takemiya continued to offer romantic accounts of various journeys at different times of year, along with more practical pieces, such as a 1983 article in which she explains how to travel by rail "Off to the Country of Your Dreams in a Premier Class Sleeping Car" and another that same year introducing various kinds of European hotels, the choice of which can set "the tone of [your] *tabi,*"[141] together evoking the 1970s JNR campaign that opens this chapter.

While *shōjo* manga magazines and other commercial publications were the primary and most far-reaching medium through which artists and fans were able to interact in this period, fan clubs and events offered a more intimate avenue for artists like Hagio and Takemiya and their fans to communicate with one another. It is difficult to overestimate the passion of *shōjo* manga artists' most devoted fans, those most likely to make an effort to go to events and actively participate in fan clubs. At an autograph-signing event for Takemiya held at a Mitsukoshi department store in Tokyo one summer in the mid-1970s, hundreds of fans gathered for a chance to meet the artist and get her autograph, lining up on the sidewalk well before the store opened.[142] Sixteen-year-old Murata Junko, an ardent fan in attendance that day, soon thereafter began to write Takemiya fan letters on a daily basis, she has claimed. This passion about—or obsession with—the artist led to an invitation to visit Takemiya at her home. Murata would go on to run the Takemiya fan club Sunroom (Sanrūmu) at the request of Masuyama Norie.[143] In keeping with Takemiya's wishes, the club's name was borrowed from the title of Takemiya's earliest *shōnen'ai* work "In the Sunroom"[144]—giving a clear emphasis to Takemiya's *shōnen'ai* manga over her many other works. From around the beginning of 1976, the club, which had as many as two thousand members while Murata was in charge, sent these members handmade zine-like newsletters, titled *Sunroom,* roughly each quarter; it also sent them monthly bulletins, titled *Wind (Kaze),* named after Takemiya's *The Song of the Wind and the Trees.*[145] Through the club, Takemiya maintained very close ties with her most devoted fans, in particular through producing letters, articles, and illustrations for its publications, along with taking part in fan club events at which she sometimes discussed her journeys to Europe.

Given the publications' titles, it is unsurprising that they are permeated with images of Takemiya's mostly European *bishōnen* characters—some drawn by the artist herself, some by her fans—not infrequently placed in romantic or erotic situations with other *bishōnen*. References to journeys to Europe taken by Takemiya, Masuyama, and other artists are also scattered throughout issues of *Sunroom*, including textual descriptions, drawings, and photographs.[146] The October 1977 issue contains a message from *shōjo* manga artist and Ōizumi guest Sasaya Nanae, who had just been summoned back from Paris, where she had been about to watch a bunch of "*homo* porno" films in rapid succession, and to which she planned to soon return to spend the rest of the year.[147] Masuyama penned several reports for *Sunroom* on European journeys she went on with Takemiya, including a report in September 1977 whose title addresses readers, "To You Who Are Going to Go on a Journey," which ends with the invitation "Won't you all go to Europe yourselves!?" and another in July 1978—in an issue with an actual photograph of Takemiya pasted on the cover—subtitled "European Travel Diary for *Shōjo*."[148] Both of these, then, encourage readers to envision the possibility of going on their own voyages to Europe. The same issue contains a transcript of a discussion between Takemiya, Masuyama, and Murata at the club's recent summer meeting, enabling even fans who were unable to attend to hear more about the trip, this time from Takemiya's perspective.[149]

Across the two pages following Masuyama's earlier travel narrative is an illustrated chart detailing the "presents" that Takemiya has "assiduously collected" during her recent European excursion for the fan club's members, to be distributed in the first of multiple such giveaways.[150] These gifts were set to be parceled out one item at a time to 150 or more members who submitted a postcard indicating which item they desire. Among these gifts are inexpensive souvenirs Takemiya may have purchased to give away, such as bookmarks, picture postcards, cheap jewelry, and a cloth badge emblazoned with "Österreich" (Austria). Most items, however, are simply mundane bits and pieces from a long journey around Europe—items any individual might have picked up or purloined as mementos of such a trip—including coins from various countries, small jars of jam from breakfast, wrapped sugar cubes, and fancy paper napkins, as well as dross like used metro tickets, a paper chopsticks wrapper emblazoned with "Lufthansa," and a used eye mask from a long-haul flight, along with Takemiya's used Eurail Pass and plane ticket booklet. The names of the lucky recipients—ultimately amounting to 184 of the over 500 members who sent in postcards—were announced in the subsequent issue.[151] For fervent fans, the provenance of these items would have endowed them with intangible value, a luster rendering the items the stuff of fantasy—particularly the rare items emblazed with Takemiya's name. Yet, placing in her fans' hands this tangible evidence of an actual journey would simultaneously have rendered such a journey all the more real for them, if not yet realistic.[152]

By the end of the 1980s, however, such journeys had indeed become realistic for an increasing number of Takemiya's fans, many of whom were now in their twenties—the age bracket constituting the largest group of females traveling overseas from Japan that decade, as noted at the outset of this chapter. And in 1989, a decade after she offered readers a *Vienna Fantasy*, Takemiya acknowledged that a significant number of her fans were either following or wanted to follow in her footsteps with the publication of a travel guide, *Still in the Mood for Europe* (*Kibun wa ima mo Yōroppa*). While containing information of use to readers planning actual trips abroad, it contains enough anecdotes and diversions to be of interest to armchair travelers as well. Even Takemiya is equivocal about what sort of book it is.[153] The book borrows its name from the title of one of the articles in Takemiya's travel series in *Grapefruit* some five years prior, and, in fact, overlaps significantly with the content of the series, which was the volume's inspiration.[154] In the preface, after bracing her readers for how inconvenient things in Europe can be compared to Japan, Takemiya recommends that readers eschew the protective bubble provided by Japanese group tours and put the necessary effort into making their own arrangements, preferably as they move from city to city, town to town, to get a taste of real, everyday daily human interactions in the places they visit.[155] And both the travel tips and tales she shares in the guide promote precisely that kind of travel, evidently with the hope that readers will learn from both her successful experiences and the mistakes she had made on her, by then, seven trips to Europe.[156] In the brief afterword, she expresses pleasure at the thought that the book—an invitation to take not a "fun, dreamlike" holiday but rather a *"tabi"* offering "real experiences"—might embolden some readers to make their own European journeys.

Fans Inspired to Embark Overseas

In the opening chapter of *Still in the Mood for Europe,* Takemiya Keiko writes as if her readers' desire to travel abroad was likely sparked by an article they had read or something they had seen on TV.[157] This inspiration may have included any combination of magazines aimed at young women or girls, such as *An An* or *Grapefruit,* TV programs or films, such as *Death in Venice* or *These Special Friendships,* or manga, such as Takemiya's "Auf Wiedersehen" or Hagio's *The Poe Clan*. What is clear is that by the time they reached an age at which they could travel abroad, fans of Takemiya and other readers of queer *shōjo* manga a generation younger than the Fabulous Forty-Niners, namely, those who grew up in the 1970s and 1980s had been exposed to an increasing amount of media promoting foreign travel, not to mention advertising within that media. And by the 1980s, this media treatment would include discourse touting the appeal of study abroad, which was increasingly targeted at young women at this time. Shimamura Mari, whose enthusiasm over Expo '70 is discussed above, herself went to the United States as a high school exchange student in 1973, a time when studying abroad was quite unusual, particularly for girls and young women.[158] Indeed, while elite young men constituted the vast majority of those from Japan who studied abroad through the 1970s, over the course of the 1980s and 1990s this was reversed to the extent that by the end of the last century, young women made up over two-thirds of students from Japan at foreign educational institutions.[159]

It is clear that the lure of the West—in particular, Western Europe and the United States—is so imbricated in the fantasy worlds of *shōnen'ai* and other queer manga of the 1970s and 1980s that it cannot but have inspired or reinforced among some fans an interest in the West, if not a desire to travel there. Nevertheless, given the media and broader cultural context just noted in which queer *shōjo* manga of this period was situated, it is impossible to tease apart the specific role that the consumption of queer *shōjo* manga played in young women's interest in foreign travel. Few fans of queer *shōjo* manga of this generation I have encountered have linked their interest in or yearning for a specific foreign country primarily to consumption of queer *shōjo* manga or related magazines. Some women with whom I have spoken, however, have named queer *shōjo* manga texts or related magazines as influencing their interest in Western culture, but usually just as part of an array of influences and experiences.

In a conversation I had with "Yamamoto Tomiko" and "Ikeda Taeko," friends born in the early 1960s who grew up in a medium-sized city in central Japan, the pair's passionate consumption of *shōnen'ai* manga in middle school blurred with their fandom of foreign male celebrities—echoing the discourse in *Allan* and *June*, as well as in some *dōjinshi*, discussed in chapter two.[160] Although both attended concerts of foreign musicians in Osaka and Nagoya, while still in middle school Yamamoto managed to use her then broken English to meet and socialize with band members, reinforcing an infatuation with American popular culture that ultimately led to her spending significant time in the United States in her twenties. Though Yamamoto has had romantic and sexual relationships with American men, she ultimately decided to live in Japan. She eventually married a Japanese man, had a child, and seems quite content with her life—albeit a life that has been unconventional, including a large contingent of foreign friends residing both in Japan and abroad, and returning to school in middle age to start a new career. The other woman, Ikeda, has traveled overseas but did not experience the same overwhelming yearning for the West. She too married and has children.

While both women, Yamamoto in particular, are critical of sexual discrimination in Japan, neither links her interest in Western culture directly with a critique of gender roles. Still, both used the imaginary Western space of early *shōnen'ai* manga as the site in which they initially explored sexuality in contravention of expectations for girls their age. And Yamamoto translated her infatuation with the West both into seeking experiences abroad and into sexual relationships with men that were not sanctioned by norms that, at the time, dictated young women should remain virgins until marriage. In the end, however, the strongest assertion I can make about these women is that their consumption of queer *shōjo* manga in their youth is part of a larger matrix of fandom and other interests tied to both their defiance of existing sexual norms and their varying degrees of interest in travel to the West.

Another woman with whom I spoke does directly link her queer *shōjo* manga consumption with her interest in Western culture and eventual move abroad, but in her case too, it is not an entirely straightforward connection. "Takeda Hiroko" was born in the mid-1960s and grew up reading queer *shōjo* manga while she was still in elementary school. These texts, including both male–male and female–female romance, were given to her by her uncle, whom she identified as gay.[161] She was particularly fond of Takemiya's manga. It is through Takemiya, she says, that she became interested in Germany and Austria and in studying German, which she began in middle school. While her favorite of Takemiya's works, including *The Song of the Wind and the Trees*, are set in France, she explained when I pressed her that it was not Takemiya's manga but the artist's interest in the Vienna Boys Choir that led to Takeda's own interest—an intriguing blurring of cultures akin to what can be seen in the origins of the *shōnen'ai* genre.[162] Takeda added that she must have also seen programs on television about these countries that helped foster this interest of hers. When Takeda was around twenty, she began to date an older man from a German-speaking country who was teaching German at the language school she attended. Eventually she married him and moved to that country. While Takeda had been living back in Japan for several years to earn a professional qualification in her field while I was doing research in 2009, enabling me to meet her, she was planning to return to Europe soon. She also told me that she had given up reading manga of any kind after getting married because her husband did not understand her interest, but clients back in Japan had gotten her into reading it again.

Based on Takeda's own narration of her life, her consumption of queer *shōjo* manga and related texts set her on a path that led to her study of German, her marrying a German-speaking man—although, at over a decade older than Takeda, he was not the kind of beautiful youth idealized in her favorite manga—and her eventual move to Europe. Such a direct correspondence between queer *shōjo* manga consumption and the choice to travel, even live abroad appears unusual. Like other women of her generation, however, Takeda grew up surrounded by discourse about travel and the appeal of Western culture. Her own qualification that television programs may have helped stimulate her interest in German-speaking countries and the German language suggests this to be the case. It seems, then, that while *shōjo* manga played a larger role in steering Takeda toward her attraction to a foreign culture than was the case for most women, Takeda—like other young women of her generation—read these manga in the context of a broader romanticization of the West in other streams of popular discourse, discourse in which travel to the West was increasingly presented as a possibility.

The word "travel," observes James Clifford, "has an inextinguishable taint of location by class, gender, race, and a certain literariness."[163] We can see all of these elements variously folded into the individual and collective experiences discussed in this chapter. Gender, in particular—or rather the challenging of gender norms—is central to all of these travels. Many of the women discussed in this chapter and with whom I have spoken in the course of researching this book engaged in travel for the purpose of transnational feminist or lesbian-feminist networking as part of a more overt questioning of gender *and* sexual norms. Thus, unsurprisingly, to Clifford's list I would add "sexuality." And here I am pointing not just to same-sex desire, but also to the erotic subjectivity that was central to Tanaka Mitsu's theory of *ūman ribu*, as well as to the broader ties between women's sexuality and reproduction that was so crucial to much *ribu* thinking and activism. Clearly, though, same-sex desire has played a significant role in many of these trips, such as the young women tourists whose experiences were published in *June* and *Allan,* for whom overseas gay male culture as well as beautiful men in general were the object of their curious and erotic gaze, and women like Wakabayashi Naeko and Sawabe Hitomi, who found in the United States new ways to be a *rezubian*. While these two women's ability to undertake their trips cannot be pulled apart from Japan's role as an economic superpower built on exploitation of former colonies, given Sawabe's and Wakabayashi's status as culturally and racially Other in a still economically and politically dominant United States, their experiences in the 1970s contrast sharply with the privileged, often exploitative "gay tourism" that has drawn the attention both of academics in the past several decades and of segments of the travel industry for still longer.[164]

In this we see that race and ethnicity are also at issue. Indeed, in spite of the then (and still) prevalent belief that Japan is culturally homogeneous in terms of race, ethnicity, and class, we can see all of these operating in the travel experiences discussed above. While I did not encounter noteworthy evidence in these spheres of a "faith in the racial and cultural superiority of the West," that Karen Kelsky found in women's "internationalist narratives" in the 1980s and 1990s,[165] in the *ribu* and *rezubian* spheres there was a clear sense that women in Japan had things they could learn from women in the United States and elsewhere. This, though, was balanced somewhat by efforts to promote the exchange rather than one-way flow of information, such as by the translation group at Ribu Shinjuku Center as well as by individuals like Takagi Sawako, who asserted that women in the West had an "obligation" to know about women in Japan and elsewhere in Asia. Race was at issue on a personal level as well, such as in Wakabayashi's romantic interest in an African American woman, which she saw as part of a larger discovery of herself as a racially "Asian" woman. It was because of this "Asianness" that a handful of women at an international conference of lesbians in Switzerland dominated by White women from Western countries decided they needed to forge stronger ties among themselves and founded Asian Lesbian Network (ALN)—although a sense of communal Asianness did not prevent expression of racism directed against ethnic Koreans in Japan by some Japanese women at the ALN meeting in Tokyo.[166] In the queer *shōjo* manga sphere, the idealization of Western beauty found in *shōnen'ai* manga as well as related magazines sometimes led to travel to Europe and romantic or sexual relationships with foreign men. It is critically important to remember, however, that this positioning of Western boys and men as either real or fictive erotic objects was, in effect, staking a claim to an erotic subjecthood on the part of these women.

Finally, while some 90 percent of Japanese people are said to have considered themselves as middle class by the 1970s, this number is belied by disparities of income and education.[167] This limited the ability to make overseas trips to individuals who, in most of the early cases, had either the financial means or sufficient time to work and save for overseas travel, or who were connected in ways that led to official invitations and sponsorship. Takagi, for instance, was able to attend the Mexico City conference because someone at the American Embassy in Tokyo saw her on an NHK television program about *ribu* after she returned to Japan from her 1973 trip to the United States, leading to an official invitation through the UN, covering most of her expenses.[168] Moreover, many of the travelers discussed above were somewhat unusual in that they held—or were in the process of obtaining—four-year degrees.[169] Although for women, a bachelor's degree did not open up many career options in the 1970s and 1980s, some of the few it did make possible involved higher wages and status and greater opportunities to travel. Such generally unremarked class distinctions were, however, mitigated by a stronger yen and a stronger Japanese economy during the peak of the economic bubble in the 1980s, as overseas travel became more affordable for an increasing portion of the population.

In the early 1970s, even as Japanese National Railways was encouraging young women to go on *tabi*, or journeys, within Japan through which they were expected to discover selves that were both women and authentically Japanese, individuals in the *ribu, rezubian,* and queer *shōjo* manga spheres were boarding trains and boats and planes to the West and back. While the motivation driving these women's voyages did not always overtly include self-discovery, travel by women in all these spheres was transformative. As we have seen in this and preceding chapters, some of this transformation was produced through the transfiguration of words, texts, and practices. Sometimes, it was individuals themselves who were, in effect, transfigured through travel. As a direct result of their own personal border crossings and encounters with people from other cultures, some women came to new understandings of themselves—as feminists, as lesbians, as women. And the ripples of change these women set in motion played a role not just in (re)shaping their self-understandings and their communities in Japan, but also the self-understandings of other women in and outside of these spheres.

Afterword

In *Transfiguring Women in Late Twentieth-Century Japan,* I have historically con-
textualized and examined the *ūman ribu* movement, the *rezubian* community, and the queer *shōjo* manga sphere in Japan in the 1970s and 1980s from
various perspectives and at various scales. My juxtaposition of these three
incongruous if overlapping communities of women and adolescent girls has
made it possible for me to explore the responses across broad swaths of the
population to restrictive gender and sexual norms during this period and to
demonstrate their cumulative cultural and social effects. Moreover, in placing the queer *shōjo* manga sphere alongside the *ribu* movement and *rezubian*
community, I have positioned artists and fans as cultural activists regardless of
how they saw themselves, thus pushing for a more expansive understanding
of activism in the late Shōwa era.

As I have shown, as part of their efforts to redefine the category "women"—
efforts building on the countless layers of transnational engagements folded
into contemporary Japanese culture—these women and girls "transfigured"
words, texts, practices, and even themselves. Notably, I have established that
the engagement of the women and girls in these spheres with Western culture
was not a matter of merely looking to the West for liberation, resulting in a
simple imitation of Western culture. Rather, their engagements with and, of
course, transfiguration of elements from Western culture was generally mea-
sured, and they were always situated within a Japan whose culture had long
been (re)constructed via such engagements. Thus, these local engagements
with the seemingly foreign were themselves *not* foreign to the Japanese culture of the time nor to those inhabiting it. And, indeed, for these women and
girls, indeed for anyone in Japan in the period upon which this book focuses,
the "foreign," particularly "Western culture," was only foreign to a degree.

Ribu activists, members of the *rezubian* community, and readers and artists
of queer *shōjo* manga did not succeed in wholly recasting gender and sexual
norms for women and girls during the 1970s and 1980s. I would argue, however, that these communities played a significant role in unsettling the idea

that girls should grow up to become "good wives and wise mothers," helping open up life-course options while strengthening and expanding women's
social and sexual agency. Their efforts also forged room for a greater diversity
of gender and sexual expression.

In the course of this study, I have introduced and demonstrated the util-
ity of the heuristic concept of "transfiguration" as an alternative to existing
framings of cultural change resulting from transnational movement of things,
of ideas, and of people. Existing concepts such as localization, glocalization,
transculturation, and hybridization, are largely premised on colonial or post-
colonial conditions or suggest unidirectional cultural flows, making them
ill-suited for a study of Japan in the late Shōwa era. Transfiguration—which I
have defined as a change in form in transit from one culture to another—calls
on us to seek out and understand processes of change as well as the acts and
actors engaged therein, with an eye toward the workings of power. Transfiguration also calls on us to examine the far-reaching ripples of change that it sets
in motion, which can extend in any direction.

In the early 2020s, some fifty years after the *ribu* movement, the *rezubian*
community, and the queer *shōjo* manga sphere emerged and more than thirty
years beyond the primary focus of this book, it is difficult to isolate the long-
term, far-reaching effects of the activities of these communities, including acts
of transfiguration, that occurred during the period I have examined here. This,
in no small part, stems from ongoing transnational engagement and transfiguration that continue to (re)shape what it means to be a woman in Japan.

Nevertheless, the queer *shōjo* manga sphere, particularly the boys love
(BL) genre, offers a fascinating window onto ripples of change engendered by
young women's acts of transfiguration in Japan in the 1970s that now extend
far beyond the borders of Japan—and even reach back again. BL is the contemporary incarnation of the genre *shōnen'ai,* which, as the chapters in this
volume repeatedly illustrate, is in part a product of the transfiguration in Japan
of a field of discourse comprised of twentieth-century European fiction and
films depicting male homosocial, sometimes homoerotic, bonds in European
settings. By the 1980s, this genre, then widely called *yaoi,* was beginning to
be discovered by fans abroad. Over the first two decades of the 2000s, BL has
developed into a truly global phenomenon with a broader fandom that seems
to include a higher proportion of queer fans and creators than in Japan.[1]

As I noted in chapter two, *shōnen'ai* fostered the liberation of ostensibly
cisgender heterosexual adolescent girl readers in Japan from restrictive patriarchal gender and sexual norms. And, as I have repeatedly made clear, I believe
the genre and its fandom have been an integral part of cultural changes that

have made it easier for girls and women to deviate from restrictive norms—norms the genre has also helped to loosen up. In addition, as a kind of ripple effect, it has made life easier for LGBT people in Japan. Prominent gay critic and writer Fushimi Noriaki, for instance, has recently described the "sympathy [toward gay men] and market power" of women who grew up reading BL as "indispensable" to the gay liberation movement of the 1990s and beyond.[2] Lesbian activist and scholar Mizoguchi Akiko has more broadly described BL as a progressive force that "moves the world forward."[3]

BL has had similarly progressive cultural effects outside Japan. It has, for instance, helped well-educated heterosexual young female fans in the Philippines rethink masculinity, femininity, and heterosexual romance; made it easier for heterosexual young men in urban China to be affectionate with one another; increased cosmopolitan young women's acceptance of LGBT people in India; and created opportunities for young female fans in Russia to explore their attraction to one another via romance shifting from online to physical fan spaces such as anime festivals and "cosplay" (costume play) events in which some "crossplay" as male characters.[4] Crossplay based on BL as well as the female–female romance genre *yuri* at cosplay as well as drag events in Israel, for example, has made it easier for trans women, trans men, and others to come to a fuller understanding of their gender identities.[5] Moreover, BL-specific and BL-related fan events, often encompassing *yuri*, have been springing up around the world since early this century, including Yaoicon, first held in San Francisco in 2001, BLush (originally Lights Out), first held in Manila in 2004, and Y/CON (originally Yaoi Yuri Con), first held in Lyon in 2011 and now held in Paris. Through such examples, we can see that a creative fan sphere spawned in Japan through transfiguration that sought to challenge gender and sexual norms has had ripple effects that continue to shape gender and sexuality far beyond Japan's shores.

While the earliest BL media consumed abroad were translated commercial and amateur works from Japan, works that continue to be popular, fans and others overseas quickly began creating BL locally, including comics, prose fiction, and even live-action TV series, including the now wildly popular Thai "series *wai*," that is "Y series," a label derived from the Japanese word *yaoi*. In so doing, they have been transfiguring the genre. In the Sinosphere, "*danmei*," originally a label for BL from Japan derived from the Japanese word "*tanbi*," now encompasses locally produced works, Japanese works, and anglophone fan fiction sometimes called "slash."[6] Outside the Sinosphere, *danmei* along with series *wai*, for instance, are sometimes treated as distinct genres, which themselves have continued to circulate beyond their places of origin.

In Vietnam, for instance, imported *danmei* fiction, locally called *"đam mỹ,"* is distinguished from Japanese BL and has led to the local creation of works in this genre.[7] Meanwhile, in the Philippines, some gay male fans see a clear distinction between "Thai BL," that is, series *wai,* which they consider to be "fundamentally Thai," and "Japanese *yaoi,*" which they see as inferior.[8] Such new forms and new understandings of BL demonstrate that, as Thomas Baudinette argues, the genre has been "dislocated" from Japan, which is no longer necessarily seen by fans as the sole origin or center of BL.[9]

Such "dislocated," or local, forms of BL—transfigured in various cultural contexts and often blurring with other forms of female-oriented male homoerotic fiction and LGBT media—is also flowing back into Japan. Fans of the Japanese *Dynasty Warriors* video game series, based on the Chinese legends of the Three Kingdoms, have been circulating their fan works between China, Taiwan, and Japan, for instance.[10] In recent years, I have also personally witnessed artists from places like Ireland and the United States selling their own BL at fan conventions in Japan. And some Indonesian BL artists have recently been pursued by Toranoana, a company best known for publishing and distributing *dōjinshi,* to license their work for publication in Japanese.[11] And by the end of the 2010s, Asian BL media, particularly the aforementioned Thai series *wai* TV dramas, had begun to see popularity in Japan, evidenced by articles and special features in and special issues of women's and general interest magazines as well as national newspapers, some of which situated this popularity as part of a global phenomenon whose roots can be traced back to Japan.[12] This kind of circulation and cross-cultural communication and exchange, whether or not Japan is included in the mix, unsettles the idea that fandoms exist as country- or even language-specific "discrete cultural communities."[13]

The BL currently being created in Japan is not unaffected by global shifts in fan practices and tastes either. If in some fan spheres overseas it has become increasingly difficult to distinguish the originally anglophone genre slash fiction and BL, there are signs that borders may be breaking down within Japan as well. In 2015, for instance, manga publisher Fusion Product began publishing a series of "Omegaverse BL" anthologies, blending BL with the Omegaverse genre. Omegaverse—which emerged in the 2000s from anglophone slash fiction in a world in which BL had already established a global fanbase—is an alternative universe genre in which males can get pregnant and that explores complex power dynamics between "alpha," "beta," and "omega" characters.[14] These character types reverberate with but are not the same as the *seme* (top) and *uke* (bottom) roles associated with Japanese BL. The cover of Fusion Product's *Omegaverse Project* volume one is adorned in large letters with *"BL wa, shinka suru,"* that is, "BL is evolving."[15] And, no doubt, through its transfiguration by Japanese fans and artists, so too is the Omegaverse genre. "Omegaverse BL" or "Omegaverse manga," defined by one English-language anime and manga distributor's website as "a sub-genre of Yaoi,"[16] is now being translated and published commercially in English. As of early 2023, the online manga rental site *Renta!* lists over 1,400 Omegaverse works available across BL and other manga categories—illustrating how porous borders have become.

In spite of increasingly blurry borders between BL and slash, BL is still widely seen as Japanese in origin. As I have shown in this volume, however, such an understanding elides the transnational engagements and acts of transfiguration that led to its creation as *shōnen'ai* in the early 1970s and its ongoing transformation. As I have argued throughout this book, such acts of transfiguration by women and girls of ostensibly foreign images, texts, practices, and the like in the 1970s and 1980s have led to a more expansive understanding of what it means to be a woman in Japan. And as I have made clear in this afterword, the effects of these transfigurations continue to ripple outward—and sometimes back again.

Notes

Chapter 1: Introduction

1. Uno, "The Death of 'Good Wife, Wise Mother'?", 303.
2. Eckert, "Language and Adolescent Peer Groups," 115.
3. Welker, "From Women's Liberation to Lesbian Feminism in Japan."
4. Kelsky, *Women on the Verge,* 4.
5. Inoue Teruko, *Joseigaku to sono shūhen,* 178–181.
6. Fujieda, "Nihon no josei undo," 3.
7. Yonezu Tomoko, interview with author, June 2009.
8. Cf. Setsu Shigematsu, who in her *Scream from the Shadows* leaves "*onna*" untranslated to emphasize the distinction between the Japanese term and "woman."
9. Muto, "The Birth of the Women's Liberation Movement in the 1970s," 158.
10. This manga was reissued as Takemiya, "Sanrūmu nite."
11. Takemiya, "Josei wa gei ga suki?"; Mizoguchi, "Mōsōryoku no potensharu"; cf. Nakano, "Yaoi hyōgen to sabetsu."
12. *Anīsu,* "Komyuniti no rekishi," 35. See also Welker, "Beautiful, Borrowed, and Bent."
13. Histories of these bars can be found in Shiba, "Shōwa rokujū [*sic*] nendai rezubian būmu"; Toyama, "Dansō no reijin no jidai," 209–221.
14. Saijō et al., "Zadankai."
15. For example, *Anīsu,* "Komyuniti no rekishi," 29.
16. Hirosawa and Rezubian Ripōto-han, "Rezubian ripōto," 151, 157.
17. Hirosawa and Rezubian Ripōto-han, "Rezubian ripōto," 284.
18. *Anīsu,* "Komyuniti no rekishi," 72.
19. Lunsing, "Gay Boom in Japan."
20. Seike, "Japan's Demographic Collapse."
21. Funabashi and Kushner, *Examining Japan's Lost Decades.*
22. Prough, *Straight from the Heart,* 43; Kinsella, *Adult Manga,* chapter four.
23. Sawabe, "The Symbolic Tree of Lesbianism in Japan," 17.
24. Binnie, *The Globalization of Sexuality,* 37–42.
25. Matt. 17:2 (King James Version).
26. Rowling, *Harry Potter and the Philosopher's Stone,* 100.
27. Gaonkar and Povinelli, "Technologies of Public Forms," 386.
28. Gaonkar and Povinelli, "Technologies of Public Forms," 387, 392–394.
29. Gaonkar and Povinelli, "Technologies of Public Forms," 386.
30. Gaonkar and Povinelli, "Technologies of Public Forms," 394, 396.

31. My use of "ripples of change" gestures to *Ripples of Change,* a documentary about a young Japanese woman who traveled to New York City and, as an effect of that voyage, came to discover the *ribu* movement almost twenty years after it faded from public discourse.

32. Appadurai, "Grassroots Globalization and the Research Imagination," 5.

33. Ortiz, *Cuban Counterpoint,* 98, 102–103.

34. Pratt, *Imperial Eyes,* 6.

35. See, for example, Bhabha, *The Location of Culture.*

36. Mizoguchi, Saeki, and Miki Sōko, *Shiryō Nihon ūman ribu shi;* Ribu Shinjuku Sentā Shiryō Hozon Kai (hereafter RSSSHK), ed., *Ribu Shinjuku Sentā shiryō shūsei 1: Ribu nyūsu: Kono michi hitosuji;* RSSSHK, ed., *Ribu Shinjuku Sentā shiryō shūsei 2: Bira hen;* RSSSHK, ed., *Ribu Shinjuku Sentā shiryō shūsei 2: Panfuretto hen.*

37. *30-nen no shisutāfuddo.*

38. Tsing, "Worlds in Motion," 11.

39. Levy, "Introduction," 1.

40. For example, Curran, Sato-Rossberg, and Tanabe, *Multiple Translation Communities in Contemporary Japan.*

Chapter 2: Trajectories

Epigraph: From the lyrics to "Fināre," in *Myūzukaru "Onna no kaihō" 1975,* by the *ribu* theater group Dotekabo Ichiza, in Dotekabo Ichiza no Bideo o Mitai Kai (hereafter DIBMK), *Dotekabo Ichiza "Myūzukaru 'Onna no kaihō' 1975" bideo/DVD kaisetsusho,* 16.

1. Gordon, *The Only Woman in the Room,* 123; Inoue, *MacArthur's Japanese Constitution,* 221–222, 238–265.

2. See, e.g., Sievers, *Flowers in Salt;* Mackie, *Feminism in Modern Japan;* and Kano, *Japanese Feminist Debates.*

3. Dower, *Embracing Defeat,* 357.

4. Gordon, *The Only Woman,* 10; cf. Koikari, *Pedagogy of Democracy,* 33. My thanks to Rio Otomo for bringing Sirota's experience to my attention.

5. Gordon, *The Only Woman,* 106–118 passim.

6. Koikari, *Pedagogy of Democracy,* 35.

7. Inoue, *MacArthur's Japanese Constitution,* 266.

8. Gluck, "Introduction," xliv.

9. Sasaki-Uemura, *Organizing the Spontaneous,* 17; see also 16–18, 23–26.

10. Sasaki-Uemura, *Organizing the Spontaneous,* 17–18.

11. Brinton, *Women and the Economic Miracle.*

12. Sasaki-Uemura, *Organizing the Spontaneous,* 198–202. Sasaki-Uemura notes here that the generation that came of age during the protests in 1959 and 1960 had a powerful influence on Zenkyōtō.

13. Schieder, *Coed Revolution;* Shigematsu, *Scream from the Shadows;* Onnatachi no Ima o Tou Kai, *Zenkyōtō kara ribu e.*

14. *Myūzukaru "Onna no kaihō" 1975.* The publication being celebrated was Ribu Shinjuku Ribu Shinjuku Sentā Shiryō Hozon Kai, *Ribu Shinjuku Sentā shiryō shūsei* (3 vols.).

15. DIBMK, *Dotekabo Ichiza,* 1; Ribu Shinjuku Sentā Shiryō Hozon Kai, ed. *Ribu Shinjuku Sentā shiryō shūsei: Ribu nyūsu: Kono michi hitosuji* (hereafter, RSSSHK, *Ribu nyūsu*), iv.

16. She describes her project and her arrest in Rokudenashiko, *Watashi no karada ga waisetsu?!*

17. DIBMK, *Dotekabo Ichiza,* 1. On discourse on infanticide (*kogoroshi*) within *ribu,* see Shigematsu, *Scream from the Shadows,* 23–28; and Castellini, *Translating Maternal Violence,* especially chapter 4.

18. DIBMK, *Dotekabo Ichiza,* 15.

19. See Asakawa's comments in *30-nen no shisutāfuddo.*

20. See Mackie, *Feminism in Modern Japan,* 147.

21. Yonezu's personal history and the history of Thought Group S.E.X. are summarized from Yonezu Tomoko, interview with author, June 20, 2009; Yonezu, "10/21 o keiki toshite Shisō Shūdan Esu Ī Ekkusu sōkatsu," 175; and Yonezu, "Mizukara no SEX."

22. Shigematsu, *Scream from the Shadows,* xxxii.

23. See section three in Tanaka Mitsu, *Inochi no onnatachi e;* and Tanaka Mitsu, "Mirai o tsukanda onnatachi," 279–283.

24. Tanaka, *Inochi no onnatachi e,* 125–126; Reich, *Sei to bunka no kakumei.*

25. Tanaka, *Inochi no onnatachi e,* 141. In this volume I translate the Japanese term "*sei,*" which can mean gender, sex, or sexuality, as "sex(uality)" to reflect its open-endedness.

26. Tanaka, *Inochi no onnatachi e,* 141.

27. For two nearly identical versions of the single-page flier, one handwritten, one typed, see Tanaka Mitsu, "Erosu kaihō sengen," 1970 (p. 7 and p. 8). While these versions circulated under the banner of Group Fighting Women, I am following Ribu Shinjuku Sentā Shiryō Hozon Kai, ed. *Ribu Shinjuku Sentā shiryō shūsei: Bira hen* (hereafter, RSSSHK, *Bira hen*), in assigning Tanaka authorship.

28. Tanaka Mitsu, "Benjo kara no kaihō." While this version circulated under the banner of Group Fighting Women, I am following RSSSHK, *Bira hen,* in assigning Tanaka authorship.

29. The year before saw hundreds of anti-war rallies around Japan. See *AMPO,* "October 21, Japan's Mightiest Anti-War Day," 4.

30. E.g., *Asahi shinbun,* "Yarimasu wa yo, 'onna kaihō.'" For an overview of Group Fighting Women, see Saeki Yōko, "Gurūpu Tatakau Onna (Tōkyō)"; Yonezu, interview.

31. *Asahi shinbun,* "Ūman ribu, 'dansei tengoku' ni jōriku."

32. Akiyama Yōko, *Ribu shishi nōto,* 8, 16–18, 23.

33. Piercy, "Idai na kūrī."

34. Ikegami's personal history is based on Ikegami Chizuko, interview with author, July 24, 2009.

35. See Ikegami, *Amerika josei kaihō shi,* iv.

36. Friedan's *The Feminine Mystique* (1963) was translated into Japanese the year Ikegami entered university: Friedan, *Atarashī josei no sōzō.* Ikegami recalls finding information on American feminism at the "American Culture Center" (Amerika no Bunka Sentā), which may be the American Center (Amerikan Sentā) in Tokyo, and at Agora, a women's resource center founded in the mid-1960s (Ikegami, interview).

37. Aki Shobō Henshūbu, *Sei sabetsu e no kokuhatsu.*

38. Ikegami, *Amerika josei kaihō shi.*

39. See *30-nen no shisutāfuddo.*

40. Miki, "Ribu gasshuku."

41. *Ribu* retreat steering committee, cited in Miki, "Ribu gasshuku." The ellipses are original.

42. *30-nen no shisutāfuddo.*
43. Miki, "Ribu gasshuku."
44. Tanaka, "Mirai o tsukanda onnatachi," 312.
45. All sixteen issues are reproduced, with minor edits to protect contributors' privacy, in RSSSHK, *Ribu nyūsu.*
46. On the history of Ribu Shinjuku Center, see RSSSHK, *Ribu nyūsu,* ii–iv, and a listing of the groups that used the space in ibid., iv–v.
47. RSSSHK, *Ribu nyūsu,* ii.
48. Norgren, *Abortion Before Birth Control,* 59–62.
49. Josei Kaihō Undō Junbi Kai, "Yūsei hogo hō kaiaku soshi e mukete no apīru"; Gurūpu Tatakau Onna, "Chūkin taisei to wa nani ka." See also Norgren, *Abortion Before Birth Control,* 65.
50. Nagano, "Women Fight for Control," 15–16.
51. Nagano, "Women Fight for Control," 17.
52. Norgren, *Abortion Before Birth Control,* 63.
53. RSSSHK, *Ribu nyūsu,* v.
54. Norgren, *Abortion Before Birth Control,* 63.
55. Chūpiren stands for Chūzetsu Kinshi Hō ni Hantai shi Piru Kaikin o Yōkyū Suru Josei Kaihō Rengō (Women's liberation collective opposing the prohibition of abortion and demanding the elimination of the prohibition on the pill). See Norgren, *Abortion Before Birth Control,* 66; and Akiyama Yōko, *Ribu shishi nōto,* 121–138.
56. *30-nen no shisutāfuddo;* Akiyama Yōko, "Piru wa hontō ni yoi mono na no ka?"
57. *30-nen no shisutāfuddo.*
58. Akiyama, *Ribu shishi nōto,* 137–138; Ōtani Junko et al., "Zadankai."
59. Atsumi, "Goals of Feminism in Modern Japan."
60. Yonezu, interview. Soshiren is an abbreviation of "82 Yūsei Hogo Hō Kaiaku Soshi Renraku Kai" (Network to prevent the worsening of the Eugenics Protection Law [in] 1982). While, as of 2023, Soshiren continues to advocate legal access to abortion as well as laws that do not encourage the use of abortion for eugenic purposes, it also focuses on issues such as women's health. See Soshiren's website: http://www.soshiren.org/.
61. See *Feminist International* [Japan], "A Brief History of 'Feminist.'" 104.
62. *Feminisuto,* "Joseigaku no akebono."
63. *Feminisuto* Henshūbu, "Onna ga, gakumon ya rekishi o, kakikae hajimeta."
64. Inoue Teruko, *Joseigaku to sono shūhen,* 230.
65. Inoue, *Joseigaku to sono shūhen,* 231.
66. Inoue, *Joseigaku to sono shūhen,* 230–231.
67. Nihon Joseigaku Kenkyūkai "Purojekuto 20," "Anata e."
68. See, e.g., Miki, "Ribu tamashī no nai joseigaku nante."
69. Inoue, *Joseigaku to sono shūhen,* 229.
70. Yonezu, interview. Soshiren's history links it to *ribu,* but it does not prominently use the term *"ribu"* about its activities.
71. *30-nen no shisutāfuddo.*
72. Hirosawa, "Nihon hatsu no rezubian sākuru," 111–112; *Shūkan bunshun,* "Jūshūnen o mukaeta rezu gurūpu hyakunin," 41–42. In the case of discrepancies between Hirosawa and *Shūkan bunshun,* I have relied on Hirosawa because of her personal investment in recording the story for posterity.

73. E.g., *Shūkan josei,* "Watashi wa 'rezubian no kai' (kaiin 80-nin) no kaichō-san."

74. *Shūkan josei,* "Watashi wa 'rezubian no kai' (kaiin 80-nin) no kaichō-san"; Hirosawa, "Nihon hatsu no rezubian sākuru," 112. She likely used the term *"resubian,"* rather than *"rezubian,"* in the early 1970s. This distinction is discussed in chapter three.

75. Suzuki Michiko, "Rezubian no kai o shusai shite jūnen," 340.

76. Suzuki Michiko, "Go-aisatsu," and "Rezubian no kai," 340.

77. Hirosawa, "Nihon hatsu no rezubian sākuru," 113.

78. Suzuki, "Rezubian no kai," 340.

79. This criticism is discussed in *Subarashī onnatachi,* "Zadankai 'Rezubian ōi ni kataru,'" 15–16.

80. Suzuki, "Go-aisatsu."

81. Welker, "From Women's Liberation to Lesbian Feminism in Japan."

82. See chapter five.

83. Asakawa, "Ribusen de deatta 'subarashī onnatachi.'" 5–6. Izumo Marou also recalls *rezubian* within *ribu* taking issue with Tanaka. See Izumo et al., "Nihon no rezubian mūvumento," 59–60.

84. *Subarashī onnatachi,* "Zasshi no hakkan ni attate," and "Zadankai 'Rezubian ōi ni kataru,'" 6. See *Subarashī onnatachi,* "Zadankai 'Rezubian ōi ni kataru'" for a transcript of the second roundtable. The survey results were included in a supplement to *Subarashī onnatachi* due to Asakawa Mari's objections: "'Resubian ni kan suru ankēto' shūkei repōto"; see especially, 6–8; see also Izumo et al., "Nihon no rezubian mūvumento," 59–60. On the number of issues sold, see Blasing, "The Lavender Kimono."

85. Suzuki Michiko, "Sōkan no kotoba," 2. The publication date is not indicated in the magazine itself; it comes from Suzuki, "Rezubian no kai," 344. On the financial difficulty leading to the group's demise, see Hirosawa, "Nihon hatsu no rezubian sākuru," 117; Hirosawa erroneously indicates the magazine was first published in 1984.

86. Wakabayashi, "Onna no nettowāku no naka de ikiru," 17, 21–25.

87. Wakabayashi, "Onna no nettowāku no naka de ikiru," 25. The article she translated is probably Barbara, "Rezubian, kono onnatachi wa nani mono da?"

88. Wakabayashi, "Onna no nettowāku no naka de ikiru," 31.

89. Izumo et al., "Nihon no rezubian mūvumento," 60; *Anīsu,* "Komyuniti no rekishi, 1971–2001," 55.

90. Sugiura, "Nihon ni okeru rezubian feminizumu no katsudō," 144, 162–163.

91. Izumo Marou, personal communication, July 9, 2009.

92. The group's name involves a layered play on words based on the fact that "dyke" rendered into Japanese is homophonous with the word for carpenter (*daiku*), as well as the expression "Sunday carpenter" (*nichiyōbi daiku*), meaning do-it-yourselfer.

93. Sugiura, "Nihon ni okeru rezubian feminizumu no katsudō," 162–163; Izumo et al., "Nihon no rezubian mūvumento," 58–62; Sawabe, "The Symbolic Tree of Lesbianism in Japan," 8–9.

94. *Za daiku,* "Hikari guruma sōkan-gō."

95. Sugiura, "Nihon ni okeru rezubian feminizumu no katsudō," 163.

96. Mackie, "Kantō Women's Groups," 108.

97. Blasing, "The Lavender Kimono"; Sawabe, "The Symbolic Tree of Lesbianism in Japan," 9; Mackie, "Kantō Women's Groups," 107–108.

98. Sawabe, *"Onna o ai suru onnatachi no monogatari* o meguru hyōgen katsudō," 39–40; Hisada, "Genki jirushi no rezubian," 122–123; Wakabayashi, "Onna no nettowāku," 27–28. For a transcript of the slideshow narration, see Sugiura, *Nihon no rezubian komyuniti,* 85–97.

99. Hisada, "Genki jirushi no rezubian." On a more recent controversy over privacy in response to the 2008 publication by Iino Yuriko of *Rezubian de aru "watashitachi" no sutōrī,* which draws heavily on *Regumi Communications,* see Regumi Sutajio Tokyo, "Iino Yuriko-san chosho *Rezubian de aru 'watashitachi' no sutōrī* ni tsuite."

100. Hisada, "Genki jirushi no rezubian," 122.

101. Hirosawa, "Sekai rezubian kaigi ni sanka shite"; Sawabe, *"Onna o ai suru onnatachi no monogatari* o meguru hyōgen katsudō," 52–54.

102. Bessatsu Takarajima, no. 64, *Onna o ai suru onnatachi no monogatari.* Many articles published under Hirosawa Yumi and other names in this volume were also penned by Sawabe, encouraged by the publisher to make the volume appear more of a collective project (personal communication, 2006).

103. Though largely absent from discussions of *rezubian* history, beginning in 1968 with her *Onna to onna,* self-identified *"resubian"* photographer Kiyooka Sumiko (1921–1991) published a series of books of essays and photos on lesbians in Japan and elsewhere.

104. Tenshin, "Media ga nakatta koro no baiburu."

105. See, e.g., Lunsing, *Beyond Common Sense,* 232–233.

106. I borrow "English-speaking lesbian community" from Peterson, "English Language Journal in Japan." This is more accurate than two other terms sometimes used: "foreign lesbian community" and "international lesbian community," which, respectively, overlook the involvement of women from Japan and the exclusion of women from abroad who do not speak English.

107. Blasing, "International Feminists of Japan," 109; Audrey Lockwood, personal correspondence, April 2009; Peterson, "Rezubian in Tokyo," 129–130; Blasing, "The Lavender Kimono."

108. *Anīsu,* "Komyuniti no rekishi," 40; Linda M. Peterson, interview with author, April 26, 2009; Izumo et al., "Nihon no rezubian mūvumento," 63.

109. Peterson, interview; Izumo et al., "Nihon no rezubian mūvumento," 62.

110. Van Dyke, *Dyketionary.*

111. Peterson, interview. Peterson and her partner, the late Amanda Hayman, from the U.K., founded an English-language newsletter called *The DD* in 1986, which members of the English-speaking lesbian community produced several per year and sometimes in abbreviated form during Weekends through the early 1990s, and sporadically thereafter through 1996.

112. Hara Minata, interview with author, July 21, 2009.

113. Peterson, interview.

114. Izumo et al., "Nihon no rezubian mūvumento," 63.

115. Welker, "Flower Tribes and Female Desire."

116. See Welker, "Flower Tribes and Female Desire," and Lunsing, "Japanese Gay Magazines and Marriage Advertisements."

117. Hirosawa, "Nihon hatsu no rezubian sākuru," 117.

118.   E.g., Itō Bungaku, "Ibu & Ibu banzai!" Several other *homo* magazines attempted to reach out to the *rezubian* community, including *The Gay* (*Za gei,* 1981–2005), published by gay rights advocate Tōgō Ken (1932–2012). In the early 1980s *The Gay* included a *rezubian* section.

119.   Nawa, "Rezubian bā no yoru to yoru," 102–103; Sawabe, "The Symbolic Tree of Lesbianism in Japan," 11–12. The bar was named after Funazaki, *Ribonnu.*

120.   *Anīsu,* "Komyuniti no rekishi," 44–45; Shinjuku ni-chōme rezu bā no Māzu bā (MARSBAR), http://www.or2.fiberbit.net/mars21/information.html (accessed December 5, 2017).

121.   Sei Ishiki Chōsa Gurūpu, *Sanbyakujū nin no sei ishiki,* 52–53, 57–58; *Anīsu,* "Komyuniti no rekishi," 75.

122.   *Anīsu,* "Rezubian no rekishi," 48. According to Kittredge Cherry, the first lesbian disco party in Japan was Space Dyke, which began in 1983; see Cherry, *Womansword,* 116.

123.   Tomita, "Rezibian bā ga toransu josei no nyūjō kyohi, shazai."

124.   *Anīsu,* "Komyuniti no rekishi," 74–75; Sei Ishiki Chōsa Gurūpu, *Sanbyakujū nin no sei ishiki,* 53, 57–58.

125.   See, e.g., Lunsing, "Gay Boom in Japan."

126.   Kakefuda, *"Rezubian" de aru to iu koto.*

127.   See, e.g., Yamashita, "Dōseikon gōhōka, 8-wari kōteiteki"; *Asahi shinbun,* "(Yōron chōsa no torisetsu) dōseikon meguri ishiki, kanjiru 'Shōwa' to henka."

128.   Sawabe, "The Symbolic Tree of Lesbianism in Japan," 6, 10, 17, 25.

129.   See, e.g., Ito, "Manga in Japanese History," 26–32.

130.   Tezuka, *Ribon no kishi;* Yonezawa, *Sengo shōjo manga shi,* 50–53.

131.   Matsutani et al., "Tezuka Osamu to Takarazuka Kageki"; Fujimoto, *Watashi no ibasho wa doko ni aru no?,* 130.

132.   Yonezawa, *Sengo shōjo manga shi,* 52. See also Fujimoto, *Watashi no ibasho,* 130.

133.   Takahashi, "Opening the Closed World of *Shōjo Manga,*" 127. See also Yonezawa, *Sengo shōjo manga shi,* 24–27.

134.   Takahashi, "Opening the Closed World of *Shōjo Manga,*"117, 118, 122.

135.   Takahashi, "Opening the Closed World of *Shōjo Manga,*" 122.

136.   Takahashi, "Opening the Closed World of *Shōjo Manga,*" 122–124, 128.

137.   Hagio Moto, interview by Fujimoto Yukari, in her *Shōjo manga damashī,* 188–189; Hagio, "The Moto Hagio Interview," 151; Matsutani et al., "Tezuka Osamu to Takarazuka Kageki," 18–19.

138.   Takahashi, "Opening the Closed World of *Shōjo Manga,*" 122–129.

139.   See, e.g., the *Yurīka* special issue: "*Shōjo* manga."

140.   Mori Mari, *Koibitotachi no mori;* Mizuno, *Faiyā!.*

141.   Minegishi, "Jūjiro."

142.   Ishida Minori, *Hisoyaka na kyōiku,* 142–143.

143.   Welker, "Drawing Out Lesbians."

144.   The writing making this case, sometimes drawing on the artists' own comments, is extensive. For representative scholarship, see McLelland et al., *Boys Love Manga and Beyond.*

145.   Mizoguchi, "Male–Male Romance by and for Women in Japan," 49.

146.   Takemiya, "Sanrūmu nite."

147.   Hagio, "Jūichigatsu no gimunajiumu."

148. Hagio, *Tōma no shinzō;* Takemiya, *Kaze to ki no uta.* The popularity of Takemiya and Hagio and their *shōnen'ai* masterpieces is evidenced by fan correspondence published in *Bessatsu shōjo komikku, Shūkan shōjo komikku,* and *Petit Flower (Puchi furawā).*

149. Takemiya, *Takemiya Keiko no manga kyōshitsu,* 244; *Josei sebun,* "Ima sugoi ninki no shōjo komikku sakka," 199; Masuyama and Sano, "Kyabetsu batake no kakumeiteki shōjo mangakatachi"; Hagio, "The Moto Hagio Interview," 160, 161.

150. In her recent memoir about the Ōizumi Salon years, *Ichido kiri no Ōizumi no hanashi,* Hagio distances herself from Takeyama and Masuyama and distances her work from *shōnen'ai* itself. While Hagio's memoir sheds light on her relationship with Takemiya and Masuyama and her past and current thoughts on her own work, based on the history I map out in this book, it has not changed how I position her work—nor, to my knowledge, has it significantly changed how fans or scholars see her work.

151. Masuyama and Sano, "Kyabetsu batake," 169; Hagio, "The Moto Hagio Interview," 160–161.

152. Terada, "70-nendai enkyori shōjo manga no jidai," 159.

153. Aoike, *Ibu no musukotachi;* Kihara, *Mari to Shingo;* Yamagishi, *Hi izuru tokoro no tenshi.*

154. Yoshida, *Banana Fish;* Akisato, *Tomoi.*

155. For instance, Fujimoto includes *Banana Fish* and *Tomoi* in the *shōnen'ai* lineage in her overview of gender-bending *shōjo* manga, *Watashi no ibasho,* 146, 148–149.

156. Komikku Māketto Junbikai, *Komikku Māketto 30's fairu,* 32.

157. See Komikku Māketto Junbikai, *Komikku Māketto 30's fairu;* and Komikku Māketto Junbikai, *Komikku Māketto 40-shūnenshi.*

158. Comiket, "Komikku Māketto 97 afutārepōto."

159. Yonezawa, "Manga/anime no kaihōka, Komike tte nani?" 15–16.

160. On the survey taken at the first Comic Market, see Shimotsuki, *Komikku Māketto sōseiki,* 12.

161. See, e.g., Shimotsuki, *Komikku Māketto sōseiki,* 21–22, 45–46, 64–68, 76–83, 96–99.

162. Shimotsuki, *Komikku Māketto sōseiki,* 20–21, 77. The anime was first screened in Shibuya, Tokyo, in 1974. See *Program: Jūichigatsu no gimunajiumu.*

163. Itō Gō, *Manga wa kawaru,* 215.

164. Quoted in Itō Gō, *Manga wa kawaru,* 216.

165. Itō, *Manga wa kawaru,* 215; Yonezawa, "Manga to dōjinshi," 41.

166. See e.g., the *dōjinshi* titled *Island* by the circle Abnorm in which readers are invited to dress up as a photograph of David Bowie in a jockstrap (pp. 35–36) and an illustration by "Layla" (dated November 8, 1977) of Jimmy Page and Robert Plant kissing (p. 23).

167. Misaki, "2007-nen no josei-kei parodi dōjinshi no dōkō," 176.

168. Takahashi Yōichi, *Kyaputen Tsubasa.*

169. Nishimura, *Aniparo to yaoi,* 32–33; Itō, *Manga wa kawaru,* 227.

170. Nishimura, *Aniparo to yaoi,* 32.

171. Nishimura, *Aniparo to yaoi,* 36.

172. Yonezawa, *Sengo ero manga shi,* 131.

173. Sagawa, "Bungaku to goraku no aida o ittari, kitari," 327.

174. Following the 1996 demise of the original *June,* its publisher produced magazines incorporating the *June* name almost continuously, including in *Comic June,* which ran from 1998 to 2013. Scholar Mori Naoko asserts that, given its distinct editorial focus, *Comic June* is

a "completely different magazine" from the original *June*. See her *Onna wa poruno o yomu,* 89n14,

175. Sagawa, "Bungaku to goraku no aida o ittari, kitari."

176. Sagawa, "Bungaku to goraku no aida o ittari, kitari," 328.

177. Ishida, *Hisoyaka na kyōiku,* 204.

178. Ishida, *Hisoyaka na kyōiku,* 222.

179. Welker, "Lilies of the Margin," 50, 61n25. Hagio, *Pō no ichizoku, Pō no ichizoku: Haru no yume, Pō no ichizoku: Yunikōn,* and *Pō no ichizoku: Hanazono.*

180. Nanbara Shirō, interview with author, June 2005.

181. For example, *Aran,* June 1983, 179; Bessatsu Takarajima, no. 64, *Onna o ai suru onnatachi no monogatari,* 109.

182. Welker, "Lilies of the Margin"; Welker, "Flower Tribes."

183. Ishida Hitoshi, "Sūji de miru *JUNE* to *Sabu,*" 170.

184. For example, *Aran,* "Ninki dōjinshi purezento."

185. Yano Keizai Kenkyūsho, "'Otaku shijō' ni kan suru chōsa o jissen 2017-nen," and "'Otaku shijō' ni kan suru chōsa kekka 2011."

186. Hester, "*Fujoshi* Emergent."

187. Galbraith, "*Moe* Talk."

Chapter 3: Terminology

Epigraph source: Foucault, "Nietzsche, Genealogy, History," 139.

1. Valentine, *Imagining Transgender,* 5.

2. Scott, "The Evidence of Experience," 778, 779.

3. Scott, "The Evidence of Experience," 792.

4. Foucault, "Nietzsche, Genealogy, History," 140.

5. Foucault, "Nietzsche, Genealogy, History," 142.

6. Flotow, "Feminist Translation," 79. See also chapter four in this volume.

7. Bhabha, *The Location of Culture,* 122.

8. Miller, "*Wasei eigo,*" 123, 124.

9. *Asahi shinbun,* "Ūman ribu, 'dansei tengoku' ni jōriku." I am drawing here from an interview and correspondence with Akiyama Yōko (March 2009), Akiyama Yōko, *Ribu shishi nōto,* 35–50; and Saitō, "'Ūman ribu to media' 'ribu to joseigaku' no dansetsu o saikō suru." Saitō's archival research, like mine, turns up no evidence of "*ūman ribu*" prior to Ninagawa's. See Saitō, "'Ūman ribu to media' 'ribu to joseigaku' no dansetsu o saikō suru," 5.

10. Although printed in the Tokyo edition and not distributed nationwide, this series would have been read by people with cultural influence, including the journalists who would write about the movement, as well as current and future *ribu* activists, in the Tokyo region.

11. Arakawa, *Gairaigo jiten,* s.v., "*ūman.*" While this dictionary may not provide a record of the precise moment when a word entered the language or appeared in print, in the case of "*ūman,*" as well "*feminizumu*" and "*feminisuto,*" its approximation is sufficient for my purposes.

12. English was compulsory at middle schools by the early twentieth century for both boys and—except from 1941 to 1945—girls; it became compulsory in high school in 1947.

See McKenzie, "The Complex and Rapidly Changing Sociolinguistic Position of the English Language in Japan," 271.

13. *Asahi shinbun,* "Buttsubuse 'dansei shakai'"; Bender, "The Women Who'd Trade in Their Pedestal for Total Equality." I found no earlier examples of *"ribu"* and "women's lib," respectively, in a search of the full-text electronic archives of the *Asahi shinbun,* the *Yomiuri shinbun,* or the *New York Times.*

14. The Redstockings were founded in 1969. The group's name represents a reclamation of "bluestocking," a term sometimes disparagingly applied to feminist intellectuals decades earlier and adopted by the early twentieth-century Japanese feminist group Seitōsha (Bluestocking Society) and their journal, *Seitō* (Bluestocking, 1911–1916).

15. Akazuka, "Shin go '70: Rabu yori ribu o!"

16. Suzuki Tadashi, "Zenkyōtō wa 'ribu' ni manabu."

17. Suzuki, "Zenkyōtō wa 'ribu' ni manabu," 184.

18. Suzuki, "Zenkyōtō wa ribu ni manabu," 185.

19. Akiyama, interview; Larry Taub, interview with author, April 2009; Akiyama, *Ribu shishi nōto,* 15–24, 139–153 passim; see also *Asahi shinbun,* "Ūman ribu, 'dansei tengoku' ni jōriku." While *ribu* may have entered Japanese prior to 1970, I have encountered no evidence thereof.

20. "Memo," in Mizoguchi, Saeki, and Miki, *Shiryō Nihon ūman ribu shi,* vol. 1, 272–273. See also *Onna kara onnatachi e* [Osaka], "Gurūpu dayori."

21. S.F., "Ribu FUKUOKA no koto," 290. While I was unable to track its introduction, the use of the women's power symbol—combining an ankh, indicating women, and a fist—likely came into circulation in the *ribu* movement early on for similar reasons. See figures 2.1 and 5.1.

22. Tanaka Mitsu, interview with author, July 2009. Multiple versions of this pamphlet were published, for example, Tanaka, "Josei kaihō e no kojinteki shiten," and Tanaka, "Benjo kara no kaihō." Note that I treat the pamphlet "Josei kaihō e no kojinteki shiten" (A personal perspective on women's liberation) as an early draft of Tanaka's "Benjo" pamphlet.

23. See., for example, Inoue et al., "Henshū ni attate."

24. Josei Kaihō Undō Junbi Kai (hereafter JKUJK), ed. *Josei kaihō undō shiryō 1,* 48.

25. The articles are McAfee and Wood, "Bread and Roses," published in Japanese as "Pan to bara"; Piercy, "The Grand Coolie Dam," published as "Idai na kūrī: Josei"; and Charlotte Bunch-Weeks, interview with Kurita Reiko.

26. *Asahi shinbun,* "Ūman ribu, 'dansei tengoku' ni jōriku."

27. Bunch-Weeks, interview, 42. Firestone and Koedt, *Notes from the Second Year,* favored "women's liberation" and "feminism"/"feminist." Whether *uimenzu ribu*/women's lib came from the interview itself or it was added by the transcriber of the interview is unclear.

28. Saitō, "'Ūman ribu to media' 'ribu to joseigaku' no dansetsu o saikō suru," 7. The distinction between *"josei," "onna,"* and *"fujin"* is discussed in chapter one.

29. Arakawa, *Gairaigo jiten,* s.v., *"feminizumu," "feminisuto"*; Matsui, Sone, and Ōya, *Kindai yōgo no jiten shūsei,* vols. 10, 12, 23, 28, 29, 30, 32, 34, 35, s.v., *"feminizumu"*; Matsui, Sone, and Ōya, *Kindai yōgo no jiten shūsei,* vols. 12, 36, s.v., *"feminisuto."*

30. *Yomiuri shinbun,* "Mi no mawari katakana no kotoba: Feminisuto."

31. Akiyama, *Ribu shishi nōto,* 58–59; Firestone and Koedt, *Notes from the Second Year.*

32. Kageyama, "Ūman pawā."

33. *Yomiuri shinbun,* "Saidoraito: Ūman pawā."

34. Tanaka, "Josei kaihō e no kojinteki shiten," 5. See also *Asahi shinbun*, "Yarimasu wa yo, 'onna kaihō'"; *Yomiuri shinbun*, "Kobushi, kyōsei roku jikan, ūman pawā sōkesshū"; *Shūkan bunshun*, "Zenbei ūman pawā no shidōsha wa Nihonjin no tsuma."

35. Saitō, "'Ūman ribu to media' 'ribu to joseigaku' no dansetsu o saikō suru," 1. While *ribu* activists and scholars looking back generally concentrate on the ridicule to which the movement was subjected, Saitō overgeneralizes academic writing on the subject. Inoue Teruko, for instance, is more nuanced in *Joseigaku to sono shūhen* than Saitō acknowledges.

36. Tanaka, interview.

37. *Radikaru Ribu Gurūpu tsūshin*, "Dai-san no sei," 111.

38. Tanaka, interview; Tanaka, *Inochi no onnatachi e*, 310–313. I borrow "disorderly" in my translation of this title from Setsu Shigematsu (personal correspondence, April 2010).

39. Miki Sōko, interview with author, July 2006.

40. *Asahi shinbun*, "Ūman ribu" (November 5, 1970); Lloyd, *Ūman ribu no hyaku nen*, and *Suffragettes International*.

41. On Tanaka's theory of *ūman ribu*, see Shigematsu, *Scream from the Shadows*; and Tanaka, *Inochi no onnatachi e*.

42. Nakanishi, *Onna no hon'ya (uimenzu bukkusutoa) no monogatari*, 161. The work in question is Mizoguchi, Saeki, and Miki, *Shiryō Nihon ūman ribu shi*.

43. Nakayama, *Gendai Nihon josei no kibun*, 15.

44. See, for example, Tabei, "Watashi no aruitekita michi," 48.

45. Atsumi et al., "Hachi nin no feminisuto ni yoru nyū feminisuto sengen."

46. *Feminisuto*, "Josei bunka no fukurami o!"; see also Mackie, *Feminism in Modern Japan*, 161.

47. Issues included interviews with figures such as Erica Jong and Yoko Ono, and articles about women's studies at US universities.

48. *Feminisuto*, "Josei no sōzō to feminizumu."

49. Dales, *Feminist Movements in Contemporary Japan*, 59, 60, 62.

50. Rich, "Compulsory Heterosexuality and Lesbian Existence," 51.

51. Brossard, *The Arial Letter*, 122.

52. *Ribu nyūsu: Kono michi hitosuji*, "Resubian"; *Subarashī onnatachi* no. 1 (1976); and Kakefuda, *"Rezubian" de aru to iu koto*.

53. Foucault, "Nietzsche, Genealogy, History," 146.

54. Reichert, *In the Company of Men*.

55. Hiruma, "Kindai Nihon ni okeru josei dōseiai no 'hakken.'" Pflugfelder, *Cartographies of Desire;* Pflugfelder, "'S' Is for Sister."

56. Pflugfelder *Cartographies of Desire*, 175, 248; Furukawa, "Dōsei 'ai' no kō."

57. Halperin, *How to Do the History of Homosexuality*, 53.

58. Cf. Ellis, "Joseikan no dōsei ren'ai"; Yoshiya, "Aishiau koto domo."

59. Robertson, "Dying to Tell," 9.

60. The veracity of this assertion hinges on translation. Namely, Robertson conflates "lesbian" with female "homosexuality," for instance rendering *"onna dōshi no dōseiai"* (homosexuality between women) as "lesbian" and *"dōseiai"* (homosexuality) "lesbian love." Compare Robertson, "Dying to Tell," 13, 16, with Yasuda, "Dōseiai no rekishikan," 150; and Saijō, "Dansō no reijin," 170.

61. Hiruma, "Kindai Nihon ni okeru josei dōseiai no 'hakken.'" 9–10.

62. For example, Sawada, *Shinpi naru dōseiai*, vol. 1, 58–59.

63. Hiruma, "Kindai Nihon ni okeru josei dōseiai no 'hakken.'"

64. Krafft-Ebing, *Hentai seiyoku shinri,* 462–464, 469, in Furukawa and Akaeda, *Senzen dōseiai kanren bunken shūsei;* cf. Krafft-Ebing, *Psychopathia Sexualis,* 321, 396, 607–611.

65. For example, Satō Kōka, *Sekai seiyokugaku jiten,* 45, 194–195.

66. *"Resubian"* as a stand-alone term can be found, for example, in Ellis, *Sei no shinri,* vol. 6, 8.

67. It lingered in other languages including English. There is an entry for "lesbian love," for instance, in *Stedman's Medical Dictionary* from at least the 1910s through the 1940s.

68. Ellis, "Joseikan no dōsei ren'ai," 4, 10; see also Pflugfelder, "'S' Is for Sister," 167–168.

69. For the prewar era, I examined dictionaries in Matsui, Sone, and Ōya, *Kindai yōgo no jiten shūsei;* Matsui and Watanabe, *Ingo jiten shūsei;* Satō, *Sekai seiyokugaku jiten;* and the dictionaries serialized in the journal *Hentai shinri* (1926–1928). On schoolgirl romance see Pflugfelder 2005, "'S' Is for Sister."

70. See Matsui, Sone, and Ōya, *Kindai yōgo no jiten shūsei,* vols. 19 (dating to 1931): 653; 23 (1933):1171; 34 (1932): 340; 36 (1933): 376; and 37 (1933): 358. See also Katō, "Sekaiteki hentai seiyoku gafu (3)," 73; Satō Kōka, "Seiyokugaku goi," part 1, 19, 95–96; and Satō, *Sekai seiyokugaku jiten,* 45, 194–195.

71. Satō, *Sekai seiyokugaku jiten.*

72. See McLelland, "From Sailor Suits to Sadists," and chapter two in McLelland, *Queer Japan from the Pacific War to the Internet Age.* Examples in contemporary dictionaries can be found in Satō, "Seiyokugaku goi," part 1, 19, 95–96; and Satō, *Sekai seiyokugaku jiten,* 45, 194–195, 261, 290.

73. Matsui, Sone, and Ōya, *Kindai yōgo no jiten shūsei,* vol. 19 (1931), 361. Sailor suits replaced the traditional *hakama* as uniforms for schoolgirls during the Taishō era. See Ōtsuka, *Shōjo minzokugaku,* 45.

74. Matsui, Sone, and Ōya, *Kindai yōgo no jiten shūsei,* vol. 19 (1931): 652–653.

75. See Pflugfelder, "'S' Is for Sister," 134–140.

76. Referring to the appearance of the *katakana* "to" (ト) and "ha" (ハ), the term "*to ichi ha ichi*" implies that in female–female sexual relations there is one (*ichi*) inserter (*to*) and one insertee (*ha*).

77. For example, Sakai, "Resubiennu."

78. Grillparzer's *Sappho: Trauerspiel in fünf Aufzüge* (*Sappho: A Tragedy in Five Acts,* 1818) was referenced in the press in the late Meiji era: for example, Kawashima, "Guriruparutsu-eru no hen'ei." Two translations of this work were published in 1922 alone: see his *Saffo: Hikyoku* and *Saffo.* Other early translations include Daudet's *Sapho* (1884), translations of which were published as early as 1913: see his *Saffuō* and *Safuo;* Baudelaire's *Les fleurs du mal* (*The Flowers of Evil,* 1857), published in translation by 1919: see his *Aku no hana;* and Louÿs's *Les chansons de Bilitis* (*The Songs of Bilitis,* 1894), published in Japanese in 1924 and 1926. Such translations can be found even in the immediate postwar period: e.g., Baudelaire, "Resubosu," a partial translation of his *Les fleurs du mal.*

79. Balakian, "Those Stigmatized Poems of Baudelaire," 276. I thank Mark McLelland for sharing this article with me.

80. Halperin, *How to Do the History of Homosexuality,* 49.

81. *Asahi shinbun,* "Byōbo o ato ni gakudan e."

82. Tanizaki, *Manji;* in English, Tanizaki, *Quicksand.*

83. For *dōseiai* see Tanizaki, *Manji,* 108; for instances of the relationship being described as between persons of the "same sex" (*dōsei*), see 37, 83, 91, 94; and for this being contrasted with relationships between members of the "opposite sex" (*isei*), see 91, 94, 106.

84. Examples of *"resubian"* used in reference to the text can be found in, for example, Kabiya, "Homo no hondana"; and Tanizaki, Wakao, and Kishida, "Zadankai." Regarding its insertion by the translator, compare Hibbett's translation, Tanizaki, *Quicksand,* 116 and 121, with Tanizaki's *Manji,* 91 and 94.

85. Ernst and Loth, *American Sexual Behavior and the Kinsey Report,* and in Japanese, *Amerika jin no sei seikatsu.*

86. Ernst and Loth, *Amerika jin no sei seikatsu,* 19; cf. Ernst and Loth, *American Sexual Behavior,* 13.

87. Kinsey and the Institute for Sex Research, *Sexual Behavior in the Human Male,* in Japanese *Ningen ni okeru dansei no sei kōi;* and *Sexual Behavior in the Human Female,* in Japanese, *Ningen josei ni okeru sei kōdō.*

88. Kinsey and the Institute for Sex Research, *Ningen josei ni okeru sei kōdō,* 15.

89. Kinsey and the Institute for Sex Research, *Ningen josei ni okeru sei kōdō,* 13.

90. Kinsey and the Institute for Sex Research, *Ningen josei ni okeru sei kōdō,* 15.

91. McLelland, "From Sailor Suits to Sadists"; McLelland, *Queer Japan.*

92. Miyagawa, *"Resubianizumu zatsuwa."*

93. Saijō et al., "Zadankai." Other examples of *"josei no homo"* include Narabayashi, *Rezubian rabu,* 9; Takahashi Tetsu, *Abu rabu,* 61. On the use of *"homo"* in this period, see McLelland, *Queer Japan.*

94. Satō, "Seiyokugaku goi," parts 1 and 2, and *Sekai seiyokugaku jiten.*

95. McLelland, *Queer Japan,* 69.

96. Higuchi, "Pari no resubiantachi." On *gei bōi* culture, see chapter three in McLelland, *Queer Japan.*

97. Kabiya, "Tōzai resubian no ai no gihō," 44, 45, 49–50.

98. Kabiya, "Tōzai resubian no ai no gihō," 44. On the use of superscript to assign a meaning to a term or to introduce a new word, see Howland, *Translating the West,* 78–82.

99. Kabiya, "Tōzai resubian no ai no gihō," 49.

100. Kawashima, "Resubosu no sasoi."

101. Pieru Rovizu [*sic,* Pierre Louÿs], "Resubiennu."

102. The latter first appeared as Sakai, "Resubiennu." The "original" is presented as a Japanese translation by Sakai Kiyoshi of a French translation from Greek by a man whose name is spelled out in Roman letters as "Pierre Lovijs [*sic*]." While both the original and plagiarized versions credit Louÿs, the dialogue does not appear in Louÿs's *Les chansons de Bilitis.* Nevertheless, Louÿs's work might have inspired Sakai to create his own invented translation from ancient Greek, via French, relying on Louÿs's name to lend an air of legitimacy or perhaps suggest to informed readers that this text too was a literary invention.

103. *Resubosu kurabu,* no. 6.

104. For example, *Yomiuri shinbun,* "Dōseiai kara shinjū"; Setouchi, "Dōseiai no onna."

105. For example, Akazuka, "Oshaberi jiten"; *Shūkan taishū,* "Otoko no tame no resubian-gaku nyūmon"; *Shūkan manga sandē,* "Fukaku shizuka ni ryūkō suru 'resubian.'"

106. Narabayashi, *Rezubian rabu.*

107. Narabayashi, *Rezubian rabu,* 3.

108. *Heibon panchi,* "Kindan no ai o motomeru rezubian no jittai," 36.

109. *Josei jishin,* "Yuganda sei no jidai o ikiru joseitachi"; *Shūkan gendai,* "BG no aida ni dōseiai ga kyūzō shiteiru!"

110. Examples of *"resubian"* from the late 1970s include *Fujin kōron,* "Kaigai josei jānaru"; and *Feminisuto,* "Nihon no josei no media."

111. The new pronunciation can be found in Firestone and Koedt, *Onna kara onna-tachi e;* Boston Women's Health Book Collective (hereafter BWHBC), *Onna no karada,* 345. And the old pronunciation is used in Aki Shobō Henshūbu, ed., *Sei sabetsu e no kokuhatsu,* 207.

112. Akiyama, interview, and *Ribu shishi nōto.*

113. For example, Tanaka, *Inochi no onnatachi e,* 311.

114. For example, Funamoto, "Shikijōteki ni, geijutsuteki ni"; Yoshihiro, "Amerika no ribu no atarashī nami"; and BWHBC, "Rezu to yobarete."

115. Yoshihiro, "Amerika no ribu," 111.

116. BWHBC, "Rezu to yobarete."

117. Amano Michimi, interview with author, March 2009.

118. Kiyooka, *Onna to onna,* 84. On Kiyooka's books, see Welker, "Toward a History of 'Lesbian History' in Japan," 153–155.

119. *Wakakusa,* "Resubian o atsukatta sakuhin," 19, 40, 41; Kiyooka, *Nichiren joyū.*

120. "Fujisaki Rie," interview with author, September 2008.

121. Hagiwara, "Furīne Key Words," 174; *Furīne,* "Phryné Key Words," 83.

122. Hara, "Yakusha atogaki," 226; Tomioka and Hara, "Yakusha kaisetsu," 392.

123. Hara Minata, interview with author, July 2009.

124. Horie, *Rezubian aidentitīzu.*

125. For example, *Fūzoku kitan,* "Josō aikō heya," 152.

126. *Kuīn,* "Josōsha kyūyū messeeji," 71.

127. *Shūkan taishū,* "Onna ga onna o kau"; *Resbosu kurabu.*

128. Kakefuda, *"Rezubian" de aru to iu koto.*

129. Kakefuda, *"Rezubian" de aru to iu koto,* 214–238.

130. Kakefuda, "Rezubian wa mainoriti ka?," 32.

131. Izumo and Maree, *Love Upon the Chopping Board,* 108.

132. Brossard, *The Arial Letter,* 122. On discomfort with *"rezubian"* into the 1990s, see Chalmers, *Emerging Lesbian Voices from Japan,* 39.

133. For example, Kita, *Shōnen'ai no renga haikai shi,* 55–56; Satō, *Sekai seiyokugaku jiten,* 235–237.

134. Kita, *Shōnen'ai no renga haikai shi.*

135. See *Nihon kokugo dai jiten,* 2nd ed., s.v., "shōnen."

136. Pflugfelder, *Cartographies of Desire,* 225.

137. Mori Ōgai, *Wita sekushuarisu.*

138. Mori, *Wita sekushuarisu,* 240. I borrow my translation of *"kōha"* as "roughneck" from Pflugfelder, *Cartographies of Desire.*

139. Iwata, *Nanshoku bunken shoshi;* Hiratsuka, *Nihon ni okeru nanshoku no kenkyū,* especially 32–35.

140. Yokota-Murakami, *Don Juan East/West,* 37.

141. Saeki Junko, "From *Iro* (Eros) to *Ai=Love,*" 81.

142. Yokota-Murakami, *Don Juan East/West,* 42–43. It merits noting that, although both Yokota-Murakami and Saeki note the existence of multiple transliterations of "love"—for example, *"rabu," "rābu,"* and *"rabbu"*—both leave unexplored the use of *"ravu,"* which also had a degree of currency by the early decades of the twentieth century, finding its way, for

instance, into the term "*resubian ravu*," discussed above. See Saeki, *"Iro" to "ai" no hikaku bunkashi,* 352n2.

143. Sawada, *Shinpi naru dōseiai.*

144. Sawada, *Shinpi naru dōseiai,* vol. 2, 119–120.

145. Morita, *Dōseiai no kenkyū,* 8.

146. Tanaka Kōgai, "Dōseiai no bunrui to kasei iseiai," 98.

147. The characters for "*nandō*" (alternatively pronounced "*dandō*") in classical Japanese represent the vernacular word "*onowarawa*," also meaning young boy. I assume Tanaka would have assigned them a Sinitic reading to match *shōnen.*

148. Satō links "*Päderastie*" with "*keikan*" and "*nanshoku* (Urning)," as well as "*sodomī* (Sodomie)," and "*pedofiria erotika* (Paedophilia erotica)" with "*shikijōsei shōni shikō*" (erotic taste for small children). See his "Seiyokugaku goi," part 2, 30, and *Sekai seiyokugaku jiten,* 235, 237.

149. Tomooka, *Jinrui sei seikatsu shi,* 160.

150. Inagaki, "Shōnen tokuhon," 248. I thank Jeffrey Angles for obtaining a copy of this article for me.

151. Angles, *Writing the Love of Boys.*

152. Inagaki, *Shōnen'ai no bigaku.* On the role of Taruho's book in naming the *shōnen'ai* genre, see Ishida, *Hisoyaka na kyōiku,* 88, 89n65. See also chapter four in this volume.

153. Kabiya, "Sodomī itsutsu no koikei," 43; *Fūzoku kitan,* "Homo no mado," 100; Kabiya, "Shōnen'ai (kunābenrībe) no hitobito."

154. Akiyama Masami, *Homo tekunikku;* Minami, *Homorojī nyūmon.*

155. For example, Takeda, "Taruho no shōmetsu no hi ni."

156. See chapter four in Mackintosh, *Homosexuality and Manliness in Postwar Japan.*

157. Takemiya, "Sanrūmu nite."

158. Fujimoto, "The Evolution of BL as 'Playing with Gender.'"

159. See the genre code lists in Komikku Māketto Junbikai, *Komikku māketto 30's fairu,* 384–389, and Komikku Māketto Junbikai, *Komikku māketto 40-shūnen shi,* 340–343.

160. Kurihara, "Tanbi shōsetsu to wa nani ka," 325; Welker, "A Brief History of *Shōnen'ai, Yaoi,* and Boys Love," 52–53.

161. Ishida Minori, *Hisoyaka na kyōiku,* 88; Takemiya, *Kaze to ki no uta.*

162. Ishida, *Hisoyaka na kyōiku,* 85–92, 296.

163. Ishida, *Hisoyaka na kyōiku,* 85.

164. Masuyama Norie, quoted in Ishida, *Hisoyaka na kyōiku,* 99–100; cf. Matsuda, *Hana moji no shisō.*

165. Welker, "Flower Tribes and Female Desire."

166. *Barazoku,* "Homo no hito to kekkon shitai."

167. Hagio, *Tōma no shinzō;* Takemiya, *Kaze to ki no uta; Death in Venice.*

168. *Barazoku,* "Homo no hito to kekkon shitai." See Welker, "Flower Tribes."

169. "Sano Rie," interview with author, March 2009.

170. For example, Kitazumi, "Homo-shi 'go-sanke' o kanzen dokuha"; *Aran,* "Shinjuku ni-chōme"; Kakinuma, "Senmonshi de shiru igai na chomeijin."

171. Welker, "Beautiful, Borrowed, and Bent."

172. For example, Nakajima, "Onna no ko o miryō suru shōnen dōshi no ai"; Nakano, "Shōjo manga no kōzō bunseki"; *Weekly pureibōi,* "Shōjo manga dai kenkyū."

173. A search of newspaper databases for *"shōnen'ai"* in the 1960s and 1970s turned up only references to Taruho's book.

174. Taniguchi, *Shōnen'aisha; Wikipedia,* s.v., *"shōnen'ai,"* http://ja.wikipedia.org/wiki/少年愛, last modified August 12, 2015, and April 12, 2023; and *Wikipedia,* s.v., *"shōnen'ai (shōjo manga),"* https://ja.wikipedia.org/wiki/少年愛_(少女漫画), last modified June 2, 2022.

175. *RAPPORI* is discussed in Hatsu, "Yaoi no moto wa 'share' deshita." Hatsu confirmed my transliteration of Ravuri into English (Hatsu Akiko, personal correspondence, November 19, 2012). See also Hagio, "The Moto Hagio Interview," 160.

176. I write "RAPPORI" in all capital letters at the request of Hatsu, listed as the primary editor of *RAPPORI: Yaoi tokushū-gō.* Hatsu explained that it is an invented word with no particular meaning (Hatsu, personal correspondence).

177. See, for example, the cover of the manga culture magazine *Manga no techō,* no. 8 (summer 1982), promoting content on "YAOI *anime*" (with *"yaoi"* in capital Roman letters).

178. On alternative meanings of the acronym, see Nishimura, *Aniparo to yaoi,* 12n3.

179. Yamamoto and BL Sapōtāzu, *Yappari, bōizu rabu ga suki,* 14.

180. *Pafu,* "Boy's Love Magazine kanzen kōryaku manyuaru."

181. Galbraith, *The Otaku Encyclopedia,* 38, 238–239.

182. Compare the treatment of these terms by different scholars in McLelland et al., *Boys Love Manga and Beyond.*

183. I base this on examinations of fan discourse and discussions with fans for over a decade.

184. Tsing, "Worlds in Motion," 11.

185. Foucault, "Nietzsche, Genealogy, History," 146.

186. Weston, "Lesbian/Gay Studies in the House of Anthropology," 349–351.

187. Welker and Kam, "Introduction: Of Queer Import(s) in Asia"; Sinnott, "Borders, Diaspora, and Regional Connections"; Chiang and Wong, "Asia Is Burning."

188. Liu, *Translingual Practice,* 26, my emphasis.

Chapter 4: Translation

Epigraph source: Levy, "Introduction," 1.

1. Mizuta, "Translation and Gender," 164.

2. On Wakamatsu Shizuko see Ortabasi, "Brave Dogs and Little Lords."

3. On translation, Seitōsha, and *Seitō,* see Bardsley, "The New Woman of Japan and the Intimate Bonds of Translation"; and Mizusaki, "Gaikoku bungaku no juyō to hyōka."

4. Levy, "Introduction," 3.

5. Levy, "Introduction," 3–4.

6. Beauvoir, *Le deuxième sexe,* first published in Japanese as *Dai ni no sei.*

7. In 1997, Inoue Takako and Kimura Nobuko published a new translation of *The Second Sex,* citing a need arising from significant errors in the original translation caused by it having been "translated from the perspective of a man at that point in time." See Inoue and Kimura, "Yakusha atogaki." I thank Julia Bullock for this information. See also Moi, "While We Wait."

8. Inoue and Kimura, "Yakusha atogaki." Some women affiliated with *ribu* who I interviewed mentioned Beauvoir's text. See also Bullock, "Fantasy as Methodology."

9. Venuti, *The Translator's Invisibility*. Although the frequent inclusion in Japanese translations of a preface or afterword from the translator mitigates the translator's invisibility, explanatory or interpretive notes by scholars or critics often overwhelm the translator's comments.

10. Gaonkar and Povinelli, "Technologies of Public Forms," 387.

11. Gaonkar and Povinelli, "Technologies of Public Forms," 393.

12. Tymoczko, *Enlarging Translation, Empowering Translators*, 97.

13. Lefevere, *Translation, Rewriting, and the Manipulation of Literary Fame*.

14. Castellini, *Translating Maternal Violence*, 93.

15. Welker, "From Women's Liberation to Lesbian Feminism in Japan."

16. See, e.g., Aoyama and Hartley, *Girl Reading Girl in Japan*.

17. Akiyama Yōko, *Ribu shishi nōto*, 52.

18. Akiyama, *Ribu shishi nōto*, 52.

19. Josei Kaihō Undō Junbi Kai (hereafter JKUJK), "Hitokoto."

20. JKUJK, *Josei kaihō undō shiryō*. Two versions of this pamphlet were produced, the original during the summer of 1970 (Akiyama, *Ribu shishi nōto*, 25). The latter includes minor corrections and the addition of a table of contents (Akiyama Yōko, personal correspondence, June 20, 2009).

21. Tymoczko, *Enlarging Translation, Empowering Translators*, 213.

22. For example, Inoue Kiyoshi, *Nihon josei shi*. See Akiyama, *Ribu shishi nōto*, 31–32.

23. Akiyama, *Ribu shishi nōto*, 31–32.

24. Akiyama, *Ribu shishi nōto*, 28. McAfee and Wood, "Bread and Roses," in Japanese, "Pan to bara"; Piercy, "The Grand Coolie Dam," in Japanese, "Idai na kūrī: josei." Akiyama received Piercy's "Grand Coolie Dam" from an American couple who introduced her to the women's liberation movement in 1969. See Akiyama, *Ribu shishi nōto*, 23–24.

25. Akiyama, *Ribu shishi nōto*, 28, 30, 32.

26. Akiyama, *Ribu shishi nōto*, 28.

27. Akiyama, *Ribu shishi nōto*, 32–33.

28. Akiyama, *Ribu shishi nōto*, 30. The interview is in JKUJK, *Josei kaihō undō shiryō*, 42–47.

29. Akiyama, *Ribu shishi nōto*, 28, 30, 32.

30. Bunch-Weeks, interview by Kurita Reiko, 46–47.

31. Aki Shobō Henshūbu, ed., *Sei sabetsu e no kokuhatsu*. N.B.: the month of publication is listed in most books published in Japan. Editor-in-chief of Aki Shobō, Kimura Takashi has characterized the press, founded in 1968, as originally producing leftist publications, adding that in recent years it has become merely left-leaning (personal correspondence, March 17, 2010). By 1971, Aki Shobō had published books on topics including student movements, peace movements, and Marxism.

32. See Inoue Teruko, *Joseigaku to sono shūhen*, 176–178, for a personal recollection of the event.

33. Inoue, *Joseigaku to sono shūhen*, 176.

34. Shortly after a woman identified as "activist (U.S.A.)" spoke (Aki Shobō Henshūbu, *Sei sabetsu e*, 70–72), a woman introduced as Diana Connolly from America spoke (81, 82). These may be the same individual.

35. Aki Shobō Henshūbu, *Sei sabetsu e*, 4–5.

36. Aki Shobō Henshūbu, *Sei sabetsu e*, 82.

37. Aki Shobō Henshūbu, *Sei sabetsu e*, 85, 87–89.

38. Aki Shobō Henshūbu, *Sei sabetsu e,* 86.

39. E.g., Aki Shobō Henshūbu, *Sei sabetsu e,* 82.

40. Aki Shobō Henshūbu, *Sei sabetsu e,* 127–180.

41. JKUJK, "Josei kaihō undō junbi kai apīru!," 130. No date is given for the release of the flier, but it introduces the American edition as forthcoming in July (1970), so it presumably dates to June 1970 or earlier.

42. Muto, "The Birth of the Women's Liberation Movement in the 1970s," 147–149.

43. Aki Shobō Henshūbu, *Sei sabetsu e,* 181–263. The translated articles are Dixon, "Naze ribu ga okiru no kaa," originally published as "Why Women's Liberation?"; Steinem, "Kanzen byōdō no yūtopia," originally "What It Would Be Like if Women Win."

44. Ikegami Chizuko, interview with author, July 24, 2009.

45. Stambler, compiler, *Women's Liberation,* translated as Millett et al., *Ūman ribu;* Firestone and Koedt, eds., *Notes from the Second Year,* in Japanese *Onna kara onnatachi e.*

46. The left-leaning orientation of Gōdō Shuppan, the Japanese publisher of *Notes,* may explain the publisher's interest in the translation project. By contrast, Hayakawa Shobō, the publisher of the Japanese version of *Women's Liberation,* is better known as a publisher of translated mysteries and science fiction.

47. Harvey, *Intercultural Movements,* 177.

48. Friedan, *The Feminine Mystique,* first translated into Japanese as *Atarashī josei no sōzō.*

49. Millett, *Sexual Politics,* in Japanese, *Sei no seijigaku;* Millett, "Sei no seijigaku," (trans. Takano Fumi).

50. *Shūkan bunshun,* "Zenbei ūman pawā no shidōsha wa Nihonjin no tsuma; Millett, "Josei kaihō no baiburu."

51. Millett et al., *Ūman ribu,* 303.

52. Morgan, *Tōtaru ūman,* originally published as *The Total Woman.*

53. Itabashi, "*Tōtaru ūman* atogaki," 258.

54. Takano, "Kaisetsu."

55. Takano, "Kaisetsu," 299.

56. Shelley, "Lesbianism and the Women's Liberation Movement."

57. Arnold, "Consciousness-Raising"; Weathers, "An Argument for Black Women's Liberation." While it might seem irrelevant to the women's movement in an ostensibly homogeneous Japan, Black feminism was sometimes referenced in discussions of feminism in the United States, possibly to display a cosmopolitan knowledge of American society.

58. Kazuko Tanaka, *A Short History of the Women's Movement in Modern Japan,* 47. See, also, e.g., Funamoto Emi's comment in *Onna erosu,* no. 2, "Henshū kōki," 213; Sarachild, "Josei kaihō no puroguramu."

59. Akiyama, *Ribu shishi nōto,* 60–61; Urufu no Kai, "Yakusha maegaki," 4–5. I use "Woolf" to reflect the name's initial inspiration.

60. Goddard, "Theorizing Feminist Discourse/Translation," 50.

61. Flotow, "Feminist Translation," 79.

62. The translation "from woman to women" is my own. While "*onna*" can mean either "woman" or "women," "*onnatachi*" is inflected with the (optional) plural marker "*tachi*" used to emphasize that there are multiple people. Akiyama says Woolf Society members

vacillated between *"onna"* and *"onnatachi."* They believed their final choice did not translate neatly into English (Akiyama, *Ribu shishi nōto,* 60). I disagree.

63. Urufu no Kai, "Yakusha maegaki," and "Onna kara onnatachi e: Zadankai."

64. Akiyama, *Ribu shishi nōto,* 33–34, 56.

65. Akiyama, *Ribu shishi nōto,* 56–57; Urufu no Kai, "Yakusha maegaki," 3.

66. Matsui Yayari, *Josei kaihō to wa nani ka?,* 40.

67. Freeman, "Bicchi sengen"; Koedt, "Wagina ōgazumu kara no kaihō"; Atkinson, "Seidoka sareta seikōshō"; Redstockings, "Redddo sutokkingu sengen"; Firestone, "Ai ni tsuite"; Millett, "Sei no seijigaku" (trans. Urufu no Kai).

68. Koedt, "Wagina ōgazumu kara no kaihō."

69. They do not, however, directly indicate that they abridged articles, such as Tax's "Woman and Her Mind," only a third of which was translated as "Onna no shinjō."

70. Akiyama, *Ribu shishi nōto,* 59.

71. Urufu no Kai, "Yakusha maegaki," 3.

72. Urufu no Kai, "Yakusha maegaki," 4.

73. The five-thousand–copy figure comes from Akiyama, *Ribu shishi nōto,* 61.

74. The translations, *From Woman to Women* and *Women's Liberation* were mentioned in *Asahi shinbun,* "Ūman ribu no ichinen."

75. Akiyama, *Ribu shishi nōto,* 69, 74; Urufu no kai, "Maegaki: 14-nin no onnatachi kara."

76. Quoted in Akiyama, *Ribu shishi nōto,* 70.

77. Cited in Akiyama, *Ribu shishi nōto,* 70–71.

78. Cited in Akiyama, *Ribu shishi nōto,* 73.

79. Cited in Akiyama, *Ribu shishi nōto,* 75.

80. Cited in Akiyama, *Ribu shishi nōto,* 73–74.

81. Akiyama, *Ribu shishi nōto,* 69.

82. Boston Women's Health Book Collective—hereafter BWHBC—*Our Bodies, Ourselves: A Book By and For Women.* This was preceded by Boston Women's Health Collective, *Women and their Bodies: A Course,* and Boston Women's Health Course Collective, *Our Bodies, Ourselves: A Course.* See Davis, *The Making of* Our Bodies, Ourselves, 22, 24.

83. The American Spanish-language edition was not published until 1977. See Davis, *The Making of* Our Bodies, Ourselves, 64–66.

84. BWHBC, *Our Bodies, Ourselves* (1973), 1.

85. *Onna kara onnatachi e* [Urufu no kai, Tokyo], "Hajime ni," no. 2 (Fall 1972), 1.

86. Urufu no Kai, "Taiken kiroku." The three issues of *From Woman to Women* are undated; I confirmed the publication dates with Akiyama Yōko (personal communication, June 21, 2009).

87. See Akiyama, Kuwahara, and Yamada, "Yakusha atogaki," 343–344; Akiyama, *Ribu shishi nōto,* 154–155, 158.

88. Akiyama, *Ribu shishi nōto,* 158–159; Akiyama, Kuwahara, and Yamada, "Yakusha atogaki," 345.

89. BWHBC, "Taikenteki piru no subete (jikken hōkoku)."

90. Akiyama, *Ribu shishi nōto,* 164.

91. After Japan and Italy in 1974, the other countries were, in chronological order, Denmark (1975), Taiwan (1976, unauthorized), France (1977), the U.K. (1978), West Germany (1980), Sweden (1980), Greece (1981), the Netherlands (1981), Israel (1982), and Spain (1982).

See Davis, *The Making of* Our Bodies, Ourselves, 52–53, 64–66. Davis downplays the first Japanese and Taiwanese versions in her narrative about the global spread of the book (60–61), perhaps because their existence runs against the standard narrative of second-wave feminism spreading from the United States to Europe before the rest of the world.

92. Akiyama, *Ribu shishi nōto,* 65.

93. BWHBC, "Nihon no mina-san e."

94. Akiyama, Kuwahara, and Yamada, "Nihongo-ban maegaki," "Iryō to watashitachi: yakusha gurūpu," "Yakusha atogaki."

95. Akiyama, Kuwahara, and Yamada, "Yakusha atogaki," 345.

96. Akiyama, Kuwahara, and Yamada, "Nihongo-ban maegaki"; the history is provided in the English version: BWHBC, "Preface," *Our Bodies, Ourselves* (1973).

97. Akiyama, Kuwahara, and Yamada, "Nihongo-ban maegaki," 3.

98. Akiyama, Kuwahara, and Yamada, "Nihongo-ban maegaki," 3.

99. Akiyama, Kuwahara, and Yamada, "Iryō to watashitachi."

100. Akiyama, Kuwahara, and Yamada, "Yakusha atogaki," 343.

101. Akiyama, Kuwahara, and Yamada, "Yakusha atogaki," 344–345.

102. Akiyama, Kuwahara, and Yamada, "Yakusha atogaki," 345.

103. BWHBC, *Onna no karada,* 101–106.

104. Davis, *The Making of* Our Bodies, Ourselves, 9.

105. Akiyama, Kuwahara, and Yamada, "Yakusha atogaki," 345; BWHBC, "Rezu to yobarete."

106. Akiyama Yōko, interview with author, March 4, 2009. The omission of this chapter from the original translation and its publication in *Onna erosu* was significant enough to be remembered twenty years later in a comment on the two volumes in a lesbian book guide produced by the Osaka-based rezubian group Kansai YLP. See the pamphlet Kansai YLP, *Rezubian no tame no dokusho annai,* 4.

107. Tanaka Mitsu, *Inochi no onnatachi e.*

108. Amano Michimi, interview with author, April 2, 2009.

109. Hisada, "Genki jirushi no rezubian," 123.

110. Wakabayashi, "'Onna no karada' renzoku tīchi in," 161.

111. Nagai et al., "Onna no karada," 114–115.

112. Ribu Shinjuku Sentā Shiryō Hozon Kai, ed., *Ribu Shinjuku Sentā shiryō shūsei 1: Ribu nyūsu: Kono michi hitosuji* (hereafter RSSHK, *Ribu nyūsu*), v; Wakabayashi, "'Onna no karada' renzoku tīchi in"; *Onna hangyaku,* "Onna no karada renzoku tīchi in."

113. On the teach-ins, see Wakabayashi, "'Onna no karada' renzoku tīchi in"; Wakabayashi, "Onna no nettowāku no naka de ikiru," 22; *Anīsu,* "Komyuniti no rekishi"; Nakayama, *Gendai Nihon josei no kibun,* 15–16.

114. *Shin chihei,* "Motto shintai aisou yo."

115. Bessatsu Takarajima, no. 4, *Onna no jiten;* Bessatsu Takarajima, no. 9, *Onna no karada.*

116. Amano, "Dōseiai," in Bessatsu Takarajima, no. 4, *Onna no jiten.*

117. See Amano's comment in *Onna erosu,* no. 8, "Henshū kōki," 190. Yūsei Hogo Hō Kaiaku o Soshi Suru Gakusei no Kai, *Onna (watashi) no karada,* 4, 18, 39. See also Kato, *Women's Rights?,* 129.

118. Yūsei Hogo Hō Kaiaku o Soshi Suru Gakusei no Kai, *Onna (watashi) no karada,* 1.

119. BWHBC, *The New Our Bodies, Ourselves.*

120. Nakanishi, *Onna no hon'ya (uimenzu bukkusutoa) no monogatari,* 90–91.

121. Akiyama, Kuwahara, and Yamada, "Yakusha atogaki," 344; Millett, *Sei no seijigaku.*

122. Nakanishi, *Onna no hon'ya (uimenzu bukkusutoa) no monogatari,* 90.

123. BWHBC, *The New Our Bodies, Ourselves,* xii; BWHBC, *Karada, watashitachi jishin,* 6; Nakanishi, *Onna no hon'ya no monogatari,* 94.

124. Ogino, "Nihon-ban ni tsuite," 8.

125. Kawano, "Onna kara onna e no messēji"; Ogino, "Nihon-ban ni tsuite"; Fujieda, "'Onna to kenkō' undō to *Karada, watashitachi jishin.*"

126. Ogino, "Nihon-ban ni tsuite," 9. Nakanishi complicates Ogino's claim. Nakanishi recalls that it would have been too difficult and expensive to obtain permission to reproduce the original photographs since there were so many different copyright holders. See Nakanishi, *Onna no hon'ya monogatari,* 100–101. See also the section on Nakanishi Toyoko in Buckley, *Broken Silence,* 184–225.

127. BWHBC, *Karada, watashitachi jishin,* 146–148.

128. BWHBC, *Karada, watashitachi jishin,* 567–595.

129. Ogino, "Nihon-ban ni tsuite," 8. Rather than the version of *kangoshi* they proposed for nurse, using the character *shi* (士) meaning a person in a profession, a man, or a samurai, a version using a more gender-neutral homophonous character (師), meaning specialist or expert, has become standard.

130. Hite, *The Hite Report.*

131. Hite, *Haito ripōto: Atarashī josei no ai to sei no shōgen* (1976).

132. *Hikari guruma,* "Sekai kara no kaze, *Haito repōto* no hon'yaku o megutte."

133. Ishikawa, "Yakusha maegaki," in Hite, *Haito ripōto,* 8.

134. Ishikawa, "Kaisetsu," in Hite, *Haito ripōto.*

135. Ishikawa, "Haito ripōto o megutte." See also Takeuchi, "The Complexity of Sexuality and *Kurowassan,*" 163–164.

136. The survey appeared in the July 1980 issue of *More: Moa,* "The More Report: Onna no sei to sei."

137. Moa Ripōto-han, *Moa ripōto: Nihon no joseitachi ga, hajimete jibuntachi no kotoba de sei o katatta;* Moa Ripōto-han, *Moa ripōto: Onnatachi no sei to sei.*

138. Moa Ripōto-han, *Moa ripōto: Nihon no joseitachi,* 3.

139. Wolfe, *Cosmo Report,* and *Kosumo ripōto.*

140. Hite, *The Hite Report on Male Sexuality,* in Japanese, *Haito ripōto: Dansei ban;* Moa Ripōto-han, ed., *Moa ripōto 2.*

141. *Onna kara onnatachi e* [Osaka], "*Haito ripōto* o yonde," 3.

142. *Onna kara onnatachi e* [Osaka], "*Haito ripōto* o yonde," 3, 5.

143. Bessatsu Takarajima, no. 64, *Onna o ai suru onnatachi no monogatari.*

144. Hirosawa and Rezubian Ripōto-han, "Rezubian ripōto." The introduction erroneously indicates that the surveys were conducted in 1981. See Sawabe Hitomi, "*Onna o ai suru onnatachi no monogatari* o meguru hyōgen katsudō," 53–56.

145. Moa Ripōto-han, *Moa ripōto,* 770–771, 786–789.

146. Frye, *The Politics of Reality: Essays in Feminist Theory* (Trumansburg, NY: Crossing Press, 1983); Hirosawa, "Sekai rezubian kaigi ni sanka shite." See also Sawabe, "*Onna o ai suru onnatachi no monogatari* o meguru hyōgen katsudō," 52–54.

147. Sawabe, "*Onna o ai suru onnatachi no monogatari* o meguru hyōgen katsudō," 52, 53.

148. Sawabe, "*Onna o ai suru onnatachi no monogatari* o meguru hyōgen katsudō," 52–58.

149. Hirosawa and Rezubian Ripōto-han, "Rezubian ripōto," 152.
150. Hirosawa and Rezubian Ripōto-han, "Rezubian ripōto," 243–244.
151. Hite, *The Hite Report,* xi.
152. Hirosawa and Rezubian Ripōto-han, "Rezubian ripōto," 151–152
153. Hirosawa and Rezubian Ripōto-han, "Rezubian ripōto," 152.
154. On the *"akarui rezubian,"* see Curran and Welker, "From the *Well of Loneliness* to the *akarui rezubian,*" 66, 75–76. I thank Beverley Curran for identifying the significance of *"akarui"* in this sphere.
155. Hirosawa and Rezubian Ripōto-han, "Rezubian ripōto," 151.
156. Hirosawa and Rezubian Ripōto-han, "Rezubian ripōto," 284–285.
157. Hirosawa and Rezubian Ripōto-han, "Rezubian ripōto," 285.
158. Hirosawa and Rezubian Ripōto-han, "Rezubian ripōto," 246–282.
159. Even in *Stories,* just five of the thirty-five works of fiction and nonfiction on its list of lesbian books are neither translations from a European language nor focused on Western cultures. See Nishihara Ryōko and Bukkurisuto-han, "Rezubian no suimyaku o tadoru bukkurisuto 35."
160. Uchiyama, "Japanese Girls' Comfort Reading of *Anne of Green Gables.*"
161. Terada, "70-nendai enkyori shōjo manga no jidai," 160–161.
162. Kelsky, *Women on the Verge,* 26.
163. Harvey, "Gay Community, Gay Identity and the Translated Text," 148, 150.
164. It was republished as Takemiya, "Sanrūmu nite." See Ishida Minori, *Hisoyaka na kyōiku,* 21, 23n14.
165. Ishida, *Hisoyaka na kyōiku,* 52.
166. Ishida, *Hisoyaka na kyōiku,* 298.
167. Ishida, *Hisoyaka na kyōiku,* 58, inter alia. Takemiya, "Sanrūmu nite," and *Kaze to ki no uta;* Hagio, "Jūichigatsu no gimunajiumu," and *Tōma no shinzō.*
168. Ishida, *Hisoyaka na kyōiku,* 70–71.
169. Takemiya, "Sanrūmu nite," 6–7; Ishida, *Hisoyaka na kyōiku,* 71.
170. Ishida, *Hisoyaka na kyōiku,* 76.
171. Ishida, *Hisoyaka na kyōiku,* 72.
172. Takemiya, *Takemiya Keiko no manga kyōshitsu,* 217; Takemiya, "Karā irasuto kagami no kuni no shōnentachi," cited in Ishida, *Hisoyaka na kyōiku,* 74.
173. Inagaki, *Shōnen'ai no bigaku.*
174. Masuyama, "*Kaze to ki no uta* no tanjō," 55.
175. Quoted in Ishida, *Hisoyaka na kyōiku,* 88.
176. Hagio, "The Moto Hagio Interview"; *Les amitiés particulières.*
177. Peyrefitte, *Les amitiés particulières: roman.*
178. *Kanashimi na tenshi Les Amitiés Particulieres* [sic].
179. Takemiya quoted in Ishida, *Hisoyaka na kyōiku,* 141. *Death in Venice.*
180. See Aoyama and Hartley, "Introduction," 5.
181. Fairclough, *Discourse and Social Change,* 85.
182. Fairclough, *Discourse and Social Change,* 102, 103.
183. See, for example, section three in Fujimoto, *Watashi no ibasho wa doko ni aru no?;* and Welker, "Beautiful, Borrowed, and Bent."
184. Quoted in Satō Masaki, "Shōjo manga to homofobia," 162.
185. Ishida, *Hisoyaka na kyōiku,* 99–100.

186. Welker, "Flower Tribes and Female Desire"; Welker "Lilies of the Margin."

187. Welker, "Drawing Out Lesbians"; Fujimoto, *Watashi no ibasho wa doko ni aru no?*

188. Yoshida, *Sakura no sono.*

189. Fujimoto, *Watashi no ibasho wa doko ni aru no?*

190. Yoshida, *Banana Fish.*

191. Welker, "From *The Cherry Orchard* to *Sakura no sono*," 163–164; Smith, *Lesbian Panic,* 2; see also Welker, "Drawing Out Lesbians," 164–168.

192. Nimiya, *Adaruto chirudoren to shōjo manga,* 35; Fujimoto, *Watashi no ibasho wa doko ni aru no?,* 205–206.

193. Quoted in *Manga yawa 4,* 154.

194. *Manga yawa 4,* 156.

195. Curran and Welker, "From the *Well of Loneliness* to the *akarui rezubian.*"

196. Nakamoto, *Chēhofu no naka no Nihon,* 7–8; Ura, "Chēhofu no bunken mokuroku."

197. Takaya, "Introduction," xxii.

198. Uno, *Chēhofu no* Sakura no sono *ni tsuite,* 16; Mizusaki, "Gaikoku bunka no juyō to hyōka," 158. Senuma is said to have been the first to translate any of Chekhov's works from Russian (see Mizusaki, "Gaikoku bunka no juyō to hyōka," 158). My thanks to Hiroko Cockerill for her efforts to verify this.

199. Chekhov, *Sakura no sono.* The translation Yoshida uses is indicated on the manga's copyright page. For a listing of postwar translations, see Uno, *Chēhofu no* Sakura no sono, 16.

200. Hirosawa, "Dandi na Roshia bungakusha Yuasa Yoshiko hōmonki."

201. See Hirosawa, "Dandi na Roshia bungakusha Yuasa Yoshiko hōmonki," 69.

202. Evdokimova, "What's So Funny about Losing One's Estate," 631.

203. Yoshida, *Sakura no sono,* 11, 82, 110–113.

204. Robertson, *Takarazuka.*

205. hoogland, *Lesbian Configurations,* 69.

206. Butler, *Gender Trouble,* 141.

207. Butler, *Gender Trouble,* 137.

208. Butler, *Gender Trouble,* 139.

209. Honda, "The Genealogy of *hirahira,*" 36.

210. Honda, "The Genealogy of *hirahira,*"34.

211. Rich, "Compulsory Heterosexuality and Lesbian Existence," 51.

212. Smith, *Lesbian Panic,* 135–136.

213. Welker, "Beautiful, Borrowed, and Bent."

214. Levy, "Introduction," 11.

215. Levy, "Introduction," 11. The point that there is, as yet, no formal discipline of translation studies in Japan is credited to Yanabu Akira, whose own many works on translation in Japan occupy several pages of the volume's annotated bibliography. See Quinn and Sturiano, "Annotated Bibliography of Translation Studies in Japan."

216. RSSSHK, *Ribu nyūsu,* iv-v; Sawabe, "*Onna o ai suru onnatachi no monogatari* o meguru hyōgen katsudō," 40.

217. Takagi Sawako, interview with author, April 2009. Examples of Femintern Press publications include Tanaka, *A Short History of the Women's Movement in Modern Japan;* Akiyama, *The Hidden Sun;* and Matsui Yayori, *Why I Oppose Kisaeng Tours.*

218. Ting (Ding) Ling and Akiyama Yōko, *Ting Ling: Purged Feminist;* Akiyama, interview.

219. "Why Have a DYKETIONARY?" (preface), in van Dyke, *Dyketionary,* 2nd ed., n.p.

220. Hagio, *The Heart of Thomas*. Scanlations of *The Heart of Thomas* and *The Song of the Wind and the Trees* were available on the website *MangaFox* when I was conducting research in 2010.

221. *Kaze to ki no uta: Sanctus seinaru kana;* Takemiya, *Il poema del vento e degli alberi;* Takemiya, *La balada del viento y los árboles.*

222. Bermann, "Introduction," 7–8.

Chapter 5: Travel

Epigraph source: Beard, *Realism in Romantic Japan,* 28. Miriam Beard was the daughter of historian and women's rights activist Mary Ritter Beard, author of *The Force of Women in Japanese History,* among the earliest English-language histories of women in Japan.

1. Ivy, *Discourses of the Vanishing,* 36–38; Fujioka, *Discover Japan,* 12. By coincidence, the subtitle of the chapter in which Ivy discusses this campaign is "Trans-Figuring Japan." While Ivy does not specify what she means by "transfiguring," as I show here, the campaign is an instance of transfiguration as I define it.

2. Kelly, "Finding a Place in Metropolitan Japan," 195 n17.

3. Fujioka, *Discover Japan,* 118.

4. Keiko Tanaka, "Japanese Women's Magazines: The Language of Aspiration," 111, 116–117; Holthus, "Sexuality, Body Images and Social Change in Japanese Women's Magazines in the 1970s and 1980s," 142.

5. Ivy, *Discourses of the Vanishing,* 36–37.

6. Guichard-Anguis, "Introduction," 2.

7. Guichard-Anguis, "Introduction," 2–3.

8. Prime Minister's Office, *Tourism White Paper* (1971), 29; Prime Minister's Office, *Tourism White Paper* (1974), 50–51; Prime Minister's Office, *Tourism White Paper* (1977), 21; Prime Minister's Office, *Tourism White Paper* (1981), 21. A breakdown by gender is first provided for 1973.

9. In 1990, women constituted 38.7 percent of nearly 11 million overseas travelers, and in 2000 the figure rose to 46.5 percent of the 17.8 million Japanese venturing overseas. See Prime Minister's Office, *Tourism White Paper* (1981), 23–24; Prime Minister's Office, *Tourism White Paper* (1991), 40; and Ministry of Land, Infrastructure, and Transport, *Tourism White Paper,* 35.

10. Prime Minister's Office, *Tourism White Paper* (1981), 23–24.

11. Fujioka, who conceived of the campaign, co-authored a book in the late 1960s about the "Discover America" campaign. See Ivy, *Discourses of the Vanishing,* 42. Fujioka has repeatedly mapped out how the campaigns were quite different in content and intent. See, e.g., Fujioka, *Disukabā Japan,* 165–168.

12. Ivy, *Discourses of the Vanishing,* 40–42.

13. Ivy, *Discourses of the Vanishing,* 39.

14. Ivy, *Discourses of the Vanishing,* 39, 42.

15. Kelsky, *Women on the Verge,* 26.

16. I am pointing here to the Conference of Asian Women Fighting Discrimination=Invasion (Shinryaku=Sabetsu to Tatakau Ajia Fujin Kaigi), founded in 1970.

In Mizoguchi, Saeki, and Miki, *Shiryō Nihon ūman ribu shi,* vol. 1, 19–65, the group is treated as an immediate precursor to *ribu.*

17. For example, Matsui Yayori, "Watashi wa naze kīsen kankō ni hantai suru no ka"; reprinted as Matsui, *Why I Oppose Kisaeng Tours.*

18. Even in the early 1970s, few Japanese people had sufficient knowledge to travel alone on extended trips abroad. See Yamaguchi, *Nippon no kaigai ryokō,* 19–20.

19. This account is based on an interview I conducted with Amano in April 2009, follow-up correspondence in May and June 2010, and August 2013, and draws from Amano, "Women in Japan: Lucy Leu Interviews Michimi."

20. British writer Angela Carter, discussed below, took a similar journey several times. See Gordon, *The Invention of Angela Carter,* 184–185.

21. Itsuki, *Seinen wa kōya o mezasu.* On the book's influence, see Yamaguchi, *Nippon no kaigai ryokō,* 55.

22. Amano, personal correspondence, August 9, 2013.

23. Tanaka Mitsu, *Inochi no onnatachi e.*

24. Amano, "Onna kaihō," 146.

25. Amano, "Onna kaihō," 147.

26. Amano, "Women in Japan."

27. Amano, "Onna kaihō," 140.

28. Amano, "Women in Japan," 39–41.

29. Amano, "Onna kaihō," 140, 141–142.

30. This description of Takagi's background and experiences comes from an interview I conducted with her in April 2009. Larry Taub, who introduced me to Takagi, was present for the first half of the interview, and helped clarify some of the details.

31. *Ribu nyūsu,* "Sukejūru."

32. See Yoshihiro, "Amerika no ribu no atarashī nami."

33. Takagi, "A Short Message from Femintern Press," 309. See also Tsurumi, "Foreword," vi.

34. A list of Femintern publications can be found in Mizoguchi, Saeki, and Miki, *Shiryō Nihon ūman ribu shi,* vol. II, 307; and a promotion for Femintern Press can be found in *Women's International Network News,* "Japan."

35. Kazuko Tanaka, *A Short History of the Women's Movement in Modern Japan.*

36. See the acknowledgment in Akiyama Yōko, *The Hidden Sun.* It was published in *International Socialist Review* at the suggestion of Evelyn Reed. See Akiyama, *The Hidden Sun,* 2.

37. Ting (Ding) Ling and Akiyama Yōko, *Ting Ling: Purged Feminist;* Matsui, *Why I Oppose Kisaeng Tours.*

38. Inoue Teruko, *Joseigaku to sono shūhen,* 229–230; Hotori Teruko [Inoue Teruko], "Amerika no josei to josei kaihō undō," 99.

39. Inoue, *Joseigaku to sono shūhen,* 230.

40. Inoue Teruko, "Atogaki ni kaete," 309–311.

41. Inoue Kiyoshi, *Nihon josei shi.* See Inoue, *Joseigaku to sono shūhen,* 216.

42. Inoue, *Joseigaku to sono shūhen,* 229.

43. Akiyama, *Ribu shishi nōto,* 8.

44. Akiyama Yōko, interview with author, March 2009.

45. Akiyama Yōko, "Sobieto kara no tegami"; Akiyama, "Soren kara."

46. López, *Seductions in Narrative,* 39.

47. Carter, *Nothing Sacred,* 28, quoted in López, *Seductions in Narrative,* 40; cf. Gordon, *The Invention of Angela Carter,* 120, 164–165.

48. Uno dedicates her influential article on the "good wife, wise mother" paradigm to her "sisters" from the Ribu Shinjuku Center, including Tanaka Mitsu and Wakabayashi Naeko. See Uno, "The Death of 'Good Wife, Wise Mother'?," 293.

49. See Wakabayashi Naeko's comment in Endō et al., "Ribusen o taguri yosete miru," 221.

50. Pharr, "Nihon no josei, Amerika no josei."

51. Bunch, "Women's Human Rights," 131; Tong, *Feminist Thought,* 228–231.

52. See Kano Mikiyo's comment, in Akiyama et al., "Tōdai tōsō kara ribu, soshite josei-gaku, feminizumu," 56.

53. Mackie, *Feminism in Modern Japan,* 175–177. The group was active as of 1980. See also Mackie, "Kantō Women's Groups," 106–107.

54. Mackie, *Feminism in Modern Japan,* 179.

55. Yamashita, "The International Movement Toward Gender Equality and Its Impact on Japan"; Kano, *Japanese Feminist Debates,* 121–125.

56. Endō et al., "Ribusen o taguri yosete miru," 209.

57. Saeki Yōko, "Tōkyō Komuunu."

58. Tanaka Mitsu, "Mirai o tsukanda onnatachi," 307.

59. Tanaka, "Mirai o tsukanda onnatachi," 280.

60. Asakawa, "Ribusen de deatta 'subarashī onnatachi.'" 8–9.

61. RSSSHK, *Ribu nyūsu,* iii–iv. Ribu Shinjuku Sentā Shiryō Hozon Kai describes this as the result of the absence of three of the managing members of the center (RSSSHK, *Ribu nyūsu,* iii), but individuals such as Asakawa, "Ribusen de deatta 'subarashī onnatachi.'" 8, suggest that it was largely Tanaka's absence that brought about the ultimate closure of the center.

62. Doi Yumi, interview with author, May 2006.

63. Doi appears in the 2004 documentary *30-nen no shisutāfuddo,* and in 2006 accompanied a tour of universities in the United States, organized by Tomomi Yamaguchi, to promote the documentary.

64. Wakabayashi's experience is summarized from Wakabayashi, "Onna no nettowāku no naka de ikiru," 17–25; *Anīsu,* "Komyuniti no rekishi," 38–41; and [Wakabayashi] Naeko, "Lesbian = Woman." See also Endo et al., "Ribusen o taguri yosete miru," 209.

65. Wakabayashi, "Onna no nettowāku," 24.

66. Wakabayashi, "Onna no nettowāku," 24–25.

67. Wakabayashi, "Lesbian = Woman," 185.

68. Information about Sawabe's experiences is drawn from Sawabe, "*Onna o ai suru onnatachi no monogatari* o meguru hyōgen katsudō," especially 39–45.

69. In "*Onna o ai suru onnatachi no monogatari* o meguru hyōgen katsudō," Sawabe recounts that her trip began in the summer of 1975 (p. 42), but she mentions elsewhere that Tanaka was still in Tokyo when she returned (p. 44). Since Tanaka had already left for Mexico by the summer, Sawabe likely went to the United States during the spring.

70. Quoted in Sawabe, "*Onna o ai suru onnatachi no monogatari* o meguru hyōgen katsudō," 42.

71. Sawabe, "*Onna o ai suru onnatachi no monogatari* o meguru hyōgen katsudō," 44.

72. Sawabe, "*Onna o ai suru onnatachi no monogatari* o meguru hyōgen katsudō," 49.

73. Sawabe participated in the roundtable *Subarashī onnatachi*, "Zadankai 'Rezubian ōi ni kataru.'" See also Sawabe, *"Onna o ai suru onnatachi no monogatari* o meguru hyōgen katsudō," 45.

74. Sawabe wrote about this experience in Hirosawa, "Sekai rezubian kaigi ni sanka shite." On the ILIS conference, see Bunch and Hinojosa, "Lesbians Travel the Roads of Feminism Globally," 3–9.

75. Wakabayashi, "Ajiakei rezubian toshite." See also Zimmerman, *Lesbian Histories and Cultures: An Encyclopedia,* s.v. "Asian Lesbian Network."

76. Bessatsu Takarajima, no. 64, *Onna o ai suru onnatachi no monogatari.*

77. Hirosawa and Rezubian Ripōto-han, "Rezubian ripōto," 217.

78. Hirosawa and Rezubian Ripōto-han, "Rezubian ripōto," 165.

79. This description of Hara's experiences abroad comes from Hara Minata, interview with author, July 2009.

80. Hara's lesbian translations include Faderman, *Resubian no rekishi,* originally *Odd Girls and Twilight Lovers;* and Califia, *Safisutorī,* originally *Sapphistry.*

81. The group's full name is Kyōsei Shakai o Tsukuru Sekushuaru Mainoriti Shien Zenkoku Nettowāku, roughly "national sexual minority support network to promote the creation of a society in which we can coexist."

82. Diehl, "Lesbians in Japan," 13.

83. Hara, interview; Diehl, "Lesbians in Japan," 14.

84. Izumo and Maree, *Love Upon the Chopping Board.*

85. Sano's experiences are summarized from an interview conducted with her in March 2009.

86. Terada, "70-nendai enkyori shōjo manga no jidai," 159.

87. Hagio, *Tōma no shinzō;* Takemiya, *Kaze to ki no uta.*

88. Matsui Yumiko, "O-atsui kappuru."

89. Matsui, "O-atsui kappuru," 261.

90. Tani, "Koibito wa kokusan (meido in Japan) yo!"

91. Tani, "Koibito wa kokusan (meido in Japan) yo!," 200–201.

92. Monden, "Layers of the Ethereal," 272.

93. Yoshimi, *Banpaku to sengo Nihon,* 58.

94. While there were pavilions representing countries and regions from around the world, including many not associated with the West, I would argue that the slippage I am engaging in here is very much a part of the discourse in Japan on foreign cultures, even more so in the 1970s than today. See also Kelsky, *Women on the Verge,* 2–6.

95. *Shōjo komikku,* "O-kaimono dai kenshō"; Tabuchi, Enomoto, and Fujio, "O-warai banpaku"; *Shōjo komikku,* "Banpaku kara konnichiwa!"

96. Shimamura, *Onna wa minna mīhā desu,* 64. While Shimamura was herself not a fan of queer *shōjo* manga (Shimamura, *Onna wa minna mīhā desu,* 162), she grew up in the same milieu as the fans of *shōnen'ai* I discuss in this section. I thank Romit Dasgupta for introducing me to Shimamura's writing.

97. Shimamura, *Onna wa minna mīhā desu,* 65–66.

98. *Shōjo komikku,* "Anata o natsu yasumi ni Hawai e go-shōtai!!"

99. *Shōjo komikku,* "Gokigen!! Hawai no bakansu."

100. Cf. *Aran,* "Honkon ierō mappu."

101. Matsuo, "Amerika no saishin GAY jijō."

102. *Aran,* "Amerikan doragu."

103. Azuma, "Itaria rezubika tansaku kikō"; Yurino, "London Lesbien Report." The article being summarized (in Yurino, "London Lesbien Report," 131–132) is Blasing, "The Lavender Kimono." Azuma seems impressed with the article overall but expresses disappointment that it does not mention "Japan's traditional secret lesbian organization, Wakakusa no Kai" (Yurino, "London Lesbien Report," 132).

104. Kakinuma, "Senmonshi de shiru igai na chomeijin."

105. Nomura, "Komyunāzu gei ando mūbī."

106. While Europe and the United States were most prominent in *Shōjo Comic* in the 1970s, Asia was not entirely absent. See, for example, *Shōjo komikku,* "Honkon izu mai hōmu."

107. Takemiya, *Kibun wa ima mo Yōroppa,* 129–153; Moto, "Konnichiwa sayonara 1," *Shōjo komikku,* 116; Takemiya, "Konnichiwa sayonara 5," 117.

108. Takemiya Keiko, quoted in Ishida Minori, *Hisoyaka na kyōiku,* 140.

109. Ishida, *Hisoyaka na kyōiku,* 140.

110. Ishida, *Hisoyaka na kyōiku,* 146.

111. Masuyama and Sano, "Kyabetsu batake no kakumeiteki shōjo mangakatachi," 171.

112. Ishida, *Hisoyaka na kyōiku,* 144.

113. Masuyama and Sano, "Kyabetsu batake," 170–171.

114. Ishida, *Hisoyaka na kyōiku,* 144.

115. Takemiya, *Sora ga suki!,* 2 vols. (1971–1972).

116. Takemiya, "Sora ga suki!" part 2, final installment, 154, 155.

117. Takemiya, "Kēko-tan no yōroppa ryokōki"; Hagio, "Konnichiwa sayonara 1"; Takemiya, "Konnichiwa sayonara 2"; Hagio and Takemiya, "Konnichiwa sayonara 3"; Moto, "Konnichiwa sayonara 4"; and Takemiya, "Konnichiwa sayonara 5."

118. Ishida, *Hisoyaka na kyōiku,* 147, 150.

119. Hagio, "Moto no Igirisu-dayori" (November 18, 1973).

120. Hagio, "Moto no Igirisu-dayori" (December 2, 1973).

121. Hagio, "Harō! Ingurando"; Hagio, "Harō! Ingurando 2"; Hagio, "Harō! Ingurando 3."

122. Hagio, "Harō! Ingurando 2."

123. Hagio, "Harō! Ingurando 2," 367.

124. Hagio, "Harō! Ingurando 3," 319.

125. Hagio, "Harō! Ingurando 3," 318.

126. *Bessatsu shōjo komikku,* "Komikku hiroba," 377. *"Sensei,"* often translated "teacher," is a respectful title used to address teachers, scholars, doctors, and manga artists, among others.

127. Hagio, *Pō no ichizoku.*

128. *Bessatsu shōjo komikku,* "Biba! Yōroppa ryokō."

129. Takemiya, *Uīn gensō.* Refer to the two-page map included in lieu of a frontispiece in Takemiya's *Kibun wa ima mo Yōroppa* for the dates of Takemiya's visits to Europe.

130. Original publication details can be found in the back of Takemiya, *Uīn gensō.*

131. Masuyama, "Fuyu no Yōroppa," 12.

132. The articles, which ran from approximately 1978 to 1984, are labeled *"shōjo no tame no seiō (yōroppa) mite aru ki"* (account of Western Europe for *shōjo*). References to Hagio's time in England appear in the magazine as well but are not the focus of features about her; see, for example, Hagio and Itō, "Ima, kaettekita *Pō no ichizoku*," 41.

133. Aoike, "Don Pedoro no Arukasaru (ōjō) to Karumona no yōsai ni kangeki." The castle Aoike discusses visiting in this article, the Alcázar del rey Don Pedro, was the setting for her long-running manga *Arukasaru—Ōjō*.

134. Takemiya, "Kēko-tan shiroi Doitsu o yuku."

135. Takemiya, "Kēko-tan shiroi Doitsu o yuku," 82.

136. Takemiya, "Kēko-tan shiroi Doitsu o yuku," 83.

137. Takemiya, "Kēko-tan shiroi Doitsu o yuku," 84.

138. Takemiya, "Kurisumasu no Uīn e konai ka," 77.

139. Takemiya, "Uīn no yūutsu."

140. Takemiya, "Uīn no yūutsu," *inter alia*.

141. Takemiya, "Tokutō shindaisha de yume no kuni e"; Takemiya, "Yōroppa hoteru monogatari," 52.

142. Murata, "Takemiya Keiko kōenkai 'Sanrūmu' tanjō no kiseki," 16.

143. Murata, "Takemiya Keiko kōenkai," 16–17.

144. Murata, "Takemiya Keiko kōenkai," 17.

145. Murata, "Takemiya Keiko kōenkai," 17; Takemiya, *Kaze to ki no uta*. Sunroom contained occasional updates on both the club's budget and its publication schedule. Each issue of *Wind* was titled after the month it was sent, for example, *April Wind (Shichi-gatsu no kaze)*.

146. I base this on having examined all issues of *Sunroom* from 1976 to 1979, as well as a handful of issues from 1980 to 1987. Note that the numbering of *Sunroom* restarts with each change in leadership.

147. Sasaya, "Gesuto kōnā."

148. Masuyama, "Kore kara tabi suru anata ni. . . . . . ," 15; Masuyama, "Fuyu no Yōroppa."

149. *Sanrūmu*, "Natsu no shūkai kanzen hōkoku!"

150. *Sanrūmu*, "Kēko-tan kara Yōroppa no kaze purezento."

151. *Sanrūmu*, "Kēko-sensei kara no Yōroppa omiyage tōsensha-san."

152. That a giveaway three years later, in 1980, included mainly items that appear to have been purchased—T-shirts, postcards, letter sets, and so forth—suggests that either the appeal of cast-off items such as used metro tickets was short lived or that Takemiya herself decided such items were no longer appropriate. See *Sanrūmu*, "Yōroppa omiyage tōsensha-san happyō."

153. Takemiya, *Kibun wa ima mo Yōroppa*, 4.

154. Takemiya, "Kibun wa ima mo Yōroppa"; Takemiya, *Kibun wa ima mo Yōroppa*, 4.

155. Takemiya, *Kibun wa ima mo Yōroppa*, 5.

156. Takemiya, *Kibun wa ima mo Yōroppa*, 159.

157. Takemiya, *Kibun wa ima mo Yōroppa*, 10.

158. Shimamura, *Bābī, anata wa doko e iku no?*, 17–40.

159. Kelsky, *Women on the Verge*, 102.

160. "Yamamoto Tomiko" and "Ikeda Taeko," group interview with author, June 2006.

161. Takeda's experience is summarized from an interview with her I conducted in July 2009. The two texts she named that she received from him were Takemiya's *Kaze to ki no uta* and Ikeda Riyoko's *Onī-sama e*.

162. On Takemiya's interest in the Vienna Boys Choir, see, for example, Takemiya, "O-egaki kyōshitsu."

163. Clifford, *Routes*, 39.

164. Puar, ed., "Queer Tourism: Geographies of Globalization."

165. Kelsky, *Women on the Verge,* 123.

166. Izumo et al., "Nihon no rezubian mūvumento," 67.

167. Aoki, "Debunking the 90%-Middle-Class Myth," 29; Gluck, "Introduction," xli.

168. Takagi, interview.

169. Fujimura-Fanselow, "College Women Today: Options and Dilemmas," 127.

Afterword

1. Welker, "Boys Love (Yaoi), and the Global Circulation of."

2. Fushimi, "Ajia ni hirogaru BL genshō."

3. Mizoguchi, *BL shinkaron.*

4. Fermin, "BL Coupling in a Different Light; Wei, "Straight Men, Gay Buddies"; Menon, "Desi Desu"; Tarasyuk, "Queer Roleplaying Practices in Russian Female BL Fandom."

5. Afriat, "Queer Cosplay in Israel."

6. Xu and Yang, "Between BL and Slash."

7. Đỗ Uyên and Nguyễn, "The Development of Boys Love in Vietnam."

8. Baudinette, "Creative Misreadings of 'Thai BL,'" 101.

9. Baudinette, "Creative Misreadings of 'Thai BL.'"

10. Saito, "From Legends to Games to Homoerotic Fiction."

11. Huang, "In Front of the Law," 126.

12. See, e.g., *Shūkan josei,* "Zen sekai o miryoku suru Tai BL dorama senpū"; *An an,* "Hot na Ajia danshi 39-nin"; *Asahi shinbun,* "Tai no dorama sekai ga koi."

13. Morimoto, "(Trans)Cutural Legibility and Online *Yuri!!! on Ice* Fandom," 154.

14. Popova, "Dogfuck Rapeworld."

15. *Omegabāsu purojekkuto 1.*

16. *Anime Planet,* search results for "omegaverse," https://www.anime-planet.com/manga/tags/omegaverse?page=1, accessed March 10, 2020.

Works Cited

30-nen no shisutāfuddo: 70-nendai no ūman ribu no onnatachi. Documentary. DVD. Dir. Yamagami Chieko and Seyama Noriko. Japan: Herstory Project, 2004.

Abnorm. *Island.* Japan: Privately printed, ca. 1979.

Afriat, Liron. "Queer Cosplay in Israel." *Mechademia: Second Arc* 13, no. 1 (2020): 171–175.

Akazuka Yukio. "Oshaberi jiten." *Yomiuri shinbun,* January 21, 1968, morning ed., 23.

———. "Shin go '70: Rabu yori ribu o!" *Yomiuri shinbun,* April 19, 1970, morning ed., 23.

Aki Shobō Henshūbu, ed. *Sei sabetsu e no kokuhatsu: Ūmanribu wa shuchō suru.* Tokyo: Aki Shobō, 1971.

Akisato Wakuni. *Tomoi.* 1986. Tokyo: Shōgakukan Bunko, 1996.

Akiyama Masami. *Homo tekunikku: Otoko to otoko no sei seikatsu.* Tokyo: Daini Shobō, 1968.

Akiyama Yōko. *The Hidden Sun: A Brief History of Japanese Women.* Tokyo: Femintern Press, 1975.

———. "Piru wa hontō ni yoi mono na no ka?" *Onna kara onnatachi e* [Urufu no kai, Tokyo], no. 2 (Fall 1972): 8–12

———. *Ribu shishi nōto: Onnatachi no jidai kara.* Tōkyō: Inpakuto Shuppankai, 1993.

———. "Sobieto kara no tegami." Parts 1 and 2. *Ribu nyūsu: Kono michi hitosuji,* no. 14 (November 1974): 8; no. 15 (February 1975): 6. In Ribu Shinjuku Sentā Shiryō Hozon Kai, *Ribu Shinjuku Sentā shiryō shūsei: Ribu nyūsu: Kono michi hitosuji,* 172, 180.

———. "Soren kara." *Onna erosu,* no. 13 (September 1979): 191–202.

Akiyama Yōko, Ikeda Sachiko, and Inoue Teruko. "Tōdai tōsō kara ribu, soshite josei-gaku, feminizumu." Roundtable discussion moderated by Ōta Kyōko and Kano Mikiyo. In Onnatachi no Ima o Tou Kai, *Zenkyōtō kara ribu e,* 38–70.

Akiyama Yōko, Kuwahara Kazuyo, and Yamada Mitsuko. "Iryō to watashitachi: Yakusha gurūpu." In Boston Women's Health Book Collective, *Onna no karada,* 339–342.

———. "Nihongo-ban maegaki." In Boston Women's Health Book Collective, *Onna no karada,* 1–3.

———. "Yakusha atogaki." In Boston Women's Health Book Collective, *Onna no karada,* 339–346.

Amano Michimi. "Dōseiai." In Bessatsu Takarajima, no. 4, *Onna no jiten,* 34–38.

———. "Onna kaihō: Yō no tōzai o mazu toeba." *Onna erosu,* no. 4 (March 1975): 138–150.

———. "Women in Japan: Lucy Leu Interviews Michimi." *The Second Wave* 3, no. 4 (Winter 1974): 37–43.

Amitiés particulières, Les. Motion picture. Dir. Jean Delannoy. France: Progéfi and LUX C.C.F., 1964.

AMPO: A Report from Japan's New Left. "October 21, Japan's Mightiest Anti-War Day." No. 1 (November 1969): 4, 12.

An an. "Hot na Ajia danshi 39-nin." September 30, 2020, 98–99.

Angles, Jeffrey. *Writing the Love of Boys: Origins of Bishōnen Culture in Modernist Japanese Literature.* Minneapolis: University of Minnesota Press, 2011.

Anīsu. "Komyuniti no rekishi, 1971–2001: Nenpyō to intabyū de furikaeru." (Summer 2001): 28–78.

Aoike Yasuko. *Arukasaru—Ōjō.* 1984–2007. 13 vols. Tokyo: Akita Shoten, 1985–2007.

———. "Don Pedoro no Arukasaru (ōjō) to Karumona no yōsai ni kangeki." *Gurēpufurūtsu,* no. 19 (December 1984): 201–203.

———. *Ibu no musukotachi.* 1976–1979. 7 vols. Tokyo: Akita Shoten, 1976–1979.

Aoki, Shigeru. "Debunking the 90%-Middle-Class Myth." *Japan Echo* 6, no. 2 (1979): 29–33.

Aoyama, Tomoko, and Barbara Hartley, eds. *Girl Reading Girl in Japan.* London: Routledge, 2010.

———. "Introduction." In their *Girl Reading Girl in Japan,* 1–14.

Appadurai, Arjun. "Grassroots Globalization and the Research Imagination." *Public Culture* 12, no. 1 (2000): 1–19.

Arakawa Soobei, ed. *Gairaigo jiten.* Tokyo: Kadokawa Shoten, 1979.

Aran. June 1983.

———. "Amerikan doragu." August 1983, 104–105.

———. "Honkon ierō mappu: Subete no korekutā ga manzoku suru fantasutikku shiti Honkon no subete!!" October 1980, 73–80.

———. "Ninki dōjinshi purezento." October 1980, 138–139.

———. "Shinjuku ni-chōme." August 1983, 9–47.

Arnold, June. "Consciousness-Raising." In Stambler, *Women's Liberation,* 155–161.

Asahi shinbun. "Buttsubuse 'dansei shakai': Bei de LIB undō." March 28, 1970, evening ed., 10.

———. "Byōbo o ato ni gakudan e: Uchida-san no seibetsu aiwa." May 7, 1928, morning ed., 4.

———. "Tai no dorama sekai ga koi," October 19, 2020, morning ed., 19.

———. "Ūman ribu." November 5, 1970, morning ed., 23.

———. "Ūman ribu, 'dansei tengoku' ni jōriku." October 4, 1970, morning ed., 24.

———. "Ūman ribu no ichinen: Amerika to Nihon." September 22, 1971, morning ed., 17.

———. "Yarimasu wa yo, 'onna kaihō': Ūman ribu Ginza ni 'otoko wa toridase' kidōtai mo tajitaji." October 22, 1970, morning ed., 3.

———. "(Yōron chōsa no torisetsu) dōseikon meguri ishiki, kanjiru 'Shōwa' to henka." March 3, 2023. https://www.asahi.com/articles/DA3S15571686.html.

Asakawa Mari. "Ribusen de deatta 'subarashī onnatachi.'" Oral history by Sugiura Ikuko. In Sugiura, *Nihon no rezubian komyuniti,* 1–16.

Atkinson, Ti-Grace. "Seidoka sareta seikōshō." Translated by Urufu no Kai. In Firestone and Koedt, *Onna kara onnatachi e,* 131–148.

Atsumi Ikuko. "Goals of Feminism in Modern Japan." *Feminist International* [Japan], no. 2 (June 1980): 96.

Atsumi Ikuko, Ōhashi Terue, Kakinuma Misachi, Kuwahara Itoko, Kobayashi Fukuko, Shima Yōko, Matsubara Junko, and Mizuta Noriko. "Hachi nin no feminisuto ni yoru nyū feminisuto sengen: Josei no gawa kara ningen kaihō shugi (feminizumu) o teigen." *Feminisuto*, no. 8 (November 1978): 56–57.

Azuma Reiko. "Itaria rezubika tansaku kikō." *Aran*, October 1983, 183.

Balakian, Anna. "Those Stigmatized Poems of Baudelaire." *The French Review* 31, no. 4 (1958): 273–277.

Barazoku. "Homo no hito to kekkon shitai." No. 46 (November 1976): 68–70.

Barbara, Lee Barbara. "Rezubian, kono onnatachi wa nani mono da?" Translated by Hazama Natsu [?Wakabayashi Naeko]. *Subarashī onnatachi*, no. 1 (November 1976): 58–61.

Bardsley, Jan. "The New Woman of Japan and the Intimate Bonds of Translation." In Levy, "The Culture of Translation," 206–225.

Baudelaire, Charles. *Aku no hana: Shishū*. 1857. Translated by Baba Mutsuo. Tokyo: Rakuyōdō, 1919.

———. "Resubosu." 1857. Translated by Satō Saku. *Mita bungaku* 20, no. 7 (September 1946): 36–44.

Baudinette, Thomas. "Creative Misreadings of 'Thai BL' by a Filipino Fan Community: Dislocating Knowledge Production in Transnational Queer Fandoms Through Aspirational Consumption," *Mechademia: Second Arc* 13, no. 1 (2020): 101–118.

Beard, Mary Ritter. *The Force of Women in Japanese History*. Washington, DC: Public Affairs Press, 1953.

Beard, Miriam. *Realism in Romantic Japan*. New York: Macmillan, 1930.

Beauvoir, Simone de. *Dai ni no sei*. 5 vols. Translated by Ikushima Ryōichi. Tokyo: Shinchōsha, 1953–1955.

———. *Dai san no sei*. Definitive edition. 2 vols. Translated by Inoue Takako and Kimura Nobuko. Tokyo: Shinchōsha, 1997.

———. *Le deuxième sexe: Les faits et les mythes* and *Le deuxième sexe: L'expérience vécue*. Paris: Gallimard, 1949.

Bender, Marylin. "The Women Who'd Trade in Their Pedestal for Total Equality." *New York Times*, February 4, 1970, Family Style: 30.

Bermann, Sandra. "Introduction." In *Nation, Language, and the Ethics of Translation*, edited by Sandra Bermann and Michael Wood, 1–10. Princeton, NJ: Princeton University Press, 2005.

Bessatsu shōjo komikku. "Biba! Yōroppa ryokō." August 1976, 337.

———. "Komikku hiroba." January 1974, 376–379.

Bessatsu Takarajima, no. 4. *Onna no jiten*. Tokyo: JICC Shuppankyoku, 1977.

———, no. 9. *Onna no karada*. Tokyo: JICC Shuppankyoku, 1978.

———, no. 64. *Onna o ai suru onnatachi no monogatari*. Tokyo: JICC Shuppankyoku, 1987.

———, no. 288. *70-nendai manga daihyakka*. Tokyo: Takarajimasha, 1996.

———, no. 358. *Watashi o komike ni tsuretette!: Kyōdai komikku dōjinshi māketto no subete*. Tokyo: Takarajimasha, 1998.

Bhabha, Homi K. *The Location of Culture*. London: Routledge, 1994.

Binnie, Jon. *The Globalization of Sexuality*. London: Sage, 2004.

Blasing, Anne. "International Feminists of Japan." *Feminist International* [Japan], no. 2 (June 1980): 109–110.

———. "The Lavender Kimono." *Connexions: An International Women's Quarterly*, no. 3 (Winter 1982): 21.

Boston Women's Health Book Collective (BWHBC). *See also* Boston Women's Health Collective, and Boston Women's Health Course Collective.

———. *Karada, watashitachi jishin*. 1984. Trans. *Karada, Watashitachi Jishin* Nihongo-ban Hon'yaku Gurūpu. Edited by *Karada, Watashitachi Jishin* Nihongo-ban Henshū Gurūpu. Kyoto: Shōkadō Shoten, 1988.

———. *The New Our Bodies, Ourselves: A Book by and for Women*. New York: Simon and Schuster, 1984.

———. "Nihon no mina-san e." In Boston Women's Health Book Collective, *Onna no karada*, i–ii.

———. *Onna no karada: Sei to ai no shinjitsu*. 1973. Translated by Akiyama Yōko, Kuwahara Kazuyo, and Yamada Mitsuko. Tokyo: Gōdō Shuppan, 1974.

———. *Our Bodies, Ourselves: A Book By and For Women*. New York: Simon and Schuster, 1973.

———. "Rezu to yobarete." Parts 1 and 2. Trans. Amano Michimi. *Onna erosu*, no. 2 (April 1974): 86–104; no. 3 (September 1974): 80–92.

———. "Taikenteki piru no subete (jikken hōkoku)." *Fujin kōron* 58, no. 11 (November 1973): 326–333.

Boston Women's Health Collective. *Women and Their Bodies: A Course*. Boston: Boston Women's Health Collective and New England Free Press, 1970.

Boston Women's Health Course Collective. *Our Bodies, Ourselves: A Course*. Boston: Boston Women's Health Course Collective and New England Free Press, 1971.

Brinton, Mary C. *Women and the Economic Miracle: Gender and Work in Postwar Japan*. Berkeley: University of California Press, 1993.

Brossard, Nicole. *The Arial Letter*. 1985. Trans. Marlene Wildeman. Toronto: Women's Press, 1988.

Buckley, Sandra. *Broken Silence: Voices of Japanese Feminism*. Berkeley: University of California Press, 1996.

Bullock, Julia C. "Fantasy as Methodology: Simone de Beauvoir and Postwar Japanese Feminism." *U.S.–Japan Women's Journal* 36 (2009): 3–21.

Bunch, Charlotte. "Women's Human Rights: The Challenges of Global Feminism and Diversity." In *Feminist Locations: Global and Local, Theory and Practice*, edited by Marianne DeKoven, 129–146. New Brunswick, NJ: Rutgers University Press, 2001.

Bunch, Charlotte, and Claudia Hinojosa. "Lesbians Travel the Roads of Feminism Globally." In *Creating Change: Sexuality, Public Policy, and Civil Rights*, edited by John D'Emilio, William B. Turner, and Urvashi Vaid, 3–16. New York: St. Martin's Press, 2000.

Bunch-Weeks, Charlotte. Interview with Kurita Reiko. In Josei Kaihō Undō Junbi Kai, *Josei kaihō undō shiryō 1*, 42–47.

Butler, Judith. *Gender Trouble: Feminism and the Subversion of Identity*. New York: Routledge, 1990.

BWHBC. *See* Boston Women's Health Book Collective.

Califia, Pat. *Safisutorī: Resubian sekushariti no tebiki*. 1980. Translated by Hara (Minako) Minata. Tokyo: Taiyōsha, 1993.

———. *Sapphistry: The Book of Lesbian Sexuality*. Tallahassee, FL: Naiad Press, 1980.

Carter, Angela. *Nothing Sacred: Selected Writing*. London: Virago, 1982.

Castellini, Alessandro. *Translating Maternal Violence: The Discursive Construction of Maternal Filicide in 1970s Japan*. London: Palgrave Macmillan, 2017.

Chalmers, Sharon. *Emerging Lesbian Voices from Japan*. Richmond, UK: Curzon, 2002.

Chekhov, Anton. *Sakura no sono*. 1904. Translated by Yuasa Yoshiko. Tokyo: Iwanami Shoten, 1950.

Cherry, Kittredge. *Womansword: What Japanese Words Say About Women*. Tokyo: Kodansha, 1987.

Chiang, Howard, and Alvin K. Wong, "Asia Is Burning: Queer Asia as Critique." *Culture, Theory and Critique* 58, no. 2 (2017): 121–126.

Clifford, James. *Routes: Travel and Translation in the Late Twentieth Century*. Cambridge, MA: Harvard University Press, 1997.

Comiket. "Komikku Māketto 97 afutārepōto." January 10, 2020. https://www.comiket .co.jp/info-a/C97/C97AfterReport.html.

Curran, Beverley, Nana Sato-Rossberg, and Kikuko Tanabe, eds. *Multiple Translation Communities in Contemporary Japan*. New York: Routledge, 2015.

Curran, Beverley, and James Welker. "From the *Well of Loneliness* to the *akarui rezubian*." In *Genders, Transgenders, and Sexualities in Japan,* edited by Mark McLelland and Romit Dasgupta, 65–80. London: Routledge, 2005.

Dales, Laura. *Feminist Movements in Contemporary Japan*. London: Routledge, 2009.

Daudet, Alphonse. *Saffuō*. 1884. Translated by Morita Sōhei. Tokyo: Seinen Gakugei Sha, 1914.

———. *Safuo*. 1884. Translated by Takebayashi Musōan. Shinchōsha, 1913.

Davis, Kathy. *The Making of* Our Bodies, Ourselves: *How Feminism Travels Across Borders*. Durham, NC: Duke University Press, 2007.

Death in Venice. Motion picture. Dir. Luchino Visconti. Italy: Alfa Cinematografica, 1971.

DIBMK. See Dotekabo Ichiza no Bideo o Mitai Kai.

Diehl, Margaret. "Lesbians in Japan." *The DD*, no. 15 (Spring 1990): 12–15.

Dixon, Marlene. "Naze ribu ga okiru no kā." 1969. Translated by Ikegami Chizuko. In Aki Shobō Henshūbu, *Sei sabetsu e no kokuhatsu*, 226–251.

———. "Why Women's Liberation?" *Ramparts*, December 1969, 57–63.

Dotekabo Ichiza no Bideo Mitai Kai. *Dotekabo Ichiza "Myūzukaru 'Onna no kaihō' 1975" bideo/ DVD kaisetsusho*. DVD pamphlet. Tokyo: Dotekabo Ichiza no Bideo Mitai Kai, 2005.

Đỗ Uyên Trịnh Minh, and Nguyễn Quốc Bình. "The Development of Boys Love in Vietnam: From Manga and Danmei Fiction to the Football Turf." *Mechademia: Second Arc* 13, no. 1 (2020): 148–152.

Dower, John W. *Embracing Defeat: Japan in the Wake of World War II*. New York: W. W. Norton & Company/The New Press, 1999.

Eckert, Penelope. "Language and Adolescent Peer Groups." *Journal of Language and Social Psychology* 22, no. 1 (2003): 112–118.

Ellis, Havelock. "Joseikan no dōsei ren'ai." Translated by Yabo. *Seitō* 4, no. 4 (February 1914). Special supplement. Reprint. Tokyo: Ryūkei Shosha, 1980.

———. *Sei no shinri*. 20 vols. Translated by Masuda Ichirō. Tokyo: Nichigetsusha, 1927–1929.

Endō Misaki, Orita Michiko, Kitamura Reiko, Takeda Miyuki, Ikuhara Reiko, Nomachi Miwa, Mori Setsuko, Yonezu Tomoko, and Wakabayashi Naeko. "Ribusen o taguri yosete miru." In Onnatachi no Ima o Tou Kai, *Zenkyōtō kara Ribu e*, 204–251.

Ernst, Morris Leopold, and David Goldsmith Loth. *American Sexual Behavior and the Kinsey Report*. New York: Greystone Press, 1948.

———. *Amerika jin no sei seikatsu*. Translated by Nakaoka Hirō. Akatsuki Shoten, 1949.

Evdokimova, Svetlana. "What's So Funny about Losing One's Estate, or Infantilism in *The Cherry Orchard*." *Slavic and East European Journal* 44, no. 4 (2000): 623–648.

Faderman, Lillian. *Odd Girls and Twilight Lovers: A History of Lesbian Life in Twentieth-Century America*. New York: Penguin, 1991.

———. *Resubian no rekishi*. Translated by Tomioka Akemi and Hara (Minako) Minata. Tokyo: Chikuma Shobō, 1996.

Fairclough, Norman. *Discourse and Social Change*. Cambridge: Blackwell Publishing, 1992.

Feminisuto. "Josei bunka no fukurami o!" No. 2 (October 1977): 1.

———. "Joseigaku no akebono." Special feature. No. 5 (April 1978): 3–37.

———. "Josei no sōzō to feminizumu." No. 7 (September 1978): 1.

———. "Nihon no josei no media: Onna no mini-media kara onnatachi e no messēji." No. 7 (September 1978): 38–41.

Feminisuto Henshūbu. "Onna ga, gakumon ya rekishi o, kakikae hajimeta: Joseigaku no akebono." *Feminisuto*, no. 5 (April 1978): 3.

Feminist International [Japan]. "A Brief History of 'Feminist.'" No. 2 (June 1980): 104–105.

Fermin, Tricia Abigail Santos. "BL Coupling in a Different Light: Filipino Fans Envisioning an Alternative Model of Intimacy." In Welker, ed., *Queer Transfigurations*, 153–166.

Firestone, Shulamith. "Ai ni tsuite." Translated by Urufu no Kai. In Firestone and Koedt, *Onna kara onnatachi e*, 85–115.

Firestone, Shulamith, and Anne Koedt, eds. *Notes from the Second Year: Women's Liberation; Major Writings of the Radical Feminists*. New York: Radical Feminism, 1970.

———. *Onna kara onnatachi e: Amerika josei kaihō undō repōto*. 1970. Translated and with commentary by Urufu no Kai. Tokyo: Gōdō Shuppan, 1971.

Flotow, Luise von. "Feminist Translation: Contexts, Practices and Theories." *TTR: traduction, terminologie, redaction* 4, no. 2 (1991): 69–84.

Foucault, Michel. "Nietzsche, Genealogy, History." Translated by Donald F. Bouchard and Sherry Simon. In *Language, Counter-Memory, and Practice: Selected Essays and Interviews*, ed. Donald F. Bouchard, 139–164. Ithaca, NY: Cornell University Press, 1977.

Freeman, Jo. "Bicchi sengen." Translated by Urufu no Kai. In Firestone and Koedt, *Onna kara onnatachi e*, 24–39.

Friedan, Betty. *Atarashī josei no sōzō.* 1963. Translated by Miura Fumiko. Tokyo: Daiwa Shoten, 1965.

———. *The Feminine Mystique.* New York: Norton, 1963.

Frye, Marilyn. *The Politics of Reality: Essays in Feminist Theory.* Trumansburg, NY: Crossing Press, 1983.

Fujieda Mioko. "Nihon no josei undō: Ribu saikō." *Joseigaku nenpō* 11 (1990): 1–7.

———. "'Onna to kenkō' undō to *Karada, watashitachi jishin.*" In Boston Women's Health Book Collective, *Karada, watashitachi jishin,* 10–11.

Fujimoto Yukari. "The Evolution of BL as 'Playing with Gender': Viewing the Genesis and Development of BL from a Contemporary Perspective." Translated by Joanne Quimby. In McLelland et al., *Boys Love Manga and Beyond,* 76–92.

———. *Watashi no ibasho wa doko ni aru no? Shōjo manga ga utsusu kokoro no katachi.* Tokyo: Gakuyō Shobō, 1998.

Fujimura-Fanselow, Kumiko. "College Women Today: Options and Dilemmas." In *Japanese Women: New Feminist Perspectives on the Past, Present, and Future,* edited by Kumiko Fujimura-Fanselow and Atsuko Kameda, 125–154. New York: The Feminist Press at the City University of New York, 1995.

Fujin kōron. "Kaigai josei jānaru." 63, no. 4 (April 1978): 350–351.

Fujioka Takao. *Discover Japan 40-nen ki'nen katarogu.* Tokyo: PHP Kenkyūsho, 2010.

———. *Disukabā Japan: Karenaru shuppatsu.* Tokyo: Mainichi Shinbunsha, 1972.

Funabashi, Yoichi, and Barak Kushner, eds. *Examining Japan's Lost Decades.* London: Routledge, 2015.

Funamoto Emi. "Shikijōteki ni, geijutsuteki ni: Han-kekkon no erosu." *Onna erosu,* no. 1 (November 1973): 40–54.

Funazaki Yoshihiko. *Ribonnu.* With illustrations by Kaneko Kuniyoshi. Tokyo: Chikuma Shobō, 1979.

Furīne. "Phryné Key Words." No. 2 (November 1995): 82–83.

Furukawa Makoto. "Dōsei 'ai' no kō." *Imago* 6, no. 12 (November 1995): 201–207.

Furukawa Makoto and Akaeda Kanako, eds. *Senzen dōseiai kanren bunken shūsei.* 3 vols. Tokyo: Fuji Shuppan, 2006.

Fushimi Noriaki. "Ajia ni hirogaru BL genshō." *Gendai sei kyōiku kenkyū jānaru,* no. 107 (February 15, 2020): 11.

Fūzoku kitan. "Homo no mado." October 1962, 100–101.

———. "Josō aikō heya." May 1961, 152–153.

Galbraith, Patrick W. "*Moe* Talk: Affective Communication among Female Fans of *Yaoi* in Japan." In McLelland et al., *Boys Love Manga and Beyond,* 153–188.

———. *The Otaku Encyclopedia: An Insider's Guide to the Subculture of Cool Japan.* Tokyo: Kodansha International, 2009.

Gaonkar, Dilip Parameshwar, and Elizabeth A. Povinelli. "Technologies of Public Forms: Circulation, Transfiguration, Recognition." *Public Culture* 15, no. 3 (2003): 385–397.

Gluck, Carol. "Introduction." In *Showa: The Japan of Hirohito,* edited by Carol Gluck and Stephen R. Graubard, xi–lxii. New York: Norton, 1992.

Goddard, Barbara. "Theorizing Feminist Discourse/Translation." *Tessera* 6 (1989): 42–53.

Gordon, Andrew. *Postwar Japan as History.* Berkeley: University of California Press, 1993.

Gordon, Beate Sirota. *The Only Woman in the Room: A Memoir.* Tokyo: Kodansha International, 1997.

Gordon, Edmund. *The Invention of Angela Carter: A Biography.* London: Chatto and Windus, 2016.

Grillparzer, Franz. *Saffo.* 1818. Translated by Kameo Eishirō. Tokyo: Ikubundō, 1922.

———. *Saffo: Hikyoku.* 1818. Translated by Yamamoto Shigeo. Tokyo: Shūeikaku, 1922.

Guichard-Anguis, Sylvie. "Introduction: The Culture of Travel (*tabi no bunka*) and Japanese Tourism." In *Japanese Tourism and Travel Culture,* edited by Sylvie Guichard-Anguis and Okpyo Moon, 1–17. London: Routledge, 2009.

Gurūpu Tatakau Onna. "Chūkin taisei to wa nani ka." In Aki Shobō Henshūbu, *Sei sabetsu e no kokuhatsu,* 163–165.

Hagio Moto. "Harō! Ingurando." *Bessatsu shōjo komikku,* December 1973, 342–343.

———. "Harō! Ingurando 2." *Bessatsu shōjo komikku,* January 1974, 366–367.

———. "Harō! Ingurando 3." *Bessatsu shōjo komikku,* February 1974, 318–319.

———. *The Heart of Thomas.* 1974. Trans. Rachel (Matt) Thorn. Seattle: Fantagraphics, 2012.

———. *Ichido kiri no Ōizumi no hanashi.* Tokyo: Kawade Shobō Shinsha, 2021.

———. Interview by Fujimoto Yukari. In Fujimoto Yukari, *Shōjo manga damashī: Ima o utsusu shōjo manga kanzen gaido & intabyū shū,* 188–206. Tokyo: Hakusensha, 2000.

———. "Jūichigatsu no gimunajiumu." 1971. In her *Jūichigatsu no gimunajiumu,* 3–48. Tokyo: Shōgakukan Bunko, 1995.

———. "Konnichiwa sayonara 1." *Shōjo komikku,* January 1, 1973, 116–117.

———. "Konnichiwa sayonara 4." *Shōjo komikku,* February 4, 1973, 115–116.

———. "The Moto Hagio Interview." By Rachel (Matt) Thorn. *The Comics Journal,* no. 269 (July 2005): 137–175.

———. "Moto no Igirisu-dayori." *Shōjo komikku,* November 18, 1973, 122.

———. "Moto no Igirisu-dayori." *Shōjo komikku,* December 2, 1973, 126.

———. *Pō no ichizoku.* 1972–1976. 3 vols. Tokyo: Shōgakukan Bunko, 1998.

———. *Pō no ichizoku: Hanazono.* 2019–2021. 2 vols. Tokyo: Shōgakukan, 2020–2021.

———. *Pō no ichizoku: Haru no yume.* 2016–2017. Tokyo: Shōgakukan, 2017.

———. *Pō no ichizoku: Yunikōn.* 2018–2019. Tokyo: Shōgakukan, 2019.

———. *Tōma no shinzō.* 1974. Tokyo: Shōgakukan Bunko, 1995.

Hagio Moto and Itō Anri. "Ima, kaettekita *Pō no ichizoku.*" *Pēpā mūn,* no. 2 (June 1976): 41–46.

Hagio Moto and Takemiya Keiko. "Konnichiwa sayonara 3." *Shōjo komikku,* January 14/ January 21, 1973, 8–10.

Hagiwara Mami. "Furīne Key Words." *Furīne,* no. 1 (June 1995): 172–174.

Halperin, David M. *How to Do the History of Homosexuality.* Chicago: University of Chicago Press, 2002.

Hara (Minako) Minata. "Yakusha atogaki." In Califia, *Safisutorī,* 225–226.

Harvey, Keith. "Gay Community, Gay Identity and the Translated Text." *TTR: traduction, terminologie, redaction* 13, no. 1 (2000): 137–165.

———. *Intercultural Movements: American Gay in French Translation.* Manchester, UK: St. Jerome Publishing, 2003.

Hatsu Akiko. "Yaoi no moto wa 'share' deshita: Hatsu kōkai: Yaoi no tanjō." *June,* no. 73 (November 1993): 136.

Heibon panchi. "Kindan no ai o motomeru rezubian no jittai." February 6, 1967, 36–40.

Hester, Jeffry T. "*Fujoshi* Emergent: Shifting Popular Representations of *Yaoi*/BL Fandom in Japan." In McLelland et al., *Boys Love Manga and Beyond,* 169–188.

Higuchi Itsuma. "Pari no resubiantachi: Resubian kurabu." *Ura mado,* February 1959, 185–189.

Hikari guruma. "Sekai kara no kaze: *Haito repōto* no hon'yaku o megutte." No. 1 (April 1978). In Mizoguchi, Saeki, and Miki, *Shiryō Nihon ūman ribu shi,* vol. III, 245.

Hiratsuka Ryōsen. *Nihon ni okeru nanshoku no kenkyū.* Tokyo: Ningen no Kagaku Sha, 1983.

Hirosawa Yumi [Sawabe Hitomi]. "Dandi na Roshia bungakusha Yuasa Yoshiko hōmonki." In Bessatsu Takarajima, no. 64, *Onna o ai suru onnatachi no monogatari,* 67–73.

———. "Nihon hatsu no rezubian sākuru: 'Wakakusa no Kai' sono jūgonen no rekishi to genzai." In Bessatsu Takarajima, no. 64, *Onna o ai suru onnatachi no monogatari,* 111–119.

———. "Sekai rezubian kaigi ni sanka shite." *Fujin kōron* 71, no. 7 (June 1986): 420–427.

Hirosawa Yumi [Sawabe Hitomi] and Rezubian Ripōto-han. "Rezubian ripōto: Nihon de hajimete! 234-nin no rezubian ni yoru shōgen." In Bessatsu Takarajima, no. 64, *Onna o ai suru onnatachi no monogatari,* 149–285.

Hiruma Yukiko. "Kindai Nihon ni okeru josei dōseiai no 'hakken.'" *Kaihō shakaigaku kenkyū* 17 (2003): 9–32.

Hisada Megumi. "Genki jirushi no rezubian: 'Regumi no Gomame' tōjō!" In Bessatsu Takarajima, no. 64, *Onna o ai suru onnatachi no monogatari,* 120–129.

Hite, Shere. *Haito ripōto: Atarashī josei no ai to sei no shōgen.* 2 vols. 1976. Translated by Ishikawa Hiroyoshi. Tokyo: Pashifika, 1977.

———. *Haito ripōto: Dansei ban.* 2 vols. 1981. Translated by Nakao Chizu. Tokyo: Chūō Kōron Sha, 1982.

———. *The Hite Report: A Nationwide Study on Female Sexuality.* New York: MacMillan, 1976.

———. *The Hite Report on Male Sexuality.* New York: Knopf, 1981.

Holthus, Barbara. "Sexuality, Body Images and Social Change in Japanese Women's Magazines in the 1970s and 1980s." In Wöhr, Satō, and Suzuki, *Gender and Modernity,* 137–161.

Honda Masuko. "The Genealogy of *hirahira:* Liminality and the Girl." Translated by Tomoko Aoyama and Barbara Hartley. In Aoyama and Hartley, *Girl Reading Girl in Japan,* 19–37.

hoogland, renée c. *Lesbian Configurations.* New York: Columbia University Press, 1997.

Horie Yuri. *Rezubian aidentitīzu.* Kyoto: Rakuhoku Shuppan, 2015.

Hotori Teruko [Inoue Teruko]. "Amerika no josei to josei kaihō undō: Ryokōsha no kaima mita Amerika." *Onna erosu,* no. 2 (April 1974): 99–104.

Howland, Douglas R. *Translating the West: Language and Political Reason in Nineteenth-Century Japan.* Honolulu: University of Hawai'i Press, 2002.

Huang, Nice. "In Front of the Law: The Production and Distribution of Boys' Love Dōjinshi in Indonesia." *Mechademia: Second Arc* 12, no. 1 (2019): 118–135.

Iino Yuriko. *Rezubian de aru "watashitachi" no sutōrī.* Tokyo: Seikatsu Shoin, 2008.

Ikeda Riyoko. *Onī-sama e.* 1974. Tokyo: Chūō Kōron Shinsha, 2002.

Ikegami Chizuko. *Amerika josei kaihō shi.* Tokyo: Aki Shobō, 1972.

Inagaki Taruho. *Shōnen'ai no bigaku.* Tokyo: Tokuma Shoten, 1968.

———. "Shōnen tokuhon." *Gurotesuku* 3, no. 1 (January 1930): 240–261.

Inoue Kiyoshi. *Nihon josei shi.* Tokyo: San'ichi Shobō, 1948.

Inoue, Kyoko. *MacArthur's Japanese Constitution: A Linguistic and Cultural Study of Its Making.* Chicago: University of Chicago Press, 1991.

Inoue Takako and Kimura Nobuko. "Yakusha atogaki." In Beauvoir, *Dai san no sei* (1997), vol. 2, n.p.

Inoue Teruko. See also Hotori Teruko.

———. "Atogaki ni kaete: Josei shakaigaku kenkyūkai no ayumi." In *Josei shakaigaku o mezashite,* edited by Josei shakaigaku kenkyūkai, 309–313. Tokyo: Kakiuchi Shuppan, 1981.

———. *Joseigaku to sono shūhen.* Tokyo: Keisō Shobō, 1980.

Inoue Teruko, Ueno Chizuko, Ehara Yumiko, and Amano Masako. "Henshū ni attate." In their *Nihon no feminizumu 1: Ribu to feminizumu,* i–ii. Tokyo: Iwanami Shoten, 1994.

Ishida Hitoshi. "Sūji de miru *JUNE* to *Sabu.*" *Yurīka* 44, no. 15 (December 2012): 159–171.

Ishida Minori. *Hisoyaka na kyōiku: "Yaoi/bōizu rabu" zenshi.* Tokyo: Rakuhoku Shuppan, 2008.

Ishikawa Hiroyoshi. "Haito ripōto o megutte." *Kurowassan* (June 1977): 177–179.

———. "Kaisetsu." In Hite, *Haito ripōto,* 631–636.

———. "Yakusha maegaki." In Hite, *Haito ripōto,* 3–8.

Itabashi Yoshie. "*Tōtaru ūman* atogaki." In Morgan, *Tōtaru ūman,* 257–262.

Itsuki Hiroyuki. *Seinen wa kōya o mezasu.* Tokyo: Bungei Shunshū, 1967.

Itō Bungaku. "Ibu & Ibu banzai!" *Barazoku,* no. 113 (June 1982): 66–67.

Itō Gō. *Manga wa kawaru: "Manga gatari" kara "manga ron" e.* Tokyo: Seidōsha, 2007.

Ito, Kinko. "Manga in Japanese History." In MacWilliams, *Japanese Visual Culture,* 26–47.

Ivy, Marilyn. *Discourses of the Vanishing: Modernity, Phantasm, Japan.* Chicago: University of Chicago Press, 1995.

Iwata Jun'ichi. *Nanshoku bunken shoshi: Fu nanshoku ishōshū (nanshoku yōgo jiten).* Toba, Japan: Iwata Sadao, 1973.

Izumo Marou and Claire Maree. *Love Upon the Chopping Board.* North Melbourne, Australia: Spinifex, 2000.

Izumo Marou, Tsuzura Yoshiko, Hara (Minako) Minata, and Ochiya Kumiko. "Nihon no rezubian mūvumento." *Gendai shisō* 25, no. 6 (May 1997): 58–83.

JKUJK. *See* Josei Kaihō Undō Junbi Kai.

Josei jishin. "Yuganda sei no jidai o ikiru joseitachi: Dōseiai, jinkō jusei, rankō o jissen suru joseitachi wa 'ai' o dō kangaeteiru ka?" February 27, 1967, 130–134.

Josei Kaihō Undō Junbi Kai. "Hitokoto." In their *Josei kaihō undō shiryō I: Amerika hen,* 48.

———. "Josei kaihō undō junbi kai apīru!" 1970. In Aki Shobō Henshūbu, *Sei sabetsu e no kokuhatsu,* 129–131.

————. *Josei kaihō undō shiryō 1: Amerika hen.* Pamphlet. Tokyo: Josei Kaihō Undō Junbi Kai, 1970.

————. "Yūsei hogo hō kaiaku soshi e mukete no apīru." In Aki Shobō Henshūbu, *Sei sabetsu e no kokuhatsu,* 159–163

Josei sebun. "Ima sugoi ninki no shōjo komikku sakka no karei-naru shi seikatsu." December 3, 1975, 194–199.

Kabiya Kazuhiko. "Homo no hondana: Tanizaki Jun'ichirō cho *Manji.*" *Fūzoku kitan,* October 1964, 114–115.

————. "Shōnen'ai (kunābenrībe) no hitobito." *Fūzoku kitan,* November 1960, 130–135.

————. "Sodomī itsutsu no koikei." *Fūzoku kagaku,* January 1954, 37–43.

————. "Tōzai resubian no ai no gihō: Joshi dōseiaisha wa donna fū ni ai shiau ka." *Fūzoku kagaku,* August 1960, 44–53.

Kageyama Yūko. "Ūman pawā: Ryō kara shitsu e no tankan, hogo kitei mo o-nimotsu ni." *Asahi shinbun,* October 31, 1968, evening ed., 7.

Kakefuda Hiroko. *"Rezubian" de aru to iu koto.* Tokyo: Kawade Shobō Shinsha, 1992.

————. "Rezubian wa mainoriti ka?" *Joseigaku nenpō* 15 (1994): 25–32.

Kakinuma Eiko. "Senmonshi de shiru igai na chomeijin, jinsei sōdan, kojin kōkoku, gei-do chekku." *June,* no. 39 (March 1988): 100.

Kakinuma Eiko, and Kurihara Chiyo, eds. *Tanbi shōsetsu, gei bungaku bukkugaido.* Tokyo: Byakuya Shobō, 1993.

Kanashimi na tenshi Les Amitiés Particulieres [sic]. Pamphlet. Tokyo: Tōhō Kabushikigai-sha Jigyōbu, 1970.

Kano, Ayako. *Japanese Feminist Debates: A Century of Contention on Sex, Love, and Labor.* Honolulu: University of Hawai'i Press, 2016.

Kansai YLP. *Rezubian no tame no dokusho annai.* Pamphlet. Osaka: Kansai YLP, 1994.

Katō Koyume. "Sekaiteki hentai seiyoku gafu (3)." *Hentai shiryō* 3, no. 2 (1928): 71–73. Reprint. Tokyo: Yumani Shobō, 2006.

Kato, Masae. *Women's Rights? The Politics of Abortion in Modern Japan.* Amsterdam: Amsterdam University Press, 2009.

Kawano Miyoko. "Onna kara onna e no messēji." In Boston Women's Health Book Collective, *Karada, watashitachi jishin,* 7–8.

Kawashima Fūkotsu. "Guriruparutsueru no hen'ei." *Yomiuri shinbun,* May 9, 1909, supplement: 2.

Kawashima Hayato. "Resubosu no sasoi." *Fūzoku kitan,* August 1960, 56–57.

Kaze to ki no uta: Sanctus seinaru kana. Dir. Yasuhiko Yoshikazu. Japan: Shōgakukan/ Herald, 1987.

Kelly, William W. "Finding a Place in Metropolitan Japan: Ideologies, Institutions, and Everyday Life." In Gordon, *Postwar Japan as History,* 189–216.

Kelsky, Karen. *Women on the Verge: Japanese Women, Western Dreams.* Durham, NC: Duke University Press, 2001.

Kihara Toshie. *Mari to Shingo.* 1977–1984. 13 vols. Tokyo: Hana to Yume Komikkusu, 1979–1984.

Kinsella, Sharon. *Adult Manga: Culture and Power in Contemporary Japanese Society.* London: Routledge, 2000.

Kinsey, Alfred C., and the Institute for Sex Research. *Ningen josei ni okeru sei kōdō*. 2 vols. 1953. Translated by Asayama Shin'ichi, Ishida Shūzō, Tsuge Hideomi, and Minami Hiroshi. Tokyo: Kosumoporitan Sha, 1954.

———. *Ningen ni okeru dansei no sei kōi*. 2 vols. 1948. Translated by Nagai Hisomu and Andō Kakuichi. Tokyo: Kosumoporitan Sha, 1950.

———. *Sexual Behavior in the Human Female*. Philadelphia: W. B. Saunders, 1953.

———. *Sexual Behavior in the Human Male*. Philadelphia: W. B. Saunders, 1948.

Kita Tadashi. *Shōnen'ai no renga haikai shi: Sugawara Michizane kara Matsuo Bashō made*. Tokyo: Chūsekisha, 1997.

Kitazumi Izumi. "Homo shi 'go-sanke' o kanzen dokuha." *Aran*, February 1983, 127–129.

Kiyooka Sumiko. *Nichiren joyū*. Tokyo: Nihon Bunkasha, 1973.

———. *Onna to onna: Resubian no sekai*. Tokyo: Naniwa Shobō, 1968.

Koedt, Anne. "Wagina ōgazumu kara no kaihō." *Fujin kōron* 56, no. 5 (May 1971): 166–174.

Koikari, Mire. *Pedagogy of Democracy: Feminism and the Cold War in the U.S. Occupation of Japan*. Philadelphia: Temple University Press, 2008.

Komikku Māketto Junbikai, ed. *Komikku Māketto 30's fairu*. Tokyo: Komiketto, 2005.

Komikku Māketto Junbikai. *Komikku Māketto 40-shūnenshi*. Tokyo: Komiketto, 2015.

Krafft-Ebing, Richard von. *Hentai seiyoku shinri*. Translated by Kurosawa Yoshitami. Tokyo: Dai Nihon Bunmei Kyōkai, 1913. In Furukawa and Akaeda, *Senzen dōseiai kanren bunken shūsei*, vol. 1, 60–186.

———. *Psychopathia Sexualis: With Especial Reference to the Antipathic Sexual Instinct: A Medico-Forensic Study*. Translated by F. J. Rebman. New York: Rebman, 1906.

Kuia Sutadīzu Henshū Iinkai, ed. *Kuia sutadīzu '96*. Tokyo: Nanatsumori Shokan, 1996.

Kuīn. "Josōsha kyūyū messēji." No. 1 (1980): 71–102.

Kurihara Chiyo. "Tanbi shōsetsu to wa nani ka." In Kakinuma and Kurihara, *Tanbi shōsetsu, gei bungaku bukkugaido*, 325–335.

Lefevere, André. *Translation, Rewriting, and the Manipulation of Literary Fame*. London: Routledge, 1992.

Les amitiés particulières. Dir. Jean Delannoy. France: Paris: Progéfi, and LUX C.C.F., 1964.

Levy, Indra. "Introduction: Modern Japan and the Trialectics of Translation." In Levy, *Translation in Modern Japan*, 1–12.

Levy, Indra, ed. *Translation in Modern Japan*. London: Routledge, 2011.

Liu, Lydia H. *Translingual Practice: Literature, National Culture, and Translated Modernity—China, 1900–1937*. Stanford, CA: Stanford University Press, 1995.

Lloyd, Trevor Owen. *Suffragettes International: The World-Wide Campaign for Women's Rights*. New York: American Heritage Press, 1971.

———. *Ūman ribu no hyaku nen: "Jūjun na" josei kara "tatakau josei" e*. 1971. Translated by Tashiro Yasuko. Tokyo: Tsuru Shoten, 1972.

López, Gemma. *Seductions in Narrative: Subjectivity and Desire in the Works of Angela Carter and Jeanette Winterson*. Youngstown, NY: Cambria Press, 2007.

Louÿs, Pierre. *Bilitis no uta kara*. 1894. Translated by Kanbara Tai. Tokyo: Nippon-no-Rômazi-sya, 1924.

———. *Birichisu no uta*. 1894. Trans. Kawaji Ryūkō. Tokyo: Kokusai Bunken Kankō Kai, 1926.

————. *Les Chansons de Bilitis: Traduites du Grec*. Paris, 1894.

Lunsing, Wim. *Beyond Common Sense: Sexuality and Gender in Contemporary Japan*. London: Kegan Paul, 2001.

————. "Gay Boom in Japan: Changing Views of Homosexuality?" *Thamyris* 4, no. 2 (1997): 267–293.

————. "Japanese Gay Magazines and Marriage Advertisements." In *Gays and Lesbians in the Pacific: Social and Human Services*, ed. Gerard Sullivan and Laurence Wai-Teng Long, 71–87. New York and London: Harrington Park Press, 1995.

Mackie, Vera. *Feminism in Modern Japan*. Cambridge: Cambridge University Press, 2003.

————. "Kantō Women's Groups." *Feminist International* [Japan], no. 2 (June 1980): 106–108.

Mackintosh, Jonathan D. *Homosexuality and Manliness in Postwar Japan*. London: Routledge, 2010.

MacWilliams, Mark Wheeler, ed. *Japanese Visual Culture: Explorations in the World of Manga and Anime*. Armonk, NY: M.E. Sharpe, 2008.

Manga no techō, no. 8 (Summer 1982).

Manga yawa 4. "Yoshida Akimi, *Sakura no sono*." Transcript of NHK BS2 Broadcast, *BS manga yawa* (August 28, 1996), 108–201. Tokyo: Kinejunpōsha, 1999.

Masuyama Norie. "Fuyu no Yōroppa: Shōjo no tame no Yōroppa tabi nikki." *Sanrūmu*, no. 9, (July 15, 1978): 10–13.

————. "*Kaze to ki no uta* no tanjō." *June*, no. 36 (September 1987): 55–56.

————. "Kore kara tabi suru anata ni. . . . . . : Non no Yōroppa senchimentaru ryokō repōto." *Sanrūmu*, no. 7 (September 15, 1977), 12–15.

Masuyama Norie and Sano Megumi. "Kyabetsu batake no kakumeiteki shōjo mangakatachi." In Bessatsu Takarajima, no. 288, *70-nendai manga daihyakka*, 166–173.

Matsuda Osamu. *Hana moji no shisō: Nihon ni okeru shōnen'ai no seishin shi*. Tokyo: Peyotoru Kōbō, 1988.

Matsui Shigekazu, Sone Hiroyoshi, and Ōya Yukiyo, eds. *Kindai yōgo no jiten shūsei*. 42 vols. Tokyo: Ōzora Sha, 1994–1996.

Matsui Shigekazu and Watanabe Tomosuke. *Ingo jiten shūsei*. 23 vols. Tokyo: Ōzora Sha, 1996–1997.

Matsui Yayori. *Josei kaihō to wa nani ka? Onnatachi no danketsu wa chikarazuyoku, kokkyō o koeru*. Tokyo: Miraisha, 1975.

————. "Watashi wa naze kīsen kankō ni hantai suru no ka: Keizai shinryaku to sei shinryaku no kōzō o abaku." *Onna erosu*, no. 2 (April 1974): 68–85.

————. *Why I Oppose Kisaeng Tours: Exposing Economic and Sexual Aggression against South Korean Women*. 1974. Translated by Lora Sharnoff. Tokyo: Femintern Press, 1975.

Matsui Yumiko. "O-atsui kappuru." *Shūkan shōjo komikku*, April 19, 1970, 235–261.

Matsuo Setsuko. "Amerika no saishin GAY jijō: Matsuo Setsuko no Nyū Yōku nikki." *Aran*, January 1981, 117–120.

Matsutani Takayuki, Ikeda Riyoko, Kusano Tadashi, Kawauchi Atsurō, and Morina Miharu. "Tezuka Osamu to Takarazuka Kageki: Myūjikaru fōramu." In *Tezuka Osamu no furusato, Takarazuka*, ed. Kawauchi Atsurō, 3–61. Kobe: Kobe Shinbun Sōgō Shuppan Sentā, 1996.

McAfee, Kathy, and Myrna Wood. "Bread and Roses." *Leviathan* 1, no. 3 (1969): 8–11, 43–44.

———. "Pan to bara." 1969. In Josei Kaihō Undō Junbi Kai, *Josei kaihō undō shiryō 1*, 2–23.

McKenzie, Robert M. "The Complex and Rapidly Changing Sociolinguistic Position of the English Language in Japan: A Summary of English Language Contact and Use." *Japan Forum* 20, no. 2 (2008): 267–286.

McLelland, Mark. "From Sailor Suits to Sadists: 'Lesbos Love' as Reflected in Japan's Postwar 'Perverse Press.'" *U.S.–Japan Women's Journal* 27 (2004): 3–26.

———. *Queer Japan from the Pacific War to the Internet Age*. Lanham, MD: Rowman and Littlefield, 2005.

McLelland, Mark, Kazumi Nagaike, Katsuhiko Suganuma, and James Welker, eds. *Boys Love Manga and Beyond: History, Culture, and Community in Japan*. Jackson: University Press of Mississippi, 2015.

Menon, Lakshmi. "Desi Desu: Sex, Sexuality, and BL Consumption in Urban India." In Welker, ed., *Queer Transfigurations*, 211–224.

Miki Sōko. "Ribu gasshuku." In Mizoguchi, Saeki, and Miki, *Shiryō Nihon ūman ribu shi*, vol. I, 315.

———. "Ribu tamashī no nai joseigaku nante." *Onna erosu*, no. 11 (October 1978): 145–149.

Miller, Laura. "*Wasei eigo*: 'Loanwords' Coined in Japan." In *The Life of Language: Papers in Linguistics in Honor of William Bright*, edited by Jane Hill, P. J. Mistry, and Lyle Campbell, 123–139. Berlin: Mouton de Gruyter, 1998.

Millett, Kate. "Josei kaihō no baiburu: Sei no seijigaku." *Fujin kōron* 55, no. 11 (November 1970): 242–253.

———. *Sei no seijigaku*. 1970. Translated by Fujieda Mioko. Tokyo: Jiyūsha, 1973.

———. "Sei no seijigaku." 1970. Translated by Takano Fumi. In Millett et al., *Ūman ribu*, 195–242

———. "Sei no seijigaku." 1970. Translated by Urufu no Kai. In Firestone and Koedt, *Onna kara onnatachi e*, 81–84.

———. *Sexual Politics*. New York: Ballentine, 1970.

Millett, Kate, et al. *Ūman ribu: Josei wa nani o kangae, nani o motomeru ka?* 1970. Translated by Takano Fumi et al. Tokyo: Hayakawa Shobō, 1971.

Minami Teishirō. *Homoroji nyūmon*. Tokyo: Dai Ni Shobō, 1972.

Minegishi Hiromi. "Jūjiro." *Fanī* 1, no. 2 (June 1969): 121–136.

Ministry of Land, Infrastructure, and Transport. *Tourism White Paper*. Tokyo: Ministry of Land, Infrastructure, and Transport, 2001.

Misaki Naoto. "2007-nen no josei-kei parodi dōjinshi no dōkō." *Yurīka* 38, no. 16 (December 2007): 176–179.

Miyagawa Yoshiko. "*Resubianizumu zatsuwa*." *Fūzoku kagaku*, February 1954: 46–52.

Mizoguchi Akiko. *BL shinkaron: Bōizurabu ga shakai o ugokasu*. Tokyo: Ōta Shuppan, 2015.

———. "Male–Male Romance by and for Women in Japan: A History and the Subgenres of *Yaoi* Fictions." *U.S.–Japan Women's Journal* 25 (2003): 49–75.

————. "Mōsōryoku no potensharu: Rezubian feminisuto janru toshite no yaoi." *Yurīka* 39, no. 7 (June 2007): 56–62.

Mizoguchi Akiyo, Saeki Yōko, and Miki Sōko, eds. *Shiryō Nihon ūman ribu shi.* 3 vols. Kyoto: Shōkadō Shoten, 1992–1995.

Mizuno Hideko. *Faiyā!* 1969–1970. 4 vols. Tokyo: Asahi Panorama, 1973.

Mizusaki Noriko. "Gaikoku bungaku no juyō to hyōka: Hon'yaku." In *Seitō o yomu,* edited by Shin Feminizumu Hihyō no Kai, 156–175. Tokyo: Gakugei Shorin, 1998.

Mizuta Noriko. "Translation and Gender: Trans/gender/lation." Translated by Judy Wakabayashi. In *Woman Critiqued: Translated Essays on Japanese Women's Writing,* edited by Rebecca L. Copeland, 159–166. Honolulu: University of Hawai'i Press, 2006.

Moa. "The More Report: Onna no sei to sei." July 1980: 155–162 and insert.

Moa Ripōto-han, ed. *Moa ripōto: Nihon no joseitachi ga, hajimete jibuntachi no kotoba de sei o katatta.* Tokyo: Shūeisha, 1983.

————, ed. *Moa ripōto: Onnatachi no sei to sei.* Tokyo: Shūeisha, 1985.

————, ed. *Moa ripōto 2: Kondo wa, dansei no gawa kara hajimete katarareta, sei to sei no shinjitsu.* Tokyo: Shūeisha, 1984.

Moi, Toril. "While We Wait: The English Translation of *The Second Sex.*" *Signs: Journal of Women in Culture and Society* 27, no. 4 (2002): 1006–1035.

Monden, Masafumi. "Layers of the Ethereal: A Cultural Investigation of Beauty, Girlhood, and Ballet in Japanese *Shōjo Manga.*" *Fashion Theory* 18, no. 3 (2014): 251–296.

Morgan, Marabel. *The Total Woman.* Old Tappan, NJ: F. H. Revell, 1973.

————. *Tōtaru ūman: Shiawase na kekkon o kizuku himitsu.* Translated by Itabashi Yoshie. Tokyo: Kōdansha, 1976.

Mori Mari. *Koibitotachi no mori.* Tokyo: Shinchōsha, 1961.

Mori Naoko. *Onna wa poruno o yomu: Josei no seiyoku to feminizumu.* Tokyo: Seikyūsha, 2010.

Mori Ōgai. *Wita sekushuarisu.* 1909. In *Mori Ōgai zenshū,* vol. 1, 209–320. Tokyo: Chikuma Shobō, 1995.

Morimoto, Lori. "(Trans)Cultural Legibility and Online *Yuri!!! on Ice* Fandom." *Mechademia: Second Arc* 12, no. 1 (2019): 136–159.

Morita Yūshū. *Dōseiai no kenkyū.* Chiba: Jinsei Sōzō Sha, 1931. In Furukawa and Akaeda, *Senzen dōseiai kanren bunken shūsei,* vol. 2, 141–226.

Murata Junko. "Takemiya Keiko kōenkai 'Sanrūmu' tanjō no kiseki." In Tokushima Kenritsu Bungaku Shodōkan, *"Takemiya Keiko no Sekai-ten" zuroku,* 16–17. Tokushima-shi: Tokushima Kenritsu Bungaku Shodōkan, 2006.

Muto Ichiyo. "The Birth of the Women's Liberation Movement in the 1970s." In *The Other Japan: Conflict, Compromise, and Resistance Since 1945,* edited by Joe Moore for the Bulletin of Concerned Asian Scholars, 147–171. Armonk, NY: M. E. Sharpe, 1997.

Myūzukaru "Onna no kaihō" 1975. DVD. Tokyo: Dotekabo Ichiza no Bideo Mitai Kai, 2005.

Nagai Reiko, Hanano Chiyo, Yamada Mitsuko, and Saeki Yōko. "Onna no karada." *Onna erosu,* no. 4 (March 1975): 114–123.

Nagano Yoshiko. "Women Fight for Control: Abortion Struggle in Japan." *AMPO: Report on Japanese People's Movements,* no. 17 (Summer 1973): 14–20.

Nakajima Azusa. "Onna no ko o miryō suru shōnen dōshi no ai." *Fujin kōron* 63, no. 7 (July 1978): 266–271.

Nakamoto Nobuyuki. *Chēhofu no naka no Nihon*. Tokyo: Daiwa Shobō, 1981.

Nakanishi Toyoko. *Onna no hon'ya (uimenzu bukkusutoa) no monogatari*. Tokyo: Domesu Shuppan, 2006.

Nakano Fuyumi. "Yaoi hyōgen to sabetsu: Onna no tame no porunogurafī o tokiho-gusu." *Josei raifusutairu kenkyū*, no. 4 (November 1994): 130–138.

Nakano Osamu. "Shōjo manga no kōzō bunseki." *Yurīka* 13, no. 9 (July 1981): 20–31.

Nakayama Chinatsu. *Gendai Nihon josei no kibun*. Tokyo: Mainichi Shinbun Sha, 1987.

Narabayashi Yasushi. *Rezubian rabu*. Tokyo: Kodama Puresu, 1967.

Nawa Kaori. "Rezubian bā no yoru to yoru." In Bessatsu Takarajima, no. 64, *Onna o ai suru onnatachi no monogatari*, 100–110.

Nihon Joseigaku Kenkyūkai "Purojekuto 20." "Anata e." In their *Watashi kara feminizumu: Nihon Joseigaku Kenkyūkai 20-shūnen ki'nenshi*, i. Osaka: Nihon Joseigaku Kenkyūkai, 1998.

Nimiya Kazuko. *Adaruto chirudoren to shōjo manga*. Tokyo: Kōsaidō, 1997.

Nishihara Ryōko and Bukkurisuto-han. "Rezubian no suimyaku o tadoru bukkurisuto 35." In Bessatsu Takarajima, no. 64, *Onna o ai suru onnatachi no monogatari*, 144–145.

Nishimura Mari. *Aniparo to yaoi*. Tokyo: Ōta Shuppan, 2002.

Nomura Fumiko. "Komyunāzu gei ando mūbī." *June*, no. 35 (July 1987): 50–52.

Norgren, Tiana. *Abortion Before Birth Control: The Politics of Reproduction in Postwar Japan*. Princeton, NJ: Princeton University Press, 2001.

Ogino Miho. "Nihon-ban ni tsuite." In Boston Women's Health Book Collective, *Karada, watashitachi jishin*, 8–9.

Omegabāsu purojekkuto 1. Tokyo: Fyūjon Purodakuto, 2015.

Onna erosu. "Henshū kōki." No. 2 (April 1974): 212–213.

———. "Henshū kōki." No. 8 (March 1977): 190–191.

Onna kara onnatachi e [Osaka]. "Gurūpu dayori." No. 1 (March 1972): 5.

———. "Haito ripōto o yonde." No. 26 (Spring 1978): 3–6

Onna kara onnatachi e [Urufu no kai, Tokyo]. "Hajime ni." No. 2 (Fall 1972): 1–2.

Onna no hangyaku. "Onna no karada renzoku tīchi in." No. 16 (March 1977): 38.

Onnatachi no Ima o Tou Kai, ed. *Zenkyōtō kara ribu e*. Tokyo: Inpakuto Shuppankai, 1996.

Ortabasi, Melek. "Brave Dogs and Little Lords: Some Thoughts on Translation, Gender, and the Debate on Childhood in Mid Meiji." In Levy, *Translation in Modern Japan*, 178–205.

Ortiz, Fernando. *Cuban Counterpoint: Tobacco and Sugar*. 1940. Translated by Harriet de Onìs. Durham, NC: Duke University Press, 1995.

Ōtani Junko, Saitō Sachie, Kitamura Mitsuko, Hatazawa Aiko, Matsumura Sachiko, and Mizoguchi Akiyo. "Zadankai: Chūpiren wa ribu datta no ka." *Onna erosu*, no. 10 (March 1978): 127–137.

Ōtsuka Eiji. *Shōjo minzokugaku: Sekimatsu no shinwa o tsumugu "miko no matsuei."* Tokyo: Kōbunsha, 1989.

Pafu. "Boy's Love Magazine kanzen kōryaku manyuaru." No. 217 (August 1994): 52–59.

Peterson, Linda M. "English Language Journal in Japan." *Lesbian News and Views* [Japan; also called *The DD*], no. 1 (May 1986): 1.

———. "Rezubian in Tokyo." In *Finding the Lesbians: Personal Accounts from Around the World*, edited by Julia Penelope and Sarah Valentine, 128–135. Freedom, CA: Crossing Press, 1990.

Peyrefitte, Roger. *Les amitiés particulières: roman*. Marseille: Jean Vigneau, 1943.

Pflugfelder, Gregory M. *Cartographies of Desire: Male–Male Sexuality in Japanese Discourse, 1600–1950*. Berkeley: University of California Press, 1999.

———. "'S' Is for Sister: Schoolgirl Intimacy and 'Same-Sex Love' in Early Twentieth-Century Japan." In *Gendering Modern Japanese History*, edited by Barbara Molony and Kathleen Uno, 133–190. Cambridge, MA: Harvard University Press, 2005.

Pharr, Susan. "Nihon no josei, Amerika no josei." Translated by Kō Mami. *Ribu nyūsu: Kono michi hitosuji*, no. 1 (September 1972): 3. In Ribu Shinjuku Sentā Shiryō Hozon Kai, *Ribu Shinjuku Sentā shiryō shūsei: Ribu nyūsu: Kono michi hitosuji*, 3.

Piercy, Marge. "The Grand Coolie Dam." *Leviathan* 1, no. 6 (1969): 16–22.

———. "Idai na kūrī: Josei." 1969. Translated by Akiyama Yōko. In Josei Kaihō Undō Junbi Kai, *Josei kaihō undō shiryō 1*, 24–43.

Popova, Milena. "'Dogfuck Rapeworld': Omegaverse Fanfiction as a Critical Tool in Analyzing the Impact of Social Power Structures on Intimate Relationships and Sexual Consent." *Porn Studies* 5, no. 2 (2018): 175–191.

Pratt, Mary Louise. *Imperial Eyes: Travel Writing and Transculturation*. London: Routledge, 1992.

Prime Minister's Office. *Tourism White Paper*. Tokyo: Prime Minister's Office, 1971.

———. *Tourism White Paper*. Tokyo: Prime Minister's Office, 1974.

———. *Tourism White Paper*. Tokyo: Prime Minister's Office, 1977.

———. *Tourism White Paper*. Tokyo: Prime Minister's Office, 1981.

———. *Tourism White Paper*. Tokyo: Prime Minister's Office, 1991.

Program: Jūichigatsu no gimunajiumu. Japan: Privately printed, 1974.

Prough, Jennifer S. *Straight from the Heart: Gender, Intimacy, and the Cultural Production of* Shōjo Manga. Honolulu: University of Hawai'i Press, 2011.

Puar, Jasbir Kaur, ed. "Queer Tourism: Geographies of Globalization." Special issue. *GLQ* 8, nos. 1–2 (2002).

Quinn, Aragorn, compiler, with Joanna Sturiano. "Annotated Bibliography of Translation Studies in Japan." In Levy, *Translation in Modern Japan*, 254–269.

Radikaru Ribu Gurūpu tsūshin. "Dai san no sei." November 29, 1970. In Mizoguchi, Saeki, and Miki, *Shiryō Nihon ūman ribu shi*, vol. I, 111–113.

Redstockings. "Redddo sutokkingu sengen." Translated by Urufu no Kai. In Firestone and Koedt, *Onna kara onnatachi e*, 212–216.

Regumi Sutajio Tokyo. "Īno Yuriko-san chosho *Rezubian de aru 'watashitachi' no sutōrī* ni tsuite." *Regumi tsūshin*, no. 250 (September 2008): 2–3.

Reich, Wilhelm. *Sei to bunka no kakumei*. Translated by Nakao Hajime. Tokyo: Keisō Shobō, 1969.

Reichert, Jim. *In the Company of Men: Representations of Male–Male Sexuality in Meiji Literature*. Stanford, CA: Stanford University Press, 2006.

Resubosu kurabu, no. 6. Tokyo: Sanwa Shuppan, 1997.

Ribu nyūsu: Kono michi hitosuji. "Resubian." No. 14 (1974): 7. In Ribu Shinjuku Sentā Shiryō Hozon Kai, *Ribu Shinjuku Sentā shiryō shūsei: Ribu nyūsu: Kono michi hitosuji,* 171.

———. "Sukejūru." No. 4 (September 1973): 24. In Ribu Shinjuku Sentā Shiryō Hozon Kai, *Ribu Shinjuku Sentā shiryō shūsei: Ribu nyūsu: Kono michi hitosuji,* 73.

Ribu Shinjuku Sentā Shiryō Hozon Kai (RSSSHK), ed. *Ribu Shinjuku Sentā shiryō shūsei: Bira hen.* Tokyo: Inpakuto Shuppankai, 2008.

———, ed. *Ribu Shinjuku Sentā shiryō shūsei: Panfuretto hen.* Tokyo: Inpakuto Shuppankai, 2008.

———, ed. *Ribu Shinjuku Sentā shiryō shūsei: Ribu nyūsu: Kono michi hitosuji.* Tokyo: Inpakuto Shuppankai, 2008.

Rich, Adrienne. "Compulsory Heterosexuality and Lesbian Existence." 1980. In her *Blood, Bread, and Poetry,* 23–75. New York: W. W. Norton, 1986.

Ripples of Change: Japanese Women's Search for Self. Documentary/DVD. Dir. Nanako Kurihara. Japan/USA: Women Make Movies, 1993.

Robertson, Jennifer. "Dying to Tell: Sexuality and Suicide in Imperial Japan." *Signs: Journal of Women in Culture and Society* 25, no. 1 (1999): 1–35.

———. *Takarazuka: Sexual Politics and Popular Culture in Modern Japan.* Berkeley: University of California Press, 1998.

Rokudenashiko. *Watashi no karada ga waisetsu?! Onna no soko dake naze ga tabū.* Tokyo: Chikuma Shobō, 2015.

Rovizu, Pieru. "Resubiennu." *Fūzoku kitan,* August 1960, 54–55.

Rowling, J. K. *Harry Potter and the Philosopher's Stone.* London: Bloomsbury, 1997.

RSSSHK. *See* Ribu Shinjuku Sentā Shiryō Hozon Kai.

Saeki Junko. "From *Iro* (Eros) to *Ai=Love:* The Case of Tsubouchi Shōyō." Translated by Indra Levy. In Levy, *Translation in Modern Japan,* 73–101.

———. "*Iro*" to "*ai*" no hikaku bunka shi. Tokyo: Iwanami Shoten, 1998.

Saeki Yōko. "Gurūpu Tatakau Onna (Tōkyō)." In Mizoguchi, Saeki, and Miki, *Shiryō Nihon ūman ribu shi,* vol. I, 209.

———. "Tōkyō Komuunu." In Mizoguchi, Saeki, and Miki, *Shiryō Nihon ūman ribu shi,* vol. II, 26.

Sagawa Toshihiko. "Bungaku to goraku no aida o ittari, kitari." Interview by Ishida Minori. In Ishida, *Hisoyaka na kyōiku,* 325–352.

Saijō Eriko. "Dansō no reijin, Masuda Fumiko no shioerabu made." *Fujin kōron* 20, no. 3 (March 1935): 168–178.

Saijō Michio, Ōgiya Afu, Ueshima Tsugi, Miwa Yōko, and Kawakami Seiko. "Zadankai: josei no homo makari tōru." *Fūzoku kagaku,* March 1955, 148–157.

Saito, Asako P. "From Legends to Games to Homoerotic Fiction: *Dynasty Warriors* BL Texts from China, Japan, and Taiwan." In Welker, ed., *Queer Transfigurations,* 257–271.

Saitō Masami. "'Ūman ribu to media' 'ribu to joseigaku' no dansetsu o saikō suru: 1970-nen aki *Asahi shinbun* tonai-ban no ribu hōdō o kiten toshite." *Joseigaku nenpō* 24 (2003): 1–20.

Sakai Kiyoshi. "Resubiennu." *Gurotesuku* 1, no. 2 (December 1928): 16–20.

Sanrūmu. "Kēko-sensei kara no Yōroppa omiyage tōsensha-san . . . kei 184mei-sama ni purezento!!" No. 8 (December 31, 1977): 26.

———. "Kēko-tan kara Yōroppa no kaze purezento." No. 7 (September 15, 1977): 16–17.

———. "Natsu no shūkai kanzen hōkoku!" No. 7 (September 15, 1977): 28–31.

———. "Yōroppa omiyage tōsensha-san happyō." No. 5 (November 24, 1980): 34.

Sarachild, Kathie. "Josei kaihō no puroguramu: Ishiki no kakumei." Translated by Urufu no Kai. In Firestone and Koedt, *Onna kara onnatachi e*, 217–224.

———. "A Program for Feminist 'Consciousness Raising.'" In Firestone and Koedt, *Notes from the Second Year*, 78–80.

Sasaki-Uemura, Wesley Makoto. *Organizing the Spontaneous: Citizen Protest in Postwar Japan*. Honolulu: University of Hawai'i Press, 2001.

Sasaya Nanae. "Gesuto kōnā: Pari kaeri no Sasaya Nanae-sensei kara mina-sama e." *Sanrūmu*, no. 3 (October 1, 1976): 20.

Satō Kōka. "Seiyokugaku goi." Part 1. *Hentai shiryō* 1, no. 3 (1926): 1–102. Reprint. Tokyo: Yumani Shobō, 2006.

———. "Seiyokugaku goi." Part 2. *Hentai shiryō* 2, no. 5 (1927), special supplement: 1–118. Reprint. Tokyo: Yumani Shobō, 2006.

———. *Sekai seiyokugaku jiten*. Tokyo: Kōbunsha, 1929.

Satō Masaki. "Shōjo manga to homofobia." In Kuia Sutadīzu Henshū Iinkai, *Kuia sutadīzu '96*, 161–169.

Sawabe Hitomi. See also Hirosawa Yumi, and Ogura Yūko.

———. "*Onna o ai suru onnatachi no monogatari* o meguru hyōgen katsudō." Oral history by Sugiura Ikuko. In Sugiura, *Nihon no rezubian komyuniti*, 38–65.

———. "The Symbolic Tree of Lesbianism in Japan: An Overview of Lesbian Activist History and Literary Works." Translated by Kimberly Hughes. In *Sparkling Rain and Other Fiction from Japan of Women Who Love Women*, edited by Barbara Summerhawk and Kimberly Hughes, 6–32. Chicago: New Victoria Publishers, 2008.

Sawada Junjirō. *Shinpi-naru dōseiai*. 2 vols. Tokyo: Kyōekisha Shuppanbu, 1923. In Furukawa and Akaeda, *Senzen dōseiai kanren bunken shūsei*, vol. 1, 187–287.

Schieder, Chelsea Szendi. *Coed Revolution: The Female Student in the Japanese New Left*. Durham, NC: Duke University Press, 2021.

Scott, Joan W. "The Evidence of Experience." *Critical Inquiry* 17, no. 4 (1991): 773–797.

Sei Ishiki Chōsa Gurūpu, ed. *Sanbyakujū nin no sei ishiki: Iseiaisha dewa nai onnatachi no ankēto chōsa*. Tokyo: Nanatsumori Shokan, 1998.

Seike Atsushi. "Japan's Demographic Collapse." In Funabashi and Kushner, *Examining Japan's Lost Decades*, 1–16.

Setouchi Harumi. "Dōseiai no onna." *Fujin kōron* 49, no. 11 (November 1964): 232–236.

S.F. "Ribu FUKUOKA no koto." 1985. In Mizoguchi, Saeki, and Miki, *Shiryō Nihon ūman ribu shi*, vol. I, 290–291.

Shelley, Martha. "Lesbianism and the Women's Liberation Movement." In Stambler, 123–129.

Shiba Fumiko. "Shōwa rokujū [sic] nendai rezubian būmu." In Kakinuma and Kurihara, *Tanbi shōsetsu, gei bungaku bukkugaido*, 290–291.

Shigematsu, Setsu. *Scream from the Shadows: The Women's Liberation Movement in Japan.* Minneapolis: University of Minnesota Press, 2012.

Shimamura Mari. *Bābī, anata wa doko e iku no? Shiteki Amerika-ron no kokoromi.* Tokyo: Magajin Hausu, 1993.

———. *Onna wa minna mīhā desu.* Tokyo: Kawade Shobō Shinsha, 2005.

Shimotsuki Takanaka. *Komikku Māketto sōseiki.* Tokyo: Asahi Shinbun Shuppan, 2008.

Shin chihei. "Motto shintai aisou yo: Ūmanzu Herusu Sentā." No. 131 (November 1985): 55.

Shōjo komikku. "Anata o natsu yasumi ni Hawai e go-shōtai!! *Shūkan shōjo komikku* aidoru māku boshū!!" July 5, 1970, 26–27.

———. "Banpaku kara konnichiwa!" July 5, 1970, 7–11.

———. "Gokigen!! Hawai no bakansu: *Shūkan shōjo komikku* aidoru māku boshū Hawai shōtai." October 11, 1970, 10.

———. "Honkon izu mai hōmu: Agnes in Hong Kong." August 19, 1973, 13–18.

———. "O-kaimono dai kenshō," March 27, 1970, 7.

Shūkan bunshun. "Jūshūnen o mukaeta rezu gurūpu hyakunin: Sono na mo 'Wakakusa no Kai.'" June 25, 1981, 41–43.

———. "Zenbei ūman pawā no shidōsha wa Nihonjin no tsuma: Josei kaihō no 'Mō goroku' o kaita Kēto Yoshimura." September 14, 1970, 30–34.

Shūkan gendai. "BG no aida ni dōseiai ga kyūzō shiteiru!" February 23, 1967, 94–98.

Shūkan josei. "Watashi wa 'rezubian no kai' (kaiin 80-nin) no kaichō-san." November 24, 1973, 173–175.

——— "Zen sekai o miryoku suru Tai BL dorama senpū." June 16, 2020, 131–133.

Shūkan manga sandē. "Fukaku shizuka ni ryūkō suru 'resubian': Onna ga onna o ai suru gendai no ijō na sei fūzoku." November 23, 1966: 54–57.

Shūkan taishū. "*Onna ga onna o kau: Otokotachi wa josō-rezu ga dai kōryū!!*" February 10, 1992: 88–91.

———. "Otoko no tame no resubian-gaku nyūmon." June 20, 1968: 100–102.

Sievers, Sharon L. *Flowers in Salt: The Beginnings of Feminist Consciousness in Japan.* Stanford, CA: Stanford University Press, 1983.

Sinnott, Megan. "Borders, Diaspora, and Regional Connections: Trends in Asian 'Queer' Studies." *Journal of Asian Studies* 69, no. 1 (February 2010): 17–31.

Smith, Patricia Juliana. *Lesbian Panic: Homoeroticism in Modern British Women's Fiction.* New York: Columbia University Press, 1997.

Stambler, Sookie, compiler. *Women's Liberation: Blueprint for the Future.* New York: Ace Books, 1970.

Steinem, Gloria. "Kanzen byōdō no yūtopia: Ribu kakumei ga umidasu shakai." Translated by Ikegami Chizuko. In Aki Shobō Henshūbu, 252–261.

———. "What It Would Be Like if Women Win." *Time,* August 31, 1970, 22, 25.

Subarashī onnatachi. No. 1 (November 1976). Also in Ribu Shinjuku Sentā Shiryō Hozon Kai, *Ribu Shinjuku Sentā shiryō shūsei: Panfuretto hen,* 480–518.

———. "'Resubian ni kan suru ankēto' shūkei repōto." No. 1 (1976), supplement.

———. "Zadankai 'Rezubian ōi ni kataru.'" No. 1 (November 1976): 6–32.

————. "Zasshi no hakkan ni attate." No. 1 (November 1976): 1.

Sugiura Ikuko. "Nihon ni okeru rezubian feminizumu no katsudō: 1970-nendai kōhan no reimeiki ni okeru." *Jendā kenkyū* [Tōkai Jendā Kenkyūsho], no. 11 (December 2008): 143–170.

————, ed. *Nihon no rezubian komyuniti: Kōjutsu no undō shi.* Tokyo: Privately printed, 2009.

Suzuki Michiko. "Go-aisatsu." *Wakakusa* (Spring 1975): 1.

————. "Rezubian no kai o shusai shite jūnen." *Fujin kōron* 68, no. 1 (January 1983): 340–344.

————. "Sōkan no kotoba." *Ibu ando ibu,* no. 1 (August 1982): 2–3.

Suzuki Tadashi. "Zenkyōtō wa 'ribu' ni manabu." *Fujin kōron* 55, no. 7 (July 1970): 184–189.

Tabei Kyōko. "Watashi no aruitekita michi." *Subarashī onnatachi* 1 (November 1976): 44–48.

Tabuchi Hideaki, Enomoto Yūya, and Fujio Puro. "O-warai banpaku." *Shōjo komikku,* March 27, 1970, 173–185.

Takagi Sawako. "A Short Message from Femintern Press: For International Communication." 1974. In Mizoguchi, Saeki, and Miki, *Shiryō Nihon ūman ribu shi,* vol. II, 308–309.

Takahashi, Mizuki. "Opening the Closed World of *Shōjo Manga.*" In MacWilliams, *Japanese Visual Culture,* 114–136.

Takahashi Tetsu. *Abu rabu: Ijō ai ripōto.* Tokyo: Seyūsha, 1966.

Takahashi Yōichi. *Kyaputen Tsubasa.* 1981–1988. 37 vols. Tokyo: Shūeisha, 1982–1989.

Takano Fumi. "Kaisetsu." In Millett et al., *Ūman ribu: Josei wa nani o kangae, nani o motomeru ka?,* 299–303.

Takaya, Ted T. "Introduction." In his *Modern Japanese Drama: An Anthology,* xv–xxxvii. New York: Columbia University Press, 1979.

Takeda Hajime. "Taruho no shōmetsu no hi ni." *Barazoku,* no. 60 (January 1978): 169.

Takemiya Keiko. *La balada del viento y los árboles.* 1976–1984. 10 vols. Translated by Marc Bernabé and Maite Madinabeitia. Asturias, Spain: Milky Way Ediciones, 2018–2020.

————. "Josei wa gei ga suki?" *Bungei shunshū* 71, no. 6 (June 1993): 82–83.

————. "Karā irasuto kagami no kuni no shōnentachi." *Pēpā mūn,* no. 14 (1978): 5–6.

————. *Kaze to ki no uta.* 1976–1984. 10 vols. Tokyo: Hakusensha Bunko, 1995.

————. "Kēko-tan shiroi Doitsu o yuku." *Pēpā mūn,* no. 14 (September 1978): 82–85.

————. "Kēko-tan no yōroppa ryokōki." *Shōjo komikku,* December 24, 1972, 206.

————. "Kibun wa ima mo Yōroppa." *Gurēpufurūtsu,* no. 16 (June 1984): 113–116.

————. *Kibun wa ima mo Yōroppa: Mai toraberu gaido.* Tokyo: Shinshokan, 1989.

————. "Konnichiwa sayonara 2." *Shōjo komikku,* January 7, 1973, 114–115.

————. "Konnichiwa sayonara 5," *Shōjo komikku,* February 11, 1973, 116–117.

————. "Kurisumasu no Uīn e konai ka." *Pēpā mūn,* no. 16 (April 1979): 76–81.

————. "O-egaki kyōshitsu." *June,* no. 15 (March 1984): 86.

————. *Il poema del vento e degli alberi.* 1976–1984. 10 vols. Translated by Marco Franca. Milan: Edizioni BD, 2018–2019.

————. "Sanrūmu nite." 1970. In her *Sanrūmu nite*, 5–54. Tokyo: San Komikkusu, 1976.

————. *Sora ga suki!* 1971–1972. 2 vols. Tokyo: Shōgakukan, 1974.

————. "*Sora ga suki!*" part 2, final installment. *Shōjo komikku*, October 8, 1972, 141–155.

————. *Takemiya Keiko no manga kyōshitsu*. Tokyo: Chikuma Shobō, 2001.

————. "Tokutō shindaisha de yume no kuni e." *Gurēpufurutsu*, no. 11 (August 1983): 166–169.

————. *Uīn gensō*. Tokyo: Hakusensha, 1979.

————. "Uīn no yūutsu." *Pēpā mūn*, no. 23 (November 1980): 102–105.

————. "Yōroppa hoteru monogatari." *Gurēpufurutsu*, no. 9 (April 1983): 52–55.

Takeuchi Keiko. "The Complexity of Sexuality and *Kurowassan*." In Wöhr, Satō, and Suzuki, *Gender and Modernity*, 163–166.

Tanaka, Kazuko. *A Short History of the Women's Movement in Modern Japan*. 3rd ed. 1975. Tokyo: Femintern Press, 1977.

Tanaka, Keiko. "Japanese Women's Magazines: The Language of Aspiration." In *The Worlds of Japanese Popular Culture: Gender, Shifting Boundaries and Global Cultures*, edited by D. P. Martinez, 110–132. Cambridge: Cambridge University Press, 1998.

Tanaka Kōgai. "Dōseiai no bunrui to kasei iseiai." *Hentai shinri* 16, no. 5 (November 1925): 97–101.

Tanaka Mitsu. "Benjo kara no kaihō." 1970. In Ribu Shinjuku Sentā Shiryō Hozon Kai, *Ribu Shinjuku Sentā shiryō shūsei: Bira hen*, 20–25.

————. "Erosu kaihō sengen." 1970. In Ribu Shinjuku Sentā Shiryō Hozon Kai, *Ribu Shinjuku Sentā shiryō shūsei: Bira hen*, 7.

————. "Erosu kaihō sengen." 1970. In Ribu Shinjuku Sentā Shiryō Hozon Kai, *Ribu Shinjuku Sentā shiryō shūsei: Bira hen*, 8.

————. *Inochi no onnatachi e: Torimidashi ūman ribu ron*. Tokyo: Tabata Shoten, 1972.

————. "Josei kaihō e no kojinteki shiten." 1970. In Ribu Shinjuku Sentā Shiryō Hozon Kai, *Ribu Shinjuku Sentā shiryō shūsei: Bira hen*, 10–16.

————. "Mirai o tsukanda onnatachi." Interview by Kitahara Minori and Ueno Chizuko. In *Sengo Nihon sutadīzu 2: 60, 70-nendai*, edited by Komori Yōichi, Narita Ryūichi, Iwasaki Minoru, Ueno Chizuko, and Kitada Akihiro, 279–334. Tokyo: Kinokuniya Shoten, 2009.

Tani Yukiko. "Koibito wa kokusan (meido in Japan) yo!" *Shōjo komikku*, May 3, 1970, 171–201.

Taniguchi Rei. *Shōnen'aisha: Shinwa to tabū ni tsutsumareta karera no hontō no suguta o saguru*. Tokyo: Tsuge Shobō Shinsha, 2003.

Tanizaki Jun'ichirō. *Manji*. 1928–1930. In his *Tanizaki Jun'ichirō zenshū*, vol. 17, 1–169. Tokyo: Chūō Kōronsha, 1959.

————. *Quicksand*. 1928–1930. Translated by Howard Hibbett. New York: Knopf, 1994.

Tanizaki Jun'ichirō, Wakao Ayako, and Kishida Kyōko. "Zadankai: *Manji* no konbi no onna no himitsu o kataru." *Fujin kōron* 49, no. 9 (September 1964): 198–204.

Tarasyuk, Yuliya. "Queer Roleplaying Practices in Russian Female BL Fandom." *Mechademia : Second Arc* 13, no. 1 (2020): 163–166.

Tax, Meredith. "Onna no shinjō." Translated by Urufu no Kai. In Firestone and Koedt, *Onna kara onnatachi e*, 15–23.

————. "Woman and Her Mind: The Story of Everyday Life." In Firestone and Koedt, *Notes from the Second Year*, 10–16.

Tenshin Ranran. "Media ga nakatta koro no baiburu." In Kuia Sutadīzu Henshū Iinkai, *Kuia sutadīzu '96*, 193–194.

Terada Kaoru. "70-nendai enkyori shōjo manga no jidai." In Bessatsu Takarajima, no. 288, *70-nendai manga daihyakka*, 158–165.

Tezuka Osamu. *Ribon no kishi*. 1953–1955. Tokyo: Kōdansha Manga Bunko, 1999.

Ting (Ding) Ling, and Akiyama Yōko. *Ting Ling: Purged Feminist*. With translations by Akiyama Yōko and Larry Taub. Tokyo: Femintern Press, 1974.

Tomioka Akemi and Hara (Minako) Minata. "Yakusha kaisetsu." In Faderman, *Resubian no rekishi*, 384–393.

Tomita Sumireko. "Rezibian bā ga toransu josei no nyūjō kyohi, shazai: LGBT tōjisha-kan no sabetsu meguru giron hirogaru." *BuzzFeed News*, June 9, 2019. https://www.buzzfeed.com/jp/sumirekotomita/gold-finger-1.

Tomooka Nobusuke. *Jinrui sei seikatsu shi*. Kyoto: Jinbun Shoin, 1932.

Tong, Rosemarie Putnam. *Feminist Thought: A More Comprehensive Introduction*. 2nd ed. Boulder, CO: Westview Press, 1998.

Toyama Hitomi. *Miss dandi: Otoko toshite ikiru joseitachi*. Tokyo: Shinchōsha, 1999.

Tsing, Anna Lowenhaupt. "Worlds in Motion." In *Words in Motion: Toward a Global Lexicon*, edited by Carol Gluck and Anna Lowenhaupt Tsing, 11–17. Durham, NC: Duke University Press, 2009.

Tsurumi, Kazuko. "Foreword." In *Women in Changing Japan*, edited by Joyce Lebra, Joy Paulson, and Elizabeth Powers, vi–vii. Stanford, CA: Stanford University Press, 1975.

Tymoczko, Maria. *Enlarging Translation, Empowering Translators*. Manchester, UK: St. Jerome Publishing, 2007.

Uchiyama, Akiko. "Japanese Girls' Comfort Reading of *Anne of Green Gables*." In *Girl Reading Girl in Japan*, edited by Tomoko Aoyama and Barbara Hartley, 92–103. New York: Routledge, 2010.

Uno Jūkichi. *Chēhofu no Sakura no sono ni tsuite*. Tokyo: Bakushūsha, 1978.

Uno, Kathleen S. "The Death of 'Good Wife, Wise Mother'?" In Gordon, *Postwar Japan as History*, 293–322.

Ura Masaharu. "Chēhofu no bunken mokuroku." *Yurīka* 10, no. 6 (June 1978): 228–231.

Urufu no Kai. "Maegaki: 14-nin no onnatachi kara." *Onna kara onnatachi e* [Urufu no kai, Tokyo], no. 1 (1972): 1.

————. "Onna kara onnatachi e: Zadankai: Yakusha no atogaki ni kaete." In Firestone and Koedt, *Onna kara onnatachi e*, 225–256.

————. "Taiken kiroku: Wa ga sei no jikken: *Onna kara onnatachi e* no hōkoku." *Fujin kōron* 58, no. 4 (April 1973): 118–133.

————. "Yakusha maegaki." In Firestone and Koedt, *Onna kara onnatachi e*, 1–5.

Valentine, David. *Imagining Transgender: An Ethnography of a Category*. Durham, NC: Duke University Press, 2007.

van Dyke, Joni. *Dyketionary*. 2nd ed. Tokyo: Privately printed, ca. 1985.

Venuti, Lawrence. *The Translator's Invisibility: A History of Translation*. 2nd ed. 1995. London: Routledge, 2008.

Wakabayashi Naeko. "Ajiakei rezubian toshite." *Imago* 6, no. 12 (November 1995): 70–74.

———. "Lesbian = Woman." In *Queer Japan, Queer Japan: Personal Stories of Japanese Lesbians, Gays, Bisexuals, and Transsexuals,* edited by Barbara Summerhawk, Cheiron McMahill, and Darren McDonald, 184–187. Norwich, VT: New Victoria, 1998.

———. "'Onna no karada' renzoku tīchi in: Onna no tame no kurinikku setsuritsu ni mukete." *Onna erosu,* no. 8 (March 1977): 161–162.

———. "Onna no nettowāku no naka de ikiru." Oral history by Sugiura Ikuko. In Sugiura, *Nihon no rezubian komyuniti,* 17–37.

Wakakusa. "Resubian o atsukatta sakuhin." Spring 1975, 19–47.

Weathers, Maryanne. "An Argument for Black Women's Liberation." In Stambler, *Women's Liberation,* 161–165.

Weekly pureibōi. "Shōjo manga dai kenkyū de jitōtto 'nurie-chikku kōsaihō' osēmasu." September 9, 1986, 64–67.

Wei, Wei. "Straight Men, Gay Buddies: The Chinese BL Boom and Its Impact on Male Homosociality." In Welker, ed., *Queer Transfigurations,* 55–67.

Welker, James. "Beautiful, Borrowed, and Bent: Boys' Love as Girls' Love in *Shōjo* Manga." *Signs: Journal of Women in Culture and Society* 31, no. 3 (2006): 841–870.

———. "Boys Love (Yaoi), and the Global Circulation of." In *Global Encyclopedia of Lesbian, Gay, Bisexual, Transgender, and Queer History,* edited by Howard Chiang, Anjali Arondekar, Marc Epprecht, Jennifer Evans, Ross Forman, Hanadi al-Samman, Emily Skidmore, and Zeb Tortorici, vol. 1, 262–268. New York: Charles Scribner & Sons, 2019.

———. "A Brief History of *Shōnen'ai, Yaoi,* and Boys' Love." In McLelland et al., *Boys Love Manga and Beyond,* 42–75.

———. "Drawing Out Lesbians: Blurred Representations of Lesbian Desire in *Shōjo* Manga." In *Lesbian Voices: Canada and the World: Theory, Literature, Cinema,* edited by Subhash Chandra, 156–184. New Delhi: Allied Publishers, 2006.

———. "Flower Tribes and Female Desire: Complicating Early Female Consumption of Male Homosexuality in *Shōjo* Manga." *Mechademia: An Annual Forum for Anime, Manga and the Fan Arts* 6 (2011): 211–228.

———. "From *The Cherry Orchard* to *Sakura no sono:* Translation and the Transfiguration of Gender and Sexuality in *Shōjo* Manga." In Aoyama and Hartley, *Girl Reading Girl in Japan,* 160–173.

———. "From Women's Liberation to Lesbian Feminism in Japan: *Rezubian Feminizumu* Within and Beyond the *Ūman Ribu* Movement in the 1970s and 1980s." In *Rethinking Japanese Feminisms,* edited by Julia Bullock, Ayako Kano, and James Welker, 50–67. Honolulu: University of Hawai'i Press, 2018.

———. "Lilies of the Margin: Beautiful Boys and Queer Female Identities in Japan." In *AsiaPacifiQueer: Rethinking Gender and Sexuality,* edited by Fran Martin, Peter A. Jackson, Mark McLelland, and Audrey Yue, 46–66. Urbana: University of Illinois Press, 2008.

———, ed. *Queer Transfigurations: Boys Love Media in Asia.* Honolulu: University of Hawai'i Press, 2022.

———. "The Revolution Cannot Be Translated: Transfiguring Discourses of Women's Liberation in 1970s–1980s Japan." In Curran, Sato-Rossberg, and Tanabe, *Multiple Translation Communities in Contemporary Japan,* 60–78.

————. "Telling Her Story: Narrating a Japanese Lesbian Community." *Japanstudien: Jahrbuch des Deutschen Instituts für Japanstudien* 16 (2004): 119–144.

————. "Toward a History of 'Lesbian History' in Japan." *Culture, Theory and Critique* 58, no. 2 (2017): 147–165.

————. "Translating Women's Liberation, Translating Women's Bodies in 1970s–1980s Japan." *Rim: Journal of the Asia-Pacific Women's Studies Association* 13, no. 2 (2012): xxviii–xxxvii.

Welker, James, and Lucetta Kam. "Introduction: Of Queer Import(s) in Asia." *Intersections: Gender and Sexuality in Asia and the Pacific* 14 (November 2006). http://intersections.anu.edu.au/issue14/introduction.htm.

Weston, Kath. "Lesbian/Gay Studies in the House of Anthropology." *Annual Review of Anthropology* 22 (1993): 339–367.

Wöhr, Ulrike. Barbara Hamill Satō, and Suzuki Sadami, eds. *Gender and Modernity: Rereading Japanese Women's Magazines*. Kyoto: International Research Center for Japanese Studies, 2000.

Wolfe, Linda. *The Cosmo Report*. New York: Arbor House, 1981.

————. *Kosumo ripōto: 10-man 6-sen nin no josei ga kattata shinjitsu no ai to sei*. Translated by Hagitani Ryō. Tokyo: Bunka Shuppankyoku, 1983.

Women's International Network News. "Japan." No. 1 (January 1975): 13.

Xu, Yanrui, and Ling Yang. "Between BL and Slash: *Danmei* Fiction, Transcultural Mediation, and Changing Gender Norms in China." In Welker, ed., *Queer Transfigurations*, 19–30.

Yamagishi Ryōko. *Hi izuru tokoro no tenshi*. 1980–1984. 11 vols. Tokyo: Hana to Yume Komikkusu, 1980–1984.

Yamaguchi Makoto. *Nippon no kaigai ryokō: Wakamono to kankō media no 50-nenshi*. Tokyo: Chikuma Shobō, 2010.

Yamamoto Fumiko and BL Sapōtāzu. *Yappari, bōizu rabu ga suki: Kanzen BL komikku gaido*. Tokyo: Ōta Shuppan, 2005.

Yamashita Tomoko. "Dōseikon gōhōka, 8-wari kōteiteki: Dentsū chōsa no 20-dai–50-dai." *Asahi shinbun* January 21, 2019. https://www.asahi.com/articles/ASM1C52Z7M1CUTIL025.html.

Yamashita Yasuko. "The International Movement Toward Gender Equality and Its Impact on Japan." Translated by Elizabeth A. Leicester. *U.S.–Japan Women's Journal*, English supplement, no. 5 (1993): 69–86.

Yano Keizai Kenkyūsho. "'Otaku shijō' ni kan suru chōsa kekka 2011: 'Otaku jinkō' no zōka = 'raito na otaku' no zōka to tomo ni shijō kibo wa kakudai." Press release. October 26, 2011. http://www.yano.co.jp/press/pdf/863.pdf.

————. "'Otaku shijō' ni kan suru chōsa o jissen 2017-nen." Press release. December 5, 2017, https://www.yano.co.jp/press/press.php/001773.

Yasuda Tokutarō. "Dōseiai no rekishikan." *Chūō kōron*, March 1935, 146–152.

Yokota-Murakami, Takayuki. *Don Juan East/West: On the Problematics of Comparative Literature*. Albany: State University of New York Press, 1998.

Yomiuri shinbun. "Dōseiai kara shinjū." January 6, 1948, morning ed., 2.

————. "Kobushi, kyōsei roku jikan, ūman pawā sōkesshū." November 15, 1970, morning ed., 13.

———. "*Mi no mawari katakana no kotoba: Feminisuto.*" August 31, 1977, morning ed., 12.

———. "*Saidoraito: Ūman pawā.*" June 17, 1969, evening ed., 1.

Yonezu Tomoko. "Mizukara no SEX o mokuteki ishikiteki ni hikiukeru naka kara 70-nendai o bokki saseyo!!" May 12, 1970. In Ribu Shinjuku Sentā Shiryō Hozon Kai, *Ribu Shinjuku Sentā shiryō shūsei: Bira hen,* 2.

———. "10/21 o keiki toshite Shisō Shūdan Esu Ī Ekkusu sōkatsu." 1970. In Mizoguchi, Saeki, and Miki, *Shiryō Nihon ūman ribu shi,* vol. I, 175–176.

Yonezawa Yoshihiro. "Manga/anime no kaihōku, komike tte nani?" Interview. In Bessatsu Takarajima, no. 358, *Watashi o komike ni tsuretette!,* 10–25.

———. "Manga to dōjinshi no sasayaka no kyōen: Komiketto no ataeta eikyō." In Bessatsu Takarajima, no. 358, *Watashi o komike ni tsuretette!,* 40–49.

———. *Sengo ero manga shi.* Tokyo: Seirin Kōgeisha, 2010.

———. *Sengo shōjo manga shi.* 1980. Tokyo: Chikuma Shobō, 2007.

Yoshida Akimi. *Banana Fish.* 1987–1994. 19 vols. Tokyo: Shōgakukan, 1987–1994.

———. *Sakura no sono.* 1985–1986. Tokyo: Hakusensha Bunko, 1994.

Yoshihiro Kiyoko. "Amerika no ribu no atarashī nami." *Onna erosu,* no. 1 (November 1973): 106–111.

Yoshimi Shunya. *Banpaku to sengo Nihon.* Tokyo: Kōdansha, 2011.

Yoshiya Nobuko. "Aishiau koto domo." *Shin shōsetsu,* October 1921, 78–80.

Yurīka. 13, no. 9 (July 1981). Special issue. "*Shōjo* manga."

Yurino Reiko [Azuma Reiko]. "London Lesbien Report: Global Lesbianism." *Aran,* October 1982, 129–132.

Yūsei Hogo Hō Kaiaku o Soshi Suru Gakusei no Kai, ed. *Onna (watashi) no karada: Hinin o kangaeru.* Rev. ed. Tokyo: Yūsei Hogo Hō Kaiaku o Soshi Suru Gakusei no Kai, ca. 1984.

Za daiku. "Hikari guruma sōkan-gō." No. 2 (June 1978): 9.

Zimmerman, Bonnie. *Lesbian Histories and Cultures: An Encyclopedia.* London: Taylor & Francis, 2000.

INDEX

Page numbers in boldface type refer to illustrations.

30 Years of Sisterhood, 14, 32

abortion, 23, 25, 28–29, 65, 102, 103, 109, 112, 113. *See also* birth control

Agora (women's center), 187n36

Akisato Wakuni, 46

Akiyama Yōko: Femintern Press and, 138, 150, 152; *Notes from the Second Year* and, 109–110; *Our Bodies, Ourselves* and, 112–115; Women's Preparation Group and, 25, 56, 59–61, 63–64, 99–102, 105; Woolf Society and, 29

akogare, 127–128, 142–143, 162–163

Alcott, Louisa May, 32, 41

Allan (Aran; magazine), 5, 48, 49–50, 89, 90–91, 161, 164–165, 175, 177

Amano Michimi, 34, 77, 79, 115, 118, 145–148, 149, 166

Amitiés particulières, les (film), 130, **131**, 175

An An (magazine) 140–141

Andreson, Björn, 130

aniparo, 48–49, 51. See also *dōjinshi*

Anise (Anīsu; magazine), 40

Anpo, 21, 25, 28

anti-war movement, 25, 100, 104, 152. *See also* Anpo; Vietnam War

Aoike Yasuko, 45, 170

Asahi shinbun, 25, 35, 56, **57**, 57–58, 59, 61–62, 194n13. *See also* Ninagawa Masao

Asakawa Mari, 23, 34, 154, 189n84, 210n61

asexual women, 8

Asian Lesbian Network (ALN), 157, 178

Atkinson, Ti-Grace, 109

Atsumi Ikuko, 30. See also *Feminist (Feminisuto;* magazine)

Austria, 20, 69, 172, 173; Vienna, 166, 168, 170, 171, 174, 176

Barazoku (magazine), 38, 86–87, 89–90. *See also* Itō Bungaku

Baudelaire, Charles, 70

Baudinette, Thomas, 183

Beard, Miriam, 140

Beauvoir, Simone de, 96, 145, 146

Bermann, Sandra, 138

Bessatsu Takarajima (book series), 37, 43, 116, **117**, 122, **123**

birth control, 112; pill: 29, 64, 102, 113, 118. *See also* abortion

birthrate, 8–9

bisexual women, 8, 37

bishōnen: female desire for, 43, 87, 128, 130, 171, 172–173; female identification with, 43; male desire for 82, 87; as a *shōjo* manga genre, 87, 167, 170

BL. *See* boys love (BL)

Black power movement, 61

Black women, 108, 155

BLush (event), 182

Boston Women's Health Book Collective. See *Our Bodies, Ourselves*

Bowie, David, 47, 164, 192n166

boys' choirs, 171. *See also* Vienna Boys Choir

boys love (BL): genre, 138, 181–184; *seme* and *uke* roles in, 129, 183; term, 5, 82, 92–93, 94. See also *shōnen'ai* (genre); *shōnen'ai* (term); *yaoi* (term)
Brossard, Nicole, 66, 81
Bunch, Charlotte, 60, 102, 103
Butler, Judith, 135

Califia, Pat, 78
capitalism, 58, 104, 109
Captain Tsubasa (*Kyaputen Tsubasa;* manga and anime), 48
Carmilla (*Kāmira;* magazine), 40
Carpenter, Edward, 85
Carter, Angela, 146, 152, 209n20
Chekhov, Anton, 95, 99, 132–137
childbirth, 28, 110, 112, 113, 154. See also abortion; birth control; pregnancy
China, 25, 87–88, 138, 150, 182, 183
Chūpiren, 29, 64
Clifford, James, 177
Cocteau, Jean, 132
Comic Market (Komiketto, Komikku Māketto; event), 6, 9, 46–48, 50–51, 87, 90, 91
communal living. See Ribu Shinjuku Center; Tokyo Komuunu
communism, 21, 149. See also capitalism; Ding Ling; Marxism; New Left; socialism
Conference of Asian Women Fighting Discrimination=Invasion (Shinryaku=Sabetsu to Tatakau Ajia Fujin Kaigi), 208–209n16
consciousness raising, 26, 36, 108, 109
Constitution of Japan, 19–20
Convention on the Elimination of All Forms of Discrimination Against Women (CEDAW), 153. See also United Nations First World Conference on Women
Cosmo Report, 121
cosplay, 182
COVID-19, 46
Croissant (*Kurowassan;* magazine), 120, 140
cross-dressing: manga and, 5, 7, 135–136; men and, 79–80; trans identity and, 80, 182; women and, 7, 156, 182. See also Peter (celebrity); Takarazuka Revue
Cuba, 12, 152

Dales, Laura, 65
danmei (term), 87–88, 182–183
danshoku. See *nanshoku*
Daudet, Alphonse, 70
Davis, Kathy, 114, 203–204n91
Death in Venice (film), 17, 89, 130, 132, 174
Delon, Alain, 49, 162
Denmark, 146, 147
Ding Ling, 138, 150
disability, 23, 28, 169
Discover Japan (campaign), 140–142, 172, 179
Doi Yumi, 23, 30, 32, 154
dōjinshi, 6, 46–50, 51, 87, 90–91, 164, 175, 183
dōseiai (term), 53, 67, 68–69, 71, 73, 74, 75; *josei (no) dōseiai,* 69, 72; *josei dōseiaisha,* 35
Dotekabo Ichiza, 19, 22–23
draft evasion, 25, 143. See also Vietnam War
drag. See cross-dressing, Takarazuka Revue
Dyke Weekends. See Weekends (event)
Dynasty Warriors (video game series), 183

Ellis, Havelock, 68, 95
Enoki Misako, 29, 64
Equal Employment Opportunity Law, 29
erotic grotesque (*eroguro*) nonsense, 75, 85
esu (term). See S (*esu;* term)
ethnic Koreans in Japan (*Zainichi Kankokujin*), xii, 178
Eugenics Protection Law (Yūsei hogo hō), 28, 30, 118. See also Soshiren
Everett, Ruppert, 164
Everyday Dyke (Mainichi Daiku), 36
Expo '70, 140, 163–164, 175

Fabulous Forty-Niners, 41–42, 46, 47, 49, 166, 175
Faderman, Lillian, 78
Fairclough, Norman, 131–132
feminism: American, 35–36, 60–66, 99–108, 125, 147, 149–151; *ribu* and, 4, 30–31, 36, 60–66. See also *The Hite Report; Our Bodies, Ourselves; Notes from the Second Year*

Feminist (*Feminisuto;* magazine), 30, 65
feminisuto (term), xi, 30, 60–61, 65–66
feminizumu (term), xi, 10, 30, 60–61, 65
Femintern Press, 138, 149–151, **150**
Firestone, Shulamith, 108, 109
Foucault, Michel, 53, 54, 66, 93
France, 24, 74, 96, 130, 145–147, 148, 176;
    Paris, 141, 146, 166, 167, 170, 171, 173,
    183
Freeman, Jo, 109, 110–111
Freud, Sigmund, 26
Friedan, Betty, 26, 106
From Woman to Women (*Onna kara*
    onnatachi e): *mini-komi* from Osaka,
    26–27, **27**, 122; *mini-komi* from Tokyo, 11;
    translation of *Our Bodies, Ourselves:* see
    Our Bodies, Ourselves
Frye, Marilyn, 123
Fujieda Mioko, 3, 118
Fujimoto Yukari, 87, 133
fujin (term), 3–4, 31, 51, 63, 103–104. See
    also *fujin kaihō* (term)
fujin kaihō (term), 3, 60, 63, 103–104
Fujin kōron (magazine), 33, 37, 58, 106, 109,
    112, 113, 124, 157
Fujin minshu shinbun, 26, 148
fujoshi (term), 51
Funny (*Fanī;* magazine), 43
Fushimi Noriaki, 182
Fūzoku kagaku (magazine), 73
Fūzoku kitan (magazine), 74, 79–80

Galbraith, Patrick W., 51
Gaonkar, Dilip, 11–12, 97
gay boom (*gei būmu*), 8, 38–39, 40, 165, 182
gay comics (*gei komikkusu*), 92
gay (*gei*) community, 8, 39–40, 50, 52, 132,
    165
gay (*gei*) magazines. See *Barazoku; Sabu*
Gekkō (magazine), 48, 49–50, 89, 164–165.
    See also *Allan* (magazine)
Genet, Jean, 88, 128, 132
Germany, 129, 170, 171, 176
Gide, André, 128
Gluck, Carol, 21
Godard, Barbara, 108
Godard, Jean-Luc, 148

good wife, wise mother (*ryōsai kenbo*), 1,
    181
Grapefruit (*Gurēpufurutsu;* magazine), 170,
    172, 174
Group Fighting Women (Gurūpu Tatakau
    Onna), 24–25, 26, 28, 63, 103, 104, 115,
    146; *rezubian* in 34, 35
Gurūpu Tatakau Onna. *See* Group Fighting
    Women
gynecology, 115, 119. *See also* obstetrics;
    Our Bodies, Ourselves; women's health
    movement

Hagio Moto: in Europe, 17–18, 165–170;
    her *The Heart of Thomas* (*Tōma no*
    shinzō), 45, 46, 89, 129, 130, 138, 139;
    her *November Gymnasium* (*Jūichigatsu*
    no gimunajiumu), 43, 47, 129, 130; her
    The Poe Clan (*Poe no ichizoku*), 49, 170,
    174; the *shōnen'ai* genre's development
    and, 17–18, 42, 43, 45, 47, 128–132, 137;
    Takemiya Keiko and, 192n148, 192n150.
    See also Ōizumi Salon
Halperin, David, 71
handicap. *See* disability
Hara Minata (Minako), 38, 78–79, 157–159
Harry Potter (series), 11
Harvey, Keith, 106, 128
Hayashi Gekkō, 50
Heibon panchi (magazine), 75, 76
Hentai shinri (magazine), 84
Hentai shiryō (magazine), 69
Hesse, Herman, 17, 88, 89, 128–130, 131
Higuchi Keiko, 149
Hikari Guruma. *See* Shining Wheel
Hiratsuka Raichō, 68, 95
Hite Report, The, 17, 37, 99, 120–127, 140
HIV/AIDS, 46
homo (term), xi; *josei no homo*, 73
homophobia: in Japan, 35–36, 40, 159; in
    ribu, 33–34, 154, 189n83; in the US, 161
homosexuality (term). See *dōseiai* (term)
Honda Masuko, 135–136
Hong Kong, 211n100, 212n106
hoogland, renée c., 135
Horie, Yuri, 79
Huxley, Aldous, 71

Ibsen, Henrik, 95
Igarashi Megumi (Rokudenashiko), 23
Iino Yuriko, 190n99
Ikeda Riyoko, 42, 213n161
Ikegami Chizuko, 25–26, 105
Image (*Imāju;* magazine), 92
Inagaki Taruho, 85, **86**, 88–89, 90, 129–130,
    131–132
India, 182
Indonesia, 183
Inoue Kiyoshi, 101, 151, 201n22
Inoue Teruko, 30–31, 151–152
International Feminist Planning
    Conference, 148–149
International Feminists of Japan (IFJ), 37
International Lesbian Information Service
    Conference, 37, 123–124, 157, 178
International Women's Year. *See* United
    Nations First International Conference
    on Women
intertextuality, 130–133
Ishida Hitoshi, 50
Ishida Minori, 43, 49, 129, 167
Ishihara Gōjin, 50
Ishikawa Hiroyoshi, 121
Israel, 182
Itabashi Yoshie, 106–107
Italy, 165, 166
Itō Bungaku, 38–39
Itsuki Hiroyuki, 146
Ivy, Marilyn, 142, 208n1

Japanese English. See *wasei Eigo*
Jong, Erica, 30, 195n47
josei (term), 3–4, 31, 103–104. See also *josei
    kaihō* (term)
Josei jishin (magazine), 74, 76
josei kaihō (term), 3–4, 59, 60, 63–64,
    103–104
Josei Kaihō Undō Junbi Kai. *See* Women's
    Preparation Group June (magazine):
    Comic Jun (magazine), 49; fan
    contributions in, 5, 6, 49, 50, 177; gay
    culture in, 89–90, 165; as a genre label,
    87, 92; history and role of, 48–51, 88, 91;
    Roman June (magazine), 50; *Shōsetsu*

    June (magazine), 49; Western culture in,
        164–165, 175, 177
joseigaku. See women's studies

Kabiya Kazuhiko, 74, 85
Kakefuda Hiroko, 40, 80
Kaneko Kuniyoshi, 39
Kansai (region), 26, 142. *See also* Kyoto;
    Osaka
katakana, use of, 58, 60, 81, 84
Kawabata Yasunari, 88
Kelsky, Karen, 2, 128, 142–143, 178
Key, Ellen, 94
Kihara Toshie, 45
Kimura Ben, 50
Kinsey, Alfred, 72, 73, 121
Kiyooka Sumiko, 78, 190n103
Koedt, Anne, 108, 109, 110
Koikari, Mire, 20
Korea, 143, 150–151. *See also* ethnic Koreans
    in Japan
Krafft-Ebing, Richard von, 67, 68, 73, 85
Krauss, Friedrich S., 69
Kurimoto Kaoru, 49
Kyoto, 14, 31, 39, 63, 111, 119, 145
Kyoto University, 58

Ladies' Home Journal (magazine), 58
LaLa (magazine), 132, 170
Led Zeppelin, 47
Lefevere, André, 98
lesbian (term). See *rezubian* (term)
lesbian feminism, xi, 35–36, 66, 77, 125, 147,
    149. See also *rezubian feminisuto* (term);
    rezubian feminisuto activism
Levy, Indra, 17, 95, 96, 137
LGBT: boys love (BL) and, 182, 183; film
    festivals, 9, 40, 165; media,183; parades
    and other events, 9, 15, 40; rights, 40;
    term, xi, 8, 9, 40
Liu, Lydia, 93
Louÿs, Pierre, 70–71, 75

Mainichi Daiku, 36
Mann, Thomas, 99, 130. See also *Death in
    Venice* (film)

marriage: as a feminist issue, 24, 26,
110; between *rezubian* and *homo*,
38; counseling, 75–76; government
encouragement of, 28; same-sex, 40;
gender roles in, 24, 26, 106–107, 110,
141, 176
Marxism, 26, 104, 145, 151, 201n31. *See
also* capitalism; communism; New Left;
socialism
Masters and Johnson, 121
masturbation, 120, 122
Masuyama Norie, 45, 88–89, 128–129,
131–132, 166–167, 170, 172, 173, 192n150
Matsui Yayori, 30–31, 109, 151
McLelland, Mark, 73
Mexico, 158. *See also* United Nations First
World Conference on Women
Miki Sōko, 10, 14, 15, 26–27, 31–32, 63–64,
65, 83, 122
Miller, Laura, 56
Millett, Kate, 30, 106, 109, 118
Minami Teishirō, 86
mini-komi. See *rezubian mini-komi; ribu
mini-komi*
Mishima Yukio, 88–89, 132
Misora Hibari, 8
Miyazaki Tsutomu, 9
Mizoguchi Akiko, 43, 182
Mizuno Hideko, 42–43, 46, 47
More (*Moa;* magazine), 120–121, 140. *See
also More Report*
More Report, 121, 122–123, 124
Morgan, Marabel, 106–107
Mori Mari, 42, 47
Mori Ōgai, 82–83
motherhood, 1, 3, 4, 21, 25, 181; lesbian
motherhood, 157

Nagoya, 14, 31, 32, 39, 111, 175
Naito Rune, 50
Nakahara Jun'ichi, 41
Nakajima Azusa, 49
Nakamura Atsuo, 101
Nakanishi Toyoko, 64, 119, 205n126
Nakayama Chinatsu, 64
Nanbara Shirō, 49–50

nanshoku, 55, 82–83, 84, 85, 86, 169
Narabayashi Yasushi, 75–76, 77
National Organization for Women (NOW), 149
New Left, 21–22, 29, 101, 105. *See also*
capitalism; communism; Marxism;
socialism; Zenkyōtō
New York Times, 57, 194n13
Nietzsche, Friedrich, 54
Nihon Kazoku Keikaku Kyōkai, 148, 149
Ninagawa Masao, 56, 59–62, 64, 99
Nishimura Mari, 48
Nomura, Gail, 151
Non-no (magazine) 140–141
Notes from the Second Year, 77, 105, 108–111
nyoshoku, 55

obstetrics, 75, 115, 119. See also *Our Bodies,
Ourselves;* women's health movement
Occupation period, 19, 20
Ōe Kenzaburō, 145
Ōizumi Salon, 45, 91, 166, 173, 192n150
Omagaverse (genre), 183–184
onna (term), 3–4, 31, 103–104
Onna erosu (magazine), 27, 31, 77, 115, 116,
118, 147–148, 149, 152
onna kaihō (term), 3–4, 59, 60, 63–64,
103–104
Onna o ai suru onna no monogatari. See
Stories of Women Who Love Women
Ono, Yōko, 30, 195n47
Ortiz, Fernando, 12
Osaka: *rezubian* and LGBT events in 33, 39,
40; *ribu* activism in 14–15, 26, 32, 111,
122, 142, 148; women's health center in,
116. *See also* Expo '70
Ōshima Yumiko, 47
Our Bodies, Ourselves, 111–120, 155; "In
Amerika They Call Us Dykes," 77,
114–115, 147
Out (*Auto;* magazine), 49

Paper Moon (*Pēpā mūn;* magazine), 170, 172
Peter (celebrity), 163, 164
Peterson, Linda, 13, 37–38
Petit Flower (*Puchi furawā;* magazine),
192n148

Pflugfelder, Gregory, 69
Pharr, Susan, 152
Philippines, 157, 158, 182, 183
Phoenix, River, 164
Phryné (*Furine;* magazine), 40, 78
Piercy, Marge, 25, 101
Playboy (magazine), 58. See also *Weekly Playboy* (magazine)
Poe, Edgar Allan, 95
postcolonial studies, 12–13, 181
Povinelli, Elizabeth, 11–12, 97
Pratt, Mary Louise, 12
pregnancy, 112, 113; male, 183. *See also* abortion; birth control; childbirth
pride (*puraido;* term), 126
privacy, 13, 36, 126, 188n45, 190n99. *See also* pseudonyms
Proust, Marcel, 132
pseudonyms, 15, 32, 37, 124. *See also* privacy

Queen (band), 47, 164
Queen (*dōjinshi*), 47
Queen (magazine), 79

Ravuri (Lovely), 91
Redstockings, 58, 109
Reed, Evelyn, 151
Regumi, 36, 115, 157, 190n99
Reich, Wilhelm, 24–25
reproduction. *See* abortion; birth control; birthrate; childbirth; *Our Bodies, Ourselves,* pregnancy; women's health movement
rezubian bars, nightclubs, and dance parties, 7, 38–39, 77, 126, 156, 191n122
rezubian community, 7–8, 32–41
rezubian feminisuto (term), xi
rezubian feminisuto activism, 2, 10, 22, 36, 122, 147; *ūman ribu* and 2, 35–36, 52, 78; Wakakusa no Kai and, 7, 8; overseas travel and, 156–161. *See also* Sawabe Hitomi; Wakabayashi Naeko
rezubian feminisuto organizations. *See* Everyday Dyke (Mainichi Dyke); Regumi; Shining Wheel (Hikari Guruma)
rezubian gender roles, 33, 126, 156

rezubian identity: as an ideological choice, 8, 35–36; applicability to Japan, 80; *shōnen'ai* manga and, 43, 50; Weekends and, 38. See also *rezubian* (term)
rezubian magazines, 9, 35, 38, 40, 78
rezubian mini-komi, 13, 36, 121, 126
rezubian organizations, 8, 126. *See also* Mainichi Dyke; Regumi; Shining Wheel
rezubian retreats. *See* Weekends (lesbian event)
rezubian spaces, 8, 14, 33, 36, 126. *See also* Weekends (lesbian event)
rezubian (term): distinction from lesbian, xi, 7, 16, 53, 66, 93–94; distinction from *resubian,* 75–79; introduction and popularization, 66–75; other uses, 71; other variants: *Resubosu no ai,* 68–69, 73–74, 75, 79–80; *bian,* 80; *rezu,* 76, 77, 80; trans women or cross-dressing men as, 79–80
ribu (term). See *ūman ribu* (term)
ribu, as distinct from feminism. *See* feminism: *ribu* and
Ribu FUKUOKA, 26, 58–59, 62–63
ribu groups. *See* Group Fighting Women (Gurūpu Tatakau Onna); Ribu FUKUOKA; Thought Collective S.E.X.
ribu magazines. See *Onna erosu* (magazine)
ribu mini-komi, 4, 13, 23, 28, 31, 33, 58–59, 64
Ribu News: This Straight Path (*Ribu nyūsu: Kono michi hitosuji;* mini-komi), 28, 152, 155
Ribu Shinjuku Center (Ribusen), foreign visitors at, 152–153; *rezubian* and, 115, 154; role in the *ribu* movement, 13, 22, 27–28, 30, 116, 149, 154; translation activities at, 36, 137–138, 149–150, 156, 178
ribu spaces, 14, 15, 116, 158, 188n46. *See also* Ribu Shinjuku Center
Rich, Adrienne, 66, 136
Richard, Cliff, 169
Ripples of Change, 186n31
Roberts, Joan, 151
Robertson, Jennifer, 67
Rokudenashiko (Igarashi Megumi), 23

Roman letters, use of, 57, 59, 84, 91–92
Russia, 146, 152, 166, 182
ryōsai kenbo, 1, 181

S (*esu;* term), 71, 74, 78–79
Sabu (magazine), 49, 50, 87
Saeki Junko, 83
Sagawa Toshihiko, 48–49
Saitō Masami, 60, 62
sapphism, 69, 73
Sappho, 68, 70–71, 72, 73, 74, 78
Sasaya Nanae, 45, 173
Satō Kōka, 69, 73
Sawabe Hitomi: *rezubian* activism and, 36,
     40, 156; *ribu* activism and, 23, 137, 156,
     159, 177–178; *Stories of Women Who Love
     Women* and, 123–125, 157
Scott, Joan, 54
Seitō (magazine), 68, 95, 134, 194n14
Senuma Kayō, 95, 134, 135
sexology, 67–70, 71, 72–74, 82, 84–85, 95
sexually transmitted diseases (STDs), 24,
     112, 113. See also HIV/AIDS
Shibusawa Tatsuhiko, 88–89, 132
Shigematsu, Setsu, 24, 185n8
Shimamura Mari, 163, 175
Shining Wheel (Hikari Guruma), 36, 121, 124
Shinryaku=Sabetsu to Tatakau Ajia Fujin
     Kaigi, 208–209n16
Shisō Shūdan Esu Ī Ekkusu. *See* Thought
     Collective S.E.X.
Shōjo Comic (*Shōjo komikku;* magazine), 45,
     162–164, 165, 167, **168**, 169, 212n106;
     Shōjo Comic Extra (*Bessatsu shōjo
     komikku;* magazine), 43, 169–170
shōjo manga magazines. See *Funny* (*Fanī*);
     Grapefruit (*Gurēpufurutsu*), *LaLa; Petit
     Flower* (*Puchi furawā*); *Shōjo Comic*
     (*Shōjo komikku*)
shōjo shōsetsu, 41, 127
shōnen'ai (genre): definition of fandom of in
     this volume, 5–6; prehistory of, 41–43;
     real homosexual men and, 45, 47,
     88–90, 173; settings of, 42, 43, 45, 48,
     127–128, 129, 130, 166, 181; translated
     literature and film and the development
     of, 128–132; overseas consumption

of, 138 (see also *shōnen'ai* [term]: use
     outside Japan); overseas travel by fans
     of, 165, 170, 173–177. See also *Allan*
     (*Aran;* magazine); *Gekkō* (magazine);
     Hagio Moto; *June* (magazine); Takemiya
     Keiko
shōnen'ai (term), xi, 16; boys love (BL) and,
     81–82, 91–93; contemporary meaning,
     90; etymology, 82–87; as a *shōjo* manga
     genre label, 81–82, 87–90; use outside
     Japan, 82, 92–93. See also boys love (BL);
     yaoi
Shōnen Jump (*Shōnen janpu;* magazine), 48
Sirota Gordon, Beate, 20
Smith, Patricia, 136
socialism, 19, 21, 150. See also capitalism;
     communism; Marxism; New Left
Soshiren, 30, 31
South Korea, 143, 150–151
Stories of Women Who Love Women (*Onna
     o ai suru onna no monogatari*), 37, 50,
     122–127, **123**, 134, 157
Students for a Democratic Society (SDS), 58
study abroad, 156, 158, 169, 170, 175
Subarashī onnatachi. See Wonderful Women
     (*mini-komi*)
Sugiura Ikuko, 35–36
Suzuki Michiko, 32–33, 35
Sweden, 25, 166
Switzerland, 37, 157, 162–163, 166, 171, 178

tabi, 141, 144, 166, 171, 172, 174, 179
Taiwan, 157, 183, 203–204n91
Takagi Sawako, 138, 148–151, 152, 159,
     178–179
Takahashi Macoto, 41
Takahashi, Mizuki, 41–42
Takano Fumi, 107–108
Takarazuka Revue, 7, 41, 135
Takemiya Keiko: fan club, 172–174; in
     Europe, 17–18, 165–169, **168**, 170–172,
     173–174; Hagio Moto and, 192n148,
     192n150; her *I Like the Sky!* (*Sora ga suki!*),
     167, 171; *June* and, 49–50; her *Song of
     the Wind and the Trees* (*Kaze to ki no
     uta*), 45, 88, 89, 129–130, 132, 138, 162,
     172, 176; her *Still in the Mood for Europe*

(*Kibun wa ima mo Yōroppa*), 174; on the *shōnen'ai* genre as *feminisuto*, 6; the *shōnen'ai* genre's development and, 17–18, 42, 45, 47, 87, 88, 128–132, 137; her *In the Sunroom* (*Sanrūmu nite*), 5, 43–44, **44**, 87, 128, 129, 130; Vienna Boys Choir and, 50, 170, 171, 177; her *Vienna Fantasy* (*Uīn gensō*), 170, 171, 174. *See also* Masuyama Norie; Ōizumi Salon

Tanaka Kazuko, 150

Tanaka Mitsu: departure from *ribu* movement, 153–154, 155; her "Liberation from the Toilet" ("*Benjo kara kaihō*") pamphlet, 24–25, 100, 194n22; on *onna* (term), 4; prominence in *ribu* movement, 24–25, 27, 34, 64, 146–147; *rezubian* and, 34, 77, 154; on *ribu* and *ūman ribu* (terms), 59, 62; on *ribu* movement as local in origin, 10, 59; in *Women's Liberation: The Musical*, 22–23; her *To Women with Spirit* (*Inochi no onnatachi e*), 63, 77, 115, 146, 177. *See also* Group Fighting Women

Tanaka Sumiko, 151

tanbi (term), 87–88, 91, 182–183

Tanizaki Jun'ichirō, 71, 88

Taruho. *See* Inagaki Taruho

Taub, Larry, 146, 147, 149, 152, 209n30

Terayama Shuji, 22

Tezuka Osamu, 8, 41–42, 43, 47

Thai BL, 183–183

theater, 7, 22–23, 101, 107, 109, 133–137

These Special Friendships. *See* *Amitiés particulières, les* (film)

Thought Collective S.E.X. (Shisō Shūdan Esu Ī Ekkusu), 24, 26, 28, 100, 154

Three Kingdoms, legends of, 183

to ichi ha ichi (term), 69, 73, 74

Tōgō Ken, 191n118

Tokyo Komuunu, 154

transfiguration (definition), 11–13, 97–98, 181

transgender identity, 8, 79–80. *See also* X-gender

transphobia, 39

Tsing, Anna Lowenhaupt, 16, 93

Tsubouchi Shōyō, 57

Tymoczko, Maria, 98, 100

Ueno Chizuko, 118

ūman ribu (term), 56–66

United Kingdom, 47, 165, 170, 190n11; London, 39, 141, 158–159, 165; England, 169–170, 212n132

United Nations First World Conference on Women, 29, 35, 138, 143, 153–155, 156, 178–179

US, 14, 25–26, 43, 46, 148–149, 150, 156, 158; California, 58, 116, 155, 156, 182; Hawai'i, 164; New York, 46, 76, 141, 143, 147, 149, 156, 165, 186n31. *See also* feminism: American

University of Tokyo, 26, 151

Uno, Kathleen, 151, 152

Urning (term), 82, 84

Valentine, David, 53

Vienna Boys Choir, 50, 164, 169, 170, 176

Vietnam War, 21, 24, 25, 102, 112, 143, 146. *See also* anti-war movement

Vietnam, 183. *See also* Vietnam War

Visconti, Luchino. See *Death in Venice* (film)

Wakabayashi Naeko, 23, 35, 36, 116, 154, 155, 156–157, 159, 177–178

Wakakusa no Kai: advertisements in *Allan* and *Gekkō*, 50; *Eve & Eve* (*Ibu & Ibu*), 35, 38; history and demise of, 6–7, 22, 32–35; Itō Bungaku and, 38; political stance of, 10, 33; *rezubian feminisuto* and, 7, 36; *ribu* and, 34–35, 78; status in *rezubian* history, 7, 212n103; *Wakakusa*, 33, **34**, 78

Waseda University, 36, 148, 156

wasei Eigo, 56, 57, 61, 81

Weekends (event), 37–38, 160

Weekly Playboy (*Weekly pureibōi;* magazine), 75

West, the: significance in Japan, 2–3, 21, 142–143, 178, 180; *ribu* and, 2–3, 10–11,

178; *rezubian* and, 2–3, 80, 161, 178, 180; *shōjo manga* and, 2–3, 47, 131–132, 137, 162–164, 175–177, 180
Weston, Kath, 93
Wilde, Oscar, 88
women (term). See *fujin* (term); *josei* (term); *onna* (term)
Women's Democratic Newspaper (*Fujin minshu shinbun*), 26, 148
women's health movement, 11, 17, 99, 155, 156, 188n60. See also *Our Bodies, Ourselves*
Women's Liberation Movement Preparation Group. See Women's Preparation Group
Women's Liberation: The Musical (*Myūzukaru "onna no kaihō"*), 22–23, 107
Women's Preparation Group (Josei Kaihō Undō Junbi Kai), 59–60, 101–102, 103, 104, 105, 109
women's studies, 30–31, 65, 97, 106, 151, 195n47
Wonderful Women (*Subarashī onnatachi; mini-komi*), 35–36, 78, 154, 157
Woolf Society (Urufu no Kai), 29, 108–112, 116
Woolf, Virginia, 108

X-gender, 159

Y/Con (event), 182
Yamada Mineko, 45
Yamagishi Ryōko, 44–45, 166
Yamaguchi, Tomomi, 14
yaoi: term origin, 6, 91; use in Japan, 6, 47–48, 51, 81–82, 91, 92, 181; use outside Japan, 82, 92–93, 182, 183, 184. See also boys love (BL); *shōnen'ai* (genre); *shōnen'ai* (term)
Yaoicon (event), 182
Year 24 Group. See Fabulous Forty-Niners
Yokota-Murakami, Takayuki, 83
Yomiuri shinbun, 58, 61, 194n13
Yonezawa Yoshihiro, 41, 46, 48. See also Comic Market
Yonezu Tomoko, 3, 13, 23, 24, 25, 30, 31, 153, 154
Yoshida Akimi, 46, 132–137
Yoshimi Shunya, 163
Yoshimoto Takaaki, 145
Yuasa Yoshiko, 134
yuri (genre), 182, 132–137
Yūsei hogo hō. See Eugenics Protection Law

Zenkyōtō, 21, 58. See also New Left

ABOUT THE AUTHOR

James Welker is professor in the Department of Cross-Cultural Studies at Kanagawa University, Yokohama, Japan. His research examines gender and sexuality in postwar and contemporary Japan with an emphasis on the consumers and producers of queer media, the lesbian community, and radical feminism, as well as the globalization of Japanese popular culture. He is the editor of *Queer Transfigurations: Boys Love Media in Asia* (2022), *BL ga hiraku tobira: Hen'yō suru Ajia no sekushuariti to jendā* (BL opening doors: Sexuality and gender transfigured in Asia; 2019), and a special issue of the journal *Mechademia*, "Second Arc on "Queer(ing)" (2020). He is also a co-editor of *Rethinking Japanese Feminisms* (2018), *Boys Love Manga and Beyond: History, Culture, and Community in Japan* (2015), *Queer Voices from Japan* (2007), and a special issue of *Intersections: Gender and Sexuality in Asia and the Pacific*, "Of Queer Import: Sexualities, Genders and Rights in Asia" (2006).